CIMA

OPERATIONAL

PAPER F1

FINANCIAL OPERATIONS

PRACTICE & REVISION KIT

This Kit is for exams in 2014.

In this Kit we:

- Discuss the **best strategies** for revising and taking your F1 exam

- Show you how to be well prepared for the **2014 exams**

- Give you **lots of great guidance** on tackling questions

- Demonstrate how you can **build your own exams**

- Provide you with **three** mock exams

- Show you how marks are awarded in the exam, using **CIMA** marking guides

FOR EXAMS IN 2014

BPP
LEARNING MEDIA

First edition 2010
Fifth edition January 2014

ISBN 9781 4453 7165 8
Previous ISBN 9781 4453 6617 3
e-ISBN 9781 4453 7192 4

British Library Cataloguing-in-Publication Data
A catalogue record for this book is available from the British
Library

Published by

BPP Learning Media Ltd
BPP House, Aldine Place
142-144 Uxbridge Road
London W12 8AA

www.bpp.com/learningmedia

Printed in the United Kingdom by Polestar Wheatons

Hennock Road
Marsh Barton
Exeter
EX2 8RP

Your learning materials, published by BPP Learning
Media Ltd, are printed on paper obtained from traceable
sustainable sources.

We are grateful to the Chartered Institute of Management
Accountants for permission to reproduce past examination
questions. The suggested solutions in the exam answer bank
have been prepared by BPP Learning Media Ltd

Marking schemes and quotes from examiner comments
(where provided for past CIMA exam questions) are sourced
from CIMA post exam guides, which can be found in full at
cimaglobal.com.

Mock exam 1

Questions 80 to 83

Mock exam 2 (September 2013 resit exam)

Questions 84 to 87

Mock exam 3 (November 2013 exam)

Questions 88 to 91

Planning your question practice

Our guidance from page xx shows you how to organise your question practice, either by attempting questions from each syllabus area or by **building your own exams** – tackling questions as a series of practice exams.

Topic index

Listed below are the key Paper F1 syllabus topics and the numbers of the questions in this Kit covering those topics.

If you need to concentrate your practice and revision on certain topics or if you want to attempt all available questions that refer to a particular subject you will find this index useful.

Using your BPP Learning Media Practice and Revision Kit

Tackling revision and the exam

You can significantly improve your chances of passing by tackling revision and the exam in the right ways. Our advice is based on feedback from CIMA. We focus on Paper F1; we discuss revising the syllabus, what to do (and what not to do) in the exam, how to approach different types of question and ways of obtaining easy marks.

Selecting questions

We provide signposts to help you plan your revision.

- A full **question index**

- A **topic index**, listing all the questions that cover key topics, so that you can locate the questions that provide practice on these topics, and see the different ways in which they might be examined

- **BPP's question plan**, highlighting the most important questions

- **Build your own exams**, showing you how you can practise questions in a series of exams

Making the most of question practice

We realise that you need more than questions and model answers to get the most from your question practice.

- Our **Top tips** provide essential advice on tackling questions and presenting answers

- We show you how you can pick up **Easy marks** on questions, as picking up all readily available marks can make the difference between passing and failing

- We include **marking guides** to show you what the examiner rewards

- We summarise **Examiner's comments** to show you how students coped with the questions

- We refer to the **BPP 2013 Study Text (for 2014 exams)** for detailed coverage of the topics covered in each question

---

Marking schemes and quotes from examiner comments (where provided for past CIMA exam questions) are sourced from CIMA post exam guides, which can be found in full at cimaglobal.com.

Attempting mock exams

There are three mock exams that provide practice at coping with the pressures of the exam day. We strongly recommend that you attempt them under exam conditions as they reflect the question styles and syllabus coverage of the exam. To help you get the most out of doing these exams, we provide guidance on how you should have approached the whole exam.

Our other products

BPP Learning Media also offers these products for practising and revising for the F1 exam:

Passcards	Summarising what you should know in visual, easy to remember, form
i-Pass	Providing computer-based testing in a variety of formats, ideal for self-assessment
Interactive Passcards	Allowing you to learn actively with a clear visual format summarising what you must know

You can purchase these products by visiting www.bpp.com/lm

Revising F1

This is a very wide-ranging syllabus, but with not a great deal of depth in some areas. The format of the paper allows the examiner to cover a large part of the syllabus, so you cannot afford to neglect any area.

The syllabus is made up as follows:

Principles of business tax	25%
Regulation and ethics of financial reporting	15%
Financial accounting and reporting	60%

Areas to concentrate your revision on are:

- Statements of cash flows. This topic is not always examined in each paper, but as seen in the November 2010, May 2011, September 2011 resit and November 2013 exam, it could form the basis of a 25 mark question, so you really need to know how to assemble a statement of cash flows.

- Leases and construction contracts. These are tricky subjects. However the questions you get on them are likely to be of a standard format. So if you practice the questions in this Kit and learn how to do the basics, you should be able to pick up at least some of the marks for questions on these topics in the exam.

- Non-current assets. You will almost always have to calculate depreciation on property, plant and equipment, and probably also deal with a revaluation. This is not a difficult topic. Make sure you practice plenty of questions so you can gain as many of the easy marks as possible in the exam.

- Taxation and deferred tax – remember that tax makes up 25% of the syllabus. Do not neglect this area. International tax and VAT appear to be favourite subjects for the examiner to test.

- The IASB *Framework.* Defining the qualitative characteristics contained in the *Framework* is a popular question. This is just rote learning so make sure you take the time to learn here.

- Single company statement of comprehensive income and statement of financial position. You must know the correct IAS 1 formats. This topic is highly examinable and has formed the basis of a Section C question in all the new syllabus exam papers. Make sure you can draw up the proformas from memory very quickly, this will help you to tackle these questions.

- Consolidated financial statements. You need to be able to calculate goodwill and put together consolidated statements of comprehensive income and consolidated statements of financial position, including equity accounting for an associate. Unrealised profit on intra-group trading is also likely to feature in consolidation questions, learn how to deal with this adjustment. You also need to understand how to classify investments, whether as subsidiaries, associates or trade investments.

Question practice

You should use the Passcards and any brief notes you have to revise these topics, but you mustn't spend all your revision time passively reading. **Question practice is vital**. Doing as many questions as you can in full will help develop your ability to analyse scenarios and produce relevant discussion and recommendations. The question plan on page xv tells you what questions cover so that you can choose questions covering a variety of topics.

Passing the F1 exam

Displaying the right qualities

The examiners will expect you to display the following qualities.

Qualities required	
Produce neat workings and readable answers	If you produce no workings, the marker can give you no credit for using the right method. If the marker cannot read what you have written they can give you no marks at all.
Carry out standard calculations	You must be able to deal with simple tax and financial instrument calculations.
Demonstrate understanding of the basics	Deferred tax and construction contracts can be complex, but you will only get fairly simple questions, so make sure you understand the principles.

Avoiding weaknesses

The examiners have identified weaknesses that occur in many students' answers at every sitting. You will enhance your chances significantly if you ensure you avoid these mistakes:

- Failing to provide what the question verbs require (discussion, evaluation, recommendations) or to write about the topics specified in the question requirements

- Inability to carry out calculations

- Not showing workings in 3-4 mark questions

- Repeating the same material in different parts of answers

- Regurgitation of definitions and lists with no application to the question

- Brain dumping all that is known about a topic (no credit is given for this)

- Failing to answer sufficient questions because of poor time management

- Not answering all parts of questions

- Not using the information provided in the question accurately

- Attempting to question spot

Using the reading time

Use the reading time to analyse the adjustments needed in the Section C questions and go over the requirements of the Section B questions deciding which parts to answer first.

Tackling questions

Numerical questions

Expect to see numbers throughout the paper. Approach them methodically and show all workings clearly.

Discussion questions

Remember that **depth of discussion** is also important. Discussions will often consist of paragraphs containing 2-3 sentences. Each paragraph should:

- **Make a point**
- **Explain the point** (you must demonstrate **why** the point is important)
- **Illustrate the point** (with material or analysis from the scenario, perhaps an example from real-life)

Gaining the easy marks

The first few marks are always the easiest to gain in any question. This applies particularly to Section B. Spend the same amount of time on each Section B question. This will give you a good chance of scoring marks on each question. Your Section C questions carry a lot of marks. Make sure you begin by getting down the format and filling in any numbers which don't require calculation.

The exam paper

Format of the paper

		Number of marks
Section A:	Around 7-10 multiple choice and other objective test questions, 2-4 marks each	20
Section B:	6 compulsory questions, 5 marks each	30
Section C:	2 compulsory questions, totalling 50 marks	50
		100

Time allowed: 3 hours plus 20 minutes reading time.

Section A will always contain some multiple choice questions but will not consist solely of multiple choice questions. For 3 or 4-mark questions, marks are given for correct workings.

Section B questions will be mainly written discussion, although some calculations may be included. This section will require breadth of syllabus knowledge and also good time management skills.

The **Section C** questions will cover statements of comprehensive income, statements of financial position, statements of cash flows for a single company and simple consolidated statement of comprehensive income and statement of financial position.

November 2013

Section A

1   Direct tax, PAYE, tax residency, deferred tax, VAT calculation, ethical code, IFRS Foundation, IASB *Conceptual Framework,* IAS 1 'presents fairly', materiality.

Section B

2a   Explain classification of subsidiaries (IFRS 10)
2b   Prepare journal entries for consolidation
2c   Explain 'indexation' and calculate capital gains tax
2d   Calculate tax payable
2e   Prepare briefing note on tax groups
2f   Explain duties of external auditor

Section C

3   Explain treatment of change in inventory accounting policy, and prepare financial statements for a single entity including purchase of own shares.

4   Explain treatment of preference shares in financial statements, calculate revised profit, and prepare statement of cash flows.

The November 2013 paper is mock exam 3 in this Kit.

September 2013 (resit exam)

Section A

1   Type of tax system, definition of tax avoidance, calculation of capital gains tax, significance of permanent establishment, withholding tax, benefit of regulating published accounts, IASB's *Conceptual Framework*, accounting standards bodies, fundamental qualitative characteristics, type of audit report.

Section B

2a   Prepare cash flows from financing activities
2b   Explain ethical issues
2c   Explain difference between bonus issue and rights issue, and prepare journal entries for rights issue
2d   Explain meaning of temporary difference (IAS 12) and calculate deferred tax
2e   Explain meaning of benefits in kind and prepare income tax computation
2f   Calculate net profit, and calculate VAT payable

Section C

3   Explain why impairment review might have been carried out, financial statements for a single entity including asset for sale and finance lease.

4   Define control (IFRS 10), consolidated statement of financial position including associate and intra-group trading.

The September 2013 paper is mock exam 2 in this Kit.

May 2013

Section A

1   Type of tax system, methods of reducing tax avoidance and evasion, methods of giving double taxation relief, calculation of capital gains tax, meaning of rollover relief, type of legal system, benefits of global harmonisation of accounting standards, IFRS Advisory Council, IASB's *Conceptual Framework*, sections of external audit report.

Section B

2a   Prepare cash flows from investing activities
2b   Explain steps to ensure adherence to CIMA Code of Ethics
2c   Explain classification of preferred shares and account for costs in accordance with IAS 39
2d   Define tax base of an asset and calculate deferred tax
2e   Calculate tax payable by an entity
2f   Explain cascade sales tax and VAT, calculate profit/loss and VAT due

Section C

3   Explain held for sale criteria (IFRS 5) and prepare financial statements for a single entity, including discontinued operations.

4   Explain treatment of post-acquisition increase in goodwill, consolidated statement of financial position including associate and intra-group trading.

March 2013

Section A

1   Tax on foreign dividends, IFRS Foundation, accounting depreciation and tax depreciation, IASB's *Framework,* adverse audit opinion, CIMA Code of Ethics, IAS 7, users of financial statements, related party transaction, IAS 18 recognition criteria.

Section B

2a List four taxes that require detailed records and identify records required for VAT returns
2b Calculate tax payable by an entity
2c Explain the effect of closure of a division and restructuring on SPLOCI (IFRS 5)
2d Explain three reasons why excise duty may be imposed
2e Explain country of residence for tax purposes and explain how profits will be taxed
2f Identify five purposes of IASB *Framework*

Section C

3 Financial statements for a single entity, including a patent, a finance lease and obsolete inventory.

4 Explanation of the circumstances that give rise to a parent/subsidiary relationship other than a majority shareholding, consolidated statement of financial position including negative goodwill and intra-group trading.

November 2012

Section A

1 Direct and indirect taxes, development process of IFRSs, deferred tax calculation, IASB *Framework* qualitative characteristics of reliability, modified audit opinion, Code of Ethics, elements of the statement of cash flows, factors influencing accounting disclosure, adjusting event under IAS 10 *Events after the reporting period*, recognition of revenue under IAS 18 *Revenue*.

Section B

2a Explain the enforcement powers given to tax authorities
2b Calculate the corporate tax payable
2c Define an operating segment and explain when a segment is reportable
2d Identify the requirements of VAT regulations and calculate net VAT balance
2e Calculate foreign tax and calculate tax due on foreign dividend
2f Explain the roles of IFRS Interpretations Committee and IFRS Advisory Council

Section C

3 Financial statements for a single entity, including adjustments to account for a patent, research costs, and an operating lease.
4 Consolidated financial statements including fair value calculation, goodwill impairment, unrealised profit on inventory and the intra-group transfer of property, plant and equipment.

September 2012 (resit exam)

Section A

1 Sources of tax rules, calculation of balancing charge, calculation of profit with VAT, scheduler system of tax, determination of residency for tax purposes, Code of Ethics, IFRS Interpretations Committee, calculation of tax on disposal of asset, accounting for a contract, IFRS 8.

Section B

2a Calculate income tax charge and explain impact of increase in tax rate on deferred tax
2b Explain methods of giving double taxation relief
2c Calculate tax payable for the year
2d Calculate revenue and cost and amount due from/to customers
2e Explain steps in IASB's standard setting process for IFRSs
2f Explain impact of two outstanding matters on the auditor's report

Section C

3   Financial statements for a single entity including suspense account and journals, outstanding litigation, and customer liquidation post-reporting date.

4   Consolidated financial statements including intra-group trading, intra-group sale of asset, goodwill calculation and an associate.

May 2012

Section A

1   OECD tax model, VAT calculation, tax on profit, list two powers of a tax authority, tax classification of VAT, CIMA's Code of Ethics, responsibilities of IASB, treatment of items in FS, IFRS 5, IAS 37.

Section B

2a   Explain benefits to users of accounts of statement of cash flows
2b   Explain deferred tax, identify reason for increase in provision, and explain what it represents
2c   Calculate corporate income tax
2d   Explain excise duty/single stage sales tax and describe characteristics suitable for excise duty
2e   Define income and equity and explain criteria for recognition
2f   Prepare briefing note on benefits of external audit

Section C

3   Financial statements for a single entity including revenue recognition and impairment of intangible non-current assets.

4   Consolidated financial statements including journal preparation and associate.

March 2012

Section A

1   Indirect tax, meaning of 'tax base', deferred tax balance, calculation of tax payable, meaning of 'hypothecation', related party, recognition of asset in FS, explain disclosure of operating segments, IAS 18 four conditions for revenue recognition.

Section B

2a   Calculate deferred tax movement and deferred tax balance
2b   Explain zero rated/exempt from VAT and calculate VAT balance
2c   Explain imputation system of corporate income tax
2d   Identify four entities involved in developing and implementing IASs
2e   Explain objective of external audit and explain three key areas of the audit report
2f   Explain ethical problem in a given scenario

Section C

3   Financial statements for a single entity including research and development.
4   Consolidated financial statements including goodwill.

November 2011

Section A

1   Principles of modern tax systems, formal/effective incidence of VAT, deferred tax, capital gains tax, definition of 'tax gap', related parties, intangible assets, events after the reporting date, IFRS 8 *Operating segments*, revenue recognition.

Section B

2a   Calculate income tax and income tax expense
2b   Calculate VAT due and profit made
2c   Explain 'tax base'
2d   Explain concepts of 'capital' and 'capital maintenance'
2e   Define materiality and issuing an audit report
2f   Ethics and the CIMA Code

Section C

3   Financial statements preparation for a single entity, including two construction contracts.
4   Preparation of consolidated statement of financial position, including the definition of control per IAS 27.

September 2011 (resit exam)

Section A

1   Direct tax, definition of capital gain, determining type of tax, definition of 'tax evasion', corporate residence for tax purposes, related parties, rights issue of shares, calculation of goodwill on acquisition, calculation of value of investment in associate, intra-group trading.

Section B

2a   Explain single-stage sales tax and VAT, calculate VAT due
2b   Explain deferred tax and how a deferred tax debit balance arises
2c   Explain worldwide approach to tax and problems caused
2d   Explain factors influencing accounting regulations
2e   Define assets/liabilities, explain recognition criteria in the *Framework*
2f   Ethics and the CIMA Code

Section C

3   Financial statements preparation for a single entity, including a finance lease, inventory adjustments, and treatment of cumulative redeemable preferred shares

4   Preparation of a property, plant and equipment note and a statement of cash flows for a single company.

May 2011

Section A

1   Type of tax system, PAYE, OECD corporate residence, excise duty and VAT, tax avoidance/evasion, change in accounting policy, reportable segments under IFRS 8, calculation of goodwill on acquisition, calculation of value of investment in associate, intra-group trading.

Section B

2a   Calculate income tax and deferred tax
2b   Explain capital gain and calculate tax due on capital gain
2c   Explain underlying tax and calculate underlying tax
2d   Principles-based vs prescriptive accounting standards
2e   Explain the objective of financial statements and the underlying assumptions in the *Framework*
2f   Ethics and the CIMA Code

Section C

3   Financial statements preparation for a single entity, including a discontinued operation.
4   Preparation of a statement of cash flows for a single company, finance lease calculation.

November 2010

Section A

1   Interaction of corporate and personal tax, employee tax, formal incidence of VAT, administration of tax, calculating VAT, audit opinions, treasury shares, IASB's *Framework*, related parties, IFRS 8 *Operating segments.*

Section B

2a   Relieving trading losses (company income tax)
2b   Withholding tax, including calculation of double tax relief
2c   *Framework*: qualitative characteristics
2d   Group accounts: calculation of goodwill and IFRS 3
2e   Group accounts: classification of investments
2f   Provisions, events after the reporting period

Section C

3   Financial statements preparation for a single entity, including an income tax computation and deferred tax.
4   Preparation of a statement of cash flows for a single company, ethical considerations.

May 2010

Section A

1   Ideal tax principles, tax rate structures, deferred tax, IASB's *Framework*, qualitative characteristics, revenue recognition, development expenditure, finance leases, discontinued operations, cash flows.

Section B

2a   Tax evasion and tax avoidance
2b   Indirect taxes
2c   International tax
2d   External audit and audit reports
2e   Construction contracts
2f   Discontinued operations, restructuring provisions, CIMA's Code of Ethics

Section C

3   Financial statements preparation for a single entity, including a share issue, operating lease and revaluation of property, plant and equipment.

4   Preparation of consolidated statement of financial position and consolidated statement of comprehensive income, calculation of income tax and deferred tax for the group.

Specimen paper

Section A

1   Tax avoidance and evasion, calculating income tax, VAT, systems of taxing corporate income, IASB Framework, CIMA Code of Ethics, external audit, IFRS 3, inventories, related parties.

Section B

2a   Tax residency
2b   VAT explanation and calculation
2c   Principles vs. rules based accounting standards
2d   Discontinued operations
2e   Accounting treatment of leases
2f   Accounting treatment of preference shares

Section C

3   Financial statements preparation for a single entity, including deferred tax calculation.

4   Preparation of consolidated statement of financial position, including the treatment of an associate in group accounts.

What the examiner means

The table below has been prepared by CIMA to help you interpret exam questions.

Learning objective	Verbs used	Definition	Examples in the Kit
1 Knowledge			
What you are expected to know	• List	• Make a list of	56(5)
	• State	• Express, fully or clearly, the details of/facts of	2(14)
	• Define	• Give the exact meaning of	16(3)
2 Comprehension			
What you are expected to understand	• Describe	• Communicate the key features of	50(10)
	• Distinguish	• Highlight the differences between	
	• Explain	• Make clear or intelligible/state the meaning or purpose of	14(b)
	• Identify	• Recognise, establish or select after consideration	70(e)
	• Illustrate	• Use an example to describe or explain something	70(a)
3 Application			
How you are expected to apply your knowledge	• Apply	• Put to practical use	55(d)
	• Calculate /compute	• Ascertain or reckon mathematically	13(b)
	• Demonstrate	• Prove the certainty or exhibit by practical means	
	• Prepare	• Make or get ready for use	13(a)
	• Reconcile	• Make or prove consistent/compatible	
	• Solve	• Find an answer to	
	• Tabulate	• Arrange in a table	
4 Analysis			
How you are expected to analyse the detail of what you have learned	• Analyse	• Examine in detail the structure of	
	• Categorise	• Place into a defined class or division	
	• Compare and contrast	• Show the similarities and/or differences between	
	• Construct	• Build up or complete	
	• Discuss	• Examine in detail by argument	17(a)
	• Interpret	• Translate into intelligible or familiar terms	
	• Prioritise	• Place in order of priority or sequence for action	
	• Produce	• Create or bring into existence	
5 Evaluation			
How you are expected to use your learning to evaluate, make decisions or recommendations	• Advise	• Counsel, inform or notify	
	• Evaluate	• Appraise or assess the value of	
	• Recommend	• Propose a course of action	

BPP LEARNING MEDIA

Planning your question practice

We have already stressed that question practice should be right at the centre of your revision. Whilst you will spend some time looking at your notes and the Paper F1 Passcards, you should spend the majority of your revision time practising questions.

We recommend two ways in which you can practise questions.

- Use **BPP Learning Media's question plan** to work systematically through the syllabus and attempt key and other questions on a section-by-section basis

- **Build your own exams** – attempt the questions as a series of practice exams

These ways are suggestions and simply following them is no guarantee of success. You or your college may prefer an alternative but equally valid approach.

BPP's question plan

The plan below requires you to devote a **minimum of 40 hours** to revision of Paper F1. Any time you can spend over and above this should only increase your chances of success.

 Review your notes and the chapter summaries in the Paper F1 **Passcards** for each section of the syllabus.

 Answer the key questions for that section. These questions have boxes round the question number in the table below and you should answer them in full. Even if you are short of time you must attempt these questions if you want to pass the exam. You should complete your answers without referring to our solutions.

 Attempt the other questions in that section.

 Attempt Mock exams 1, 2 and 3 under strict exam conditions.

Syllabus section	2013 Passcards chapters	Questions in this Kit	Comments	Done ☑
The regulatory framework	1	1 4	The MCQs are fairly simple here. The Section B questions invite you to spend a lot of time, so *don't do it* – practise answering these question with notes and bullet points.	☐
External audit and ethics	2, 3	2-3 5, 6	Make sure you know the different types of audit report qualification and be very strict and to the point on the Section B questions.	☐
Financial accounts – presentation	4,5	7-8	This area is very important – IAS 1 and IAS 8. Do all of the MCQs. Make sure you can write out the formats.	☐
Statements of cash flows	9	9, 10	These are good revision for the various components of the statement, so do them before attempting the longer questions.	☐
Statements of cash flows	9	11-14	These are Section C questions on statements of cash flows. Question 11 is a preparatory question which you should attempt first.	☐
Non-current assets, inventories and construction contracts	6, 7, 11	15–18	These are fairly complex topics. If you have trouble with the MCQs, go back to the Study Text and revise the area.	☐
Capital transactions and financial instruments	12	19	These MCQs cover most of the important issues in this area. Make sure you understand how to deal with redemption of capital and purchase of own shares.	☐
Accounting standards	8, 10	20-23	These questions cover IAS 10, IAS 24, IAS 37 and IAS 17. These are all important because they are relatively *easy* to learn and apply, so if they come up they will be easy marks. Make sure you can calculate finance lease interest payments using both methods.	☐
Financial statements	4, 5	24-35	Section C will have an accounts preparation question, so practice on these.	☐
Group financial statements	13, 14, 15, 16	36-48	This is a new topic at this level so it needs a lot of practice.	☐
General principles of taxation	17, 18	49-51	Answer all of these MCQs. There will be more than one question on each topic, so you will get lots of practice.	☐
		53, 54	These are Section B-type questions. Make sure you do not spend more than 9 minutes on each.	☐
Company taxation	19	51-52	Answer all of these MCQs. Make sure you really understand the adjustments necessary to get from accounting profit to taxable profit and can do it easily.	☐
		55	These are Section B questions on company tax. Deferred tax is the most difficult aspect. Just make sure you understand the basics.	☐

Build your own exams

Having revised your notes and the BPP Passcards, you can attempt the questions in the Kit as a series of practice exams. You can organise the questions in the following way:

	Marks
7-10 objective test questions	20
6 Section B questions	30
2 Section C questions	50
	100

The easiest way to do this is to do one of the past exam papers in full.

Once you have completed the real exams you can make your own exams as follows.

For Section A of your exam, select from each of these banks (1 – 3, 7, 9, 15, 16, 19 – 21, 36, 49 – 52) to a total of 20 marks. Tax usually features heavily in section A, so choose around 4 or 5 questions from banks 49 – 52. If you do a 3 or 4-mark question, reduce the number of questions accordingly.

For Section B, do 6 sub-questions from the following questions – 4, 5, 6, 8, 10, 17, 22, 23, 53 - 55. Make sure you do at least one question from Part A, one from Part B, one from Part C and one from Part D – see the Question and Answer Checklist.

Then chose two section C questions, one from questions 28 – 35, then one from either 12 – 14 or 37 – 48.

Also make sure you do the **three mock exams**.

IMPORTANT NOTE ON TERMINOLOGY

An amendment to IAS 1 was published in June 2011, applicable to annual periods beginning on or after 1 July 2012. This amendment changes the name of the full statement of comprehensive income to the 'statement of profit or loss and other comprehensive income'. The part of the statement previously known as the income statement becomes the 'statement of profit or loss'. The revised terminology is not mandatory, so you will still meet the terms income statement and statement of comprehensive income not only in this Practice and Revision Kit but in other publications and possibly in your F1 exam.

You may also hear or see the statement of financial position referred to as the balance sheet, and the statement of cash flows referred to as the cash flow statement.

IMPORTANT NOTE ON IASB *Conceptual Framework for Financial Reporting*

From May 2013 CIMA have been examining the new *Conceptual Framework for Financial Reporting* and questions in this 2014 Practice and Revision Kit have been updated to reflect this. The Study Text, however, was published before this change was introduced by CIMA and it is therefore based on the previous version of the *Framework*.

QUESTIONS

2

Part A: Regulation and Ethics of Financial Reporting

Questions 1 to 6 cover Regulation and Ethics of Financial Reporting, the subject of Part A of the BPP Study Text for F1.

1 Objective test questions: The regulatory framework   92 mins

1   Which one of the following bodies is responsible for reviewing new financial reporting issues and issuing guidance on the application of IFRSs?

    A   The IASB
    B   The IFRS Foundation
    C   The IFRS Interpretations Committee
    D   The IFRS Advisory Council   **(2 marks)**

2   Which of the following is **not** an advantage of global harmonisation of accounting standards?

    A   Priority given to different user groups in different countries
    B   Easier transfer of accounting staff across national borders
    C   Ability to comply with the requirements of overseas stock exchanges
    D   Better access to foreign investor funds   **(2 marks)**

3   Which of the following bodies is responsible for the development of 'Draft Interpretations' for public comment?

    A   The IFRS Advisory Council
    B   The IFRS Foundation
    C   The International Accounting Standards Board
    D   The IFRS Interpretations Committee   **(2 marks)**

4   The International Accounting Standards Board's *Conceptual Framework for Financial Reporting (2010)* defines five elements of financial statements. Three of the elements are asset, liability and income.

List the other **two** elements.   **(2 marks)**

5   Which of the following, per the IASB's *Conceptual Framework*, is an underlying assumption relating to financial statements?

    A   The accounts have been prepared on an accruals basis
    B   Users are assumed to have sufficient knowledge to be able to understand the financial statements
    C   The business is expected to continue in operation for the foreseeable future
    D   The information is free from material error or bias   **(2 marks)**

6   Which two of the following are **not** elements of financial statements per the IASB's *Conceptual Framework*?

    1   Profits
    2   Assets
    3   Income
    4   Equity
    5   Losses
    6   Expenses

    A   2 and 4
    B   1 and 5
    C   3 and 4
    D   5 and 6   **(2 marks)**

7   According to the IASB's *Conceptual Framework*, the statement of profit or loss and other comprehensive income shows an entity's:

   A   Economic resources
   B   Financial performance
   C   Changes in resources and claims
   D   Financial adaptability   **(2 marks)**

8   Which of the following is an underlying assumption in the IASB's *Conceptual Framework for Financial Reporting (2010)*?

   A   Accruals
   B   Relevance
   C   Timeliness
   D   Going concern   **(2 marks)**

9   The IASB's *Conceptual Framework for Financial Reporting (2010)* defines elements of financial statements. One of the elements defined by the *Conceptual Framework* is an 'asset'.

   In no more than **30** words **define** an asset.   **(2 marks)**

10 The term GAAP is used to mean:

   A   Generally accepted accounting procedures
   B   General accounting and audit practice
   C   Generally agreed accounting practice
   D   Generally accepted accounting practice   **(2 marks)**

11 Which one of the following is responsible for governance and fundraising in relation to the development of International Financial Reporting Standards?

   A   International Accounting Standards Board
   B   IFRS Interpretations Committee
   C   IFRS Foundation Trustees
   D   IFRS Advisory Council   **(2 marks)**

12 The setting of International Financial Reporting Standards is carried out by co-operation between a number of committees and boards, which include:

   1   IFRS Foundation
   2   IFRS Advisory Council
   3   IFRS Interpretations Committee

   Which of the above reports to, or advises, the International Accounting Standards Board (IASB)?

	Reports to:	*Advises:*
A	1 and 3	2
B	1 and 2	3
C	3	2
D	2	1

                                                                                (2 marks)

13 The IASB's *Conceptual Framework for Financial Reporting (2010)* provides definitions of the elements of financial statements. One of the elements defined by the *Conceptual Framework* is 'expenses'.

   In no more than **40** words, **define** expenses.   **(2 marks)**

14 According to the International Accounting Standards Board's *Conceptual Framework for Financial Reporting (2010)*, what is the objective of financial reporting?

   Write your answer in no more than **35** words.   **(2 marks)**

15   Which of the following correctly defines 'equity' according to the IASB's *Conceptual Framework for Financial Reporting (2010)*?

    A   Equity is a present obligation of the entity arising from past events, the settlement of which is expected to result in an outflow from the entity of resources embodying economic benefit

    B   Equity is a resource controlled by an entity as a result of past events and from which future economic benefits are expected to flow to the entity

    C   Equity is the residual interest in the assets of the entity after deducting all its liabilities

    D   Equity is increases in economic benefits during the accounting period in the form of inflows or enhancements of assets or decreases of liabilities   **(2 marks)**

16   Which of the following are the responsibilities of the IFRS Foundation Trustees?

    1   Issuing International Financial Reporting Standards

    2   Approving the annual budget of the IASB

    3   Enforcing International Financial Reporting Standards

    4   Reviewing the strategy of the IASB and its effectiveness

    5   Appointing the members of the IASB, the IFRS Interpretations Committee and the IFRS Advisory Council

    A   1, 2 and 5
    B   2 and 4
    C   1, 3 and 5
    D   2, 4 and 5   **(2 marks)**

17   The International Accounting Standards Board's *Conceptual Framework for Financial Reporting (2010)* categorises the qualitative characteristics of financial information as fundamental or enhancing.

    State the fundamental qualitative characteristics.   **(2 marks)**

18   Which of the following statements is/are true?

    1   The IFRS Interpretations Committee is a forum for the IASB to consult with the outside world.

    2   The IFRS Foundation produces IFRSs. The IFRS Foundation is overseen by the IASB.

    3   One of the objectives of the IFRS Foundation is to bring about convergence of national accounting standards and IFRSs.

    A   1 and 3 only
    B   2 only
    C   2 and 3 only
    D   3 only   **(2 marks)**

19   The process leading to the publication of an International Financial Reporting Standard (IFRS) has a number of stages.

    List the **four** stages normally involved in developing an IFRS.   **(3 marks)**

20   According to the IASB's *Conceptual Framework* which of the following is *not* an objective of financial statements?

    A   Providing information regarding the economic resources and claims of a business
    B   Providing information regarding the performance of a business
    C   Enabling users to assess the performance of management to aid decision making
    D   Helping to assess the going concern status of a business   **(2 marks)**

21 According to the IASB's *Conceptual Framework*, which **two** of the following make information a faithful representation?

    1   It is free from bias
    2   It is relevant
    3   It is complete
    4   It is verifiable

    A   1 and 2
    B   2 and 4
    C   1 and 3
    D   3 and 4   (2 marks)

22 Listed below are some characteristics of financial information.

    1   Comparability
    2   Relevance
    3   Completeness
    4   Timeliness

    Which of these characteristics are qualitative characteristics of useful financial information according to the IASB's *Conceptual Framework for Financial Reporting (2010)*?

    A   1, 2 and 3 only
    B   1, 2 and 4 only
    C   1, 3 and 4 only
    D   2, 3 and 4 only   (2 marks)

23 According to the IASB's *Conceptual Framework for Financial Reporting (2010),* which of the following are enhancing characteristics of useful financial information?

    A   Timeliness, completeness, understandability, materiality
    B   Relevance, comparability, verifiability, materiality
    C   Completeness, timeliness, understandability, verifiability
    D   Verifiability, understandability, comparability, timeliness   (2 marks)

24 Which body issues International Financial Reporting Standards?

    A   The IFRS Advisory Council
    B   The IFRS Foundation
    C   The International Accounting Standards Board
    D   The IFRS Interpretations Committee   (2 marks)

25 Which of the following provides advice to the International Accounting Standards Board (IASB) as well as informing the IASB of the implications of proposed standards for users and preparers of financial statements?

    A   The IFRS Advisory Council
    B   The IFRS Interpretations Committee
    C   The IFRS Foundation
    D   The Trustees   (2 marks)

                                                                       (Total = 51 marks)

2   Objective test questions: External audit   56 mins

1   An external audit:

   A   Guarantees that the financial statements are free from misstatements.

   B   Provides reasonable assurance that the financial statements are free from misstatements.

   C   Guarantees that the financial statements are free from material misstatements.

   D   Provides reasonable assurance that the financial statements are free from material misstatements.

                                                                                  (2 marks)

2   An external auditor gives a modified audit opinion that is a 'disclaimer of opinion'.

    This means that the auditor:

   A   Has been unable to agree with an accounting treatment used by the directors in relation to a material item.

   B   Has been prevented from obtaining sufficient appropriate audit evidence and concludes the effects of undetected misstatements could be both material and pervasive.

   C   Has found extensive errors in the financial statements that are material and pervasive and so concludes that they do not show a true and fair view.

   D   Has discovered a few immaterial differences that do not affect the auditor's opinion.   **(2 marks)**

3   There is a major uncertainty facing Z, a limited liability company. Actions are pending against the company for allegedly supplying faulty goods, causing widespread damage.

    The directors have fully described the circumstances of the case in a note to the financial statements.

    What form of audit opinion is appropriate in this case?

   A   Qualified opinion – unable to obtain sufficient appropriate audit evidence

   B   Disclaimer of opinion

   C   Unmodified opinion with an additional emphasis of matter paragraph

   D   Qualified opinion – misstatements are material, but not pervasive   **(2 marks)**

4   Which of the following matters are normally covered by the auditors' report?

   1   Whether the company has kept proper accounting records

   2   Whether the accounts are in agreement with the accounting records

   3   Whether the accounts have been prepared in accordance with the relevant legislation and accounting standards

   4   Whether other information presented with the financial statements is consistent with them

   A   1 and 2 only

   B   1, 2 and 3 only

   C   3 and 4 only

   D   All four matters are normally covered   **(2 marks)**

5   A company's auditors find insufficient evidence to substantiate the company's cash sales, which are material in amount.

    What form of modification of the audit opinion would normally be appropriate in this situation?

   A   Qualified opinion – misstatements are material, but not pervasive

   B   Qualified opinion – unable to obtain sufficient appropriate audit evidence

   C   Disclaimer of opinion

   D   Adverse opinion   **(2 marks)**

6   A company's accounting records were largely destroyed by fire shortly after the year end. As a result, the financial statements contain a number of figures based on estimates.

What form of modification of the audit opinion would be appropriate in this situation?

A   Qualified opinion – misstatements are material, but not pervasive
B   Qualified opinion – unable to obtain sufficient appropriate audit evidence
C   Disclaimer of opinion
D   Adverse opinion   **(2 marks)**

7   Who is responsible for the preparation and fair presentation of financial statements of a company?

A   External auditors of the company
B   The finance department of the company
C   Management of the company
D   External auditors and Management are jointly responsible   **(2 marks)**

8   When carrying out an audit an external auditor must satisfy himself of a number of matters. Which of the following are **not** one of those matters?

A   The accounts have been prepared by a qualified accountant

B   Proper accounting records have been kept

C   The accounts have been prepared in accordance with local legislation and relevant accounting standards

D   The accounts are in agreement with accounting records   **(2 marks)**

9   If an external auditor does not agree with the directors' treatment of a material item in the accounts, the first action they should take is to:

A   Give a qualified opinion of the financial statements
B   Give an unmodified opinion of the financial statements
C   Force the directors to change the treatment of the item in the accounts
D   Persuade the directors to change the treatment of the item in the accounts   **(2 marks)**

10 The external auditor has a duty to report on the truth and fairness of the financial statements and to report any reservations. The auditor is normally given a number of powers by statute to enable the statutory duties to be carried out.

List three powers that are usually granted to the auditor by statute.   **(3 marks)**

11 Which one of the powers listed below is unlikely to be granted to the auditor by legislation?

A   The right access at all times to the books, records, documents and accounts of the entity

B   The right to be notified of, attend and speak at meetings of equity holders

C   The right to correct financial statements if the auditor believes the statements do not show a true and fair view

D   The right to require officers of the entity to provide whatever information and explanations thought necessary for the performance of the duties of the auditor   **(2 marks)**

12 Which of the following is the most appropriate definition of an external audit?

A   An external audit is an exercise carried out by auditors in order to give an opinion on whether the financial statements of a company are true and fair.

B   An external audit is an exercise carried out by auditors in order to give assurance to shareholders on the effectiveness and efficiency of management.

C   An external audit is performed by management to identify areas of deficiency within a company and to make recommendations to mitigate those deficiencies.

D   The external audit is an exercise performed by auditors to provide assurance that the company will continue to operate in the future.   **(2 marks)**

13 The external auditors have completed the audit of GQ for the year ended 30 June 20X8 and have several outstanding differences of opinion that they have been unable to resolve with the management of GQ. The senior partner of the external auditors has reviewed these outstanding differences and concluded that individually and in aggregate the differences are not material.

Which **one** of the following audit opinions will the external auditors use for GQ's financial statements for the year ended 30 June 20X8?

A An unmodified opinion
B An adverse opinion
C An emphasis of matter
D A qualified opinion **(2 marks)**

14 In no more than 25 words, state the objective of an external audit. **(2 marks)**

15 The external auditors have completed the audit of SR. The auditors disagree with the accounting treatment of a material item in the financial statements and have concluded that the effect of this issue is material, but not pervasive to the financial statements.

Which **one** of the following audit opinions will the external auditors use for SR's financial statements?

A An unmodified opinion
B An adverse opinion
C An emphasis of matter
D A qualified opinion **(2 marks)**

(Total = 31 marks)

3 Objective test questions: Ethics 40 mins

1 A professional accountant in business may be involved in a wide variety of work. Which of these functions will he **not** be carrying out?

A Preparing financial statements
B Auditing financial statements
C Preparing budgets and forecasts
D Preparing the management letter provided to the auditors **(2 marks)**

2 A professional accountant is required under the CIMA Code to comply with five fundamental principles. These include:

A Integrity, Objectivity, Reliability
B Professional competence and due care, Confidentiality, Integrity
C Morality, Objectivity, Professional behaviour
D Efficiency, Confidentiality, Professional competence and due care **(2 marks)**

3 A qualified accountant holds a number of shares in his employing company, and has become eligible for a profit-related bonus for the first time. What type of threat could this represent to his objectivity when preparing the company's financial statements?

A Self-interest
B Self-review
C Intimidation
D Familiarity **(2 marks)**

4 Three of the following are recognised advantages of a principles based approach to ethical codes. Which is the exception?

A Encourages proactive discussion of issues
B Encourages consistent application of rules
C Suits complex situations and evolving environments
D Encourages professional development **(2 marks)**

5   While out to lunch, you run into a client at the sandwich bar. In conversation, she tells you that she expects to inherit from a recently deceased uncle, and asks you how she will be affected by inheritance tax, capital gains tax and other matters – which you have not dealt with, in detail, for some years.

Which of the following principles of the CIMA Code of Ethics is raised by this scenario?

A   Professional competence and due care
B   Integrity
C   Professional behaviour
D   Confidentiality   **(2 marks)**

6   While at a party at the weekend, you meet a client of yours who is clearly very concerned about some VAT issues. You know enough about VAT to carry out your daily work, but you are not an expert on the areas of imports and exports on which your client is asking your opinion.

What ethical issue does this situation raise?

A   Objectivity
B   Professional competence and due care
C   Professional behaviour
D   Confidentiality   **(2 marks)**

7   The CIMA Code of Ethics for Professional Accountants sets out five principles that a professional accountant is required to comply with. Three of these principles are professional behaviour, integrity and objectivity. List the other two.   **(2 marks)**

8   Which of the following is an advantage of a principles-based ethical code?

A   It can easily be legally enforced.

B   It provides rules to be followed in all circumstances

C   It encourages compliance by requiring a professional person to actively consider the issues.

D   It can be narrowly interpreted, making it easy for the professional to see whether or not the Code has been violated.   **(2 marks)**

9   What is meant by the fundamental principle of 'professional behaviour'?

A   Compliance with relevant laws and regulations and avoidance of any action that discredits the profession

B   Being straightforward and honest in all professional and business relationships

C   Not allowing professional judgement to be affected by bias, undue influence or business considerations

D   Maintaining a high level of technical expertise through continuing professional development
                                                                                       (2 marks)

10   Which of the following is **not** a circumstance where disclosure of confidential information is permitted under the CIMA Code?

A   Disclosure of information when authorised by the client
B   Disclosure of information to advance the interests of a new client
C   Disclosure of information to protect the professional interests of an accountant in a legal action
D   Disclosure of information when required by law   **(2 marks)**

11   Which of these is **not** a source of ethical codes for accountants?

A   IFAC
B   CIMA
C   APB
D   HMRC   **(2 marks)**

                                                                          (Total = 22 marks)

4 Section B questions: Regulation   45 mins

(a)   The International Accounting Standards Board (IASB')'s *Conceptual Framework for Financial Reporting (2010)* defines the elements of financial statements.

     Required

     Explain each of the elements, illustrating each with an example.   **(5 marks)**

     `P7 5/08`

(b)   The IASB's *Conceptual Framework* identifies four enhancing qualitative characteristics of useful financial information.

     Required

     Identify and **explain** each of the four enhancing qualitative characteristics of financial information listed in the IASB's *Conceptual Framework*.   **(5 marks)**

     `P7 11/05`

(c)   C is a small developing country which passed legislation to create a recognised professional accounting body two years ago. At the same time as the accounting body was created, new regulations governing financial reporting requirements of entities were passed. However, there are currently no accounting standards in C.

     C's government has asked the new professional accounting body to prepare a report setting out the country's options for developing and implementing a set of high quality local accounting standards. The government request also referred to the work of the IASB and its International Financial Reporting Standards.

     Required

     As an advisor to the professional accounting body, **outline** three options open to C for the development of a set of high quality local accounting standards. **Identify one** advantage and **one** disadvantage of each option.   **(5 marks)**

     `P7 5/06`

(d)   *The Conceptual Framework for Financial Reporting* was first published in 1989 and was amended in 2010. It has been adopted by The International Accounting Standards Board (IASB)

     Explain the purposes of the *Conceptual Framework*.   **(5 marks)**

     `P7 5/07`

(e)   The IFRS Foundation oversees a number of other International committees, two of which are the IFRS Advisory Council and the IFRS Interpretations Committee.

     Required

     Explain the role of the IFRS Advisory Council and the IFRS Interpretations Committee in assisting with developing and implementing International Financial Reporting Standards.   **(5 marks)**

     `P7 11/08`

(Total = 25 marks)

5   Section B questions: External audit   36 mins

(a)   Selected balances in HF's financial records at 30 April 20X9 were as follows:

	$'000
Revenue	15,000
Profit	1,500
Property, plant and equipment – net book value	23,000
Inventory	1,500

After completing the required audit work the external auditors of HF had the following observations:

(1)   Inventory with a book value of $500 is obsolete and should be written off.

(2)   Development expenditure net book value of $600,000, relating to the development of a new product line, has been capitalised and amortised in previous years but the project has now been abandoned, (after 30 April X9).

(3)   Decommissioning costs relating to HF's production facilities, estimated to be $5,000,000 in 17 years time is being provided for, over 20 years, at $250,000 a year.

Assume there are no other material matters outstanding.

As external auditor you have just completed a meeting with HF management. At the meeting HF management decided the following:

- Item (1) is not material, so it is not necessary to write off the obsolete inventory.
- Item (2) the development expenditure should be written off against current year profits.
- Item (3) the decommissioning cost will continue to be provided for over 20 years.

Required

(i)   **Explain** whether or not the management's decisions taken in the meeting are correct for items (1) and (2).   **(2 marks)**

(ii)   **Explain** whether you agree with the management's treatment of the decommissioning costs in item (3) and **explain** the type of audit opinion that should be issued, giving your reasons.   **(3 marks)**

                                                (Total = 5 marks)

                                                   `P7 5/09`

(b)   **Explain** the circumstances in which an audit report will express each of the following:

(i)   A qualified opinion
(ii)   A disclaimer of opinion
(iii)   An adverse opinion   **(5 marks)**

(c)   An auditor, in carrying out his statutory duty, may sometimes find himself to be in conflict with the directors of the company. What statutory rights does he have to assist him in discharging his responsibility to the shareholders?   **(5 marks)**

(d)   DC is carrying out three different construction contracts. The balances and results for the year to 30 September 20X6 were as follows:

Contract	1	2	3
Contract end date	30 Sept 20Y3	31 Dec 20Y0	30 Sept 20Y0
	$m	$m	$m
Profit/(loss) recognised for year	2	2.3	(0.6)
Expected total profit/(loss) on contract	12	5.0	(3.0)

DC's management have included $3.7m profit in the profit for the year ended 30 September 20X6. DC's financial statements show a profit for the year of $16.32m.

No allowance has been made in the statement of profit or loss and other comprehensive income for the future loss expected to arise on contract 3, as management consider the loss should be offset against the expected profits on the other two contracts.

EA & Co are DC's external auditors. EA & Co consider that the profit in relation to long term contracts for the year ended 30 September 20X6 should be $1.3m, according to IAS 11 *Construction Contracts*. EA & Co have been unable to persuade DC's management to change their treatment of the construction contract profit/loss.

Required

(i)   **Explain** the objective of an external audit.

(ii) **Identify**, with reasons, the type of audit opinion that would be appropriate for EA & Co to use for DC's financial statements for the year ended 30 September 20X6. Briefly **explain** what information should be included in the audit report in relation to the contracts.

(5 marks)

(Total = 20 marks)

6   Section B questions: Ethics   27 mins

(a)   The CIMA Code of Ethics sets out fundamental principles and a conceptual framework for applying them. How does this approach work and how does it differ from a rules-based system?   **(5 marks)**

(b)   The CIMA Code of Ethics sets out five fundamental principles. **List** and briefly **explain** each of these principles.   **(5 marks)**

(c)   The CIMA Code of Ethics is principles based. **Describe** the advantages and disadvantages of a principles-based ethical code.   **(5 marks)**

(Total = 15 marks)

7 Objective test questions: Presentation   43 mins

1   Which, if any, of the following statements about limited liability companies are correct, according to IAS 1 (revised)?

   1   Companies must produce their financial statements within one year after their reporting period.

   2   The accounting policies adopted by a company must be disclosed by note.

   3   The accounting records of a limited liability company must be open to inspection by a member of the company at all times.

   A   2 only
   B   2 and 3 only
   C   1 and 3 only
   D   None of the statements is correct   **(2 marks)**

2   Which of the following items can appear in a company's statement of changes in equity, according to IAS 1 (revised) *Presentation of financial statements?*

   1   Total comprehensive income for the period
   2   Dividends paid
   3   Surplus on revaluation of properties
   4   Proceeds of issuance of share capital

   A   All four items
   B   1, 2 and 3 only
   C   1, 3 and 4 only
   D   2 and 4 only   **(2 marks)**

3   Which of the following items are required by IAS 1 (revised) *Presentation of financial statements* to be disclosed in the financial statements of a limited liability company?

   1   Authorised share capital
   2   Finance costs
   3   Staff costs
   4   Depreciation

   A   1 and 4 only
   B   1 , 2 and 3 only
   C   2, 3 and 4 only
   D   All four items   **(2 marks)**

4   Which of the following constitute a change of accounting policy according to IAS 8 *Accounting policies, changes in accounting estimates and errors?*

   1   A change in the basis of valuing inventory

   2   A change in depreciation method

   3   Depreciation that was previously treated as part of cost of sales is now shown under administrative expenses

   4   Adopting an accounting policy for a new type of transaction not previously dealt with

   A   1 and 2
   B   2 and 3
   C   1 and 3
   D   2 and 4   **(2 marks)**

5   Which of the following items would qualify for treatment as a change in accounting estimate, according to IAS 8 *Accounting policies, changes in accounting estimates and errors?*

1   Provision for obsolescence of inventory
2   Correction necessitated by a material error
3   A change as a result of the adoption of a new International Accounting Standard
4   A change in the useful life of a non-current asset

A   All four items
B   2 and 3 only
C   1 and 3 only
D   1 and 4 only   **(2 marks)**

6   A change in accounting policy is accounted for by:

A   Changing the current year figures but not previous year's figures
B   Retrospective application
C   No alteration of any figures but disclosure in the notes
D   No alteration of any figures nor disclosure in the notes   **(2 marks)**

7   Which one of the following would be regarded as a change of accounting policy under IAS 8 *Accounting policies, changes in accounting estimates and errors*?

A   An entity changes its method of depreciation of machinery from straight line to reducing balance.

B   An entity has changed its method of valuing inventory from FIFO to weighted average.

C   An entity changes its method of calculating the provision for warranty claims on its products sold.

D   An entity disclosed a contingent liability for a legal claim in the previous year's accounts. In the current year, a provision has been made for the same legal claim.   **(2 marks)**

8   Shah changes the depreciation method for its motor vehicles from the straight line method to the reducing balance method. How would this be treated in the financial statements?

A   Changing the current year figures but not previous year's figures
B   Retrospective application
C   No alteration of any figures but disclosure in the notes
D   No alteration of any figures nor disclosure in the notes   **(2 marks)**

9   IAS 8 *Accounting Policies, Changes in Accounting Estimates and Errors* specifies the definition and treatment of a number of different items. Which of the following is NOT specified by IAS 8?

A   The effect of a change in an accounting estimate
B   Prior period adjustments
C   Provisions
D   Errors   **(2 marks)**

10   IAS 1 (revised) *Presentation of financial statements* requires some items to be disclosed on the face of the financial statements and others to be disclosed in the notes.

1   Depreciation
2   Revenue
3   Closing inventory
4   Finance cost
5   Dividends

Which two of the above have to be shown on the face of the statement of profit or loss and other comprehensive income, rather than in the notes:

A   1 and 4
B   3 and 5
C   2 and 3
D   2 and 4   **(2 marks)**

11   IAS 1 (revised) *Presentation of Financial Statements* encourages an analysis of expenses to be presented on the face of the statement of profit or loss and other comprehensive income. The analysis of expenses must use a classification based on either the nature of expense, or its function, within the entity such as:

1   Raw materials and consumables used
2   Distribution costs
3   Employee benefit costs
4   Cost of sales
5   Depreciation and amortisation expense

Which of the above would be disclosed on the face of the statement of profit or loss and other comprehensive income if a manufacturing entity uses analysis based on function?

A   1, 3 and 4
B   2 and 4
C   1 and 5
D   2, 3 and 5

(2 marks)

12   Which one of the following would be regarded as a change of accounting estimate according to IAS 8 *Accounting policies, changes in accounting estimates and errors*?

A   An entity started valuing inventory using the weighted average cost basis. Inventory was previously valued on the FIFO basis.

B   An entity started revaluing its properties, as allowed by IAS 16 *Property, plant and equipment*. Previously, all property, plant and equipment had been carried at cost less accumulated depreciation.

C   A material error in the inventory valuation methods caused the closing inventory at 31 March 2008 to be overstated by $900,000.

D   An entity created a provision for claims under its warranty of products sold during the year. 5% of sales revenue had previously been set as the required provision amount. After an analysis of three years sales and warranty claims the calculation of the provision amount has been changed to a more realistic 2% of sales.

(2 marks)

(Total = 24 marks)

8   Section B questions: Presentation   18 mins

(a)   Suggest reasons why companies should be expected to publish accounts using standard formats saying why and to whom the specific information shown in the formats would be useful.   **(5 marks)**

(b)   The following is an extract from the trial balance of CE at 31 March 20X6:

	$'000	$'000
Administration expenses	260	
Cost of sales	480	
Interest paid	190	
Interest bearing borrowings		2,200
Inventory at 31 March 20X6	220	
Property, plant and equipment at cost	1,500	
Property, plant and equipment, depreciation to 31 March 20X5		540
Distribution costs	200	
Revenue		2,000

Notes

(i)   Included in the closing inventory at the year end was inventory at a cost of $35,000, which was sold during April 20X6 for $19,000.

(ii)   Depreciation is provided for on property, plant and equipment at 20% per year using the reducing balance method. Depreciation is regarded as cost of sales.

(iii)   A member of the public was seriously injured while using one of CE's products on 4 October 20X5. Professional legal advice is that CE will probably have to pay $500,000 compensation.

Required

Prepare CE's statement of profit or loss and other comprehensive income for the year ended 31 March 20X6 down to the line 'profit before tax'.   **(5 marks)**

P7 5/06

(Total = 10 marks)

9   Objective test questions: Statements of cash flows   43 mins

1   The following is an extract from a statement of cash flows prepared by a trainee accountant.

	$'000
Cash flows from operating activities	
Profit before taxation	3,840
Adjustments for	
Depreciation	(1,060)
Loss on sale of building	210
	2,990
Increase in inventories	(490)
Decrease in trade payables	290
Net cash from operating activities	2,790

Which of the following criticisms of this extract are correct?

1   Depreciation should have been added, not deducted.
2   Loss on sale of building should have been deducted, not added.
3   Increase in inventories should have been added, not deducted.
4   Decrease in trade payables should have been deducted, not added.

A   1 and 4
B   2 and 3
C   1 and 3
D   2 and 4   **(2 marks)**

2   In the year ended 31 December 20X4 a company sold some plant which had cost $100,000 for $20,000. At the time of sale the carrying value of the plant was $18,000.

Which of the following correctly states the treatment of the transaction in the company's statement of cash flows?

	Proceeds of sale	*Profit on sale*
A	Cash inflow under financing activities	Deducted from profit in calculating cash flow from operating activities.
B	Cash inflow under investing activities	Added to profit in calculating cash flow from operating activities.
C	Cash inflow under financing activities	Added to profit in calculating cash flow from operating activities.
D	Cash inflow under investing activities	Deducted from profit in calculating cash flow from operating activities. **(2 marks)**

3   Which of the following items should not appear in a company's statement of cash flows?

   1   Proposed dividends
   2   Dividends received
   3   Bonus issue of shares
   4   Surplus on revaluation of a non-current asset
   5   Proceeds of sale of an investment not connected with the company's trading activities

   A   1, 2, 3 and 5
   B   3 and 4 only
   C   1, 3 and 4
   D   2 and 5   (2 marks)

---

4   Which, if any, of the following statements about statements of cash flows are correct according to IAS 7 *Statement of cash flows*?

   1   The direct and indirect methods produce different figures for operating cash flow.

   2   In calculating operating cash flow using the indirect method, an increase in inventory is added to operating profit.

   3   Figures shown in the statement of cash flows should include sales taxes.

   4   The final figure in the statement of cash flows is the increase or decrease in cash at bank.

   A   1 and 4
   B   2 and 3
   C   2 only
   D   None of the statements is correct.   (2 marks)

---

5   The statement of financial position of R, a limited liability company, at 31 December 20X3 and 20X4 included these figures.

	31 December	
	20X3	*20X4*
	$m	$m
Property, plant and equipment: cost	40	50
Accumulated depreciation	(10)	(14)
	30	36

The statement of profit or loss and other comprehensive income for the year ended 31 December 20X4 showed the following figures.

Depreciation charge for year	$6m
Loss on sales of property, plant and equipment	$1m

The company purchased new property, plant and equipment costing $16m during the year.

What figure should appear in the company's statement of cash flows for 20X4 for receipts from the sale of property, plant and equipment?

   A $3m
   B $5m
   C $4m
   D   The figure cannot be calculated from the information provided.   (2 marks)

6 A statement of cash flows shows the increase or decrease in cash and cash equivalents in the period.

Which of the following items are included in this movement?

1 Cash at bank

2 Overdraft at bank

3 Current asset investments readily convertible into known amounts of cash and which can be sold without disrupting the company's business.

4 Equity investments.

A All four items
B 1, 2 and 3 only
C 1 and 2 only
D 1 and 3 only   **(2 marks)**

---

7 Which of the following should appear in a statement of cash flows according to IAS 7 *Statement of cash flows*?

1 Dividends paid on preference shares
2 Interest capitalised as part of the cost of a non-current asset
3 Cash flows resulting from share issues

A All three items
B 1 and 2 only
C 1 and 3 only
D 2 and 3 only   **(2 marks)**

---

8 The IAS 7 format for a statement of cash flows using the indirect method opens with adjustments to net profit before taxation to arrive at cash flow from operating activities.

Which of the following lists consists only of items that would be deducted in that calculation?

A Loss on sale of non-current assets, increase in inventories, decrease in trade payables
B Depreciation, increase in trade receivables, decrease in trade payables
C Increase in trade receivables, profit on sale of non-current assets, decrease in trade payables
D Profit on sale of non-current assets, increase in trade payables, decrease in trade receivables

(2 marks)

---

9 A company's accounting records contain the following figures.

	$'000
Sales for year	3,600
Purchases for year	2,400
Receivables: 31 December 20X2	600
31 December 20X3	700
Payables: 31 December 20X2	300
31 December 20X3	450
Salaries and other expenses paid during 20X3, excluding interest	760

What figure should appear in the company's statement of cash flows for 20X3 for cash generated from operations, based on these figures?

A $490,000
B $390,000
C $1,250,000
D None of these figures   **(2 marks)**

10 At 30 September 20X5, BY had the following balances, with comparatives:

As at 30 September	20X5	20X4
	$'000	$'000
Non-current tangible assets		
Property, plant and equipment	260	180
Equity and reserves		
Property, plant and equipment revaluation surplus	30	10

The statement of profit or loss and other comprehensive income for the year ended 30 September 20X5 included:

Gain on disposal of an item of equipment	$10,000
Depreciation charge for the year	$40,000

Notes to the accounts:

Equipment disposed of had cost $90,000. The proceeds received on disposal were $15,000.

Required

Calculate the property, plant and equipment purchases that BY would show in its statement of cash flows for the year ended 30 September 20X5, as required by IAS 7 *Statement of cash flows*. **(4 marks)**

11 At 1 October 20X4, BK had the following balance:

Accrued interest payable $12,000 credit

During the year ended 30 September 20X5, BK charged interest payable of $41,000 to its statement of profit of loss and other comprehensive income. The closing balance on accrued interest payable account at 30 September 20X5 was $15,000 credit.

How much interest paid should BK show on its statement of cash flows for the year ended 30 September 20X5?

A $38,000
B $41,000
C $44,000
D $53,000   **(2 marks)**

(Total = 24 marks)

10 Section B questions: Statements of cash flows   9 mins

(a)   The following financial information relates to FC for the year ended 31 March 20X8.

FC
STATEMENT OF PROFIT OR LOSS AND OTHER COMPREHENSIVE INCOME

FOR THE YEAR ENDED 31 MARCH 20X8

	$'000
Revenue	445
Cost of sales	(220)
Gross profit	225
Other income	105
	330
Administrative expenses	(177)
Finance costs	(20)
Profit before tax	133
Income tax expense	(43)
Profit for the year	90

The following administrative expenses were incurred in the year.

	$'000
Wages	70
Other general expenses	15
Depreciation	92
	177

Other income:	
Rentals received	45
Gain on disposal of non-current assets	60
	105

Statement of financial position extracts at:

	31 March 20X8 $'000	31 March 20X7 $'000
Inventories	40	25
Trade receivables	50	45
Trade payables	(30)	(20)

Required

Prepare FC's statement of cash flows for the year ended 31 March 20X8, down to the line 'Cash generated from operations', using the **direct method**. **(5 marks)**

P7 5/08

Statements of cash flows – section C questions

The following tax regime data is applicable to questions 11 – 14, which cover the preparation of statements of cash flows.

Country X – Tax regime

Relevant tax rules

Corporate Profits

Unless otherwise specified, only the following rules for taxation of corporate profits will be relevant, other taxes can be ignored:

(a)   Accounting rules on recognition and measurement are followed for tax purposes.

(b)   All expenses other than depreciation, amortisation, entertaining, taxes paid to other public bodies and donations to political parties are tax deductible.

(c)   Tax depreciation is deductible as follows:

- 50% of additions to property, plant and equipment in the accounting period in which they are recorded

- 25% per year of the written-down value (ie cost minus previous allowances) in subsequent accounting periods except that in which the asset is disposed of

- No tax depreciation is allowed on land

(d)   The corporate tax on profits is at a rate of 25%.

(e)   No indexation is allowable on the sale of land.

(f)   Tax losses can be carried forward to offset against future taxable profits from the same business.

Value Added Tax

Country X has a VAT system which allows entities to reclaim input tax paid. In Country X the VAT rates are:

Zero rated	0%
Standard rated	15%

11 Dickson   27 mins

Below are the statements of financial position of Dickson Co as at 31 March 20X6 and 31 March 20X5, together with the statement of profit or loss and other comprehensive income for the year ended 31 March 20X6.

STATEMENTS OF FINANCIAL POSITION AS AT 31 MARCH

	20X6 $'000	20X5 $'000
Non-current assets		
Property, plant and equipment	825	637
Goodwill	100	100
Development expenditure	290	160
	1,215	897
Current assets		
Inventories	360	227
Trade receivables	274	324
Investments	143	46
Cash	29	117
	806	714
Total assets	2,021	1,611
Equity		
Share capital – $1 ordinary shares	500	400
Share premium	350	100
Revaluation surplus	160	60
Retained earnings	151	152
	1,161	712
Non-current liabilities		
6% loan notes	150	100
Finance lease liabilities	100	80
Deferred tax	48	45
	298	225
Current liabilities		
Trade payables	274	352
Finance lease liabilities	17	12
Current tax	56	153
Loan note interest	5	–
Dividends	78	103
Bank overdraft	132	54
	562	674
Total equity and liabilities	2,021	1,611

STATEMENT OF PROFIT OR LOSS AND OTHER COMPREHENSIVE INCOME

FOR THE YEAR ENDED 31 MARCH 20X6

	$'000
Revenue	1,476
Cost of sales	(962)
Gross profit	514
Other expenses	(157)
Finance costs	(15)
Profit before tax	342
Income tax expense	(162)
Profit for the year	180

Notes

(1) Goodwill arose on the acquisition of unincorporated businesses. During the year ended 31 March 20X6 expenditure on development projects totalled $190,000.

(2) During the year ended 31 March 20X6 items of property, plant and equipment with a carrying value of $103,000 were sold for $110,000. Depreciation charged in the year on property, plant and equipment totalled $57,000. Dickson purchased $56,000 of property, plant and equipment by means of finance leases, payments being made in arrears on the last day of each accounting period.

(3) The current asset investments are government bonds and management has decided to class them as cash equivalents.

(4) The new loan notes were issued on 1 April 20X5. Finance cost includes loan note interest and finance lease finance charges only.

(5) During the year Dickson made a 1 for 8 bonus issue capitalising its retained earnings followed by a rights issue.

(6) Dividends declared during the period totalled $131,000.

Required

Prepare a statement of cash flows for the year ended 31 March 20X6 for Dickson Co in accordance with IAS 7 *Statement of cash flows,* using the indirect method. Your answer should include notes for Property, plant and equipment and for Cash and cash equivalents. **(15 marks)**

---

12 UV (9/11)   45 mins

UV's draft financial statements for the year ended 30 June 2011 and financial statements for the year ended 30 June 2010 are as follows:

STATEMENTS OF FINANCIAL POSITION AS AT 30 JUNE

	Other Information	2011	2010
Non-current assets		$'000	$'000
Property, plant & equipment	(i) to (v)	5,675	4,785
Deferred development expenditure	(vi)	170	69
		5,845	4,854
Current assets			
Inventory		95	80
Trade receivables		190	145
Cash and cash equivalents		95	160
		380	385
		6,225	5,239
Equity and liabilities			
Equity			
Share capital	(vii)	910	760
Share premium	(vii)	665	400
Revaluation reserve		600	0
Retained earnings		2,899	1,982
		5,074	3,142
Non-current liabilities			
Deferred tax		410	0
Long-term loans		250	1,500
		660	1,500
Current liabilities			
Trade payables		60	85
Income tax		321	305
Interest payable		5	32
Provision for restructuring costs	(ix)	0	100
Provision for legal claim	(viii)	105	75
		491	597
		6,225	5,239

STATEMENT OF PROFIT OR LOSS AND OTHER COMPREHENSIVE INCOME

FOR THE YEAR ENDED 30 JUNE 2011

	$'000
Revenue	2,300
Cost of Sales	(450)
Gross profit	1,850
Administration expenses and distribution costs	(200)
Loss on disposal of plant	(15)
Profit from operations	1,635
Interest payable	(95)
Profit before tax	1,540
Income tax	(455)
Profit after tax	1,085
Other comprehensive income	
Revaluation of property, net of deferred tax	600
Total comprehensive income	1,685

Other information:

(i) Non-current assets – property, plant and equipment, balances at 30 June 2010 were:

Cost or valuation:	$'000	$'000
Property	4,150	
Plant	2,350	
Equipment	985	
		7,485
Depreciation:		
Property	450	
Plant	1,350	
Equipment	900	
		2,700
Carrying amount		4,785

(ii) Equipment was purchased during the year at a cost of $275,000 and plant was purchased for $215,000.

(iii) During the year UV disposed of plant with a carrying amount of $30,000 and accumulated depreciation of $60,000.

(iv) On 1 July 2010 property was revalued to $4,500,000. At that time the average remaining life of property was 90 years. Property is depreciated on a straight line basis.

(v) Depreciation for the year was $280,000 and $40,000 for plant and equipment respectively.

(vi) Development expenditure incurred during the year to 30 June 2011 was $114,000. Deferred development expenditure is amortised over its useful economic life.

(vii) UV issued equity shares during the year at a premium.

(viii) Provision was made by UV for outstanding legal claims against the entity at the year end.

(ix) The restructuring costs relate to a comprehensive restructuring and reorganisation of the entity that began in 2009. UV's financial statements for the year ended 30 June 2010 included a provision for restructuring costs of $100,000. Restructuring costs incurred in the year to 30 June 2011 were $160,000. No further restructuring and reorganisation costs are expected to occur. UV treats restructuring costs as a cost of sales.

Required

(a) **Prepare** a property, plant and equipment note for UV for the year ended 30 June 2011, in accordance with the requirements of IAS 16 *Property, plant and equipment*. **(6 marks)**

(b) **Prepare** a statement of cash flows, for UV for the year ended 30 June 2011 using the indirect method, in accordance with the requirements of IAS 7 *Statement of Cash Flows*. **(19 marks)**

(Total = 25 marks)

13 OP (5/11)   45 mins

Extracts of OP's financial statements for the year ended 31 March 20X1 are as follows.

OP STATEMENTS OF FINANCIAL POSITION AS AT:

	31 March 20X1		31 March 20X0	
Assets	$'000	$'000	$'000	$'000
Non-current assets				
Property, plant and equipment	977		663	
Development expenditure	60		65	
Brand name	30		40	
		1,067		768
Current assets				
Inventory	446		450	
Trade receivables	380		310	
Cash and cash equivalents	69		35	
		895		795
Total assets		1,962		1,563
Equity and liabilities				
Equity shares of $1 each	400		200	
Share premium	200		100	
Revaluation reserve	30		95	
Retained earnings	652		423	
		1,282		818
Non-current liabilities				
Long term borrowings	100		250	
Deferred tax	130		120	
		230		370
Current liabilities				
Trade payables	150		95	
Current tax	250		260	
Accrued interest	10		20	
Other provisions	40		0	
		450		375
Total equity and liabilities		1,962		1,563

OP STATEMENT OF PROFIT OR LOSS AND OTHER COMPREHENSIVE INCOME

FOR THE YEAR ENDED 31 MARCH 20X1

	$'000	$'000
Revenue		10,400
Cost of sales		(4,896)
Gross profit		5,504
Distribution costs		(1,890)
Administrative expenses		(2,510)
Finance cost		(15)
Profit before tax		1,089
Taxation		(280)
Profit for the year		809
Other comprehensive income		
Loss on revaluation of property		(65)
Total comprehensive income		744

Additional information

(i)   Property, plant and equipment comprises:

	Cost at 31 March 20X1	Cost at 31 March 20X0	Depreciation to 31 March 20X0
	$'000	$'000	$'000
Land	426	320	0
Buildings	840	610	366
Plant and equipment	166	180	81
	1,432	1,110	447

(ii)   Depreciation for the year ended 31 March 20X1 was:

	$'000
Buildings	17
Plant and equipment	25

(iii)   Plant and equipment disposed of during the year had a carrying amount of $11,000 (cost $45,000). The loss on disposal of $6,000 is included in cost of sales.

(iv)   All land was revalued on 31 March 20X1, the decrease in value of $65,000 was deducted from the revaluation reserve.

(v)   Cost of sales includes $15,000 for development expenditure amortised during the year and $10,000 for impairment of the purchased brand name.

(vi)   On 1 November 20X0, OP issued $1 equity shares at a premium. No other finance was raised during the year.

(vii)   OP paid a dividend during the year.

(viii) Other provisions relate to legal claims made against OP during the year ended 31 March 20X1. The amount provided is based on legal opinion at 31 March 20X1 and is included in cost of sales.

Required

(a)   **Prepare** a statement of cash flows, using the indirect method, for OP for the year ended 31 March 20X1, in accordance with IAS 7 *Statement of cash flows.*   **(19 marks)**

The following information should not be included in your answer to part (a). It is only required for your answer to part (b) of the question.

OP's directors acquired equipment on 1 April 20X1 on a finance lease.

The finance lease terms are:

•   Lease for a ten year period
•   Rentals paid annually in arrears on 31 March

- Each annual rental is $44,000
- Original cost of the equipment was $248,610
- The interest rate implicit in the lease is 12% per year

Required

(b) Calculate the amounts in respect of this finance lease that would be included in OP's:

    (i)   Statement of profit or loss and other comprehensive income for the year ended 31 March 20X2
    (ii)   Statement of financial position as at 31 March 20X2
    (ii)   Statement of cash flows for the year ended 31 March 20X2   **(6 marks)**

(Total = 25 marks)

14 YG (11/10)   45 mins

The financial statements of YG are given below.

STATEMENTS OF FINANCIAL POSITION AS AT:

	31 OCTOBER 20X9		31 OCTOBER 20X8	
	$'000	$'000	$'000	$'000
Assets				
Non-current assets				
Property, plant and equipment	4,676		4,248	
Development expenditure	417		494	
		5,093		4,742
Current assets				
Inventory	606		509	
Trade receivables	456		372	
Cash and cash equivalents	1,989		205	
		3,051		1,086
Total assets		8,144		5,828
Equity and liabilities				
Equity shares of $1 each		3,780		2,180
Share premium		1,420		620
Revaluation surplus		560		260
Retained earnings		1,314		1,250
		7,074		4,310
Non-current liabilities				
Long term borrowings	360		715	
Deferred tax	210		170	
		570		885
Current liabilities				
Trade payables	425		310	
Current tax	70		170	
Accrued interest	5		3	
Provision for redundancy costs	0		150	
		500		633
Total equity and liabilities		8,144		5,828

STATEMENT OF PROFIT OR LOSS AND OTHER COMPREHENSIVE INCOME

FOR THE YEAR ENDED 31 OCTOBER 20X9

	$'000
Revenue	6,640
Cost of sales	(3,530)
Gross profit	3,110
Administrative expenses	(2,040)
Distribution costs	(788)
Finance cost	(16)
Profit before tax	266
Income tax expense	(120)
Profit for the year	146
Other comprehensive income:	
Gain on revaluation of property, plant and equipment	300
Total comprehensive income for the year	446

Additional information:

(i) On 1 November 20X8, YG issued 1,600,000 $1 ordinary shares at a premium of 50%. No other finance was raised during the year.

(ii) YG paid a dividend during the year.

(iii) Plant and equipment disposed of in the year had a carrying amount of $70,000; cash received on disposal was $66,000. Any gain or loss on disposal has been included under cost of sales.

(iv) Cost of sales includes $145,000 for development expenditure amortised during the year.

(v) Depreciation charged for the year was $250,000.

(vi) The income tax expense for the year to 31 October 20X9 is made up as follows:

	$'000
Corporate income tax	80
Deferred tax	40
	120

(vii) During the year to 31 October 20X8 YG set up a provision for redundancy costs arising from the closure of one of its activities. During the year to 31 October 20X9, YG spent $177,000 on redundancy costs, the additional cost being charged to administrative expenses.

Required

(a) **Prepare** a statement of cash flows, using the indirect method, for YG for the year ended 31 October 20X9, in accordance with IAS 7 *Statement of cash flows*. **(20 marks)**

(b) Someone you have known for many years has heard that you work for YG, a well known international entity. There are rumours in the press that YG's latest share issue was to raise cash to enable it to launch a takeover bid for another entity. Your friend wants to treat you to dinner at an expensive local restaurant, so that you can give him details of the proposed takeover before it is made public.

Explain how you would respond to your friend. Your answer should include reference to CIMA's Code of Ethics for Professional Accountants. **(5 marks)**

(Total = 25 marks)

15 Objective test questions: Non-current assets, inventories and construction contracts I 49 mins

1 The components of the cost of a major item of equipment are given below.

	$
Purchase price	780,000
Import duties	117,000
Sales tax (refundable)	78,000
Site preparation	30,000
Installation	28,000
Initial operating losses before the asset reaches planned performance	50,000
Estimated cost of dismantling and removal of the asset, recognised as a provision under IAS 37 *Provisions, contingent liabilities and contingent assets*	100,000
	1,183,000

What amount may be recognised as the cost of the asset, according to IAS 16 *Property, plant and equipment?*

A $956,000
B $1,105,000
C $1,055,000
D $1,183,000   **(2 marks)**

2 Which of the following statements about IAS 36 *Impairment of assets* are correct?

1   Non-current assets must be checked annually for evidence of impairment.

2   An impairment loss must be recognised immediately in the statement of profit or loss and other comprehensive income, except that all or part of a loss on a revalued asset should be charged against any related revaluation surplus.

3   If individual assets cannot be tested for impairment, it may be necessary to test a group of assets as a unit.

A   1 and 2 only
B   1 and 3 only
C   2 and 3 only
D   1, 2 and 3   **(2 marks)**

3 Which of the following statements is/are correct?

1   Negative goodwill should be shown in the statement of financial position as a deduction from positive goodwill.

2   IAS 38 allows goodwill to be written off immediately against reserves as an alternative to capitalisation.

3   As a business grows, internally generated goodwill may be revalued upwards to reflect that growth.

4   Internally developed brands must not be capitalised.

A   1 and 4
B   2 and 3
C   3 only
D   4 only   **(2 marks)**

4   Which of the following accounting policies would contravene International Financial Reporting Standards if adopted by a company?

1   Goodwill on acquisitions is written off immediately against reserves.

2   Land on which the company's buildings stand is not depreciated.

3   Internally generated brands are capitalised at fair value as advised by independent consultants.

4   In calculating depreciation, the estimated useful life of an asset is taken as half the actual estimated useful life as a measure of prudence.

A   1, 3 and 4
B   2 and 4 only
C   1 and 3 only
D   All four are unacceptable   **(2 marks)**

5   Which of the following items should be included in arriving at the cost of the inventory of finished goods held by a manufacturing company, according to IAS 2 *Inventories?*

1   Carriage inwards on raw materials delivered to factory
2   Carriage outwards on goods delivered to customers
3   Factory supervisors' salaries
4   Factory heating and lighting
5   Cost of abnormally high idle time in the factory
6   Import duties on raw materials
A   1, 3, 4 and 6
B   1, 2, 4 ,5 and 6
C   3, 4 and 6
D   2, 3 and 5   **(2 marks)**

6   Which of the following statements about IAS 2 *Inventories* is/are correct?

1   Production overheads should be included in cost on the basis of a company's actual level of activity in the period.

2   In arriving at the net realisable value of inventories, trade discounts and settlement discounts must be deducted.

3   In arriving at the cost of inventories, FIFO, LIFO and weighted average cost formulas are acceptable.

4   It is permitted to value finished goods inventories at materials plus labour cost only, without adding production overheads.

A   1 only
B   2 only
C   3 only
D   None of them   **(2 marks)**

7   The position of a construction contract at 30 June 20X6 is as follows.

	$
Contract price	900,000
At 30 June 20X6	
Costs to date	720,000
Estimated costs to completion	480,000
Progress payments invoiced and received	400,000
Percentage complete	60%

What figures should appear for this contract in the accounts at 30 June 20X6, according to IAS 11 *Construction contracts*?

		SPLOCI		Statement of financial position	
A		Sales revenue	$540,000	Receivables	$140,000
		Costs	$840,000		
B		Sales revenue	$540,000		
		Costs	$720,000		
C		Sales revenue	$540,000	Amount due from customer	$20,000
		Costs	$840,000		
D		Sales revenue	$540,000	Receivables	$140,000
		Costs	$720,000		

(2 marks)

8   The following measures relate to a non-current asset:

(i)	Net book value	$20,000
(ii)	Net realisable value	$18,000
(iii)	Value in use	$22,000
(iv)	Replacement cost	$50,000

The recoverable amount of the asset is

A $18,000
B $20,000
C $22,000
D $50,000   **(2 marks)**

9   BL started a contract on 1 November 20X4. The contract was scheduled to run for two years and has a sales value of $40 million.

At 31 October 20X5, the following details were obtained from BL's records:

	$m
Costs incurred to date	16
Estimated costs to completion	18
Percentage complete at 31 October 20X5	45%

Applying IAS 11 *Construction contracts*, how much revenue and profit should BL recognise in its statement of profit or loss and other comprehensive income for the year ended 31 October 20X5?

(2 marks)

10   CI purchased equipment on 1 April 20X2 for $100,000. The equipment was depreciated using the reducing balance method at 25% per year. CI's year end is 31 March.

Depreciation was charged up to and including 31 March 20X6. At that date, the recoverable amount was $28,000.

Calculate the impairment loss on the equipment according to IAS 36 *Impairment of assets*.   **(3 marks)**

The following data is to be used for sub-questions 11 and 12 below

CN started a three year contract to build a new university campus on 1 April 20X5. The contract had a fixed price of $90 million.

CN incurred costs to 31 March 20X6 of $77 million and estimated that a further $33 million would need to be spent to complete the contract.

CN uses the percentage of cost incurred to date to total cost method to calculate stage of completion of the contract.

11   Calculate revenue earned on the contract to 31 March 20X6, according to IAS 11 *Construction contracts*.
(2 marks)

12   State how much gross profit/loss CN should recognise in its statement of profit or loss and other comprehensive income for the year ended 31 March 20X6, according to IAS 11 *Construction contracts*.
(2 marks)

13   IAS 16 *Property, plant and equipment* requires an asset to be measured at cost on its original recognition in the financial statements.

EW used its own staff, assisted by contractors when required, to construct a new warehouse for its own use.

Which **one** of the following costs would **not** be included in attributable costs of the non-current asset?

A   Clearance of the site prior to work commencing.

B   Professional surveyors' fees for managing the construction work.

C   EW's own staff wages for time spent working on the construction.

D   An allocation of EW's administration costs, based on EW staff time spent on the construction as a percentage of the total staff time.   **(2 marks)**

(Total = 27 marks)

16   Objective test questions: Non-current assets, inventories and construction contracts II   63 mins

1   A company purchased a machine for $50,000 on 1 January 20X1. It was judged to have a 5-year life with a residual value of $5,000. On 31 December 20X2 $15,000 was spent on an upgrade to the machine. This extended its remaining useful life to 5 years, with the same residual value. During 20X3, the market for the product declined and the machine was sold on 1 January 20X4 for $7,000.

What was the loss on disposal?

A $31,000
B $35,000
C $31,600
D $35,600   **(2 marks)**

2   A cash generating unit comprises the following:

	$m
Building	20
Plant and equipment	10
Goodwill	5
Current assets	10
	45

Following a downturn in the market, an impairment review has been undertaken and the recoverable amount of the cash generating unit is estimated to be $25m.

What is the carrying value of the building after adjusting for the impairment loss?

A $11m
B $10m
C $12.5m
D $20m   **(2 marks)**

3   In less than **30** words, **define** 'impairment'.   **(2 marks)**

4   Which of the following is *not* true regarding IAS 2 *Inventories*?

     A   Fixed production overheads must be allocated to items of inventory on the basis of the normal level of production.

     B   Plant lying idle will lead to a higher fixed overhead allocation to each unit.

     C   An abnormally high level of production will lead to a lower allocation of fixed production overhead to each unit

     D   Unallocated overheads must be recognised as an expense in the period in which they are incurred.

                 (2 marks)

---

5   In less than **20** words, **define** 'fair value'.   **(2 marks)**

The following data is to be used to answer sub-questions 6 and 7 below

X acquired the business and assets from the owners of an unincorporated business: the purchase price was satisfied by the issue of 10,000 equity shares with a nominal market value of $10 each and $20,000 cash. The market value of X shares at the date of acquisition was $20 each.

The assets acquired were:

- Net tangible non-current assets with a book value of $20,000 and current value of $25,000.

- Patents for a specialised process valued by a specialist valuer at $15,000.

- Brand name, valued by a specialist brand valuer on the basis of a multiple of earnings at $50,000.

- Publishing rights of the first text from an author that the management of X expects to become a best seller. The publishing rights were a gift from the author to the previous owners at no cost. The management of X has estimated the future value of the potential best seller at $100,000. However, there is no reliable evidence available to support the estimate of the management.

---

6   In no more than **30 words**, **explain** the accounting treatment to be used for the publishing rights of the first text.   **(2 marks)**

---

7   **Calculate** the value of goodwill to be included in the accounts of X for this purchase.   **(4 marks)**

---

8   An item of plant and equipment was purchased on 1 April 20X1 for $100,000. At the date of acquisition its expected useful life was 10 years. Depreciation was provided on a straight line basis, with no residual value.

     On April 1 20X3, the asset was revalued to $95,000. On 1 April 20X4, the useful life of the asset was reviewed and the remaining useful life was reduced to 5 years, a total useful life of 8 years.

     Calculate the amounts that would be included in the statement of financial position for the asset cost/valuation and provision for accumulated depreciation at 31 March 20X5.   **(4 marks)**

---

9   IAS 16 *Property, plant and equipment* provides definitions of terms relevant to non-current assets. Complete the following sentence, **in no more than 10 words**.

        'Depreciable amount is ...'   **(2 marks)**

10 Which **one** of the following items would CM recognise as subsequent expenditure on a non-current asset and capitalise it as required by IAS 16 *Property, plant and equipment*?

    A   CM purchased a furnace five years ago, when the furnace lining was separately identified in the accounting records. The furnace now requires relining at a cost of $200,000. When the furnace is relined it will be able to be used in CM's business for a further five years.

    B   CM's office building has been badly damaged by a fire. CM intends to restore the building to its original condition at a cost of $250,000.

    C   CM's delivery vehicle broke down. When it was inspected by the repairers it was discovered that it needed a new engine. The engine and associated labour costs are estimated to be $5,000.

    D   CM closes its factory for two weeks every year. During this time, all plant and equipment has its routine annual maintenance check and any necessary repairs are carried out. The cost of the current year's maintenance check and repairs was $75,000. **(2 marks)**

---

11 DS purchased a machine on 1 October 20X2 at a cost of $21,000 with an expected useful economic life of six years, with no expected residual value. DS depreciates its machines using the straight line basis.

The machine has been used and depreciated for three years to 30 September 20X5. New technology was invented in December 20X5, which enabled a cheaper, more efficient machine to be produced; this technology makes DS's type of machine obsolete. The obsolete machine will generate no further economic benefit or have any residual value once the new machines become available. However, because of production delays, the new machines will not be available on the market until 1 October 20X7.

Calculate how much depreciation DS should charge to profit or loss for the year ended 30 September 20X6, as required by IAS 16 *Property, plant and equipment*. **(3 marks)**

---

12 IAS 38 *Intangible assets* sets out six criteria that must be met before an internally generated intangible asset can be recognised.

List four of IAS 38's criteria for recognition. **(4 marks)**

---

13 Details from DV's long-term contract, which commenced on 1 May 20X6, at 30 April 20X7:

	$'000
Invoiced to client for work done	2,000
Costs incurred to date:	
Attributable to work completed	1,500
Inventory purchased, but not yet used	250
Progress payment received from client	900
Expected further costs to complete project	400
Total contract value	3,000

DV uses the percentage of costs incurred to total costs to calculate attributable profit.

Calculate the amount that DV should recognise in its statement of profit or loss and other comprehensive income for the year ended 30 April 20X7 for revenue, cost of sales and attributable profits on this contract according to IAS 11 *Construction contracts*. **(4 marks)**

(Total = 35 marks)

17 Section B questions: Non-current assets, inventories and construction contracts
63 mins

(a) (i) **Discuss** the criteria which IAS 38 *Intangible assets* states should be used when considering whether research and development expenditure should be written off in an accounting period or carried forward.

(ii) **Discuss** to what extent these criteria are consistent with the fundamental accounting assumptions within IAS 1. **(5 marks)**

(b) 'The cost of inventories should comprise all costs of purchase, costs of conversion and other costs incurred in bringing the inventories to their present location and condition' (IAS 2).

This statement results in problems of a practical nature in arriving at the amount at which inventories and short term work in progress are stated in the accounts.

Required

Comment on the above statement **identifying** and **discussing** both the accounting policy and the problems 'of a practical nature' that may arise when computing the amount at which inventories and short term work in progress are stated in financial accounts. **(5 marks)**

(c) A new type of delivery vehicle, when purchased on 1 April 20X0 for $20,000, was expected to have a useful life of four years. It now appears that the original estimate of the useful life was too short, and the vehicle is now expected to have a useful life of six years, from the date of purchase. All delivery vehicles are depreciated using the straight-line method and are assumed to have zero residual value.

Required

As the trainee management accountant, draft a memo to the transport manager **explaining** whether it is possible to change the useful life of the new delivery vehicle. Using appropriate International Financial Reporting Standards, **explain** how the accounting transactions relating to the delivery vehicle should be recorded in the statement of profit or loss and other comprehensive income for the year ended 31 March 20X3 and the statement of financial position at that date **(5 marks)**

P7 Pilot paper

(d) BI owns a building which it uses as its offices, warehouse and garage. The land is carried as a separate non-current tangible asset in the statement of financial position.

BI has a policy of regularly revaluing its non-current tangible assets. The original cost of the building in October 20X2 was $1,000,000; it was assumed to have a remaining useful life of 20 years at that date, with no residual value. The building was revalued on 30 September 20X4 by a professional valuer at $1,800,000.

BI also owns a brand name which it acquired 1 October 20X0 for $500,000. The brand name is being amortised over 10 years.

The economic climate had deteriorated during 20X5, causing BI to carry out an impairment review of its assets at 30 September 20X5. BI's building was valued at a market value of $1,500,000 on 30 September 20X5 by an independent valuer. A brand specialist valued BI's brand name at market value of $200,000 on the same date.

BI's management accountant calculated that the brand name's value in use at 30 September 20X5 was $150,000.

Required

Explain how BI should report the events described above and **quantify** any amounts required to be included in its financial statements for the year ended 30 September 20X5. **(5 marks)**

P7 11/05

(e) DV purchased two buildings on 1 September 1996. Building A cost $200,000 and had a useful economic life of 20 years. Building B cost $120,000 and had a useful life of 15 years. DV's accounting policies are to revalue buildings every five years and depreciate them over their useful economic lives on the straight line basis. DV does not make an annual transfer from revaluation surplus to retained profits for excess depreciation.

DV received the following valuations from its professionally qualified external valuer:

31 August 2001	Building A	$180,000
	Building B	$75,000
31 August 2006	Building A	$100,000
	Building B	$30,000

Required

Calculate the gains or impairments arising on the revaluation of Buildings A and B at 31 August 2006 and identify where they should be recognised in the financial statements of DV. **(5 marks)**

(f) HS, a contractor, signed a two year fixed price contract on 31 March 20X8 for $300,000 to build a bridge. Total costs were originally estimated at $240,000.

At 31 March 20X9, HS extracted the following figures from its financial records:

	$'000
Contract value	300
Costs incurred to date	170
Estimated costs to complete	100
Progress payments received	130
Value of work completed	165

HS calculates the stage of completion of contracts using the value of work completed as a proportion of total contract value.

Required

Calculate the following amounts for the contract that should be shown in HS's financial statements:

Statement of profit or loss and other comprehensive income:

- Revenue recognised for the year ended 31 March 20X9
- Profit recognised for the year ended 31 March 20X9

Statement of financial position:

- Gross amount due to/from the customer at 31 March 20X9, stating whether it is an asset or liability **(5 marks)**

(g) EK publishes various types of book and occasionally produces films which it sells to major film distributors.

(i) On 31 March 20X7, EK acquired book publishing and film rights to the next book to be written by an internationally acclaimed author, for $1 million. The author has not yet started writing the book but expects to complete it in 20X9.

(ii) Between 1 June and 31 July 20X7, EK spent $500,000 exhibiting its range of products at a major international trade fair. This was the first time EK had attended this type of event. No new orders were taken as a direct result of the event, although EK directors claim to have made valuable contacts that should generate additional sales or additional funding for films in the future. No estimate can be made of additional revenue at present.

(iii) During the year, EK employed an external consultant to redesign EK's corporate logo and to create advertising material to improve EK's corporate image. The total cost of the consultancy was $800,000.

EK's directors want to treat all of the above items of expenditure as assets.

Required

Explain how EK should treat these items of expenditure in its financial statements for the year ended 31 October 20X7 with reference to the International Accounting Standard Board's *Conceptual Framework for Financial Reporting (2010)* and relevant International Financial Reporting Standards. **(5 marks)**

P7 5/08

(Total = 35 marks)

18 Geneva 27 mins

Geneva Co is a company involved in the building industry and often has a number of major construction contracts which fall into two or more accounting periods.

During the year ended 31 December 20X8, Geneva Co enters into three construction contracts as follows:

		Contract	
	Lausanne	*Bern*	*Zurich*
	$'000	$'000	$'000
Fixed contract price	2,000	2,000	2,000
Payments on account	1,080	950	800
Costs incurred to date	1,000	1,100	640
Estimated costs to complete the contract	600	1,100	1,160
Estimate percentage of work completed	60%	50%	35%

Required

Show how each contract would be reflected in the statement of financial position and statement of profit or loss and other comprehensive income of Geneva Co for the year ended 31 December 20X8. **(5 marks each)**

(Total = 15 marks)

19 Objective test questions: Capital transactions and financial instruments
43 mins

1   A company made an issue of 100,000 ordinary shares of 50c at $1.10 each. The cash received was correctly recorded in the cash book but the whole amount was entered into ordinary share capital account.

Which of the following journal entries will correct the error made in recording the issue?

		Debit $	Credit $
A	Share capital account	10,000	
	Share premium account		10,000
B	Cash	60,000	
	Share premium account		60,000
C	Share capital account	60,000	
	Share premium account		60,000
D	Share premium account	60,000	
	Share capital account		60,000

(2 marks)

2   A company issued 1,000,000 $1 shares at $1.50 each payable as follows.

On application (including premium)	70c
On allotment	30c
First and final call	50c

All monies were received except for the call due from a holder of 10,000 shares. These shares were subsequently forfeited and reissued at $1.60 per share.

What *total* will be credited to share premium account as a result of this issue?

A $501,000
B $506,000
C $511,000
D   None of the above   **(2 marks)**

3   At 1 January 20X4, a company's share capital consisted of 1,000,000 ordinary shares of 50c each, and there was a balance of $800,000 on its share premium account.

During 20X4, the following events took place.

1 March	The company made a bonus issue of 1 share for every 2 held, using the share premium account.
1 July	The company issued 600,000 shares at $2 per share.
1 October	The company made a rights issue of 1 share for every 3 held at $1.80 per share.

What are the balances on the company's share capital and share premium accounts at 31 December 20X4?

	Share capital $	Share premium $
A	1,400,000	2,860,000
B	2,800,000	1,460,000
C	1,800,000	2,320,000
D	1,400,000	2,360,000

(2 marks)

4   Which of the following statements regarding share issues is **incorrect**?

A   Application is where potential shareholders apply for shares in the company and send cash to cover their application

B   Allotment is when the company allocates shares to the successful applicants and returns cash to unsuccessful applicants

C   A call is where the purchase value is payable in instalments. The company will 'call' for instalments.

D   If a shareholder fails to pay a call his allotment is cancelled and his money returned to him. His shares may then be reissued.

(2 marks)

5   An entity has the following categories of funding in its statement of financial position:

1   A preference share that is redeemable for cash at a 10% premium on 30 May 2015.
2   An ordinary share which is not redeemable and has no restrictions on receiving dividends.
3   A loan note that is redeemable at par in 2020.
4   A cumulative preference share that is entitled to receive a dividend of 7% a year.

Applying IAS 32 *Financial instruments: presentation*, how would **each** of the above be categorised on the statement of financial position?

	As an equity instrument	As a financial liability
A	1 and 2	3 and 4
B	2 and 3	1 and 4
C	2	1, 3 and 4
D	1, 2 and 3	4

(2 marks)

6   BN purchased 100,000 of its own equity shares in the market and classified them as treasury shares. BN still held the treasury shares at the year end.

How should BN classify the treasury shares on its closing statement of financial position in accordance with IAS 32 *Financial instruments: presentation*?

A   As a non-current asset investment.
B   As a deduction from equity.
C   As a current asset investment.
D   As a non-current liability.

(2 marks)

The following data applies to questions 7 and 8.

On 1 January 20X7 PX issued 10m 7% $1 preference shares, redeemable after 4 years at a 5% premium. Issue charges amount to $500,000 and the effective interest rate is 10%.

7   **Calculate** the total finance charge on the issue of the preference shares.   **(3 marks)**

8   **Calculate** the amount the preference shares will be shown at in the statement of financial position at 31 December 20X8.   **(3 marks)**

9   Which **one** of the following gives the true meaning of "treasury shares"?

A   Shares owned by a country's Treasury
B   An entity's own shares purchased by the entity and still held at the period end
C   An entity's own shares purchased by the entity and resold before the period end at a gain
D   An entity's own shares purchased by the entity and cancelled

(2 marks)

10   At 31 December 20X1 the capital structure of a company was as follows:

	$
Ordinary share capital	
100,000 shares of 50c each	50,000
Share premium account	180,000

During 20X2 the company made a bonus issue of 1 share for every 2 held, using the share premium account for the purpose, and later issued for cash another 60,000 shares at 80c per share.

What is the company's capital structure at 31 December 20X2?

	Ordinary share capital	Share premium account
	$	$
A	130,000	173,000
B	105,000	173,000
C	130,000	137,000
D	105,000	137,000

(2 marks)

11   At 30 June 20X2 a company's capital structure was as follows:

	$
Ordinary share capital	
500,000 shares of 25c each	125,000
Share premium account	100,000

In the year ended 30 June 20X3 the company made a rights issue of 1 share for every 2 held at $1 per share and this was taken up in full. Directly attributable issue costs amounted to $1,200. Later in the year the company made a bonus issue of 1 share for every 5 held, using the share premium account for the purpose.

Calculate the balance on the share premium account at 30 June 20X3.   (2 marks)

(Total = 24 marks)

20 Objective test questions: Accounting standards I   65 mins

1   A company leases some plant on 1 January 20X4. The cash price of the plant is $9,000, and the company leases it for four years, paying four annual instalments of $3,000 beginning on 31 December 20X4.

The company uses the sum-of-the-digits method to allocate interest.

What is the interest charge for the year ended 31 December 20X5?

A $900
B $600
C $1,000
D $750   (2 marks)

2   A company leases some plant on 1 January 20X4. The cash price is $9,000, and the company is to pay four annual instalments of $3,000, beginning on 1 January 20X4.

The company uses the sum-of-the-digits method to allocate interest.

What is the interest charge for the year ended 31 December 20X5?

A $750
B $500
C $900
D $1,000   (2 marks)

3   Which of the following statements about IAS 10 *Events after the reporting period* are correct?

1   A material event that occurs before the financial statements are authorised that provides more evidence of conditions that already existed at the reporting date should be adjusted for in the financial statements.

2   The notes to the financial statements must give details of non-adjusting events affecting the users' ability to understand the company's financial position.

3   Financial statements should not be prepared on a going concern basis if after the end of the reporting period but before the financial statements are authorised the directors have decided to liquidate the company.

A   All three statements are correct.
B   1 and 2 only
C   1 and 3 only
D   2 and 3 only   (2 marks)

4   A company's statement of profit or loss and other comprehensive income showed a profit before tax of $1,800,000

After the year end and before the financial statements were authorised for issue, the following events took place.

1   The value of an investment held at the year end fell by $85,000.

2   A customer who owed $116,000 at the year end went bankrupt owing a total of $138,000.

3   Inventory valued at cost $161,000 in the statement of financial position was sold for $141,000.

4   Assets with a carrying value at the year end of $240,000 were unexpectedly expropriated by government.

What is the company's profit after making the necessary adjustments for these events?

A $1,399,000
B $1,579,000
C $1,664,000
D   None of these figures   (2 marks)

5   Which of the following events after the reporting period would normally be classified as *adjusting*, according to IAS 10 *Events after the reporting period*?

1   Destruction of a major non-current asset
2   Issue of shares and loan notes
3   Discovery of error or fraud
4   Evidence of impairment in value of a property as at the year end
5   Purchases and sales of non-current assets

A   1, 2 and 5 only
B   3 and 4 only
C   3, 4 and 5 only
D   1, 3 and 4 only   (2 marks)

6   Which of the following events after the reporting period would normally be classified as *non-adjusting*, according to IAS 10 *Events after the reporting period*?

1   Opening new trading operations
2   Sale of goods held at the year end for less than cost
3   A customer is discovered to be insolvent
4   Announcement of plan to discontinue an operation
5   Expropriation of major assets by government

A   2 and 3 only
B   1, 2 and 3 only
C   2, 3, 4 and 5 only
D   1, 4 and 5 only   (2 marks)

7   In compiling its financial statements, the directors of a company have to decide on the correct treatment of the following items.

1   An employee has commenced an action against the company for wrongful dismissal. The company's solicitors estimate that the ex-employee has a 40 per cent chance of success in the action.

2   The company has guaranteed the overdraft of another company, not at present in any financial difficulties. The possibility of a liability arising is thought to be remote.

3   Shortly after the year end, a major installation owned by the company was destroyed in a flood. The company's going concern status is not affected.

What are the correct treatments for these items, assuming all are of material amount?

A   All three should be disclosed by note.
B   A provision should be made for item 1 and items 2 and 3 disclosed by note.
C   Items 1 and 3 should be disclosed by note, with no disclosure for item 2.
D   Item 1 should be disclosed by note. No disclosure is required for items 2 and 3.   **(2 marks)**

8   Which of the following statements about IAS 37 *Provisions, contingents liabilities and contingent assets* are correct?

1   Provisions should be made for constructive obligations (those arising from a company's pattern of past practice) as well as for obligations enforceable by law.

2   Discounting may be used when estimating the amount of a provision if the effect is material.

3   A restructuring provision must include the estimated costs of retraining or relocating continuing staff.

4   A restructuring provision may only be made when a company has a detailed plan for the reconstruction and a firm intention to carry it out.

A   All four statements are correct
B   1, 2 and 4 only
C   1, 3 and 4 only
D   2, 3 and 4 only   **(2 marks)**

9   Which of the following criteria must be present in order for a company to recognise a provision?

1   There is a present obligation as a result of past events.
2   It is probable that a transfer of economic benefits will be required to settle the obligation.
3   A reliable estimate of the obligation can be made.

A   All three criteria must be present.
B   1 and 2 only
C   1 and 3 only
D   2 and 3 only   **(2 marks)**

10   Which **one** of the following would be treated as a non-adjusting event after the reporting period, as required by IAS 10 *Events after the reporting period*, in the financial statements of AN for the period ended 31 January 20X5? The financial statements were approved for publication on 15 May 20X5.

A   Notice was received on 31 March 20X5 that a major customer of AN had ceased trading and was unlikely to make any further payments.

B   Inventory items at 31 January 20X5, original cost $30,000, were sold in April 20X5 for $20,000.

C   During 2004, a customer commenced legal action against AN. At 31 January 20X5, legal advisers were of the opinion that AN would lose the case, so AN created a provision of $200,000 for the damages claimed by the customer. On 27 April 20X5, the court awarded damages of $250,000 to the customer.

D   There was a fire on 2 May 20X5 in AN's main warehouse which destroyed 50% of AN's total inventory.   **(2 marks)**

11 DT's final dividend for the year ended 31 October 20X5 of $150,000 was declared on 1 February 20X6 and paid in cash on 1 April 20X6. The financial statements were approved on 31 March 20X6.

The following statements refer to the treatment of the dividend in the accounts of DT:

1 The payment clears an accrued liability set up as at 31 October 20X5.

2 The dividend is shown as a deduction in the statement of profit or loss and other comprehensive income for the year ended 31 October 20X6.

3 The dividend is shown as an accrued liability as at 31 October 20X6.

4 The $150,000 dividend was shown in the notes to the financial statements at 31 October 20X5.

5 The dividend is shown as a deduction in the statement of changes in equity for the year ended 31 October 20X6.

Which of the above statements reflect the correct treatment of the dividend?

A 1 and 2
B 1 and 4
C 3 and 5
D 4 and 5 **(2 marks)**

12 List the **three** criteria specified in IAS 37 *Provisions, contingent liabilities and contingent assets* that must be satisfied before a provision is recognised in the financial statements. **(3 marks)**

13 DH has the following two legal claims outstanding:

• A legal action against DH claiming compensation of $700,000, filed in February 20X7. DH has been advised that it is probable that the liability will materialise.

• A legal action taken by DH against another entity, claiming damages of $300,000, started in March 20X4. DH has been advised that it is probable that it will win the case.

How should DH report these legal actions in its financial statements for the year ended 30 April 20X7?

	Legal action against DH	Legal action taken by DH
A	Disclose by a note to the accounts	No disclosure
B	Make a provision	No disclosure
C	Make a provision	Disclose as a note
D	Make a provision	Accrue the income

(2 marks)

14 Define an operating segment as per IFRS 8 *Operating segments*. **(3 marks)**

15 Which **one** of the following is a criteria for determining a reportable segment under IFRS 8 *Operating segments*?

A Its revenue is 15% or more of the total revenue of all segments
B Its revenue is 10% or more of the total revenue of all operating segments
C Its assets are 10% or more of the combined assets of all operating segments
D Its assets are 15% or more of the combined assets of all operating segments **(2 marks)**

16 Which **one** of the following material items would be classified as a non-adjusting event in HL's financial statements for the year ended 31 December 20X8 according to IAS 10 *Events after the reporting period*?

HL's financial statements were approved for publication on 8 April 20X9.

A On 1 March 20X9, HL's auditors discovered that, due to an error during the count, the closing inventory had been undervalued by $250,000.

B Lightning struck one of HL's production facilities on 31 January 20X9 and caused a serious fire. The fire destroyed half of the factory and its machinery. Output was severely reduced for six months.

C One of HL's customers commenced court action against HL on 1 December 20X8. At 31 December 20X8, HL did not know whether the case would go against it or not. On 1 March 20X9, the court found against HL and awarded damages of $150,000 to the customer.

D On 15 March 20X9, HL was advised by the liquidator of one of its customers that it was very unlikely to receive any payments for the balance of $300,000 that was outstanding at 31 December 20X8. **(2 marks)**

17 Which of the following are required by IFRS 8 *Operating segments* to be disclosed in an entity's financial statements, if they are included in the measure of segment profit or loss to be reported to the chief operating decision maker?

(i) Revenues from transactions with other operating segments within the entity
(ii) Cost of sales
(iii) Amortisation
(iv) Income tax expense
(v) Administrative expenses and distribution costs

A (i), (ii) and (v)
B (ii), (iii) and (iv)
C (ii), (iii) and (v)
D (i), (iii) and (iv)

(2 marks)

(Total = 36 marks)

21 Objective test questions: Accounting standards II   86 mins

1 IAS 37 *Provisions, contingent liabilities and contingent assets* governs the recognition of contingent items. Which of the following statements about contingencies, if any, are correct according to IAS 37?

1 A contingent liability should be disclosed by note if it is probable that an obligation will arise and its amount can be estimated reliably.

2 A contingent asset should be disclosed by note if it is probable that it will arise.

3 An entity should not recognise a contingent asset.

A None of the statements is correct.
B 1 and 2
C 2 and 3
D All of the statements are correct. **(2 marks)**

2   IAS 24 *Related party disclosures* governs disclosures required for transactions between a company and parties deemed to be related to it.

Which of the following parties will normally be held to be related parties of a company?

1   Its subsidiary companies
2   Its directors
3   Close family of the company's directors
4   Providers of finance to the company
5   A customer or supplier with whom the company has a significant volume of business

A   All of the parties listed
B   1, 2, 3 and 4 only
C   1, 2 and 3 only
D   3, 4 and 5 only   (2 marks)

3   Which of the following statements defines a finance lease?

A   A short term hire agreement

B   A long term hire agreement where the legal title in the asset passes on the final payment

C   A long term hire agreement where substantially all the risks and rewards of ownership are transferred

D   A long term hire agreement where the hirer is responsible for maintenance of the asset   **(2 marks)**

4   An asset is hired under a finance lease with a deposit of $30,000 on 1 January 20X1 plus 8 six monthly payments in arrears of $20,000 each. The fair value of the asset is $154,000. The finance charge is to be allocated using the sum-of-the-digits method.

What is the finance charge for the year ending 31 December 20X3?

A $7,000
B $8,000
C $10,000
D $11,000   **(2 marks)**

5   The directors of Robin (year end 31 December 20X6) were informed on 27 February 20X7 that a serious fire at one of the company's factories had stopped production there for at least six months to come. On 3 March 20X7 the directors of Robin were informed that a major customer had gone into liquidation owing a substantial amount to Robin as at the year end. The liquidator was pessimistic about the prospect of recovering anything for unsecured creditors. The financial statements for the year ended 31 December 20X6 were approved on 20 March 20X7.

In accordance with IAS 10 *Events after the reporting period*, how should the two events be treated in the financial statements?

	Fire	Liquidation
A	Accrued in accounts	Disclosed in notes
B	Disclosed in notes	Disclosed in notes
C	Accrued in accounts	Accrued in accounts
D	Disclosed in notes	Accrued in accounts

(2 marks)

6   In which of the following circumstances would a provision be recognised under IAS 37 *Provisions, contingent liabilities and contingent assets* in the financial statements for the year ending 31 March 20X6?

    1   A board decision was made on 15 March to close down a division with potential costs of $100,000. At 31 March the decision had not been communicated to managers, employees or customers.

    2   There are anticipated costs from returns of a defective product in the next few months of $60,000. In the past all returns of defective products have always been refunded to customers.

    3   It is anticipated that a major refurbishment of the company Head Office will take place from June onwards costing $85,000.

    A   1 and 2 only
    B   2 and 3 only
    C   2 only
    D   3 only   **(2 marks)**

7   According to IAS 24 *Related party disclosures*, which of the following would be presumed to be a related party of Fredo unless it can be demonstrated otherwise?

    A   The bank which has given a loan to Fredo
    B   The husband of the managing director of Fredo
    C   Fredo's major supplier
    D   The assistant accountant of Fredo   **(2 marks)**

8   **List** the three criteria set out in IAS 37 *Provisions, contingent liabilities and contingent assets* for the recognition of a provision.   **(3 marks)**

9   AP has the following two legal claims outstanding:

    •   A legal action claiming compensation of $500,000 filed against AP in March 20X4.

    •   A legal action taken by AP against a third party, claiming damages of $200,000 was started in January 20X3 and is nearing completion.

In both cases, it is more likely than not that the amount claimed will have to be paid.

How should AP report these legal actions in its financial statements for the year ended 31 March 20X5?

	Legal action against AP	Legal action by AP
A	Disclose by a note	No disclosure
B	Make a provision	No disclosure
C	Make a provision	Disclose as a note
D	Make a provision	Accrue the income

    (2 marks)

10 Which one of the following would be regarded as a related party of BS?

    A   BX, a customer of BS.

    B   The president of the BS Board, who is also the chief executive officer of another entity, BU, that supplies goods to BS.

    C   BQ, a supplier of BS.

    D   BY, BS's main banker.   **(2 marks)**

11 An item of machinery leased under a five year finance lease on 1 October 20X3 had a fair value of $51,900 at date of purchase.

The lease payments were $12,000 per year, payable in arrears.

If the sum of digits method is used to apportion interest to accounting periods, **calculate** the finance cost for the year ended 30 September 20X5.   **(3 marks)**

12   Which one of the following would require a provision to be created by BW at its year end of 31 October 20X5?

    A   The government introduced new laws on data protection which come into force on 1 January 20X6. BW's directors have agreed that this will require a large number of staff to be retrained. At 31 October 20X5, the directors were waiting on a report they had commissioned that would identify the actual training requirements.

    B   At the year end, BW is negotiating with its insurance provider about the amount of an insurance claim that it had filed. On 20 November 20X5, the insurance provider agreed to pay $200,000.

    C   BW makes refunds to customers for any goods returned within 30 days of sale, and has done so for many years.

    D   A customer is suing BW for damages alleged to have been caused by BW's product. BW is contesting the claim and, at 31 October 20X5, the directors have been advised by BW's legal advisers it is very unlikely to lose the case.   **(2 marks)**

13   IAS 18 *Revenue* defines when revenue may be recognised on the sale of goods.

    List four of the five conditions that IAS 18 requires to be met for income to be recognised.   **(4 marks)**

The following data is given for sub-questions 14 and 15 below

CS acquired a machine, using a finance lease, on 1 January 20X4. The machine had an expected useful life of 12,000 operating hours, after which it would have no residual value.

The finance lease was for a five-year term with rentals of $20,000 per year payable in arrears. The cost price of the machine was $80,000 and the implied interest rate is 7.93% per year. CS used the machine for 2,600 hours in 20X4 and 2,350 hours in 20X5.

14   Using the actuarial method, **calculate** the non-current liability and current liability figures required by IAS 17 *Leases* to be shown in CS's statement of financial position at 31 December 20X5.   **(3 marks)**

15   Calculate the non-current asset – property, plant and equipment net book value that would be shown in CS's statement of financial position at 31 December 20X5. **Calculate** the depreciation charge using the machine hours method.   **(2 marks)**

16   On 31 March 20X7, DT received an order from a new customer, XX, for products with a sales value of $900,000. XX enclosed a deposit with the order of $90,000.

On 31 March 20X7, DT had not completed credit referencing of XX and had not despatched any goods. DT is considering the following possible entries for this transaction in its financial statements for the year ended 31 March 20X7.

    1   Include $900,000 in statement of profit or loss and other comprehensive income revenue for the year

    2   Include $90,000 in statement of profit or loss and other comprehensive income revenue for the year

    3   Do not include anything in statement of profit of loss and other comprehensive income revenue for the year

    4   Create a trade receivable for $810,000

    5   Create a trade payable for $90,000

According to IAS 18 *Revenue*, how should DT record this transaction in its financial statements for the year ended 31 March 20X7?

    A   1 and 4
    B   2 and 5
    C   3 and 4
    D   3 and 5   **(2 marks)**

The following data is to be used in sub questions 17 and 18 below

Company X closed **one** of its divisions 12 months ago. It has yet to dispose of **one** remaining machine. The carrying value of the machine at the date when business ceased was $750,000. It was being depreciated at 25% on a reducing balance basis. Company X has been advised that the fair value of the machine is $740,000 and expects to incur costs of $10,000 in making the sale. It has located a probable buyer but the sale will not be completed before the year end.

17   At what amount should the machine be shown in the year end financial statements of Company X?

     A $750,000
     B $562,500
     C $740,000
     D $730,000   **(2 marks)**

18   Where should the carrying value of the machine be shown in Company X's statement of financial position?

     A   Under non-current assets
     B   Under current assets
     C   Included within inventory
     D   Included within receivables   **(2 marks)**

19   GD's financial reporting period is 1 September 2007 to 31 August 2008.

Which **one** of the following would be classified as a non-adjusting event according to IAS 10 *Events after the reporting period*?

Assume all amounts are material and that GD's financial statements have not yet been approved for publication.

     A   On 30 October 2008, GD received a communication stating that one of its customers had ceased trading and gone into liquidation. The balance outstanding at 31 August 2008 was unlikely to be paid.

     B   At 31 August 2008, GD had not provided for an outstanding legal action against the local government administration for losses suffered as a result of incorrect enforcement of local business regulations. On 5 November 2008, the court awarded GD $50,000 damages.

     C   On 1 October 2008, GD made a rights issue of 1 new share for every 3 shares held at a price of $175. The market price on that date was $200.

     D   At 31 August 2008, GD had an outstanding insurance claim of $150,000. On 10 October 2008, the insurance company informed GD that it would pay $140,000 as settlement.   **(2 marks)**

20   Which **one** of the following would **not** normally be treated as a related party of HJ in accordance with IAS 24 *Related party disclosures*?

     A   XX, HJ's largest customer, accounts for 75% of HJ's turnover
     B   HJ2, a subsidiary of HJ, that does not trade with HJ
     C   HJA, an associate of HJ
     D   A shareholder of HJ, holding 25% of HJ's equity shares   **(2 marks)**

21   HP entered into an operating lease for a machine on 1 May 20X7 with the following terms:

     •   Five years non-cancellable lease
     •   12 months rent free period from commencement
     •   Rent of $12,000 per annum payable at $1,000 a month from month 13 onwards
     •   Machine useful life 15 years

Calculate the amount that should be charged to profit or loss in HP's financial statements in respect of the lease, for each of the years ended 30 April 20X8 and 30 April 20X9.   **(3 marks)**

(Total = 48 marks)

22   Section B questions: Accounting standards I   72 mins

(a)   The following definitions have been taken from the IASB's *Conceptual Framework for Financial Reporting*.

   •   'An asset is a resource controlled by the entity as a result of past events and from which future economic benefits are expected to flow to the entity.'

   •   'A liability is a present obligation of the entity arising from past events, the settlement of which is expected to result in an outflow from the entity of resources embodying economic benefits.'

   IAS 17 *Leases* requires lessees to capitalise finance leases in their financial statements.

   Required

   Explain how IAS 17's treatment of finance leases applies the definitions of assets and liabilities.

                                                                                        (5 marks)

(b)   NDL drilled a new oil well, which started production on 1 March 20X3. The licence granting permission to drill the new oil well included a clause that requires NDL to 'return the land to the state it was in before drilling commenced'.

   NDL estimates that the oil well will have a 20-year production life. At the end of that time, the oil well will be de-commissioned and work carried out to reinstate the land. The cost of this de-commissioning work is estimated to be $20 million.

   Required

   As the trainee management accountant, draft a memo to the production manager **explaining** how NDL must treat the de-commissioning costs in its financial statements for the year to 31 March 20X3. Your memo should refer to appropriate International Financial Reporting Standards.   **(5 marks)**

                                                                                        `P7 Pilot paper`

(c)   BJ is an entity that provides a range of facilities for holidaymakers and travellers.

   At 1 October 20X4 these included:

   •   A short haul airline operating within Europe; and
   •   A travel agency specialising in arranging holidays to more exotic destinations, such as Hawaii and Fiji.

   BJ's airline operation has made significant losses for the last two years. On 31 January 20X5, the directors of BJ decided that, due to a significant increase in competition on short haul flights within Europe, BJ would close all of its airline operations and dispose of its fleet of aircraft. All flights for holiday makers and travellers who had already booked seats would be provided by third party airlines. All operations ceased on 31 May 20X5.

   On 31 July 20X5, BJ sold its fleet of aircraft and associated non-current assets for $500 million, the carrying value at that date was $750 million.

   At the reporting date, BJ were still in negotiation with some employees regarding severance payments. BJ has estimated that in the financial period October 20X5 to September 20X6, they will agree a settlement of $20 million compensation.

   The closure of the airline operation caused BJ to carry out a major restructuring of the entire entity. The restructuring has been agreed by the directors and active steps have been taken to implement it. The cost of restructuring to be incurred in year 20X5/20X6 is estimated at $10 million.

   Required

   Explain how BJ should report the events described above and quantify any amounts required to be included in its financial statements for the year ended 30 September 20X5. (Detailed disclosure notes are not required.)   **(5 marks)**

                                                                                        `P7 11/05`

(d) CB is an entity specialising in importing a wide range of non-food items and selling them to retailers. George is CB's president and founder and owns 40% of CB's equity shares:

- CB's largest customer, XC, accounts for 35% of CB's revenue. XC has just completed negotiations with CB for a special 5% discount on all sales.

- During the accounting period, George purchased a property from CB for $500,000. CB had previously declared the property surplus to its requirements and had valued it at $750,000.

- George's son, Arnold, is a director in a financial institution, FC. During the accounting period, FC advanced $2 million to CB as an unsecured loan at a favourable rate of interest.

Required

Explain, with reasons, the extent to which each of the above transactions should be classified and disclosed in accordance with IAS 24 *Related party disclosures* in CB's financial statements for the period.

(5 marks)

`P7 5/06`

(e) CR issued 200,000 $10 redeemable 5% preference shares at par on 1 April 20X5. The shares were redeemable on 31 March 20Y0 at a premium of 15%. Issue costs amounted to $192,800.

Required

(i) **Calculate** the total finance cost over the life of the preference shares. **(2 marks)**

(ii) **Calculate** the annual charge to the statement of profit or loss and other comprehensive income for finance expense, as required by IAS 39 *Financial instruments: recognition and measurement*, for each of the five years 20X6 to 20Y0. Assume the constant annual rate of interest as 10%.

(3 marks)

(Total = 5 marks)

`P7 5/06`

(f) You are in charge of the preparation of the financial statements for DF. You are nearing completion of the preparation of the accounts for the year ended 30 September 20X6 and two items have come to your attention.

(i) Shortly after a senior employee left in April 20X6, a number of accounting discrepancies were discovered. With further investigation, it became clear that fraudulent activity had been going on. DF has calculated that, because of the fraud, the profit for the year ended 30 September 20X5 had been overstated by $45,000.

(ii) On 1 September 20X6, DF received an order from a new customer enclosing full payment for the goods ordered; the order value was $90,000. DF scheduled the manufacture of the goods to commence on 28 November 20X6. The cost of manufacture was expected to be $70,000. DF's management want to recognise the $20,000 profit in the statement of profit or loss and other comprehensive income for the year ended 30 September 20X6. It has been suggested that the $90,000 should be recognised as revenue and a provision of $70,000 created for the cost of manufacture.

DF's statement of profit of loss and other comprehensive income for the year ended 30 September 20X5 showed a profit of $600,000. The draft statement of profit of loss and other comprehensive income for the year ended 30 September 20X6 showed a profit of $700,000. The 30 September 20X5 accounts were approved by the directors on 1 March 20X6.

Required

Explain how the events described above should be reported in the financial statements of DF for the years ended 30 September 20X5 and 20X6. **(5 marks)**

`P7 11/06`

(g) On 1 June 20X6 the directors of DP commissioned a report to determine possible actions they could take to reduce DP's losses. The report, which was presented to the directors on 1 December 20X6, proposed that DP cease all of its manufacturing activities and concentrate on its retail activities. The directors formally approved the plan to close DP's factory. The factory was gradually shut down, commencing on 5 December 20X6, with production finally ceasing on 15 March 20X7. All employees had ceased working or had been transferred to other facilities in the company, by 29 March 20X7. The plant and equipment was removed and sold for $25,000 (net book value $95,000) on 30 March 20X7.

The factory and building are being advertised for sale but had not been sold by 31 March 20X7. The carrying value of the land and building at 31 March 20X7, based on original cost, was $750,000. The estimated net realisable value of the land and building at 31 March 20X7 was $1,125,000.

Closure costs incurred (and paid) up to 31 March 20X7 were $620,000.

The cash flows, revenues and expenses relating to the factory were clearly distinguishable from DP's other operations. The output of the factory was sold directly to third parties and to DP's retail outlets. The manufacturing facility was shown as a separate segment in DP's segmental information.

Required

With reference to relevant International Financial Reporting Standards, **explain** how DP should treat the factory closure in its financial statements for the year ended 31 March 20X7.   **(5 marks)**

P7 5/07

(h) On 1 September 20X7, the Directors of EK decided to sell EK's retailing division and concentrate activities entirely on its manufacturing division.

The retailing division was available for immediate sale, but EK had not succeeded in disposing of the operation by 31 October 20X7. EK identified a potential buyer for the retailing division, but negotiations were at an early stage. The Directors of EK are certain that the sale will be completed by 31 August 20X8.

The retailing division's carrying value at 31 August 20X7 was:

	$'000
Non-current tangible assets – property, plant and equipment	300
Non-current tangible assets – goodwill	100
Net current assets	43
Total carrying value	443

The retailing division has been valued at $423,000, comprising:

	$'000
Non-current tangible assets – property, plant and equipment	320
Non-current tangible assets – goodwill	60
Net current assets	43
Total carrying value	423

EK's directors have estimated that EK will incur consultancy and legal fees for the disposal of $25,000.

Required

(i)   **Explain** whether EK can treat the sale of its retailing division as a 'discontinued operation', as defined by IFRS 5 *Non-current assets held for sale and discontinued operations*, in its financial statements for the year ended 31 October 20X7.   **(3 marks)**

(ii) **Explain** how EK should treat the retailing division in its financial statements for the year ended 31 October 20X7, assuming the sale of its retailing division meets the classification requirements for a disposal group (IFRS 5).   **(2 marks)**

(Total = 5 marks)

P7 11/07

(Total = 40 marks)

23 Section B questions: Accounting standards II   72 mins

(a) IAS 37 defines the meaning of a provision and sets out when a provision should be recognised.

Required

Using the IAS 37 definition of a provision, **explain** how a provision meets the International Accounting Standards Board's *Conceptual Framework for Financial Reporting* definition of a liability.   **(5 marks)**

P7 Pilot paper

(b) A lessee leases a non-current asset on a non-cancellable lease contract of five years, the details of which are:

• The asset has a useful life of five years.
• The rental is $21,000 per annum payable at the end of each year.
• The lessee also has to pay all insurance and maintenance costs.
• The fair value of the asset was $88,300.

The lessee uses the sum of digits method to calculate finance charges on the lease.

Required

Prepare statement of profit of loss and other comprehensive income and statement of financial position extracts for years **one** and two of the lease.   **(5 marks)**

P7 Pilot paper

(c) AE has a three year contract which commenced on 1 April 20X4. At 31 March 20X5, AE had the following balances in its ledger relating to the contract:

	$'000	$'000
Total contract value		60,000
Cost incurred up to 31 March 20X5:		
Attributable to work completed	21,000	
Inventory purchased for use in 20X5/6	3,000	24,000
Progress payments received		25,000

Other information:
Expected further costs to completion   19,000

At 31 March 20X5, the contract was certified as 50% complete.

Required

Prepare the statement of profit of loss and other comprehensive income and statement of financial position extracts showing the balances relating to this contract, as required by IAS 11 *Construction contracts*.   **(5 marks)**

P7 5/05

(d) A five year finance lease commenced on 1 April 20X3. The annual payments are $30,000 in arrears. The fair value of the asset at 1 April 20X3 was $116,000. Use the sum of digits method for interest allocations and assume that the asset has no residual value at the end of the lease term.

Required

In accordance with IAS 17 *Leases*:

(i) **Calculate** the amount of finance cost that would be charged to the statement of profit of loss and other comprehensive income for the year ended 31 March 20X5

(ii) **Prepare** statement of financial position extracts for the lease at 31 March 20X5.   **(5 marks)**

P7 5/05

(e) CD is a manufacturing entity that runs a number of operations including a bottling plant that bottles carbonated soft drinks. CD has been developing a new bottling process that will allow the bottles to be filled and sealed more efficiently.

The new process took a year to develop. At the start of development, CD estimated that the new process would increase output by 15% with no additional cost (other than the extra bottles and their contents).

Development work commenced on 1 May 20X5 and was completed on 20 April 20X6. Testing at the end of the development confirmed CD's original estimates.

CD incurred expenditure of $180,000 on the above development in 20X5/X6.

CD plans to install the new process in its bottling plant and start operating the new process from 1 May 20X6.

CD's year end is 30 April.

Required

(i)   **Explain** the requirements of IAS 38 *Intangible assets* for the treatment of development costs.

(3 marks)

(ii) **Explain** how CD should treat its development costs in its financial statements for the year ended 30 April 20X6.   **(2 marks)**

(Total = 5 marks)

`P7 5/06`

(f)   On 1 April 20X5, DX acquired plant and machinery with a fair value of $900,000 on a finance lease. The lease is for five years with the annual lease payments of $228,000 being paid in advance on 1 April each year. The interest rate implicit in the lease is 13.44%. The first payment was made on 1 April 20X5.

Required

(i)   **Calculate** the finance charge in respect of the lease that will be shown in DX's statement of profit or loss and other comprehensive income for the year ended 31 March 20X7.

(ii) **Calculate** the amount to be shown as a current liability and a non-current liability in DX's statement of financial position at 31 March 20X7.

(All workings should be to the nearest $'000.)   **(5 marks)**

`P7 5/07`

(g)   The objective of IAS 24 *Related party disclosures* is to ensure that financial statements disclose the effect of the existence of related parties.

Required

With reference to IAS 24, **explain** the meaning of the terms 'related party' and 'related party transaction'.

(5 marks)

`P7 11/07`

(h)   EJ publishes trade magazines and sells them to retailers. EJ has just concluded negotiations with a large supermarket chain for the supply of a large quantity of several of its trade magazines on a regular basis.

EJ has agreed a substantial discount on the following terms:

*   The same quantity of each trade magazine will be supplied each month;
*   Quantities can only be changed at the end of each six month period;
*   Payment must be made six monthly in advance.

The supermarket paid $150,000 on 1 September 20X7 for six months supply of trade magazines to 29 February 20X8. At 31 October 20X7, EJ had supplied two months of trade magazines.

EJ estimates that the cost of supplying the supermarket each month is $20,000.

Required

(i)   **State** the criteria in IAS 18 *Revenue* for income recognition.   **(2 marks)**

(ii) **Explain**, with reasons, how EJ should treat the above in its financial statements for the year ended 31 October 20X7.   **(3 marks)**

(Total = 5 marks)

`P7 11/07`

(Total = 40 marks)

Published accounts – section C questions

The following tax regime data is applicable to questions 24 – 35 which cover the preparation of financial statements for single companies.

Country X – Tax regime

Relevant tax rules

Corporate Profits

Unless otherwise specified, only the following rules for taxation of corporate profits will be relevant, other taxes can be ignored:

(a) Accounting rules on recognition and measurement are followed for tax purposes.

(b) All expenses other than depreciation, amortisation, entertaining, taxes paid to other public bodies and donations to political parties are tax deductible.

(c) Tax depreciation is deductible as follows:

- 50% of additions to property, plant and equipment in the accounting period in which they are recorded

- 25% per year of the written-down value (ie cost minus previous allowances) in subsequent accounting periods except that in which the asset is disposed of

- No tax depreciation is allowed on land

(d) The corporate tax on profits is at a rate of 25%.

(e) No indexation is allowable on the sale of land.

(f) Tax losses can be carried forward to offset against future taxable profits from the same business.

Value Added Tax

Country X has a VAT system which allows entities to reclaim input tax paid. In Country X the VAT rates are:

Zero rated	0%
Standard rated	15%

24   SA (5/13)   45 mins

SA has two divisions, division A and division B. On 31 March 2013, SA's management board agreed to dispose of its loss-making division B. In previous accounting periods the two divisions had been classified as separate operating segments in accordance with IFRS 8 *Operating Segments.*

On 31 March 2013 division B was classified as "held for sale" in accordance with IFRS 5 *Noncurrent assets held for sale and discontinued operations.* All net assets, income and expenditure of division B are included in the trial balance.

SA trial balance at 31 March 2013 is shown below:

	Notes	$000	$000
Long term borrowings	(vii)		450
Administrative expenses	(vi)	263	
Cash and cash equivalents		202	
Distribution costs	(vi)	145	
Equity dividend paid		55	
Inventory at 31 March 2013		68	
Buildings at valuation	(i); (iv)	995	
Loan interest paid		13	
Ordinary shares $1 each			800
Plant and equipment at cost	(i); (iv)	1,010	
Provision for deferred tax at 31 March 2012	(ii)		72
Provision for plant & equipment depreciation at 31 March 2012	(iii); (iv)		360
Provision for buildings depreciation at 31 March 2012	(iii); (iv)		50
Retained earnings at 31 March 2012			183
Revaluation reserve at 31 March 2012			80
Sales revenue – division B			185
Sales revenue – division A			2,784
Cost of goods sold – division B		230	
Cost of goods sold – division A		1900	
Trade payables			51
Division B disposal costs		78	
Trade receivables		56	
		5,015	5,015

Additional information:

(i)   There were no sales of non-current assets during the year ended 31 March 2013.

(ii)   The tax due for the year ended 31 March 2013 is estimated to be $50,000. This includes a tax reduction of $40,000 that relates to discontinued operations. The deferred tax provision relates to division A and should be reduced to $69,000.

(iii)   Plant and equipment depreciation is provided at 20% per year on the reducing balance basis. Buildings are depreciated at 2.5% per year on a straight line basis. All depreciation is charged to administrative expenses. SA's policy is to charge a full year's depreciation in the year of acquisition and no depreciation in the year of disposal.

(iv)   Division B's assets included in the trial balance at 31 March 2013 are:

The plant and equipment cost and related provision for depreciation include the following amounts for division B:

- Plant and equipment cost $180,000
- Plant and equipment, provision for depreciation $140,000

The buildings balances in the trial balance include:

	Cost $000	Depreciation $000
Factory – division B	460	23

Division B has no further assets at 31 March 2013.

(v)   The fair value of division B's net assets at 31 March 2013 was $431,000.

(vi) The running costs of division B for the period 1 April 2012 to 31 March 2013 (included in the trial balance) are:

- Administrative expenses $30,000
- Distribution costs $125,000

(vii) The long term borrowings incur an annual interest rate of 6%.

Required

(a) **Explain** the criteria that have to be met in order to classify division B as "held for sale" in accordance with IFRS 5 *Non-current assets held for sale and discontinued operations*. **(3 marks)**

(b) **Prepare** the statement of profit or loss and a statement of changes in equity for SA for the year to 31 March 2013 and a statement of financial position at that date, in accordance with the requirements of International Financial Reporting Standards. **(22 marks)**

Notes to the financial statements are not required, but all workings must be clearly shown. Do *not prepare a statement of accounting policies.*

(Total = 25 marks)

25 CQ (3/13) — 45 mins

CQ's trial balance at 31 December 2012 is shown below:

	Notes	$000	$000
Bank loan	(i)		375
Administrative expenses		395	
Cash and cash equivalents		192	
Distribution costs		140	
Equity dividend paid		30	
Finance lease payment	(iii)	12	
Income tax	(iv)	32	
Inventory at 31 December 2011	(v)	196	
Land and buildings at cost at 1 January 2012	(vi)	1,415	
Bank loan interest paid	(i)	30	
Equity shares $1 each, fully paid at 1 January 2012			500
Patent	(ii)	180	
Amortisation of patent at 1 January 2012	(ii)		90
Plant and equipment at cost at 1 January 2012	(vii)	482	
Provision for deferred tax at 1 January 2012	(viii)		210
Accumulated depreciation - buildings at 1 January 2012	(vi)		120
Accumulated depreciation - plant and equipment at 1 January 2012	(vii)		279
Purchase of goods for resale		996	
Retained earnings at 1 January 2012			168
Sales revenue			1,992
Share premium			150
Trade payables			140
Trade receivables		249	
Proceeds of issue of equity shares	(ix)		325
		4,349	4,349

Additional information:

(i) The bank loan is a 10 year 8% loan received in 2007 and repayable in 2017. Interest is paid annually in December.

(ii) The patent was purchased on 1 January 2007, it was estimated to have a useful life of 10 years with no residual value. At 31 December 2012 the fair value of the patent was $65,000. Amortisation should be included in cost of sales.

(iii)　CQ acquired a motor vehicle on a finance lease on 1 January 2012. The present value of the minimum lease payments are $46,260 and legal title will not pass to CQ at the end of the lease. The lease terms are 5 annual payments of $12,000 due on 1 January commencing 1 January 2012. The rate of interest implicit in the lease is 15%. Depreciation on vehicles should be included in cost of sales. The only entry made for this transaction was to record the first rental payment.

(iv)　The income tax balance in the trial balance is a result of the under provision of tax for the year ended 31 December 2011.

(v)　An inventory count at 31 December 2012 valued inventory at $183,000. This value includes inventory that had originally cost $15,000 but it is now obsolete and its estimated scrap value is $2,000.

(vi)　Depreciation is charged on buildings using the straight line method at 3% per annum. The cost of land included in land and buildings is $1,015,000. Buildings depreciation is treated as an administrative expense. There were no sales of non-current assets during the year ended 31 December 2012.

(vii)　Depreciation is charged on owned plant and equipment using the reducing balance method at 25% per year. Plant and equipment depreciation should be included as a cost of sales.

(viii)　The tax due for the year ended 31 December 2012 is estimated at $77,000 and the deferred tax provision should be decreased by $42,000.

(ix)　On 30 September 2012 CQ issued 250,000 $1 equity shares at a premium of 30%. The proceeds were received before 31 December 2012.

Required

Prepare the statement of comprehensive income and a statement of changes in equity for CQ for the year to 31 December 2012 and a statement of financial position at that date, in accordance with the requirements of International Financial Reporting Standards.

Notes to the financial statements are not required, but all workings must be clearly shown.

Do not prepare a statement of accounting policies.

(Total = 25 marks)

26 YZ (11/12)   45 mins

YZ is a manufacturing entity which produces and sells a range of products.

YZ's trial balance at 30 September 2012 is shown below:

	Note	$'000	$'000
Administrative expenses		910	
Borrowings @ 7% per year			3,000
Buildings at cost at 30 September 2011		3,400	
Cash and cash equivalents		130	
Cash received on disposal of machinery	(i)		8
Cost of raw materials purchased in year to 30 September 2012		2,220	
Direct production labour costs		670	
Distribution costs		515	
Equity dividend paid		170	
Equity shares $1 each, fully paid at 30 September 2012	(xi)		1,700
Income tax	(viii)	30	
Inventory of finished goods at 30 September 2011	(vii)	190	
Inventory of raw materials at 30 September 2011	(vii)	275	
Land at valuation at 30 September 2011	(ii)	9,000	
Loan interest paid		210	
Plant and equipment at cost at 30 September 2011	(i)	3,900	
Production overheads (excluding depreciation)		710	
Provision for deferred tax at 30 September 2011	(ix)		430
Accumulated depreciation at 30 September 2011:			
Buildings	(iii)		816
Plant and equipment	(iv)		2,255
Patent	(v)	526	
Retained earnings at 30 September 2011			3,117
Revaluation reserve at 30 September 2011			1,800
Sales revenue			9,820
Share premium			100
Trade payables			940
Trade receivables		1,130	
		23,986	23,986

Additional information:

(i)   During the year YZ disposed of obsolete machinery for $8,000. The cash received is included in the trial balance. The obsolete machinery had originally cost $35,000 and had accumulated depreciation of $32,000.

(ii)   On 30 September 2012 YZ revalued its land to $9,500,000.

(iii)   Buildings are depreciated at 2% per annum on the straight line basis. Buildings depreciation should be treated as an administrative expense. No buildings were fully depreciated at 30 September 2011.

(iv)   Plant and equipment is depreciated at 25% per annum using the reducing balance method and is treated as a production overhead.

(v)   The patent for one of YZ's products was purchased on 1 October 2009. The patent had a useful life of 10 years when it was purchased and is being amortised on a straight line basis with no residual value anticipated. Amortisation of the patent is treated as cost of sales when charged to the statement of profit or loss and other comprehensive income. Research is carried out on a continuous basis to develop the patented process and ensure that the product range continues to meet customer demands. The patent figure in the trial balance is made up as follows:

	$'000
Original cost of patent	420
less amortisation to 30 September 2011	(84)
	336
Research costs incurred in the year to 30 September 2012	190
Total	526

(vi) YZ's accounting policy for amortisation and depreciation is to charge a full year in the year of acquisition and none in the year of disposal.

(vii) Inventory of raw materials at 30 September 2012 was $242,000. Inventory of finished goods at 30 September 2012 was $180,000.

(viii) The directors estimate the income tax charge on the year's profits at $715,000. The balance on the income tax account represents the under-provision for the previous year's tax charge.

(ix) The deferred tax provision is to be reduced by $47,000.

(x) YZ entered into a non-cancellable 4 year operating lease on 1 October 2011, to acquire machinery to replace the old machinery sold. Under the terms of the lease YZ will pay no rent for the first year. $8,000 is payable for each of 3 years commencing on 1 October 2012. The machine is estimated to have a useful economic life of 10 years.

(xi) During the year YZ issued 200,000 $1 equity shares at a premium of 50%. The total proceeds were received before 30 September 2012 and are reflected in the trial balance figures.

Required

Prepare YZ's statement of profit or loss and other comprehensive income and a statement of changes in equity for the year to 30 September 2012 and a statement of financial position at that date, in accordance with the requirements of International Financial Reporting Standards. (All workings should be to the nearest $'000).

Notes to the financial statements are not required, but all workings must be clearly shown. Do not prepare a statement of accounting policies.

(Total = 25 marks)

27 QWE (9/12)   45 mins

QWE's trial balance at 31 March 2012 is shown below:

	Notes	$'000	$'000
4% Loan notes (redeemable 2020)			500
Administrative expenses		190	
Amortisation of deferred development expenditure			30
Cash and cash equivalents		42	
Deferred development expenditure	(i)	150	
Distribution costs		72	
Equity dividend paid 1 September 2011		62	
Income tax	(ii)	8	
Inventory at 31 March 2012		214	
Cost of sales		1,605	
Land and buildings at cost at 1 April 2011		2,410	
Loan interest paid		10	
Ordinary Shares $1 each, fully paid at 1 April 2011			930
Plant and equipment at cost at 1 April 2011		560	
Provision for deferred tax at 1 April 2011	(iii)		86
Provision for buildings depreciation at 1 April 2011	(v)		386
Provision for plant and equipment depreciation at 1 April 2011	(v)		185
Retained earnings at 1 April 2011			621
Sales revenue			2,220
Share premium at 1 April 2011			310
Trade payables			190
Trade receivables		130	
Suspense account	(iv)	5	
		5,458	5,458

Additional information:

(i)   Deferred development expenditure is being amortised at 10% pa on the straight line basis.

(ii)   The income tax balance in the trial balance is a result of the under provision of tax for the year ended 31 March 2011.

(iii)   The tax due for the year ended 31 March 2012 is estimated at $83,000 and the deferred tax provision needs to be increased by $25,000.

(iv)   The suspense account is comprised of two items:

- Expenditure of $20,000 incurred during the year on original research aimed at possibly finding a new material for QWE to use in manufacturing its products.

- $15,000 cash received from disposal of some plant and equipment that had an original cost of $82,000 and a carrying value of $3,000.

The only entries made in QWE's ledgers for these items were in cash and cash equivalents and suspense account.

(v)   Depreciation is charged on buildings using the straight line method at 3% per annum. The cost of land included in land and buildings is $800,000. Buildings depreciation should be included in administrative expenses.

Depreciation of plant and equipment is at 12.5% on the reducing balance basis and is treated as part of the cost of sales.

QWE's policy is to charge a full year's depreciation in the year of acquisition and no depreciation in the year of disposal.

(vi)   On 1 July 2011 one of QWE's customers started litigation against QWE, claiming damages caused by an allegedly faulty product. QWE has been advised that it will probably lose the case and the claim for $25,000 will probably succeed.

(vii)   On 1 August 2012 QWE was advised that one of its customers, that had been in some financial difficulties at 31 March 2012, had gone into liquidation and that the $32,000 balance outstanding at 31 March 2012 was very unlikely to be paid.

(viii) QWE has not previously made any provisions for legal claims or irrecoverable debts.

Required

(a)   Prepare journal entries, with a short narrative, to eliminate the balance on QWE's suspense account.   **(3 marks)**

(b)   Prepare the statement of profit or loss and other comprehensive income and a statement of changes in equity for QWE for the year to 31 March 2012 and a statement of financial position at that date, in accordance with the requirements of International Financial Reporting Standards.

Notes to the financial statements are not required, but all workings must be clearly shown. Do not prepare a statement of accounting policies.   **(22 marks)**

(Total = 25 marks)

28 DFG (5/12)   45 mins

DFG's trial balance at 31 March 2012 is shown below:

	Notes	$'000	$'000
5% Loan notes (issued 2010, redeemable 2020)			280
Administrative expenses		180	
Amortisation of patent at 1 April 2011			27
Cash and cash equivalents			56
Cost of sales		554	
Distribution costs		90	
Equity dividend paid 1 September 2011		55	
Income tax	(i)	10	
Inventory at 31 March 2012		186	
Land and buildings at cost	(ii)	960	
Loan interest paid		7	
Ordinary Shares $1 each, fully paid at 1 April 2011			550
Patent	(vii)	90	
Plant and equipment at cost	(ii)	480	
Provision for deferred tax at 1 April 2011	(iii)		75
Provision for buildings depreciation at 1 April 2011	(iv)		33
Provision for plant and equipment depreciation at 1 April 2011	(v)		234
Retained earnings at 1 April 2011			121
Sales revenue	(vi)		1,200
Share premium			110
Trade payables			61
Trade receivables		135	
		2,747	2,747

Additional information:

(i)   The income tax balance in the trial balance is a result of the under provision of tax for the year ended 31 March 2011.

(ii)   There were no sales of non-current assets during the year ended 31 March 2012.

(iii) The tax due for the year ended 31 March 2012 is estimated at $52,000 and the deferred tax provision should be increased by $15,000.

(iv)   Depreciation is charged on buildings using the straight line method at 3% per annum. The cost of land included in land and buildings is $260,000. Buildings depreciation is treated as an administrative expense.

(v)   Up to 31 March 2011 all plant and equipment was depreciated using the straight line method at 12.5%. However some plant and equipment has been wearing out and needing to be replaced on average after six years. DFG management have therefore decided that from 1 April 2011 the expected useful life of this type of plant and equipment should be changed to a total of six years from acquisition. The plant and equipment affected was purchased on 1 April 2007 and had an original cost of $120,000. This plant and equipment is estimated to have no residual value. All plant and equipment depreciation should be charged to cost of sales.

(vi)   The sales revenue for the year to 31 March 2012 includes $15,000 received from a new overseas customer. The $15,000 was a 10% deposit for an order of $150,000 worth of goods. DFG is still waiting for the results of the new customer's credit reference and at 31 March 2012 has not despatched any goods.

(vii) On 1 April 2008 DFG purchased a patent for a secret recipe and manufacturing process for one of its products. Due to recent world economic difficulties DFG has carried out an impairment review of its patent. At 31 March 2012 the patent was found to have the following values:

  •   Value in use $50,000
  •   Fair value less cost to sell $47,000

(viii) On 1 July 2011 one of DFG's customers started litigation against DFG, claiming damages caused by an allegedly faulty product. DFG has been advised that it will probably lose the case and that the claim for $35,000 will probably succeed.

Required

(a)   Briefly **explain** how items (vi) and (vii) should be treated by DFG in its financial statements for the year ended 31 March 2012.   **(6 marks)**

(b)   **Prepare** DFG's statement of profit or loss and other comprehensive income and statement of changes in equity for the year to 31 March 2012 AND a statement of financial position at that date in accordance with the requirements of International Financial Reporting Standards.

(19 marks)

Notes to the financial statements are not required, but all workings must be clearly shown. Do not prepare a statement of accounting policies.

(Total = 25 marks)

29 RTY (3/12)   45 mins

RTY's trial balance at 31 January 2012 is shown below:

	Notes	$'000	$'000
Administrative expenses		1,225	
Cash and cash equivalents		142	
Cash received on disposal of non-current assets	(i)		2,068
Cost of goods sold		1,939	
Distribution costs		679	
Equity dividend paid	(iii)	138	
Equity Shares $1 each, fully paid at 31 January 2011			1,375
Income tax	(vi)	35	
Interest paid – half year to 31 July 2011		69	
Inventory at 31 January 2012		330	
Long term borrowings (redeemable 2025)	(v)		2,740
Plant and equipment at cost 31 January 2011	(i)	5,750	
Property at valuation 31 January 2011	(i)	17,120	
Provision for deferred tax at 31 January 2011	(vii)		1,064
Provision for plant and equipment depreciation at 31 January 2011	(i)		3,900
Provision for property depreciation at 31 January 2011	(i)		2,610
Research and development	(ii)	689	
Retained earnings at 31 January 2011			2,785
Revaluation reserve at 31 January 2011			2,900
Sales revenue			9,320
Share premium at 31 January 2011			2,750
Trade payables			1,080
Trade receivables	(iv)	1,476	
		32,592	32,592

Additional information provided:

(i)   **Property, plant and equipment**

The property valuation at 31 January 2011 of $17,120,000 consisted of land $6,220,000 and buildings $10,900,000. On 1 February 2011 RTY revalued its properties to $15,750,000 (land $6,850,000 and buildings $8,900,000).

During the year RTY disposed of non-current assets as follows:

•   A piece of surplus land was sold on 1 March 2011 for $2,060,000.
•   Obsolete plant was sold for $8,000 scrap value on the same date.
•   All the cash received is included in the trial balance.
•   Details of the assets sold were:

Asset type	Cost	Revalued amount	Accumulated depreciation
Land	$1,000,000	$1,800,000	$0
Plant and equipment	$820,000		$800,000

Buildings are depreciated at 5% per annum on the straight line basis. No buildings were fully depreciated at 31 January 2011. Plant and equipment is depreciated at 25% per annum using the reducing balance method. All depreciation is treated as a cost of sales. RTY charges a full year's depreciation in the year of acquisition and none in the year of disposal.

(ii) **Research and development**

RTY carries out research and development on a continuous basis to ensure that its product range continues to meet customer demands. The research and development figure in the trial balance is made up as follows:

	$'000
Development costs capitalised in previous years	1,199
Less amortisation to 31 January 2011	744
	455
Research costs incurred in the year to 31 January 2012	163
Development costs (all meet IAS 38 *Intangible Assets* criteria) incurred in the year to 31 January 2012	71
Total	689

Development costs are amortised on a straight line basis at 20% per year. No development costs were fully amortised at 31 January 2011. Research and development costs are treated as cost of sales when charged to the statement or profit or loss and other comprehensive income. RTY charges a full year's amortisation in the year of acquisition.

(iii) During the year RTY paid a final dividend for the year to 31 January 2012.

(iv) On 1 March 2012, RTY was informed that one of its customers, BVC, had ceased trading. The liquidators advised RTY that it was very unlikely to receive payment of any of the $48,000 due from BVC at 31 January 2012.

(v) The long term borrowings incur annual interest at 5% per year paid six monthly in arrears.

(vi) The income tax balance in the trial balance is a result of the under provision of tax for the year ended 31 January 2011. The directors estimate the income tax charge on the year's profits to 31 January 2012 at $765,000.

(vii) The deferred tax provision is to be decreased by $45,000.

Required

Prepare RTY's statement of profit of loss and other comprehensive income and statement of changes in equity for the year to 31 January 2012 AND a statement of financial position at that date in accordance with the requirements of International Financial Reporting Standards.

Notes to the financial statements are not required, but all workings must be clearly shown. Do not prepare a statement of accounting policies.

(25 marks)

30 ABC (11/11) 45 mins

ABC sells goods to the building industry and carries out construction contracts for clients. ABC's trial balance at 30 September 2011 is shown below:

	Notes	$'000	$'000
Administrative expenses		1,020	
Cash and cash equivalents		440	
Cash received on account from construction contract clients during year to 30 September 2011 — contract 1	(i)		4,000
Cash received on account from construction contract clients during year to 30 September 2011 — contract 2	(i)		1,800
Cash received on disposal of plant and equipment	(iii)		15
Construction contract 1 - work in progress for year to 30 September 2011	(i)	3,750	
Construction contract 2 - work in progress for year to 30 September 2011	(i)	2,250	
Distribution costs		590	
Equity dividend paid	(viii)	250	
Equity Shares $1 each, fully paid at 30 September 2011			2,500
Income tax	(v)	15	
Interest paid – half year to 31 March 2011		58	
Inventory at 30 September 2011 (excluding construction contracts)		310	
Long term borrowings (redeemable 2021)	(iv)		2,300
Plant and equipment at cost 30 September 2011	(iii)	4,930	
Property at valuation 30 September 2010	(ii)	11,000	
Provision for deferred tax at 30 September 2010	(vi)		250
Provision for plant and equipment depreciation at 30 September 2010	(iii)		2,156
Provision for property depreciation at 30 September 2010	(ii)		3,750
Cost of goods sold (excluding construction contracts)		3,210	
Retained earnings at 30 September 2010			627
Sales revenue			9,500
Share premium at 30 September 2011			1,500
Trade payables			235
Trade receivables	(viii)	810	
		28,633	28,633

Additional information provided:

(i) At 30 September 2011 ABC had two construction contracts in progress.

	Contract 1	Contract 2
Contract length	3 years	2 years
Date commenced	1 October 2010	1 April 2011
Fixed contract value	$11,000,000	$8,000,000

Contract detail for year ended 30 September 2011

	Contract 1	Contract 2
Proportion of work certified as completed	40%	25%
	$'000	$'000
Construction contract work in progress	3,750	2,250
Estimated cost to complete contract	5,400	6,750
Cash received on account from construction contract clients during year	4,000	1,800

Both contracts use the value of work completed method to recognise attributable profit for the year.

(ii) Property consists of land $3,500,000 and buildings $7,500,000. Buildings are depreciated at 5% per year on the straight line basis. No buildings were fully depreciated at 30 September 2011.

(iii) Plant and equipment is depreciated at 25% per year using the reducing balance method. During the year to 30 September 2011 ABC sold obsolete plant for $15,000. The plant had cost $75,000 and had been depreciated by $65,000. All depreciation is considered to be part of cost of sales. ABC's policy is to charge a full year's depreciation in the year of acquisition and no depreciation in the year of disposal. This disposal has not been accounted for in the trial balance.

(iv) The long term borrowings incur annual interest at 5% paid six monthly in arrears.

(v) The income tax balance in the trial balance is a result of the under provision of tax for the year ended 30 September 2010. The directors estimate the income tax charge on the profit of the year to 30 September 2011 at $910,000.

(vi) The deferred tax provision is to be increased by $19,000.

(vii) On 1 August 2011, ABC was informed that one of its customers, EF, had ceased trading. The liquidators advised ABC that it was very unlikely to receive payment of any of the $25,000 due from EF at 30 September 2011.

(viii) ABC made no new share issues during the year. ABC paid a final dividend for the year to 30 September 2010.

Required

Prepare ABC's statement of profit of loss and other comprehensive income and statement of changes in equity for the year to 30 September 2011 AND a statement of financial position at that date in accordance with the requirements of International Financial Reporting Standards.

Notes to the financial statements are not required, but all workings must be clearly shown. Do not prepare a statement of accounting policies. **(25 marks)**

31 ZY (9/11) 45 mins

ZY's trial balance at 30 June 2011 is shown below:

	Notes	$'000	$'000
Administrative expenses		338	
Cash and cash equivalents		229	
Cash received on disposal of vehicles	(ii)		10
Distribution costs		221	
Equity dividend paid	(v)	90	
Equity Shares $1 each, fully paid at 30 June 2011			500
Finance lease rental paid	(iii)	30	
Income tax	(viii)	15	
Interest paid – half year to 31 December 2010		8	
Inventory at 30 June 2010	(vii)	358	
Long term borrowings (repayable 2020)	(iv)		320
Plant and equipment at 30 June 2010		864	
Preferred shares, 4% cumulative redeemable 2021	(vi)		150
Property at valuation 30 June 2010	(i)	844	
Provision for deferred tax at 30 June 2010	(ix)		45
Provision for plant and equipment depreciation at 30 June 2010	(i)		249
Provision for property depreciation at 30 June 2010	(i)		8
Purchase of goods for resale		987	
Retained earnings at 30 June 2010			288
Revaluation reserve at 30 June 2010	(i)		220
Sales revenue			2,084
Share premium at 30 June 2011			270
Trade payables			120
Trade receivables	(x)	280	
		4,264	4,264

Additional information provided:

(i) Property is depreciated at 1% per year and plant and equipment is depreciated at 20% per year straight line. Depreciation is charged to cost of sales. ZY's policy is to charge a full year's depreciation in the year of acquisition and no depreciation in the year of disposal. Property is revalued every three years.

(ii) ZY disposed of its old vehicles on 1 October 2010 for $10,000. The original cost was $95,000 and the net book value at the date of disposal was zero. Vehicles are included in plant and equipment. No adjusting entries have yet been made to ZY's plant and equipment for this disposal.

(iii)   ZY purchased new vehicles using a finance lease on 1 July 2010. The finance lease terms are:

- Lease for a five year period
- Rentals paid annually in arrears on 30 June
- Each annual rental is $30,000
- The fair value of the vehicles was $120,000
- The interest rate implicit in the lease is 7.93% per year

(iv)   The long term borrowings incur annual interest at 5% per year, and is paid six monthly in arrears.

(v)   During the current accounting period ZY paid a final dividend for the year ended 30 June 2010 of $50,000 and an interim dividend for the year ended 30 June 2011 of $40,000.

(vi)   On 1 January 2011 ZY issued $150,000 4% cumulative redeemable preferred shares. At 30 June 2011 no dividend had been paid.

(vii)   Inventory at 30 June 2011 amounted to $390,000 at cost. A review of inventory items revealed the need for some adjustments for two inventory lines.

- Items which had cost $100,000 and which would normally sell for $220,000 were found to have deteriorated. Remedial work costing $30,000 would be needed to enable the items to be sold for $110,000.

- Some items sent to customers on sale or return terms had been omitted from inventory and included as sales in June 2011. The cost of these items was $15,000 and they were included in sales at $30,000. On 30 June 2011, the items were returned in good condition by the customers but no entries have been made to record this.

(viii) The income tax balance in the trial balance is a result of the under provision of tax for the year ended 30 June 2010. The directors estimate the income tax charge on the profits of the year ended 30 June 2011 at $56,000.

(ix)   The deferred tax provision is to be reduced to $38,000.

(x)   On 1 August 2011, ZY was informed that one of its customers, X, had ceased trading. The liquidators advised ZY that it was very unlikely to receive payment of any of the $48,000 due from X at 30 June 2011.

Required

Prepare ZY's statement of profit or loss and other comprehensive income and statement of changes in equity for the year to 30 June 2011 AND a statement of financial position at that date, in accordance with the requirements of International Financial Reporting Standards.

Notes to the financial statements are not required, but all workings must be clearly shown. Do not prepare a statement of accounting policies.

(25 marks)

32 MN (5/11)   45 mins

MN operates a number of retail outlets around the country. **One** retail outlet was closed on 31 March 20X1 when trading ceased and the outlet was put up for sale. All income and expenses of the outlet are included in the trial balance. The retail outlet is regarded as a cash generating unit, all its assets are being sold as **one** unit. At 31 March 20X1 the directors are certain that the outlet meets the requirements of IFRS 5 *Non-current Assets Held for Sale and Discontinued Operations* for treatment as non-current assets held for sale.

MN's trial balance at 31 March 20X1 is shown below:

	Further information	$'000	$'000
Administration expenses	(ii)	160	
Cash and cash equivalents			14
Cost of goods sold	(ii)	622	
Distribution costs	(ii)	170	
Equity dividend paid		30	
Inventory at 31 March 20X1		65	
Long term borrowings	(vii)		300
Equity shares $1 each, fully paid			600
Property, plant and equipment			
net book value at 31 March 20X0	(i) to (iii)	2,073	
Provision for deferred tax at 31 March 20X0	(vi)		83
Provision for repairs under warranty at 31 March 20X0	(iv)		76
Retained earnings at 31 March 20X0			777
Revenue	(ii)		1,120
Share premium at 31 March 20X0			200
Trade payables			51
Trade receivables		101	
		3,221	3,221

Further information

(i)   The book values of the property, plant and equipment at 31 March 20X0 were as follows:

Asset type	Cost – continuing activities	Cost – discontinued operations	Accumulated depreciation – continuing activities	Accumulated depreciation – discontinued operations	Net book value
	$'000	$'000	$'000	$'000	$'000
Land	1,220	150	0	0	1,370
Buildings	700	40	140	20	580
Plant & equipment	240	60	142	35	123
	2,160	250	282	55	2,073

(ii) The fair value less cost to sell of the assets of the closed retail outlet at 31 March 20X1 was $176,000.

The results of the closed outlet for the period 1 April 20X0 to 31 March 20X1 were as follows:

	$'000
Revenue	80,000
Cost of sales	(130,000)
Administration expenses	(40,000)
Distribution costs	(90,000)

(iii) MN depreciates buildings at 5% per annum on the straight-line basis and plant and equipment at 20% per annum using the reducing balance method. Depreciation is included in cost of sales.

(iv) MN sells electronic goods with a one year warranty. At 31 March 20X0 MN created a provision of $76,000 for the cost of honouring the warranties at that date. On 31 March 20X1 the outstanding warranties were reviewed and the following estimates prepared:

Scenario	Probability	Anticipated cost
Worst case	10%	$190,000
Best case	15%	$20,000
Most likely	75%	$80,000

All warranties relate to continuing activities. Actual repair costs incurred during the year were charged to cost of sales.

(v)   The directors estimate the income tax charge on the year's profits at $67,000, of this a tax reduction of $10,000 relates to discontinued operations.

(vi) The deferred tax provision is to be reduced to $78,000.

(vii) The long term borrowings incur annual interest at 4% per year paid annually in arrears.

Required

Prepare MN's statement of profit or loss and other comprehensive income and statement of changes in equity for the year to 31 March 20X1 AND a statement of financial position at that date, in a form suitable for presentation to the shareholders and in accordance with the requirements of International Financial Reporting Standards.

Notes to the financial statements are not required, but all workings must be clearly shown. Do not prepare a statement of accounting policies.

(25 marks)

33 XB (11/10)   45 mins

XB's trial balance at 31 October 20Y0 is shown below:

	Notes	$'000	$'000
Administrative expenses		185	
Cash and cash equivalents		216	
Cost of sales		237	
Distribution costs		62	
Donations to political party		5	
Entertaining expenses		12	
Equity dividend paid	(i)	50	
Interest paid	(ii)	3	
Inventory at 31 October 20Y0		18	
Land at cost – 31 October 20X9	(iii)	730	
Long term borrowings	(ii)		200
Ordinary Shares $1 each, fully paid at 31 October 20Y0	(iv)		630
Property, plant and equipment – at cost 31 October 20X9	(iii)	320	
Provision for deferred tax at 31 October 20X9			10
Provision for property, plant and equipment depreciation at 31 October 20X9	(v)		192
Purchase of property, plant and equipment during the year	(v)	110	
Retained earnings at 31 October 20X9			168
Revenue			690
Share premium at 31 October 20Y0	(iv)		99
Suspense	(vi)	3	
Taxation	(vii)	6	
Trade payables			77
Trade receivables		109	
		2,066	2,066

Additional information provided:

(i)   The final dividend for the year to 31 October 20X9 of $50,000 was paid on 31 March 20Y0.

(ii) Long-term borrowings consist of a loan taken out on 1 May 20X9 at 3% interest per year. Six months loan interest has been paid in the year to 31 October 20Y0.

(iii) At 31 October 20X9 the tax written down value of XB's assets was $90,000. None of these assets were fully depreciated at this date.

(iv) XB issued 330,000 equity shares on 30 June 20Y0 at a premium of 30%.

(v)   Property, plant and equipment is depreciated at 20% per annum using the straight line method. Depreciation of property, plant and equipment is considered to be part of cost of sales. XB's policy is to charge a full year's depreciation in the year of acquisition and no depreciation in the year of disposal.

(vi) Purchased goods, invoiced at $3,000 received in September 20Y0 were returned to the supplier in October. At 31 October 20Y0 the supplier had not issued a credit note. XB had correctly deducted the amount from purchases with the corresponding double entry posted to the suspense account.

(vii) The balance on the taxation account is the income tax underestimated in the previous year's financial statements.

(viii) XB is resident in Country X.

Required

(a) **Prepare** XB's statement of profit or loss and other comprehensive income for the year to 31 October 20Y0, including a **calculation** of income tax expense.

(*Note there are up to 8 marks available for the taxation computation*) **(14 marks)**

(b) **Prepare** XB's statement of changes in equity for the year to 31 October 20Y0 **and** a statement of financial position at that date. **(11 marks)**

All statements should be in a form suitable for presentation to the shareholders and in accordance with the requirements of International Financial Reporting Standards.

Notes to the financial statements are not required, but all workings must be clearly shown. Do not prepare a statement of accounting policies.

Note. **Your answer should be to the nearest $'000.**

(Total = 25 marks)

34 EZ (5/10) — 45 mins

EZ's trial balance at 31 March 20X9 is shown below:

	Notes	$'000	$'000
Administrative expenses		86	
Cash and cash equivalents		22	
Cost of goods sold		418	
Distribution costs		69	
Equity dividend paid	(v)	92	
Inventory at 31 March 20X9		112	
Land market value – 31 March 20X8	(i)	700	
Lease	(ix)	15	
Long term borrowings	(vii)		250
Equity Shares $1 each, fully paid at 31 March 20X9	(vi)		600
Property, plant and equipment – at cost 31 March 20X8	(iii)	480	
Provision for deferred tax at 31 March 20X8	(ii)		30
Provision for property, plant and equipment dep'n at 31 March 20X8	(iv)		144
Retained earnings at 31 March 20X8			181
Revaluation reserve at 31 March 20X8			10
Revenue			720
Share premium at 31 March 20X9	(vi)		300
Suspense	(iii)		2
Trade payables			32
Trade receivables	(viii)	275	
		2,269	2,269

Additional information provided:

(i) Land is carried in the financial statements at market value. The market value of the land at 31 March 20X9 was $675,000. There were no purchases or sales of land during the year.

(ii) The tax due for the year ended 31 March 20X9 is estimated at $18,000. Deferred tax is estimated to decrease by $10,000.

(iii) During the year EZ disposed of old equipment for $2,000. No entry has been made in the accounts for this transaction except to record the cash received in the cash book and in the suspense account. The original cost of the equipment sold was $37,000 and its book value at 31 March 20X8 was $7,000.

(iv) Property, plant and equipment is depreciated at 10% per year straight line. Depreciation of property, plant and equipment is considered to be part of cost of sales. EZ's policy is to charge a full year's depreciation in the year of acquisition and no depreciation in the year of disposal.

(v) During the year EZ paid a final dividend of $92,000 for the year ended 31 March 20X8.

(vi) EZ issued 200,000 equity shares on 30 September 20X8 at a premium of 50%.

(vii) Long term borrowings consist of a loan taken out on 1 April 20X8 at 4% interest per year. No loan interest has been paid at 31 March 20X9.

(viii) On 22 April 20X9 EZ discovered that ZZZ, its largest customer, had gone into liquidation. EZ has been informed that it is very unlikely to receive any of the $125,000 balance outstanding at 31 March 20X9.

(ix) On 1 April 20X8 EZ acquired additional vehicles on a 2½ year (30 months) operating lease. The lease included an initial 6 months rent-free period as an incentive to sign the lease. The lease payments were $2,500 per month commencing on 1 October 20X8.

Required

Prepare EZ's statement of profit or loss and other comprehensive income and statement of changes in equity for the year to 31 March 20X9 and a statement of financial position at that date, in a form suitable for presentation to the shareholders and in accordance with the requirements of International Financial Reporting Standards.

Notes to the financial statements are NOT required, but all workings must be clearly shown. Do **not** prepare a statement of accounting policies.

(25 marks)

---

35 XY (Specimen paper)   45 mins

XY's trial balance at 31 March 20X9 is shown below:

	Notes	$'000	$'000
Administrative expenses		303	
Available for sale investments	(ii)	564	
Cash and cash equivalents		21	
Cash received on disposal of land			48
Cost of goods sold		908	
Distribution costs		176	
Equity dividend paid	(ix)	50	
Income tax	(iii)	12	
Inventory at 31 March 20X9		76	
Land at cost – 31 March 20X8	(v)	782	
Long term borrowings	(viii)		280
Ordinary Shares $1 each, fully paid at 31 March 20X9	(vii)		500
Property, plant and equipment – at cost 31 March 20X8	(vi)	630	
Provision for deferred tax at 31 March 20X8	(iv)		19
Property, plant and equipment depreciation at 31 March 20X8	(vi)		378
Retained earnings at 31 March 20X8			321
Revaluation surplus at 31 March 20X8			160
Revenue			1,770
Share premium at 31 March 20X9			200
Trade payables			56
Trade receivables		210	
		3,732	3,732

Additional information provided:

(i)   XY is resident in Country X.

(ii)   Available for sale investments are carried in the financial statements at market value. The market value of the available for sale investments at 31 March 20X9 was $608,000.There were no purchases or sales of available for sale investments during the year.

(iii)   The income tax balance in the trial balance is a result of the underprovision of tax for the year ended 31 March 20X8.

(iv)   The taxation due for the year ended 31 March 20X9 is estimated at $96,000. The tax depreciation cumulative allowances at 31 March 20X8 for property, plant and equipment were $453,000.

(v)   Land sold during the year had a book value of $39,000. The fair value of the remaining land at 31 March 20X9 was $729,000.

(vi)   Property, plant and equipment is depreciated at 20% per annum straight line. Depreciation of property, plant and equipment is considered to be part of cost of sales. XY's policy is to charge a full year's depreciation in the year of acquisition and no depreciation in the year of disposal.

(vii)   XY issued 100,000 equity shares on 31 October 20X8 at a premium of 50%. The cash received was correctly entered into the financial records and is included in the trial balance.

(viii) Long term borrowings consist of a loan taken out on 1 April 20X8 at 5% interest per year. No loan interest has been paid at 31 March 20X9.

(ix)   XY paid a final dividend of $50,000 for the year ended 31 March 20X8.

Required

(a)   **Calculate** the deferred tax amounts relating to property, plant and equipment, that are required to be included in XY's statement of profit or loss and other comprehensive income for the year ended 31 March 20X9 and its statement of financial position at that date. Ignore all other deferred tax implications.

(5 marks)

(b)   **Prepare** XY's statement of profit or loss and other comprehensive income and statement of changes in equity for the year to 31 March 20X9 and a statement of financial position at that date, in a form suitable for presentation to the shareholders and in accordance with the requirements of International Financial Reporting Standards.   **(20 marks)**

Notes to the financial statements are NOT required, but all workings must be clearly shown. Do **not** prepare a statement of accounting policies.

(Total = 25 marks)

Part C: Group Financial Statements

Questions 36 to 48 cover Group Financial Statements, the subject of Part C of the BPP Study Text for F1.

36 Objective test questions: Group financial statements   38 mins

1   Fanta acquired 100% of the ordinary share capital of Tizer on 1 October 20X7.

On 31 December 20X7 the share capital and retained earnings of Tizer were as follows:

	$'000
Ordinary shares of $1 each	400
Retained earnings at 1 January 20X7	100
Retained profit for the year ended 31 December 20X7	80
	580

The profits of Tizer have accrued evenly throughout 20X7. Goodwill arising on the acquisition of Tizer was $30,000.

What was the cost of the investment in Tizer?

A $400,000
B $580,000
C $610,000
D $590,000   **(2 marks)**

2   Mercedes has owned 100% of Benz for many years. At 31 March 20X9 the retained earnings of Mercedes were $450,000 and the consolidated retained earnings of the group were $560,000. Mercedes has no other subsidiaries.

During the year ended 31 March 20X9, Benz had sold goods to Mercedes for $50,000. Mercedes still had these goods in inventory at the year end. Benz uses a 25% mark up on all goods.

What were the retained earnings of Benz at 31 March 20X9?

A $110,000
B $60,000
C $170,000
D $120,000   **(2 marks)**

3   Oldsmobile, a company with subsidiaries, purchased 35% of the ordinary share capital of Chevrolet for $50,000 on 1 April 20X8.

Chevrolet's statement of financial position at 31 March 20X9 was as follows:

	$'000
Net assets	55
Ordinary share capital ($1 shares)	15
Retained earnings at 1 April 20X8	20
Net profit for the year ended 31 March 20X9	20
	55

During the year to 31 March 20X9 Chevrolet paid out a total dividend to its shareholders of $10,000. Oldsmobile considers that its investment in Chevrolet has been impaired by $6,000.

At what amount should Oldsmobile's investment in Chevrolet be shown in its consolidated statement of financial position as at 31 March 20X9?

A $57,000
B $50,500
C $47,500
D $44,000   **(2 marks)**

4   Ruby owns 30% of Emerald. During the year to 31 December 20X8 Emerald sold goods to Ruby for
     $160,000. Emerald applies a one-third mark up on cost. Ruby still had 25% of these goods in inventory
     at the year end.

     What amount should be deducted from consolidated retained earnings in respect of this transaction?

     A $40,000
     B $3,000
     C $10,000
     D $4,000   **(2 marks)**

5   Colossal acquired 100% of the $100,000 ordinary share capital of Enormous for $300,000 on 1 January
     20X9 when the retained earnings of Enormous were $156,000. At the date of acquisition the fair value
     of plant held by Enormous was $20,000 higher than its carrying value. This plant had a remaining life of
     4 years at the acquisition date.

     At 31 December 20X9 retained earnings are as follows:

	$
Colossal	275,000
Enormous	177,000

     Colossal considers that goodwill on acquisition is impaired by 50%.

     What are group retained earnings at 31 December 20X9?

     A $279,000
     B $284,000
     C $296,000
     D $291,000   **(3 marks)**

6   On 1 April 20X7 Rhino acquired 40% of the share capital of Hippo for $120,000, when the retained
     earnings of Hippo were $80,000. During the year Rhino sold goods to Hippo for $30,000, including a
     profit margin of 25%. These goods were still in inventory at the year end.

     At 31 March 20X8 the retained earnings of Hippo were $140,000.

     At what amount should Rhino's interest in Hippo be shown in the consolidated statement of financial
     position at 31 March 20X8?

     A $173,000
     B $144,000
     C $141,000
     D $105,000   **(2 marks)**

The following information is relevant for questions 7 and 8

On 1 January 20X6 A purchased 100,000 ordinary shares in B for $210,000. At that date B's retained
earnings amounted to $90,000 and the fair value of its assets was equal to their book values.

Four years later, on 31 December 20X9, the statements of financial position of the two companies were:

	A	B
	$	$
Sundry net assets	200,000	260,000
Shares in B	210,000	-
	410,000	260,000
Ordinary shares of $1	200,000	100,000
Retained earnings	210,000	160,000
	410,000	260,000

The share capital of B has remained unchanged since 1 January 20X6. Goodwill is impaired by 50%.

7   What amount should appear in the group consolidated statement of financial position at 31 December
     20X9 for goodwill?

     A $25,000
     B $20,000
     C $10,000
     D $14,000   (2 marks)

8   What amount should appear in the consolidated statement of financial position at 31 December 20X9 for
     group retained earnings?

     A $270,000
     B $338,000
     C $370,000
     D $280,000   (2 marks)

The following information is relevant for questions 9 and 10

H acquired 100% of the share capital of S on 1 January 20X9 for $350,000.

The statements of financial position of the two companies at 31 December 20X9 were as follows:

	H $	S $
Sundry assets	590,000	290,000
Investment in S	350,000	-
	940,000	290,000
Issued share capital - $1 shares	400,000	140,000
Share premium account	320,000	50,000
Retained earnings at 1 January 20X9	140,000	60,000
Profit for year to 31 December 20X9	80,000	40,000
	940,000	290,000

There have been no changes in the share capital or share premium account of either company since 1
January 20X9. There was no impairment of goodwill.

9   What figure for goodwill should appear in the consolidated statement of financial position of the H group
     at 31 December 20X9?

     A $60,000
     B $100,000
     C $150,000
     D $160,000   (2 marks)

10   What figure for group retained earnings should appear in the consolidated statement of financial position
     of the H group at 31 December 20X9?

     A $260,000
     B $220,000
     C $320,000
     D $200,000   (2 marks)

                                                                          (Total = 21 marks)

Group Financial Statements – section C questions

The following tax regime data is applicable to questions 37 – 48 which cover the preparation of group financial statements.

Country X – Tax regime

Relevant tax rules

Corporate Profits

Unless otherwise specified, only the following rules for taxation of corporate profits will be relevant, other taxes can be ignored:

(a) Accounting rules on recognition and measurement are followed for tax purposes.

(b) All expenses other than depreciation, amortisation, entertaining, taxes paid to other public bodies and donations to political parties are tax deductible.

(c) Tax depreciation is deductible as follows:

  • 50% of additions to property, plant and equipment in the accounting period in which they are recorded

  • 25% per year of the written-down value (ie cost minus previous allowances) in subsequent accounting periods except that in which the asset is disposed of

  • No tax depreciation is allowed on land

(d) The corporate tax on profits is at a rate of 25%.

(e) No indexation is allowable on the sale of land.

(f) Tax losses can be carried forward to offset against future taxable profits from the same business.

Value Added Tax

Country X has a VAT system which allows entities to reclaim input tax paid. In Country X the VAT rates are:

Zero rated	0%
Standard rated	15%

---

37 Club, Green and Tee (5/13)   45 mins

The draft statements of financial position at 31 March 2013 and statements of profit or loss for the year ended 31 March 2013 for three entities, are given below:

Statements of financial position as at 31 March 2013

	Notes	Club $000	Green $000	Tee $000
Non-current Assets				
Property, plant and equipment	(vi)	50,050	30,450	28,942
Investments:				
17,370,000 Ordinary shares in Green at cost	(i);(ii);(iii)	35,610		
3,980,000 Ordinary shares in Tee at cost	(iv)	8,000		
		93,660	30,450	28,942
Current Assets				
Inventory	(v)	34,910	9,310	2,580
Trade receivables		38,790	16,530	2,660
Cash and cash equivalents	(vii)	5,010	1,480	318
		78,710	27,320	5,558
Total Assets		172,370	57,770	34,500

Equity and Liabilities

Equity shares of $1 each	112,620	17,370	15,920
Share premium	0	3,470	0
Retained earnings	15,630	10,650	3,590
	128,250	31,490	19,510
Non-current liabilities			
Long term borrowings	32,000	15,000	9,140
Current liabilities			
Trade payables	11,320	10,830	5,530
Loan interest payable	800	450	320
	12,120	11,280	5,850
Total equity and liabilities	172,370	57,770	34,500

Summarised statements of profit or loss for the year ended 31 March 2013

	Club	Green	Tee
	$000	$000	$000
Revenue	130,000	67,410	31,890
Cost of sales	(75,470)	(40,470)	(18,920)
Gross profit	54,530	26,940	12,970
Expenses	(37,660)	(20,230)	(9,460)
	16,870	6,710	3,510
Finance cost	(1,600)	(900)	(640)
	15,270	5,810	2,870
Income tax expense	(3,050)	(1,160)	(580)
Profit for the year	12,220	4,650	2,290

Additional information:

(i) Club acquired all of Green's equity shares on 1 April 2011 in a share for share exchange. The agreed purchase consideration was $35,610,000. Green's retained earnings were $3,000,000 on 1 April 2011.

(ii) The fair value of Green's property, plant and equipment on 1 April 2011 exceeded its carrying value by $1,200,000. The excess of fair value over carrying value was attributed to buildings owned by Green. At the date of acquisition these buildings had a remaining useful life of 12 years. Club's accounting policy is to depreciate all property, plant and equipment using the straight line basis with no residual value.

(iii) Club carried out an impairment review of the goodwill arising on acquisition of Green and found that as at 31 March 2013 the goodwill had NOT been impaired but had actually increased in value by $50,000.

(iv) Club purchased its shareholding in Tee on 1 April 2012 for $8,000,000. The fair value of Tee's net assets was the same as its carrying value at that date. Club exercises significant influence over all aspects of Tee's financial and operating policies.

(v) Club occasionally trades with Green. During February 2013 Club sold Green goods for $960,000. Green had not paid for the goods by 31 March 2013. Club uses a mark-up of 33⅓% on cost. 20% of the goods had been sold by Green at 31 March 2013.

(vi) Club sold a piece of machinery to Green on 1 April 2012 for $115,000. The machinery had previously been used in Club's business and had been included in Club's property, plant and equipment at a carrying value of $90,000. Club had recognised the profit on disposal in revenue. The machinery had a remaining useful life of 5 years on 1 April 2012.

(vii) Green transferred $115,000 to Club on 31 March 2013 which was not recorded by Club until April 2013.

Required

(a) **Explain** how a post acquisition increase in goodwill, for example in note (iii) above, should be treated in consolidated financial statements. **(2 marks)**

(b) **Prepare** the consolidated statement of financial position for Club as at 31 March 2013, in accordance with the requirements of International Financial Reporting Standards. **(23 marks)**

Notes to the financial statements are not required, but all workings must be clearly shown.

(Total = 25 marks)

38 TX, SX and LW (3/13)   45 mins

The draft statements of financial position at 31 December 2012 for three entities, TX, SX and LW are given below:

Statements of Financial Position as at 31 December 2012:

	Notes	TX $000	SX $000	LW $000
Non-current Assets				
Property, plant and equipment		545	480	468
Investments at cost:				
SX	(i),(ii)	530	0	0
LW (150,000 equity shares)	(iii)	190	0	0
		1,265	480	468
Current Assets				
Inventory	(iv)	221	55	170
Trade receivables		98	75	124
Cash and cash equivalents	(v)	72	0	110
Total Assets		391	130	404
		1,656	610	872
Equity and Liabilities				
Equity shares of $1 each		800	360	500
Share premium		400	0	100
Retained earnings		300	140	120
		1,500	500	720
Current liabilities				
Trade payables		156	47	152
Bank overdraft		0	63	0
		156	110	152
Total Equity and Liabilities		1,656	610	872

Additional information:

(i)   TX acquired all of SX's equity shares on 1 January 2012 for an agreed purchase consideration of $530,000. SX's retained earnings were $110,000 on 1 January 2012.

(ii)   The fair value of SX's property on 1 January 2012 exceeded its carrying value by $72,000. The excess of fair value over carrying value was attributed to buildings with a remaining useful life of 18 years. TX's accounting policy is to depreciate buildings using the straight line basis with no residual value.

(iii)   TX purchased its shareholding in LW on 1 January 2012 for $190,000 when LW's retained earnings were $70,000. The fair value of all LW's net assets was the same as their carrying value at that date. TX exercises significant influence over all aspects of LW's financial and operating policies.

(iv)   During September 2012 TX sold SX goods for $44,000 at a mark up of 33$\frac{1}{3}$% on cost. At 31 December 2012 all the goods remained in SX's closing inventory. At 31 December 2012 TX had not recorded any payment for the goods.

(v)   SX made a part payment to TX for $15,000 on 29 December 2012 which was not recorded by TX until 4 January 2013.

Required

(a)   If an entity, TX, owns more than half the equity (voting) shares of another entity, SX, then SX will be deemed to be the subsidiary of TX. However a parent/subsidiary relationship can exist even when the parent owns less than 50% of the equity shares.

        Explain the circumstances that can give rise to a parent/subsidiary relationship other than a majority shareholding.   **(5 marks)**

(b) **Prepare** the consolidated statement of financial position for TX as at 31 December 2012, in accordance with the requirements of International Financial Reporting Standards. **(20 marks)**

Notes to the financial statements are not required, but all workings must be clearly shown.

(Total = 25 marks)

39 AZ, PQ and SY (11/12)   45 mins

The draft statements of financial position at 30 September 2012 for three entities, AZ, PQ and SY are given below:

Statements of Financial Position at 30 September 2012:

	Notes	AZ $'000	PQ $'000	SY $'000
Non-current Assets				
Property, plant and equipment	(vii)	400	297	380
Investments:				
100,000 Equity shares in PQ at cost	(i) to (iii)	500	–	–
80,000 Equity shares in SY at cost	(iv)	125		
		1,025	297	380
Current Assets				
Inventory	(vi)	190	60	160
Trade receivables		144	63	88
Cash and cash equivalents	(viii)	48	21	73
		382	144	321
Total Assets		1,407	441	701
Equity and Liabilities				
Equity shares of $1 each		900	100	400
Share premium		300	50	100
Retained earnings	(v)	111	112	95
Revaluation reserve			60	
		1,311	322	595
Current liabilities				
Trade payables		96	119	106
Total Equity and Liabilities		1,407	441	701

Additional information:

(i)   AZ acquired all of PQ's equity shares on 1 October 2010 for $500,000. PQ's retained earnings at 1 October 2010 were $38,000.

(ii)   AZ commissioned a professional valuer to value PQ's net assets at 1 October 2010. The results were as follows:

	Original Cost $'000	Carrying value $'000	Valuation $'000
Property	100	200	300
Plant and equipment	200	97	117
All other assets and liabilities			Equal to carrying value

Plant and equipment had an average remaining useful life of 5 years at 1 October 2010.

AZ's accounting policy is to depreciate plant and equipment using the straight line basis with no residual value.

(iii)   AZ carried out an impairment review of the goodwill arising on acquisition of PQ and found that as at 30 September 2012 the goodwill had been impaired by $20,000.

(iv)   AZ purchased its shareholding in SY on 1 October 2011 for $125,000. The fair value of all SY's net assets was the same as their carrying value at that date. AZ exercises significant influence over all aspects of SY's financial and operating policies.

(v)   The Statements of Profit or Loss and Other Comprehensive Income for the year ended 30 September 2012 showed the following amounts for the profit for the year for each entity:

	$'000
AZ	67
PQ	49
SY	55

(vi)   During August 2012 PQ sold goods to AZ for $52,000 at a mark up of 33⅓% on cost. At 30 September 2012 all of the goods remained in AZ's closing inventory and AZ had not paid for the goods.

(vii)   AZ sold a piece of machinery to PQ on 1 October 2011 for $74,000. The machinery had previously been used in AZ's business and had been included in AZ's property, plant and equipment at a carrying value of $50,000. The machinery had a remaining useful life of 4 years at that date. Profit on disposal was included in revenue.

(viii)   AZ made a payment to PQ for $60,000 on 30 September 2012 which was not recorded by PQ until 5 October 2012.

Required

(a)   (i)   **Explain** the meaning of fair value according to IFRS 13 *Fair value measurement*.

(ii)   **Calculate** the fair value of PQ's net assets acquired by AZ on 1 October 2010.   **(4 marks)**

(b)   **Prepare** the consolidated statement of financial position for AZ as at 30 September 2012, in accordance with the requirements of International Financial Reporting Standards.   **(21 marks)**

Notes to the financial statements are not required, but all workings must be clearly shown.

(Total = 25 marks)

40   Wood, Plank and Bush (9/12)   45 mins

The draft statements of financial position at 31 March 2012 and statements of profit or loss and other comprehensive income for the year ended 31 March 2012 for three entities, Wood, Plank and Bush are given below:

Statements of financial position at 31 March 2012

	Notes	Wood $'000	Plank $'000	Bush $'000
Non-current Assets				
Property, plant and equipment	(iii)/(vii)	11,820	7,240	6,730
Investments:				
6,000,000 Ordinary shares in				
Plank at cost	(ii)	9,200		
Loan to Plank	(ii)	3,100		
1,540,000 Ordinary shares in Bush at cost	(v)	2,420		
		26,540	7,240	6,730
Current Assets				
Inventory	(vi)	12,060	3,215	890
Trade receivables		13,400	5,710	920
Cash and cash equivalents	(ix)	1,730	510	110
		27,190	9,435	1,920
Total Assets		53,730	16,675	8,650
Equity and Liabilities				
Equity shares of $1 each		38,900	6,000	5,500
Share premium		5,520	0	0
Retained earnings		5,400	3,680	1,240

	49,820	9,680	6,740

Non-current liabilities

Loan from Wood	0	3,100	0

Current liabilities

Trade payables	3,910	3,740	1,910
Loan interest payable	0	155	0
	3,910	3,895	1,910
Total Equity and Liabilities	53,730	16,675	8,650

Statements of profit or loss and other comprehensive income for the year ended 31 March 2012

	Wood	Plank	Bush
	$'000	$'000	$'000
Revenue	15,500	6,900	2,300
Cost of sales	(8,700)	(3,080)	(840)
Gross profit	6,800	3,820	1,460
Expenses	(1,250)	(750)	(340)
	5,550	3,070	1,120
Finance cost	(810)	(440)	(120)
	4,740	2,630	1,000
Tax	(1,250)	(230)	(170)
Profit for the year	3,490	2,400	830

Additional information:

(i)   Wood holds shares in two other entities, Plank and Bush.

(ii)   Wood acquired all of Plank's equity shares on 1 April 2011 for $9,200,000 when Plank's retained earnings were $1,280,000. Wood also advanced Plank a 10 year loan of $3,100,000 on 1 April 2011.

(iii)   The fair value of Plank's property, plant and equipment on 1 April 2011 exceeded its carrying value by $1,350,000. The excess of fair value over carrying value was attributed to buildings owned by Plank. At the date of acquisition these buildings had a remaining useful life of 15 years. Wood's accounting policy is to depreciate buildings using the straight line basis with no residual value.

(iv)   Wood carried out an impairment review of the goodwill arising on acquisition of Plank and found that as at 31 March 2012 the goodwill had been impaired by $80,000.

(v)   Wood purchased its shareholding in Bush on 1 April 2011 for $2,420,000 when Bush's retained earnings were $410,000. The fair value of Bush's net assets was the same as its carrying value at that date. Wood exercises significant influence over all aspects of Bush's financial and operating policies.

(vi)   Wood occasionally trades with Plank. During February 2012 Wood sold Plank goods for $520,000. Wood uses a mark up of 100% on cost. At 31 March 2012 all the goods remained in Plank's closing inventory and Plank had not paid for the goods.

(vii)   Wood sold a piece of machinery to Plank on 30 September 2011 for $95,000. The machinery had previously been used in Wood's business and had been included in Wood's property, plant and equipment at a carrying value of $75,000. The machinery had a remaining useful life of ten years at 30 September 2011.

(viii) At 31 March 2012 $155,000 loan interest was due and had not been paid. Plank had accrued the loan interest due at the year-end but Wood had not accrued any interest income.

(ix)   Plank posted a cheque to Wood for $210,000 on 31 March 2012 which did not arrive until 5 April 2012.

Required

(a)   Explain how item (vii) above should be treated in Wood's consolidated financial statements for the year ended 31 March 2012.   **(3 marks)**

(b) Prepare the consolidated statement of profit or loss and other comprehensive income for Wood for the year ended 31 March 2012 AND the consolidated statement of financial position for Wood as at 31 March 2012, in accordance with the requirements of International Financial Reporting Standards. **(22 marks)**

Notes to the financial statements are not required but all workings must be shown.

(Total = 25 marks)

41 Loch, River and Stream (5/12)   45 mins

The draft statements of financial position at 31 March 2012 and statements of profit or loss and other comprehensive income for the year ended 31 March 2012 for three entities, Loch, River and Stream are given below:

STATEMENTS OF FINANCIAL POSITION AS AT 31 MARCH 2012:

	Notes	Loch $'000	River $'000	Stream $'000
Non-current Assets				
Property, plant and equipment	(iv)	1,193	767	670
Investments:				
Loan to River	(iii)	300	0	0
156,000 Ordinary shares	(vi)			
in Stream at cost		223	0	0
		1,716	767	670
Current Assets				
Inventory	(vii)	1,107	320	87
Trade receivables		1,320	570	90
Current a/c with River	(viii)	101	0	0
Cash and cash equivalents		62	58	14
		2,590	948	191
Total Assets		4,306	1,715	861
Equity and Liabilities				
Equity shares of $1 each		3,500	600	520
Retained earnings		413	385	125
		3,913	985	645
Non-current liabilities				
Loan from Loch	(iii)	0	300	0
Current liabilities				
Trade payables		393	340	216
Loan interest payable	(ix)	0	15	0
Current a/c with Loch	(viii)	0	75	0
		393	430	216
Total Equity and Liabilities		4,306	1,715	861

STATEMENTS OF PROFIT OR LOSS AND OTHER COMPREHENSIVE INCOME

FOR THE YEAR ENDED 31 MARCH 2012

	Loch $'000	River $'000	Stream $'000
Revenue	1,500	693	227
Cost of sales	(865)	(308)	(84)
Gross profit	635	385	143
Expenses	(124)	(70)	(35)
	511	315	108
Finance cost	(80)	(40)	(12)
	431	275	96
Income tax expense	(118)	(20)	(16)
Profit for the year	313	255	80

Additional information:

(i)   Loch holds shares in two other entities, River and Stream.

(ii)   Loch acquired all of River's equity shares on 1 April 2011 in a share for share exchange. The agreed purchase consideration was $950,000, however Loch has not yet recorded the acquisition in its accounting records. On the 1 April 2011 Loch's shares had a market value of $2.00 each. River's retained earnings were $130,000 on 1 April 2011.

(iii)   On 1 April 2011 Loch advanced River a 10 year loan of $300,000.

(iv)   The fair value of River's property, plant and equipment on 1 April 2011 exceeded its carrying value by $144,000. The excess of fair value over carrying value was attributed to buildings owned by River. At the date of acquisition these buildings had a remaining useful life of 12 years. Loch's accounting policy is to depreciate buildings using the straight line basis with no residual value.

(v)   Loch carried out an impairment review of the goodwill arising on acquisition of River and found that as at 31 March 2012 the goodwill had been impaired by $20,000.

(vi)   Loch purchased its shareholding in Stream on 1 April 2011 for $223,000 when Stream's retained earnings were $45,000. The fair value of Stream's net assets was the same as its carrying value at that date. Loch exercises significant influence over all aspects of Stream's financial and operating policies.

(vii)   Loch occasionally trades with River. During September 2011 Loch sold River goods for $220,000. Loch uses a mark-up of 50% on cost. At 31 March 2012 all the goods remained in River's closing inventory.

(viii) River posted a cheque to Loch for $26,000 on 29 March 2012 which did not arrive until 7 April 2012.

(ix)   At 31 March 2012 $15,000 loan interest was due and had not been paid. River had accrued the loan interest due at the year end but Loch had not accrued any interest income.

Required

(a)   Prepare the journal entry to record the purchase of River in Loch's accounting records.   **(3 marks)**

(b)   Prepare the consolidated statement of profit or loss and other comprehensive income for Loch for the year ended 31 March 2012 AND a consolidated statement of financial position for Loch as at 31 March 2012, in accordance with the requirements of International Financial Reporting Standards.   **(22 marks)**

Notes to the financial statements are not required, but all workings must be clearly shown.

(Total = 25 marks)

---

42   Tree, Branch and Leaf (3/12)   45 mins

The draft statements of financial position at 31 January 2012 and statements of profit or loss and other comprehensive income for the year ended 31 January 2012 for three entities, Tree, Branch and Leaf are given below:

STATEMENTS OF FINANCIAL POSITION AT 31 JANUARY 2012

	Notes	Tree $'000	Branch $'000	Leaf $'000
Non-current Assets				
Property, plant and equipment		1,535	1,155	1,025
Investments:				
790,000 Ordinary shares in Branch at cost	(ii); (iii)	1,500		
Loan to Branch	(ii)	600		
332,000 Ordinary shares in Leaf at cost	(iv)	550		
		4,185	1,155	1,025
Current Assets				
Inventory	(v)	1,360	411	123
Current account with Branch	(vii)	123	0	0
Trade receivables		1,540	734	142
Cash and cash equivalents		47	75	55
		3,070	1,220	320
Total Assets		7,255	2,375	1,345

Equity and Liabilities

		Tree	Branch	Leaf
Equity shares of $1 each		3,900	790	830
Retained earnings		665	495	220
		4,565	1,285	1,050
Non-current liabilities				
Long term borrowings		0	600	0
Current liabilities				
Trade payables		2,690	365	295
Loan interest payable	(vi)	0	30	0
Current account with Tree	(vii)	0	95	0
		2,690	490	295
Total Equity and Liabilities		7,255	2,375	1,345

STATEMENTS OF PROFIT OR LOSS AND OTHER COMPREHENSIVE INCOME
FOR THE YEAR ENDED 31 JANUARY 2012

	Tree $'000	Branch $'000	Leaf $'000
Revenue	2,200	777	411
Cost of sales	1,112	456	146
Gross profit	1,088	321	265
Expenses	221	115	62
	867	206	203
Finance cost	102	59	34
	765	147	169
Taxation	145	32	19
Profit for the year	620	115	150

Additional information:

(i) Tree holds shares in two other entities, Branch and Leaf.

(ii) Tree acquired all of Branch's equity shares on 1 February 2011 for $1,500,000 when Branch's retained earnings were $380,000. Tree also advanced Branch a ten year loan of $600,000 on 1 February 2011.

(iii) The fair value of Branch's property, plant and equipment on 1 February 2011 exceeded its book value by $240,000. The excess of fair value over book value was attributed to buildings owned by Branch. At the date of acquisition these buildings had a remaining useful life of 10 years. Tree's accounting policy is to depreciate buildings using the straight line basis.

(iv) Tree purchased its shareholding in Leaf on 1 February 2011 for $550,000 when Leaf's retained earnings were $70,000. The fair value of Leaf's net assets was the same as its net book value at that date. Tree exercises significant influence over all aspects of Leaf's strategic and operational decisions.

(v) Tree occasionally trades with Branch. During September 2011 Tree sold Branch goods for $180,000. Tree uses a mark up of fifty percent on cost. By 31 January 2012 Branch had sold one third of the goods, $120,000 being included in Branch's closing inventory.

(vi) At 31 January 2012 $30,000 loan interest was due and had not been paid. Branch had accrued this amount at the year end but Tree had not accrued any interest income.

(vii) Branch posted a cheque to Tree for $28,000 on 29 January 2012 which did not arrive until 7 February 2012.

(viii) No dividends are proposed by any of the entities.

Required

Prepare a consolidated statement of profit of loss and other comprehensive income for the Tree group of entities for the year ended 31 January 2012 AND a consolidated statement of financial position for the Tree group of entities as at 31 January 2012, in accordance with the requirements of International Financial Reporting Standards.

Notes to the financial statements are not required but all workings must be shown.

(25 marks)

43 PH, SU and AJ (11/11)   45 mins

The Draft summarised Statements of Financial Position at 30 September 2011 for three entities, PH, SU and AJ are given below:

	PH $'000	SU $'000	AJ $'000
Non-current Assets			
Property, plant and equipment	50,390	57,590	41,270
Investments:			
48,000,000 Ordinary shares in SU at cost	75,590		
Loan to SU	12,600		
8,000,000 Ordinary shares in AJ at cost	16,400		
	154,980	57,590	41,270
Current Assets			
Inventory	10,160	14,410	10,260
Current account with SU	10,000		
Trade receivables	21,400	13,200	11,940
Cash and cash equivalents	1,260	3,600	3,580
	42,820	31,210	25,780
Total Assets	197,800	88,800	67,050
Equity and Liabilities			
Equity shares of $1 each	126,000	48,000	24,000
Retained earnings	26,500	15,600	28,800
	152,500	63,600	52,800
Non-current liabilities			
Long term borrowings	32,700	12,600	11,800
Current liabilities			
Trade payables	12,600	5,400	2,450
Current account with PH	0	7,200	0
	12,600	12,600	2,450
Total Equity and Liabilities	197,800	88,800	67,050

Additional information:

(i)   PH acquired all of SU's equity shares on 1 October 2010 for $75,590,000 when SU's retained earnings were $7,680,000. PH also advanced SU a ten year loan of $12,600,000 on 1 October 2010.

(ii)   The fair value of SU's property, plant and equipment on 1 October 2010 exceeded its book value by $1,300,000. The excess of fair value over book value was attributed to buildings owned by SU. At the date of acquisition these buildings had a remaining useful life of 20 years. PH's accounting policy is to depreciate buildings using the straight line basis.

(iii)   At 30 September 2011 $90,000 loan interest was due on the loan made by PH to SU and had not been paid. Both PH and SU had accrued this amount at the year end.

(iv)   PH purchased 8,000,000 of AJ's equity shares on 1 October 2010 for $16,400,000 when AJ's retained earnings were $24,990,000. PH exercises significant influence over all aspects of AJ's strategic and operational decisions.

(v)   SU posted a cheque to PH for $2,800,000 on 29 September 2011 which did not arrive until 7 October 2011.

(vi)   No dividends are proposed by any of the entities.

(vii)   PH occasionally trades with SU. In September 2011 PH sold SU goods for $4,800,000. PH uses a mark-up of one third on cost. On 30 September 2011 all the goods were included in SU's closing inventory.

Required

(a)   **Define** what is meant by control and **explain** how this is determined according to IFRS 10 *Consolidated financial statements*.   **(5 marks)**

(b)   **Prepare** the consolidated statement of financial position for the PH group of entities as at 30 September 2011, in accordance with the requirements of International Financial Reporting Standards.

Notes to the financial statements are not required but all workings must be shown.

(20 marks)

(Total = 25 marks)

44   AX (5/10)   45 mins

AX holds shares in two other entities, AS and AA.

AX purchased 100% of AS shares on 1 April 20X8 for $740,000, when the fair value was $75,000 more than book value. The excess of fair value over book value was attributed to land held by AS.

At 1 April 20X8 the retained earnings of AS showed a debit balance of $72,000.

AX purchased 120,000 ordinary shares in AA on 1 April 20X8 for $145,000 when AA's retained earnings were $49,000. AX is able to exercise significant influence over all aspects of AA's strategic and operational decisions. At 1 April 20X8 the fair values of AA's assets were the same as their net book value.

The draft summarised financial statements for the three entities as at 31 March 20X9 are given below.

DRAFT SUMMARISED STATEMENTS OF FINANCIAL POSITION AS AT 31 MARCH 20X9

	AX		AS		AA	
	$'000	$'000	$'000	$'000	$'000	$'000
Non-current Assets						
Property, plant and equipment	1,120		700		740	
Investments:						
600,000 Ordinary shares in AS at cost	740		–		–	
120,000 Ordinary shares in AA at cost	145		–		–	
		2,005		700		740
Current Assets						
Inventory	205		30		14	
Trade receivables	350		46		30	
Cash and cash equivalents	30		–		11	
		585		76		55
Total Assets		2,590		776		795
Equity and Liabilities						
Equity shares of $1 each		1,500		600		550
Retained earnings		518		15		100
		2,018		615		650
Non-current liabilities						
Borrowings	360		80		109	
Deferred tax	120		16		10	
		480		96		119
Current liabilities						
Trade payables	92		29		15	
Tax (see additional information (i))	–		16		11	
Bank overdraft	–		20		–	
		92		65		26
Total Equity and Liabilities		2,590		776		795

SUMMARISED STATEMENTS OF PROFIT OR LOSS AND OTHER COMPREHENSIVE INCOME
FOR THE YEAR ENDED 31 MARCH 20X9

	AX $'000	AS $'000	AA $'000
Revenue	820	285	147
Cost of sales	(406)	(119)	(52)
	414	166	95
Administrative expenses	(84)	(36)	(14)
Distribution costs	(48)	(22)	(11)
	(282)	(108)	(70)
Finance cost	(18)	(5)	(8)
	264	103	62
Income Tax (see additional information (i))		(16)	(11)
Profit for the year		87	51

Additional information:

(i)   AX is deemed resident in Country X for tax purposes.

(ii)   AX has not yet calculated its tax charge for the year to 31 March 20X9. AX's cost of sales includes a depreciation charge of $31,000 for property, plant and equipment. Included in administrative expenses are entertaining expenses of $4,000. AX's property, plant and equipment qualified for tax depreciation allowances of $49,000 for the year ended 31 March 20X9.

(iii)   In the year since acquisition AS sold goods for $55,000 to AX of which $25,000 remained in AX's closing inventory at 31 March 20X9. AS uses a mark up of 25% on cost. All invoices from AS for the goods had been paid by the year end.

(iv)   No dividends are proposed by any of the entities.

Required

(a)   **Calculate** the estimated amount of corporate income tax that AX will be due to pay for the year ended 31 March 20X9 and any required adjustment to the provision for deferred tax at that date.

(5 marks)

(b)   **Prepare** a consolidated statement of profit or loss and other comprehensive income for the AX Group of entities for the year ended 31 March 20X9 and a consolidated statement of financial position as at that date.

Notes to the financial statements are not required but all workings must be shown.   **(20 marks)**

(Total = 25 marks)

---

45   PSA (Specimen Paper)   45 mins

The draft summarised statements of financial position at 31 March 20X9 for three entities, P, S and A are given below.

	P $'000	P $'000	S $'000	S $'000	A $'000	A $'000
Non-current Assets						
Property, plant and equipment		40,000		48,000		34,940
Investments:						–
40,000 Ordinary shares in S at cost		60,000		–		–
Loan to S		10,000		–		–
8,000 Ordinary shares in A at cost		13,000		–		–
		123,000		48,000		34,940
Current Assets						
Inventory	8,000		12,000		8,693	
Current a/c with S	8,000		–		–	
Trade receivables	17,000		11,000		10,106	
Cash and cash equivalents	1,000		3,000		3,033	
		34,000		26,000		21,832
Total Assets		157,000		74,000		56,772

Equity and Liabilities					
Equity shares of $1 each		100,000	40,000		20,000
Retained earnings		21,000	13,000		7,800
		121,000	53,000		27,800
Non-current liabilities					
Borrowings		26,000	10,000		10,000
Current liabilities					
Trade payables	10,000		5,000	18,972	
Current a/c with P	–		6,000	–	
		10,000	11,000		18,972
Total Equity and Liabilities		157,000	74,000		56,772

Additional information:

(i)   P acquired all of S's equity shares on 1 April 20X8 for $60,000,000 when S's retained earnings were $6,400,000. P also advanced S a ten year loan of $10,000,000 on 1 April 20X8.

(ii)   The fair value of S's property, plant and equipment on 1 April 20X8 exceeded its book value by $1,000,000. The excess of fair value over book value was attributed to buildings owned by S. At the date of acquisition these buildings had a remaining useful life of 20 years. P's accounting policy is to depreciate buildings using the straight line basis.

(iii)   At 31 March 20X9 $250,000 loan interest was due and had not been paid. Both P and S had accrued this amount at the year end.

(iv)   P purchased 8,000,000 of A's equity shares on 1 April 20X8 for $13,000,000 when A's retained earnings were $21,000,000. P exercises significant influence over all aspects of A's strategic and operational decisions.

(v)   S posted a cheque to P for $2,000,000 on 30 March 20X9 which did not arrive until 7 April 20X9.

(vi)   No dividends are proposed by any of the entities.

(vii)   P occasionally trades with S. In March 20X9 P sold S goods for $4,000,000. P uses a mark up of one third on cost. On 31 March 20X9 all the goods were included in S's closing inventory and the invoice for the goods was still outstanding.

(viii)   P's directors do not want to consolidate A. They argue that they do not control A, therefore it does not need to be consolidated. They insist that A should appear in the consolidated statement of financial position at cost of $13,000,000.

Required

(a)   Draft a response that **explains** to P's directors the correct treatment of A in the consolidated financial statements. Include comments on any ethical issues involved.   **(5 marks)**

(b)   **Prepare** a consolidated statement of financial position for the P Group of entities as at 31 March 20X9, in accordance with the requirements of International Financial Reporting Standards.   **(20 marks)**

Notes to the financial statements are not required but all workings must be shown.

Total = 25 marks)

46 Parsley   45 mins

You are provided with the following financial statements for Parsley, a limited liability company, and its subsidiary Sage.

STATEMENTS OF PROFIT OR LOSS AND OTHER COMPREHENSIVE INCOME
FOR THE YEAR ENDED 31 DECEMBER 20X9

	Parsley $'000	Sage $'000
Sales revenue	135,000	74,000
Cost of sales	(70,000)	(30,000)
Gross profit	65,000	44,000
Distribution costs	(7,500)	(6,200)
Administrative expenses	(19,000)	(7,784)
Income from Sage: loan note interest	4	–
dividends	8,000	–
Interest payable	–	(16)
Profit before tax	46,504	30,000
Income tax expense	(10,000)	(9,000)
Profit for the year	36,504	21,000

STATEMENTS OF FINANCIAL POSITION AS AT 31 DECEMBER 20X9

	Parsley $'000	Parsley $'000	Sage $'000	Sage $'000
Assets				
Non-current assets				
Property, plant and equipment		74,000		39,050
Investments:				
$1 ordinary shares in Sage at cost		30,000		–
Sage loan notes		50		–
		104,050		39,050
Current assets				
Inventory	10,630		4,498	
Receivables	18,460		12,230	
Bank	13,400		1,344	
		42,490		18,072
Total assets		146,540		57,122
Equity and liabilities				
Equity				
$1 ordinary shares		80,000		25,000
Retained earnings		37,540		15,000
		117,540		40,000
Non-current liabilities				
8% Loan note		–		200
Current liabilities				
Payables	6,000		1,922	
Tax	11,000		7,000	
Dividends payable	12,000		8,000	
		29,000		16,922
Total equity and liabilities		146,540		57,122

The following information is also available:

(a)   Parsley purchased 100% of the $1 ordinary shares in Sage on 1 January 20X8. At that date Sage's retained earnings were $2,000,000.

(b)   Parsley's annual impairment review of goodwill on acquisition of Sage valued it at $2,250,000 at 31 December 20X9.

(c)   During the year ended 31 December 20X9 Parsley sold goods which originally cost $8,000,000 to Sage for $12,000,000. Sage still had 25% of these goods in inventory at 31 December 20X9.

(d) Sage owed Parsley $1,800,000 at 31 December 20X9 for some of the goods Parsley supplied during the year.

(e) Parsley owns $50,000 of Sage's loan notes. The interest is paid annually in arrears at 31 December. Interest for the year ended 31 December 20X9 is included in Sage's payables. Parsley has also included the interest in its receivables.

(f) All dividends were declared but not paid prior to the year end.

Required

(a) **Calculate** the goodwill arising on the acquisition of Sage.   **(2 marks)**

(b) **Prepare** the following financial statements for Parsley:

    (i) The consolidated statement of profit or loss and other comprehensive income for the year ended 31 December 20X9.   **(6 marks)**

    (ii) The consolidated statement of financial position as at 31 December 20X9.

    Note. A working should be included for the retained earnings. Disclosure notes are not required.

(14 marks)

(c) **Explain** the accounting treatment of intra-group trading in consolidated accounts.   **(3 marks)**

(Total = 25 marks)

47 Tom, Dick and Harry   45 mins

The following statements of financial position have been prepared as at 31 October 20X9.

	Tom		Dick		Harry	
	$'000	$'000	$'000	$'000	$'000	$'000
Non-current assets						
Property, plant and equipment		205		120		220
Investments						
100,000 shares in Dick Ltd at cost		200		–		–
60,000 shares in Harry Ltd at cost		115		–		–
Current assets						
Inventory	100		70		90	
Receivables	170		40		70	
Bank	190		30		50	
		460		140		210
		980		260		430
Equity and liabilities						
Equity						
$1 ordinary shares		500		100		200
Retained earnings		370		130		150
		870		230		350
Current liabilities						
Trade payables		110		30		80
		980		260		430

Additional information

(a) Tom purchased all the share capital of Dick on 1 November 20X8 for $200,000. The previous owners of Dick needed to sell quickly as they were in financial difficulty. The book value of Dick's net assets on the date of acquisition was $190,000. A valuation exercise performed by a reputable firm showed that the fair value of Dick's property, plant and equipment at that date was $50,000 greater than book value. The increase in fair value was not accounted for in the books of Dick. If Dick had re-valued its non-current assets at 31 October 20X8, an addition of $2,000 would have been made to the depreciation charged for 20X8/20X9.

(b) Tom sold goods for $25,000 to Dick during the year. The price included a 25% mark up. 40% of them are still held in inventory by Dick.

(c) Tom's investment in Harry was acquired on 31 October 20X5 when the retained earnings of Harry were $130,000. The fair value of Harry's assets were the same as their net book value at the date of acquisition. At 31 October 20X9, the investment in Harry is impaired by $4,000.

Required

(a) (i) **Calculate** the goodwill on acquisition of Dick.

   (ii) **Explain** the treatment required by IFRS 3 for a bargain purchase that creates negative goodwill.

(6 marks)

(b) **Prepare** the consolidated statement of financial position for the Tom Group as at 31 October 20X9.

(19 marks)

(Total = 25 marks)

---

48 ZA   45 mins

ZA is the parent company of ZB and owns 30% of ZC. The following are the financial statements for all three companies as at 31 October 20X7.

STATEMENTS OF PROFIT OR LOSS AND OTHER COMPREHENSIVE INCOME
FOR THE YEAR ENDED 31 OCTOBER 20X7

	ZA	ZB	ZC
	$'000	$'000	$'000
Sales revenue	870	285	148
Cost of sales	(540)	(119)	(60)
Gross profit	330	166	88
Distribution costs	(54)	(36)	(12)
Administrative expenses	(78)	(22)	(15)
Interest payable	–	(10)	(16)
Profit before tax	198	98	45
Income tax expense	(40)	(25)	(5)
Profit for the year	158	73	40

STATEMENTS OF FINANCIAL POSITION AS AT 31 OCTOBER 20X7

	ZA	ZB	ZC
	$'000	$'000	$'000
Assets			
Non-current assets			
Property, plant and equipment	3,000	3,300	2,000
Investments: shares in ZB at cost	4,545		–
shares in ZC at cost	800	–	–
Current assets			
Inventory	1,500	800	400
Receivables	1,800	750	300
Bank	600	350	150
	3,900	1,900	850
Total assets	12,245	5,200	2,850
Equity and liabilities			
Equity			
$1 ordinary shares	9,000	4,000	2,260
Retained earnings	1,325	200	340
	10,325	4,200	2,600
Current liabilities			
Payables	1,220	200	150
Tax	700	800	100
Total equity and liabilities	12,245	5,200	2,800

The following information is also available.

(a) ZA purchased all of the shares in ZB some years ago when ZB had retained earnings of $60,000. All goodwill on acquisition has been fully written off as impaired in prior years. ZA purchased its shares in ZC on 1 November 20X6 when ZC had retained earnings of $300,000.

(b) During the year ZA sold goods with an invoice value of $240,000 to ZB. These goods were invoiced at cost plus 20%. Half of the goods are still in ZB's inventory at the year end.

(c) ZB owes ZA $30,000 at 31 October 20X7 for goods it purchased during the year.

(d) ZA wants to recognise an impairment of $100,000 in respect of its investment in ZC.

Required

(a) **Calculate** the goodwill on acquisition of ZB.   **(2 marks)**

(b) **Prepare** a consolidated statement of profit or loss and other comprehensive income for the ZA group of entities for the year ended 31 October 20X7 and a consolidated statement of financial position as at that date.

   Note. A working should be included for group retained earnings. Disclosure notes are not required.
                                                                                          (20 marks)

(c) A company that owns less than 50% of the shares of another company will regard it as an 'associate' if it is able to exert 'significant influence'. **Identify** three circumstances that might demonstrate 'significant influence'.
                                                                                          (3 marks)

                                                                            (Total = 25 marks)

Part D: Principles of Business Taxation

Questions 49 to 55 cover Principles of Business Taxation, the subject of Part D of the BPP Study Text for F1.

Unless otherwise specified, the following data is applicable to questions 49 - 55.

Country X – Tax regime

Relevant tax rules

Corporate Profits

Unless otherwise specified, only the following rules for taxation of corporate profits will be relevant, other taxes can be ignored:

(a)   Accounting rules on recognition and measurement are followed for tax purposes.

(b)   All expenses other than depreciation, amortisation, entertaining, taxes paid to other public bodies and donations to political parties are tax deductible.

(c)   Tax depreciation is deductible as follows:

- 50% of additions to property, plant and equipment in the accounting period in which they are recorded

- 25% per year of the written-down value (ie cost minus previous allowances) in subsequent accounting periods except that in which the asset is disposed of

- No tax depreciation is allowed on land

(d)   The corporate tax on profits is at a rate of 25%.

(e)   No indexation is allowable on the sale of land.

(f)   Tax losses can be carried forward to offset against future taxable profits from the same business.

Value Added Tax

Country X has a VAT system which allows entities to reclaim input tax paid. In Country X the VAT rates are:

Zero rated	0%
Standard rated	15%

49 Objective test questions: General principles of taxation   65 mins

1   Which of the following powers is *not* available to tax authorities.

   A   Power to review and query filed returns
   B   Power to detain company officials
   C   Power to request special returns
   D   Power to enter and search premises   **(2 marks)**

2   Complete the blanks:

   Direct taxation is charged directly on the .... or .... that is intended to pay the tax.   **(2 marks)**

3   The economist, Adam Smith, proposed that an acceptable tax should meet four characteristics. Three of these characteristics were certainty, convenience and efficiency.

   Identify the FOURTH characteristic.

   A   Neutrality
   B   Transparency
   C   Equity
   D   Simplicity   **(2 marks)**

4   In no more than 20 words, **define** tax evasion.   **(2 marks)**

5   **List** (using no more than five words per item) the four main sources of tax rules in a country.   **(4 marks)**

6   The effective incidence of a tax is on:

    A   the date the tax is actually paid.
    B   the person or entity that finally bears the cost of the tax.
    C   the date the tax assessment is issued.
    D   the person or entity receiving the tax assessment.   **(2 marks)**

7   In no more than 15 words, **define** the meaning of competent jurisdiction.   **(2 marks)**

8   Which **one** of the following powers is a tax authority least likely to have granted to them?

    A   Power of arrest.
    B   Power to examine records.
    C   Power of entry and search.
    D   Power to give information to other country's tax authorities.   **(2 marks)**

9   An entity sells furniture and adds a sales tax to the selling price of all products sold. A customer purchasing furniture from the entity has to pay the cost of the furniture plus the sales tax. The customer therefore bears the cost of the sales tax.

    This is referred to as:

    A   Formal incidence
    B   Indirect incidence
    C   Effective incidence
    D   Direct incidence   **(2 marks)**

10   **List** three possible reasons why governments set deadlines for filing returns and/or paying taxes.   **(3 marks)**

11   What is 'hypothecation'?

    A   Process of earmarking tax revenues for specific types of expenditure
    B   Estimation of tax revenue made by the tax authorities for budget purposes
    C   Refund made by tax authorities for tax paid in other countries
    D   Payment of taxes due to tax authorities, net of tax refunds due from tax authorities   **(2 marks)**

12   **Explain** briefly **three** major principles of modern taxation.   **(3 marks)**

13   Which **one** of the following is **not** an advantage for the tax authority of deduction of tax at source?

    A   The total amount of tax due for the period is easier to calculate
    B   Tax is collected earlier
    C   Administration costs are borne by the entity deducting tax
    D   Tax is deducted before income is paid to the taxpayer   **(2 marks)**

14   HD sells office stationery and adds a sales tax to the selling price of all products sold. A customer purchasing goods from HD has to pay the cost of the goods plus the sales tax.

    HD pays the sales tax collected to the tax authorities.

    From the perspective of HD the sales tax would be said to have

    A   Formal incidence
    B   Effective incidence
    C   Informal incidence
    D   Ineffective incidence   **(2 marks)**

15 The 'tax gap' is the difference between:

A   When a tax payment is due and the date it is actually paid

B   The tax due calculated by the entity and the tax demanded by the tax authority

C   The amount of tax due to be paid and the amount actually collected

D   The date when the entity was notified by the tax authority of the tax due and the date the tax should be paid   **(2 marks)**

16 Which of the following is a source of tax rules?

A   International accounting standards
B   Local company legislation
C   International tax treaties
D   Domestic accounting practice   **(2 marks)**

(Total = 36 marks)

50 Objective test questions: Types of taxation I   85 mins

1 Country X uses a Pay-As-You-Earn (PAYE) system for collecting taxes from employees. Each employer is provided with information about each employee's tax position and tables showing the amount of tax to deduct each period. Employers are required to deduct tax from employees and pay it to the revenue authorities on a monthly basis

From the perspective of the government, **list three** advantages of the PAYE system.   **(3 marks)**

2 Where is employee tax recorded in a set of financial accounts?

A   Charged to employee costs in the statement of profit or loss and other comprehensive income
B   Charged to cost of sales in the statement of profit of loss and other comprehensive income
C   Included as a payable in the statement of financial position
D   Included as a receivable in the statement of financial position   **(2 marks)**

3 Complete the following equation.

Accounting profit + ? – non-taxable income – tax allowable expenditure = ?   **(2 marks)**

4 A withholding tax is:

A   Tax withheld from payment to the tax authorities.
B   Tax paid less an amount withheld from payment.
C   Tax deducted at source before payment of interest or dividends.
D   Tax paid on increases in value of investment holdings.   **(2 marks)**

5 BM has a taxable profit of $30,000 and receives a tax assessment of $3,000.

BV has a taxable profit of $60,000 and receives a tax assessment of $7,500.

BM and BV are resident in the same tax jurisdiction.

This tax could be said to be

A   A progressive tax
B   A regressive tax
C   A direct tax
D   A proportional tax   **(2 marks)**

6 **State** two reasons why a group of entities might want to claim group loss relief rather than use the loss in the entity to which it relates.   **(2 marks)**

7   DR makes a taxable profit of $400,000 and pays an equity dividend of $250,000. DR is resident in Country X. In Country X, equity shareholders pay tax on their dividend income at a rate of 30%.

     If DR and its equity shareholders pay a total of $175,000 tax between them, what method of corporate income tax is being used in that country?

     A   The classical system
     B   The imputation system
     C   The partial imputation system
     D   The split rate system   **(2 marks)**

8   A full imputation system of corporate income tax is one where an entity is taxable on:

     A   All of its income and gains whether they are distributed or not. The shareholder is liable for taxation on all dividends received.

     B   All of its income and gains whether they are distributed or not, but all the underlying corporation tax on the distribution is passed to the shareholder as a tax credit.

     C   All of its income and gains whether they are distributed or not, but only part of the underlying corporation tax is passed to the shareholder as a tax credit.

     D   Its retained profits at one rate and on its distributed profits at another (usually lower) rate of tax.
                                                                                                  (2 marks)

9   Company Z has a factory in Malaysia with retail outlets in Hong Kong. The company's registered office is in London but the head office is located in the Cayman Islands. All board meetings take place in the Cayman Islands. Where is Company Z's country of residence?

     A   Malaysia
     B   Hong Kong
     C   England
     D   Cayman Islands   **(2 marks)**

10   The European Union (EU) is an example of a supranational body. In not more than 20 words, **describe** the effect the EU has on its member states' tax rules.   **(2 marks)**

11   **List** four payments that are usually affected by withholding tax.   **(2 marks)**

12   **List** three methods of giving double taxation relief.   **(2 marks)**

13   Double tax relief is used to:

     A   Ensure that you do not pay tax twice on any of your income.
     B   Mitigate taxing overseas income twice.
     C   Avoid taxing dividends received from subsidiaries in the same country twice.
     D   Provide relief where a company pays tax at double the normal rate.   **(2 marks)**

14   Corporate residence for tax purposes can be determined in a number of ways, depending on the country concerned.

     Which **one** of the following is **not** normally used to determine corporate residence for tax purposes?

     A   The country from which control of the entity is exercised.
     B   The country of incorporation of the entity.
     C   The country where management of the entity hold their meetings.
     D   The country where most of the entity's products are sold.   **(2 marks)**

15 An entity, DP, in Country A receives a dividend from an entity in Country B. The gross dividend of $50,000 is subject to a withholding tax of $5,000 and $45,000 is paid to DP.

Country A levies a tax of 12% on overseas dividends.

Country A and Country B have both signed a double taxation treaty based on the OECD model convention and both apply the credit method when relieving double taxation.

How much tax would DP be expected to pay in Country A on the dividend received from the entity in Country B?

A $400
B $1,000
C $5,400
D $6,000   (2 marks)

16 Where a resident entity runs an overseas operation as a branch of the entity, certain tax implications arise.

Which **one** of the following does not usually apply in relation to an overseas branch?

A   Assets can be transferred to the branch without triggering a capital gain
B   Corporate income tax is paid on profits remitted by the branch
C   Tax depreciation can be claimed on any qualifying assets used in the trade of the branch
D   Losses sustained by the branch are immediately deductible against the resident entity's income.
                                                                                              (2 marks)

17 The following details relate to EA:

•   Incorporated in Country A.
•   Carries out its main business activities in Country B.
•   Its senior management operate from Country C and effective control is exercised from Country C.

Assume countries A, B and C have all signed double tax treaties with each other, based on the OECD model tax convention.

Which country will EA be deemed to be resident in for tax purposes?

A   Country A
B   Country B
C   Country C
D   Both Countries B and C   (2 marks)

18 The OECD Model tax convention defines a permanent establishment.

Which **one** of the following is **not** specifically listed as a "permanent establishment" by the OECD Model tax convention?

A   An office
B   A factory
C   An oil well
D   A site of an 11 month construction project   (2 marks)

19 Developed countries generally use three tax bases. One tax base widely used is income.

List the other **two** widely used bases.   (2 marks)

20 The following details are relevant:

- HC carries out its main business activities in Country A

- HC is incorporated in Country B

- HC's senior management exercise control from Country C, but there are no sales or purchases made in Country C

- HC raises its finance and is quoted on the stock exchange in Country D.

Assume Countries A, B, C and D have all signed double taxation treaties with each other, based on the OECD model tax convention.

Which country will HC be deemed to be resident in for tax purposes?

A Country A
B Country B
C Country C
D Country D

(2 marks)

21 EB has an investment of 25% of the equity shares in XY, an entity resident in a foreign country.

EB receives a dividend of $90,000 from XY, the amount being after the deduction of withholding tax of 10%.

XY had profits before tax for the year of $1,200,000 and paid corporate income tax of $200,000.

Calculate how much underlying tax can EB claim for double taxation relief.   **(3 marks)**

22 A company resident in Country X purchased land and buildings in January 20X5 for $155,000, of which $55,000 was attributed to the land. The company incurred in the same month $50,000 for refurbishment of the building, which was classified as capital expenditure according to local tax regulations.

The land and buildings were sold for $425,000 in January 20X9, $100,000 of this price was attributable to the land. The company paid $8,000 in disposal costs which were allowable for tax purposes.

Local tax regulations allow for indexation of the purchase and refurbishment costs of the building. The index has increased by 35% between January 20X5 and January 20X9. Capital gains are taxed at the corporate income tax rate applicable in Country X.

Required

Calculate the capital gain arising on the sale of the land and buildings and the tax payable. Work to the nearest $1.   **(3 marks)**

(Total = 47 marks)

51 Objective test questions: Types of taxation II   99 mins

1 Excise duties are deemed to be most suitable for commodities that have certain specific characteristics.

List three characteristics of a commodity that, from a revenue authority's point of view, would make that commodity suitable for an excise duty to be imposed.   **(3 marks)**

2 Which of the following is an indirect tax?

A Withholding tax
B Employee tax
C Sales tax
D Company income tax

(2 marks)

3 The cost of a sales tax is borne by which person?

    A   The supplier of raw materials
    B   The end consumer
    C   The retailer
    D   The wholesaler   **(2 marks)**

4 DA and DB are entities resident in Country X. DA is a manufacturer and sells products to DB, a retailer, for $500 excluding VAT. DB sells the products to customers for a total of $1,000 excluding VAT.

DA paid $200 plus VAT for the manufacturing cost of its products. All VAT is charged at the standard rate.

Calculate the net VAT due to be paid by DA and DB for the products.   **(2 marks)**

5 Country E uses a multi-stage sales tax system, where a cumulative sales tax is levied every time a sale is made. The tax rate is 15% and tax paid on purchases is not recoverable. ZA and ZB are entities resident in Country E.

ZA is a manufacturer and sells products to ZB, a retailer, for $500 excluding sales tax. ZB sells the products to customers for a total of $1,000 excluding sales tax.

ZA paid $200 plus sales tax for the manufacturing cost of its products.

Calculate the total sales tax due to be paid on all of the sales of the products.   **(2 marks)**

6 Which of the following types of taxes is regarded as an indirect tax?

    A   Taxes on income.
    B   Taxes on capital gains.
    C   Taxes on inherited wealth.
    D   Sales tax (Value added tax).   **(2 marks)**

7 AE purchases products from a foreign entity and imports them into Country X. On import, the products are subject to an excise duty of $5 per item and Value Added Tax (VAT).

AE purchased 200 items for $35 each and after importing them sold all of the items for $50 each plus VAT. AE is resident in Country X. All VAT is charged at the standard rate.

How much is due to be paid to the tax authorities in Country X for these transactions?

    A $450
    B $1,450
    C $2,050
    D $2,500   **(3 marks)**

8 BZ is resident in Country X.

During the last VAT period, BZ, purchased materials and services costing $100,000, excluding VAT. All materials and services were subject to VAT a the standard rate.

BZ converted the materials into two products Z and L. Product Z is zero rated and product L is standard rated for VAT purposes.

During the VAT period, BZ made the following sales, excluding VAT:

	$
Z	60,000
L	120,000

At the end of the period, BZ paid the net VAT due to the tax authorities.

Assuming BZ had no other VAT-related transactions, **calculate** how much VAT BZ paid.   **(2 marks)**

9   CU and CZ are entities resident in Country X.

CU is a manufacturer and pays $115 including VAT for the raw materials to manufacture a batch of clothing. CU sells the batch of clothing to a retailer CZ for $250 plus VAT. CZ unpacks the clothing and sells the items separately to various customers for a total of $690 including VAT. VAT on clothing and raw materials is charged at the standard rate.

Calculate how much VAT CU and CZ each have to pay to the tax authorities in respect of this **one** batch of clothing.   **(2 marks)**

10   GW is resident in Country X.

During the last VAT period GW purchased materials and services costing $138,000 including VAT. All materials and services were at standard rate VAT.

GW converted the materials into two products A and B; product A is zero rated and product B is standard rated for VAT purposes.

During the VAT period, GW made the following sales, including VAT:

	$
A	70,000
B	253,000

At the end of the period, GW paid the net VAT due to the tax authorities.

Assume no opening or closing inventory balances.

Assuming GW had no other VAT-related transactions, **calculate** GW's gross profit and the amount of VAT that GW paid.   **(4 marks)**

11   HN purchases products from a foreign country. The products cost $14 each and are subject to excise duty of $3 per item and VAT at the standard rate. HN is resident in Country X.

If HN imports 1,000 items, how much does it pay to the tax authorities for this transaction?

A $2,100
B $5,100
C $5,550
D $19,550   **(2 marks)**

12   FE owns and runs a small retail store and is resident in Country X. The store's sales include items that are zero rated, standard rated and exempt. FE's electronic cash register provides an analysis of sales. The figures for the three months to 30 April 20X8 were:

	Sales value, including VAT where appropriate $
Zero rated	13,000
Standard rated	18,400
Exempt	11,000
Total	42,400

FE's analysis of expenditure for the same period provided the following:

	Expenditure, excluding VAT $
Zero rated purchases	6,000
Standard rated purchases relating to standard rate outputs	10,000
Standard rated purchases relating to zero rate outputs	4,000
Standard rated purchases relating to exempt outputs	5,000
	25,000

Calculate the VAT due to/from FE for the three months ended 30 April 20X8.   **(3 marks)**

13   Company G makes an accounting profit of $350,000 during the year. This includes non-taxable income of $25,000 and depreciation of $30,000. In addition, $15,000 of the expenses are disallowable for tax purposes. If the tax allowable depreciation totals $32,000, what is the taxable profit?

        A $323,000
        B $338,000
        C $352,000
        D $362,000   **(2 marks)**

14   Company G makes a taxable profit of $350,000 during the year. This includes adjustments for non-taxable income of $25,000, depreciation of $30,000 and $15,000 disallowed expenses. If the tax allowable depreciation totals $32,000, what is the accounting profit?

        A $323,000
        B $338,000
        C $352,000
        D $362,000   **(2 marks)**

15   Company G makes an accounting loss of $350,000 during the year. This includes non-taxable income of $25,000 and depreciation of $30,000. In addition, $400,000 of the expenses are disallowable for tax purposes. If the tax allowable depreciation totals $32,000, what is the taxable amount?

        A $23,000 profit
        B $23,000 loss
        C $123,000 profit
        D $123,000 profit   **(2 marks)**

16   Company W makes a taxable profit of $50m during the year. This is after adjustments for non-taxable income of $3m, depreciation of $15m and $1m disallowed expenses. If the tax allowable depreciation totals $4m, what is the accounting profit?

        A $38m
        B $41m
        C $58m
        D $59m   **(2 marks)**

17   Company M is resident in Country X and makes an accounting profit of $250,000 during the year. This includes depreciation of $45,000 and disallowable expenses of $20,000. If the tax allowable depreciation totals $30,000, what is the tax payable?

        A $66,250
        B $53,750
        C $60,000
        D $71,250   **(2 marks)**

18   Company B is resident in Country X and makes an accounting profit of $360,000 during the year. This includes non-taxable income of $35,000 and depreciation of $40,000. In addition, $10,000 of the expenses are disallowable for tax purposes. If the tax allowable depreciation totals $30,000, what is the tax payable?

        A $90,000
        B $93,750
        C $86,250
        D $92,500   **(2 marks)**

19   Company RE is resident in Country X and makes an accounting profit of $500,000 during the year. This includes non-taxable income of $25,000 and depreciation of $50,000.

The finance director finds that $5,000 of the expenses are disallowable for tax purposes. If the tax allowable depreciation totals $60,000, what is the tax payable?

A $116,250
B $117,500
C $123,750
D $132,500   **(2 marks)**

20   Company G is resident in Country X and makes an accounting profit of $250,000 during the year. This is after charging depreciation of $40,000 and tax disallowable expenses of $2,000. If the tax allowable depreciation totals $30,000, what is the tax payable?

A $65,000
B $59,500
C $62,500
D $65,500   **(2 marks)**

21   E has an accounting profit before tax of $95,000. E is resident in Country X. The accounting profit included non-taxable income from government grants of $15,000 and non-tax allowable expenditure of $10,000 on entertaining expenses.

Calculate how much tax is E due to pay for the year.   **(2 marks)**

22   AC made the following payments during the year ended 30 April 20X5:

	$'000
Operating costs (excluding depreciation)	23
Finance costs	4
Capital repayment of loans	10
Payments for the purchase of new computer equipment for use in AC's business	20

AC's revenue for the period was $45,000. AC is resident in Country X.

Calculate AC's tax payable for the year ended 30 April 20X5.   **(3 marks)**

23   Country B has a corporate income tax system that treats capital gains/losses separately from trading profits/losses. Capital gains/losses cannot be offset against trading profits/losses. All losses can be carried forward indefinitely, but cannot be carried back to previous years. Trading profits and capital gains are both taxed at 25%.

BD is resident in Country B and had no brought forward losses on 1 October 20X2. BD's results for 20X3 to 20X5 were as follows:

	Trading profit/(loss)	Capital gains/(loss)
	$'000	$'000
Year to September 20X3	200	(100)
Year to September 20X4	(120)	0
Year to September 20X5	150	130

Calculate BD's corporate income tax due for each of the years ended 30 September 20X3 to 20X5.

(3 marks)

24 DZ recognised a tax liability of $290,000 in its financial statements for the year ended 30 September 20X5. This was subsequently agreed with and paid to the tax authorities as $280,000 on 1 March 20X6. The directors of DZ estimate that the tax due on the profits for the year to 30 September 20X6 will be $320,000. DZ has no deferred tax liability.

What is DZ's tax charge in its statement of profit or loss and other comprehensive income for the year ended 30 September 20X6?

A $310,000
B $320,000
C $330,000
D $600,000

(2 marks)

(Total = 55 marks)

52 Objective test questions: Deferred tax   77 mins

1 A company had a credit balance brought forward on current tax of $20,000. During the year it paid tax of $18,000 and it has a provision for the current year of $50,000. It has increased the deferred tax provision by $5,000. What is the total charge to tax for the year in the statement of profit or loss and other comprehensive income?

A $53,000
B $55,000
C $57,000
D $68,000

(2 marks)

2 A company had a debit balance brought forward on current tax of $2,000. During the year it has paid no tax and received a tax refund of $1,800. It has a provision for the current year of $30,000. It has decreased the deferred tax provision by $5,000. What is the total charge to tax for the year in the statement of profit or loss and other comprehensive income?

A $23,200
B $24,800
C $25,200
D $35,200

(2 marks)

3 In accounting for deferred tax, which of the following items can give rise to temporary differences?

1 Differences between accounting depreciation and tax allowances for capital expenditure

2 Expenses charged in the statement of profit or loss and other comprehensive income but disallowed for tax

3 Revaluation of a non-current asset

4 Unrelieved tax losses

A 1, 3 and 4 only
B 1 and 2 only
C 3 and 4 only
D All four items

(2 marks)

4   Which of the following are examples of assets or liabilities whose carrying amount is always equal to their tax base?

1   Accrued expenses that will never be deductible for tax purposes

2   Accrued expenses that have already been deducted in determining the current tax liability for current or earlier periods

3   Accrued income that will never be taxable

4   A loan payable in the statement of financial position at the amount originally received, which is also the amount eventually repayable

A   1 and 3 only
B   1 and 2 only
C   2 and 4 only
D   All four items   **(2 marks)**

5   Which of the following statements about IAS 12 *Income taxes* are correct?

1   Companies may discount deferred tax assets and liabilities if the effect would be material.

2   The financial statements must disclose an explanation of the relationship between tax expense and accounting profit.

3   Deferred tax may not be recognised in respect of goodwill unless any impairment of that goodwill is deductible for tax purposes.

4   The tax base of an asset or liability is the amount attributed to that asset or liability for tax purposes.

A   All the statements are correct
B   2, 3 and 4 only are correct
C   1 and 4 only are correct
D   None of the statements is correct.   **(2 marks)**

6   The following information relates to an entity.

•   At 1 January 20X8, the net book value of non-current assets exceeded their tax written down value by $850,000.

•   For the year ended 31 December 20X8, the entity claimed depreciation for tax purposes of $500,000 and charged depreciation of $450,000 in the financial statements.

•   During the year ended 31 December 20X8, the entity revalued a freehold property. The revaluation surplus was $250,000. The entity has no plans to sell the property and realise the gain in the foreseeable future.

•   The entity is resident in Country X.

Calculate the provision for deferred tax required by IAS 12 *Income taxes* at 31 December 20X8.
                                                                                   (2 marks)

7   A company had a credit balance brought forward on current tax of $25,000. During the year it has paid no tax and received a tax refund of $2,500. It has a provision for the current year of $30,000. It has decreased the deferred tax provision by $10,000. What is the total charge to tax for the year in the statement of profit or loss and other comprehensive income?

A $5,000 debit
B $5,000 credit
C $7,500 debit
D $7,500 credit   **(2 marks)**

8   A company had a credit balance brought forward on current tax of $25,000. During the year it paid tax of $27,800. It has a provision for the current year of $28,000. It has increased the deferred tax provision by $5,000. What is the total charge to tax for the year in the statement of profit or loss and other comprehensive income?

   A $31,200
   B $33,000
   C $33,800
   D $35,800   **(2 marks)**

9   BC, a small entity, purchased its only non-current tangible asset on 1 October 20X3. The asset cost $900,000, all of which qualified for tax depreciation.

   BC's accounting depreciation policy is to depreciate the asset over its useful economic life of five years, assuming a residual value of $50,000.

   BC is resident in Country X.

   Calculate BC's deferred tax balance required in the statement of financial position as at 30 September 20X5 according to IAS 12 *Income taxes*.   **(4 marks)**

10   On 31 March 20X6, CH had a credit balance brought forward on its deferred tax account of $642,000. There was also a credit balance on its corporate income tax account of $31,000, representing an over-estimate of the tax charge for the year ended 31 March 20X5.

   CH's taxable profit for the year ended 31 March 20X6 was $946,000. CH's directors estimated the deferred tax provision required at 31 March 20X6 to be $759,000. CH is resident in Country X.

   Calculate the income tax expense that CH will charge in its statement of profit of loss and other comprehensive income for the year ended 31 March 20X6, as required by IAS 12 *Income taxes*.
                                                                                                    (3 marks)

11   FD purchased an item of plant and machinery costing $600,000 on 1 April 20X5.

   FD's policy in respect of plant and machinery is to charge depreciation on a straight line basis over five years, with no residual value.

   On 1 April 20X7, FD carried out an impairment review of all its non-current assets. This item of plant and machinery was found to have a value in use of $240,000. FD adjusted its financial records and wrote the plant and machinery down to its value in use on 1 April 20X7.

   FD is resident in Country X and there are no other temporary differences in the period.

   Calculate the amount of any deferred tax balances outstanding at 31 March 20X7 and 31 March 20X8. (Work to the nearest $1,000.)   **(4 marks)**

12   EE reported accounting profits of $822,000 for the period ended 30 November 20X7. This was after deducting entertaining expenses of $32,000 and a donation to a political party of $50,000, both of which are disallowable for tax purposes.

   EE's reported profit also included $103,000 government grant income that was exempt from taxation. EE paid dividends of $240,000 in the period.

   Assume EE had no temporary differences between accounting profits and taxable profits.

   EE is resident in Country X where a classical tax system applies.

   Calculate EE's tax payable on its profits for the year to 30 November 20X7.   **(2 marks)**

13   ED purchased new machinery for $400,000 on 1 October 20X5. For accounting purposes ED depreciated the machinery on the reducing balance basis at 25% per year.

   ED is resident in Country X.

   Assume ED had no other temporary differences.

   Calculate the amount of deferred tax that ED would show in its statement of financial position at 30 September 20X7.   **(3 marks)**

14 HF purchased an asset on 1 April 20X7 for $220,000. HF depreciates the asset over eight years using straight line depreciation, assuming no residual value. On 1 April 20X8, HF revalued the asset and increased the net book value by $50,000. The asset's useful life was not affected. HF is resident in Country X and there are no other temporary differences in the period.

Calculate the amount of deferred tax movement in the year ended 31 March 20X9 and the deferred tax balance at 31 March 20X9, in accordance with IAS 12 *Income taxes*. (4 marks)

15 CY had the following amounts for 20X3 to 20X5:

Year ended 31 December:	20X3	20X4	20X5
	$	$	$
Accounting depreciation for the year	1,630	1,590	1,530
Tax depreciation allowance for the year	2,120	1,860	1,320

At 31 December 20X2, CY had the following balances brought forward:

	$
Cost of property, plant and equipment qualifying for tax depreciation	20,000
Accounting depreciation	5,000
Tax depreciation	12,500

CY had no non-current asset acquisitions or disposals during the period 20X3 to 20X5.

CY is resident in Country X.

Calculate the deferred tax provision required by IAS 12 *Income taxes* at 31 December 20X5. (3 marks)

16 DD purchased an item of plant and machinery costing $500,000 on 1 April 20X4.

DD's policy in respect of plant and machinery is to charge depreciation on a straight line basis over five years, with no residual value. On 1 April 20X6, DD revalued the item of plant and machinery to $420,000.

DD is resident in Country X and there are no other capital transactions in the three year period.

Calculate the amount of deferred tax to be included in DD's tax charge for the year ended 31 March 20X7, and the deferred tax provision to be included in its statement of financial position at 31 March 20X7. (4 marks)

(Total = 43 marks)

53 Section B questions: Taxation I   45 mins

(a) Briefly explain the following taxation terminology:

   (i)   Competent jurisdiction
   (ii)   Hypothecation
   (iii) Taxable person
   (iv)   Regressive tax structure
   (v)   Tax gap.   (5 marks)

(b) (i)   Give a definition of an indirect tax and explain how it works.   (3 marks)
     (ii) There are two types of indirect taxes. State what these are and give two examples of each.
                                                                      (2 marks)

(Total = 5 marks)

(c)   On 1 January 20X3, SPJ had an opening credit balance of $5,000 on its tax account, which represented the balance on the account after settling its tax liability for the previous year. SPJ had a credit balance on its deferred tax account of $1·6 million at the same date.

SPJ has been advised that it should expect to pay $1 million tax on its trading profits for the year ended 31 December 20X3 and increase its deferred tax account balance by $150,000.

Required

Prepare extracts from the statement of profit or loss and other comprehensive income for the year ended 31 December 20X3, statement of financial position at that date and notes to the accounts showing the tax entries required.

(5 marks)

P7 Pilot paper

(d)   CW owns 40% of the equity shares in Z, an entity resident in a foreign country. CW receives a dividend of $45,000 from Z; the amount received is after deduction of withholding tax of 10%. Z had before tax profits for the year of $500,000 and paid corporate income tax of $100,000.

Required

(i)   **Explain** the meaning of 'withholding tax' and 'underlying tax.'   (2 marks)

(ii)   **Calculate** the amount of withholding tax paid by CW.   (1 mark)

(iii)   **Calculate** the amount of underlying tax that relates to CW's dividend.   (2 marks)

(Total = 5 marks)

P7 5/06

(e)   EF is resident in Country X and imports perfumes and similar products in bulk. EF repackages the products and sells them to retailers. EF is registered for Value Added Tax (VAT).

EF imports a consignment of perfume priced at $10,000 (excluding excise duty and VAT) and pays excise duty of 20% and VAT on the total (including duty) at standard rate.

EF pays $6,900 repackaging costs, including VAT at the standard rate and then sells all the perfume for $40,250 including VAT at the standard rate.

EF has not paid or received any VAT payments to/from the VAT authorities for this consignment.

Required

(i)   **Calculate** EF's net profit on the perfume consignment.

(ii)   **Calculate** the net VAT due to be paid by EF on the perfume consignment.   (Total = 5 marks)

P7 11/07

(Total = 25 marks)

---

54   Section B questions: Taxation II   45 mins

(a)   Governments use a range of specific excise duties as well as general sales taxes on goods.

Required

(i)   **Explain** the reasons why a government might apply a specific excise duty to a category of goods.

(3 marks)

(ii)   **Explain** the difference between a single stage and a multi-stage sales tax.   (2 marks)

(Total = 5 marks)

P7 5/09

(b)   Tax authorities have various powers to enforce compliance with the tax rules.

State what these powers are and give examples of each.   (5 marks)

(c)   What is withholding tax and why do tax authorities use it? Give two examples of payments affected by withholding tax.   **(5 marks)**

(d)   Why do countries need to enter into double taxation agreements? What are the three main methods of giving double taxation relief?   **(5 marks)**

(e)   (i)   **Explain** the difference between tax avoidance and tax evasion.   **(2 marks)**

      (ii)   **Briefly explain** the methods that governments can use to reduce tax avoidance and tax evasion.

      (3 marks)

(Total = 5 marks)

(Total = 25 marks)

55   Section B questions: Taxation III   45 mins

(a)   H is a major manufacturing entity. According to the entity's records, temporary differences of $2.00 million had arisen at 30 April 20X4 because of differences between the carrying amount of non-current assets and their tax base, due to H claiming accelerated tax relief in the earlier years of the asset lives.

At 30 April 20X3, the temporary differences attributable to non-current assets were $2.30 million.

H is resident in Country X.

Required

Prepare the note in respect of deferred tax as it would appear in the financial statements of H for the year ended 30 April 20X4. (Your answer should be expressed in $ million and you should work to two decimal places.)   **(5 marks)**

(b)   B is a retail entity resident in Country X. It has a current tax liability brought forward from the year ended 30 April 20X3 of $750,000 and a deferred tax liability of $250,000.

On 30 April 20X4, the estimated tax charge for the year ended 30 April 20X4 was $1,400,000. The actual tax charge for the year ended 30 April 20X3 was agreed with the tax authority and settled with a payment of $720,000. The deferred tax liability needs to be increased to $300,000 as at 30 April 20X4.

Required

Prepare the notes in respect of current and deferred tax as they would appear in the financial statements of B for the year ended 30 April 20X4. (Your answer should be expressed in $ million and you should work to two decimal places.)   **(5 marks)**

(c)   DG purchased its only non-current tangible asset on 1 October 20X2. The asset cost $200,000, all of which qualified for tax depreciation. DG's accounting depreciation policy is to depreciate the asset over its useful economic life of five years on a straight-line basis, assuming no residual value, charging a full year's depreciation in the year of acquisition and no depreciation in the year of disposal.

DG sold the asset on 30 September 20X6 for $60,000.

DG's accounting period is 1 October to 30 September. DG is resident in Country X. No tax depreciation is given in the year of disposal in Country X.

Required

(i)   **Calculate** DG's deferred tax balance at 30 September 20X5.

(ii)   **Calculate** DG's accounting profit/loss that will be recognised in its statement of profit or loss and other comprehensive income on the disposal of the asset, in accordance with IAS 16 *Property, plant and equipment.*

(iii)   **Calculate** DG's tax balancing allowance/charge arising on the disposal of the asset.   **(5 marks)**

P7 11/06

(d) AB acquired non-current assets on 1 April 20X3 costing $250,000. AB depreciates all non-current assets at 20% a year on the straight line basis.

AB is resident in Country X.

Required

Apply IAS 12 *Income taxes* and **calculate**:

(i)   the deferred tax balance required at 31 March 20X4
(ii) the deferred tax balance required at 31 March 20X5
(iii) the charge or credit to the statement of profit or loss and other comprehensive income for the year ended 31 March 20X5   **(5 marks)**

`P7 5/05`

(e) FB commenced trading on 1 May 20X5 when it purchased all its non-current assets.

FB's non-current asset balances were:

	Cost 1 May 20X5 $	Net book value 1 May 20X7 $	Tax written down value 1 May 20X7 $
Land	20,000	20,000	–
Buildings	80,000	73,600	30,000
Plant and equipment	21,000	1,000	7,875
Furniture and fittings	15,000	5,000	5,625

FB did not purchase any non-current assets between 1 May 20X5 and 30 April 20X7. On 2 May 20X7, FB disposed of all its plant and equipment for $5,000 and purchased new plant and equipment for $30,000. FB is resident in Country X.

FB STATEMENT OF PROFIT OR LOSS AND OTHER COMPREHENSIVE INCOME

FOR THE YEAR ENDED 30 APRIL 20X8

	$
Gross profit	210,000
Administrative expenses	(114,000)
Gain on disposal of plant and equipment	4,000
Depreciation – furniture and fittings	(5,000)
Depreciation – buildings	(3,200)
Depreciation – plant and equipment	(6,000)
Distribution costs	(49,000)
	36,800
Finance cost	(7,000)
Profit before tax	29,800

Required

Calculate FB's corporate income tax due for the year ended 30 April 20X8.   **(5 marks)**

(Total = 25 marks)

Mixed question banks

The following tax regime data is applicable to the mixed question banks.

Country X – Tax regime

Relevant tax rules

Corporate Profits

Unless otherwise specified, only the following rules for taxation of corporate profits will be relevant, other taxes can be ignored:

(a)   Accounting rules on recognition and measurement are followed for tax purposes.

(b)   All expenses other than depreciation, amortisation, entertaining, taxes paid to other public bodies and donations to political parties are tax deductible.

(c)   Tax depreciation is deductible as follows:

- 50% of additions to property, plant and equipment in the accounting period in which they are recorded

- 25% per year of the written-down value (ie cost minus previous allowances) in subsequent accounting periods except that in which the asset is disposed of

- No tax depreciation is allowed on land

(d)   The corporate tax on profits is at a rate of 25%.

(e)   No indexation is allowable on the sale of land.

(f)   Tax losses can be carried forward to offset against future taxable profits from the same business.

Value Added Tax

Country X has a VAT system which allows entities to reclaim input tax paid. In Country X the VAT rates are:

Zero rated   0%
Standard rated   15%

56 Mixed objective test questions bank 1 (Specimen Paper) 36 mins

1   Which of the following statements is correct?

A   Tax evasion is legally arranging affairs so as to minimise the tax liability. Tax avoidance is the illegal manipulation of the tax system to avoid paying taxes due.

B   Tax evasion is legally arranging affairs so as to evade paying tax. Tax avoidance is tax planning, legally arranging affairs so as to minimise the tax liability.

C   Tax evasion is using loop holes in legislation to evade paying tax. Tax avoidance is the illegal manipulation of the tax system to avoid paying taxes due.

D   Tax evasion is the illegal manipulation of the tax system to avoid paying taxes due. Tax avoidance is tax planning, legally arranging affairs so as to minimise the tax liability.   **(2 marks)**

2   A has been trading for a number of years and is resident for tax purposes in Country X. The tax written down value of A's property, plant and equipment was $40,000 at 31 March 20X8. A did not purchase any property, plant and equipment between 1 April 20X8 and 31 March 20X9.

A's statement of profit or loss and other comprehensive income for the year ended 31 March 20X9 is as follows:

	$
Gross profit	270,000
Administrative expenses	(120,000)
Depreciation - property, plant and equipment	(12,000)
Distribution costs	(55,000)
	83,000
Finance cost	(11,000)
Profit before tax	72,000

Administration expenses include entertaining of $15,000.

What is A's income tax due for the year ended 31 March 20X9?

A   8,750
B   13,750
C   15,500
D   22,250   **(2 marks)**

3   B buys goods from a wholesaler, paying the price of the goods plus VAT. B sells goods in its shop to customers. The customers pay the price of the goods plus VAT.

From the perspective of B, the VAT would have

A   Effective incidence
B   Formal incidence
C   Ineffective incidence
D   Informal incidence   **(2 marks)**

4   CT has taxable profits of $100,000 and pays 50% as dividends.

The total tax due is calculated as:

CT's corporate income tax ($100,000 × 25%)	$25,000
CT's shareholder's personal income tax on dividends received ($50,000 × 20%)	$10,000
Total tax due	$35,000

The tax system in use here would be classified as a:

A   Imputation tax system
B   Partial imputation tax system
C   Classical tax system
D   Split rate tax system   **(2 marks)**

5   The International Accounting Standards Board's *Conceptual Framework for Financial Reporting (2010)* sets out four enhancing qualitative characteristics.

Timeliness and verifiability are two; **state** the other two.   **(2 marks)**

6   The CIMA Code of Ethics for Professional Accountants sets out five principles that a professional accountant is required to comply with. Two principles are objectivity and professional competence/due care, **list** the other two.   **(2 marks)**

7   The purpose of an external audit is to:

A   Check the accounts are correct and to approve them.

B   Enable the auditor to express an opinion as to whether the financial statements give a true and fair view of the entity's affairs.

C   Search for any fraud taking place in the entity.

D   Check that all regulations have been followed in preparing the financial statements and to authorise the financial statements.   **(2 marks)**

8   Goodwill arising on acquisition is accounted for according to IFRS 3 *Business combinations*. Goodwill arising on acquisition is:

A   Carried at cost, with an annual impairment review
B   Written off against reserves on acquisition
C   Amortised over its useful life
D   Revalued to fair value at each year end   **(2 marks)**

9   IT has 300 items of product ABC2 in inventory at 31 March 20X9. The items were found to be damaged by a water leak. The items can be repaired and repackaged for a cost of $1.50 per item. Once repackaged, the items can be sold at the normal price of $3.50 each.

The original cost of the items was $2.20 each. The replacement cost at 31 March 20X9 is $2.75 each.

What value should IT put on the inventory of ABC2 in its statement of financial position at 31 March 20X9?

A $600
B $660
C $810
D $825   **(2 marks)**

10   (i)   CD is Z's main customer.

(ii)   FE is a supplier of Z.

(iii) ST is Z's chairman of the board and a major shareholder of Z.

(iv)   K is Z's banker and has provided an overdraft facility and a $1,000,000 loan.

(v)   JT is the owner of a building entity that has just been awarded a large building contract by Z. JT is also the son of ST.

Which two of the above can be regarded as a related party of Z?

A   (i) and (iii)
B   (ii) and (iv)
C   (iii) and (v)
D   (iv) and (v)   **(2 marks)**

(Total = 20 marks)

57 Mixed objective test questions bank 2 (5/10)   36 mins

1   An ideal tax system should conform to certain principles. Which one of the following statements *is not* generally regarded as a principle of an ideal tax?

A   It should be fair to different individuals and should reflect a person's ability to pay.
B   It should not be arbitrary, it should be certain.
C   It should raise as much money as possible for the government.
D   It should be convenient in terms of timing and payment.   **(2 marks)**

2   Which one of the following could be said to be a progressive tax?

    A   Property sales tax at 1% of the selling price of all properties sold.

    B   Value added tax at a rate of 0%, 10% or 15% depending on the type of goods or services provided.

    C   Corporate wealth tax at 2% of total net assets up to $10 million then at 0.5% on total net assets greater than $10 million.

    D   Personal income tax at 10% on earnings up to $10,000, then at 15% from $10,001 up to $100,000 and 25% over $100,000.   **(2 marks)**

3   An item of equipment cost $60,000 on 1 April 20X6. The equipment is depreciated at 20% per annum on a reducing balance basis.

    The amount of deferred tax relating to this asset that should be recognised in the statement of financial position as at 31 March 20X9 is:

    A $1,781
    B $3,461
    C $3,975
    D $13,845   **(2 marks)**

4   The International Accounting Standards Board's (IASB)'s *Conceptual Framework for Financial Reporting (2010)* provides the framework for preparing financial information. Which one of the following does the *Conceptual Framework* **not** cover?

    A   The format of financial statements
    B   The objective of financial statements
    C   Concepts of capital maintenance
    D   The elements of financial statements   **(2 marks)**

5   The IASB's *Conceptual Framework* identifies faithful representation as one of the fundamental qualitative characteristics of useful financial information. Which one of the following is not an element of faithful representation?

    A   Information should be timely
    B   Information should be free from material error
    C   Information should be free from bias
    D   Information must be complete   **(2 marks)**

6   OC signed a contract to provide office cleaning services for an entity for a period of one year from 1 October 20X8 for a fee of $500 per month.

    The contract required the entity to make **one** payment to OC covering all twelve months' service in advance. The contract cost to OC was estimated at $300 per month for wages, materials and administration costs.

    OC received $6,000 on 1 October 20X8.

    How much profit/loss should OC recognise in its statement of profit or loss and other comprehensive income for the year ended 31 March 20X9?

    A $600 loss
    B $1,200 profit
    C $2,400 profit
    D $4,200 profit   **(2 marks)**

7   Which one of the following could be classified as deferred development expenditure in M's statement of financial position as at 31 March 20X9 according to IAS 38 *Intangible assets*?

     A $120,000 spent on developing a prototype and testing a new type of propulsion system for trains. The project needs further work on it as the propulsion system is currently not viable.

     B   A payment of $50,000 to a local university's engineering faculty to research new environmentally friendly building techniques.

     C $35,000 spent on consumer testing a new type of electric bicycle. The project is near completion and the product will probably be launched in the next twelve months. As this project is the first of its kind for M it is expected to make a loss.

     D $65,000 spent on developing a special type of new packaging for a new energy efficient light bulb. The packaging is expected to be used by M for many years and is expected to reduce M's distribution costs by $35,000 a year.   **(2 marks)**

---

8   A finance lease for 6 years has an annual payment in arrears of $24,000. The fair value of the lease at inception was $106,000. Using the sum of digits method, the liability for the lease at the end of year 2 is:

       $'000
     A   58.0
     B   77.9
     C   86.1
     D   115.9   **(2 marks)**

---

9   PQ has ceased operations overseas in the current accounting period. This resulted in the closure of a number of small retail outlets.

     Which **one** of the following costs would be *excluded* from the loss on discontinued operations?

     A   Loss on the disposal of the retail outlets
     B   Redundancy costs for overseas staff
     C   Cost of restructuring head office as a result of closing the overseas operations
     D   Trading losses of the overseas retail outlets up to the date of closure   **(2 marks)**

---

10   The following balances were extracted from N's financial statements:

STATEMENT OF FINANCIAL POSITION (EXTRACT)

	As at 31 December 20X8	As at 31 December 20X7
	$'000	$'000
Non Current liabilities		
Deferred tax	38	27
Current Liabilities		
Current tax payable	119	106

STATEMENT OF PROFIT OR LOSS AND OTHER COMPREHENSIVE INCOME

FOR THE YEAR ENDED 31 DECEMBER 20X8 (EXTRACT)

	$'000
Income tax expense	122

The amount of tax paid that should be included in N's statement of cash flows for the year ended 31 December 20X8 is:

       $'000
     A   98
     B   109
     C   122
     D   241   **(2 marks)**

         (Total = 20 marks)

58 Mixed objective test questions bank 3 (11/10)   36 mins

1   CR is resident in Country X. CR makes a taxable profit of $750,000 and pays an equity dividend of $350,000.

Equity shareholders pay tax on their dividend income at a rate of 30%.

If CR and its equity shareholders pay a total of $205,000 tax between them, what method of corporate income tax is being used in Country X?

     A   The classical system
     B   The imputation system
     C   The partial imputation system
     D   The split rate system   **(2 marks)**

2   Which **one** of the following is **not** a benefit of pay-as-you-earn (PAYE) method of tax collection?

     A   It makes payment of tax easier for the tax payer as it is in instalments.
     B   It makes it easier for governments to forecast tax revenues.
     C   It benefits the tax payer as it reduces the tax payable.
     D   It improves governments cash flow as cash is received earlier.   **(2 marks)**

3   In relation to a Value Added Tax (VAT) system, which **one** of the following would be classified as the formal incidence of VAT?

     A   The entity submitting a VAT return and making payment to the tax authorities.
     B   The date the tax is actually paid.
     C   The person that pays a retail entity for the goods plus VAT.
     D   A retail entity paying a wholesale entity for goods plus VAT.   **(2 marks)**

4   Which **one** of the following is **not** a reason for governments to set deadlines for filing tax returns and payment of taxes?

     A   To enable governments to enforce penalties for late payments.
     B   To ensure tax deducted at source by employers is paid over promptly.
     C   To ensure tax payers know when they have to make payment.
     D   To ensure that the correct amount of tax revenue is paid.   **(2 marks)**

5   UF manufactures clothing and operates in Country X. UF and ZF are both registered for VAT.

UF manufactures a batch of clothing and pays expenses (taxable inputs at standard rate) of $1,000 plus VAT. UF sells the batch of clothing to a retailer ZF for $2,875 including VAT at standard rate. ZF sells the clothing items separately to various customers for a total of $6,900 including VAT at standard rate.

Calculate how much VAT UF and ZF each has to pay in respect of the above transactions.   **(2 marks)**

6   An external auditor has completed an audit and is satisfied that proper records have been maintained and that the financial statements reflect those transactions. However the auditor has one disagreement with the management of the entity. The disagreement involves the treatment of one large item of expenditure that has been classified by management as an increase in non-current assets. The auditor is of the opinion that the item should have been classified as maintenance and charged as an expense to the statement of profit or loss and other comprehensive income. The amount is material in the context of the reported profit for the year.

Assuming that the management refuse to change their approach, which **one** of the following modified audit reports should the auditor use?

     A   Emphasis of matter
     B   "Except for" qualification
     C   Adverse opinion
     D   Disclaimer of opinion   **(2 marks)**

7   TS purchased 100,000 of its own equity shares in the market and classified them as treasury shares. At the end of the accounting period TS still held the treasury shares.

Which **one** of the following is the correct presentation of the treasury shares in TS's closing statement of financial position in accordance with IAS 32 *Financial instruments: presentation?*

A   As a current asset investment
B   As a non-current liability
C   As a non-current asset
D   As a deduction from equity   **(2 marks)**

8   Which **one** of the following is **not** a topic included in the International Accounting Standards Board (IASB)'s *Conceptual Framework for Financial Reporting (2010)?*

A   The objective of financial statements
B   Concepts of capital maintenance
C   Regulatory bodies governing financial statements
D   Measurement of the elements of financial statements   **(2 marks)**

9   Which **one** of the following would be regarded as a related party of Z in accordance with IAS 24 *Related party disclosures?*

A   FG is Z's banker and has provided an extensive overdraft facility on favourable terms.
B   JK is Z's principal customer, accounting for 60% of its revenue.
C   MN is Z's marketing director who holds 20% of Z's equity shares.
D   QR is Z's main supplier, supplying nearly 50% of Z's purchases by value.   **(2 marks)**

10 Which **one** of the following is **not** included in the definition of an operating segment in accordance with IFRS 8 *Operating Segments?*

A   A component of an entity that earns the majority of its revenue from sales to external customers.

B   A component of an entity that engages in business activities from which it may earn revenues and incur expenses.

C   A component of an entity whose operating results are regularly reviewed by the entity's chief operating decision maker, to make decisions about resource allocations and assess performance.

D   A component of an entity for which discrete financial information is available.   **(2 marks)**

                                                                          (Total = 20 marks)

59 Mixed objective test questions bank 4 (5/11)   36 mins

1   In Country Y, A earns $75,000 profit for the year and receives a tax bill for $17,000.

B earns $44,000 profit for the year and receives a tax bill for $4,800.

Country Y's income tax could be said to be a:

A   Regressive tax
B   Proportional tax
C   Progressive tax
D   Fixed rate tax   **(2 marks)**

2   Tax deducted at source by employers from employees' earnings and paid to government, often called pay-as-you-earn (PAYE) has a number of advantages.

     (i)   Most of the administration costs are borne by the employer.
     (ii)   Employers may delay payment or fail to pay over PAYE deducted from employees.
     (iii)   Employers may be inefficient and not deduct any tax or deduct the wrong amount from employees.
     (iv)   Government receives a higher proportion of the tax due as defaults and late payments are fewer.

    Which **two** of the above are **not** likely to be seen as an advantage of PAYE by the Government?

     A   (i) and (ii)
     B   (ii) and (iii)
     C   (ii) and (iv)
     D   (iii) and (iv)   **(2 marks)**

3   The Organisation for Economic Co-operation and Development's (OECD) model tax convention defines corporate residence.

    In no more than 15 words complete the following sentence:

    Under the OECD model an entity will have residence....   **(2 marks)**

4   P is a trader resident in Country X. P imports products from a foreign country. Each unit costs $15.00 to purchase and on import is subject to an excise duty of $3.00 per unit. P also has to pay VAT at standard rate on all imports. If P imports 2,000 units how much would the tax authorities be due on import?

     A $4,500
     B $6,000
     C $10,500
     D $11,400   **(2 marks)**

5   Which **two** of the following are most likely to encourage an increase in the incidence of tax avoidance or tax evasion?

     (i)   High penalties for any tax evasion
     (ii)   Imprecise and vague tax laws
     (iii)   A tax system that is seen as fair to everyone
     (iv)   Very high tax rates

     A   (i) and (ii)
     B   (ii) and (iii)
     C   (ii) and (iv)
     D   (iii) and (iv)   **(2 marks)**

6   According to IAS 8 *Accounting policies, changes in accounting estimates and errors*, which **one** of the following is a change in accounting policy requiring a retrospective adjustment in financial statements for the year ended 31 December 20X0?

     A   The depreciation of the production facility has been reclassified from administration expenses to cost of sales in the current and future years.

     B   The depreciation method of vehicles was changed from straight line depreciation to reducing balance.

     C   The provision for warranty claims was changed from 10% of sales revenue to 5%.

     D   Based on information that became available in the current period a provision was made for an injury compensation claim relating to an incident in a previous year.   **(2 marks)**

7   According to IFRS 8 *Operating Segments* which **two** of the following apply to reportable segments?

(i)   The results of the segment must be prepared using the same accounting policies as are used for the financial statements.

(ii)   A reportable segment is a component of the entity whose operating results are regularly reviewed by the entity's chief operating decision maker in order to make decisions about resource allocations.

(iii)   Information for reportable segments is required to be prepared based on products and geographical areas.

(iv)   A reportable segment is every segment that accounts for 10% or more of the sales revenue.

A   (i) and (ii)
B   (i) and (iii)
C   (ii) and (iii)
D   (ii) and (iv)   **(2 marks)**

8   HA acquired 100% of SB's equity shares on 1 April 20X0 for $185,000. The values of SB's assets at that date were:

	Book value $'000	Fair value $'000
Property	100	115
Plant and equipment	75	70

On 1 April 20X0 all other assets and liabilities had a fair value approximately equal to their book value.

SB's equity at 1 April 20X0 was:

	$'000
$1 equity shares	150
Share premium	15
Retained earnings	(22)

Calculate the goodwill arising on the acquisition of SB.   **(2 marks)**

9   The HC group acquired 30% of the equity share capital of AF on 1 April 20X0 paying $25,000.

At 1 April 20X0 the equity of AF comprised:

	$
$1 equity shares	50,000
Share premium	12,500
Retained earnings	10,000

AF made a profit for the year to 31 March 20X1 (prior to dividend distribution) of $6,500 and paid a dividend of $3,500 to its equity shareholders.

Calculate the value of HC's investment in AF for inclusion in HC's statement of financial position at 31 March 20X1.   **(2 marks)**

10   HB sold goods to S2, its 100% owned subsidiary, on 1 November 20X0. The goods were sold to S2 for $33,000. HB made a profit of 25% on the original cost of the goods.

At the year end, 31 March 20X1, 50% of the goods had been sold by S2. The remaining goods were included in inventory.

Calculate the amount of the adjustment required to inventory in the consolidated statement of financial position at 31 March 20X1.   **(2 marks)**

(Total = 20 marks)

60 Mixed objective test questions bank 5 (9/11)   36 mins

1   The following are common taxes used in many countries:

(i)   Value added tax/sales tax
(ii)   Corporate income tax
(iii)   Import duty payable on petroleum and other products
(iv)   Individual income tax deducted at source (such as PAYE)

Which of the above would normally be defined as a direct tax?

A   (i) and (ii)
B   (i) and (iv)
C   (ii) and (iii)
D   (ii) and (iv)   **(2 marks)**

2   Which **one** of the following defines a taxable capital gain?

A   The growth in value of an investment in shares in another entity.
B   Gains made on disposal of various types of investments or other assets.
C   Gain made by an increase in an entity's own shares.
D   Income from capital investments, for example dividends.   **(2 marks)**

3   A country has a duty that is levied on all imported petroleum products. This levy is $5 per litre. This duty could be said to be:

A   General consumption tax
B   Value added tax
C   Specific unit tax
D   Ad valorem tax   **(2 marks)**

4   Define the meaning of "tax evasion".   **(2 marks)**

5   Corporate residence for tax purposes can be determined in different ways by different countries.

Which **one** of the following is **not** normally used to determine corporate residence for tax purposes?

A   The country where management of the entity hold their meetings.
B   The country of incorporation of the entity.
C   The country where most of the entity's products are sold.
D   The country from which control of the entity is exercised.   **(2 marks)**

6   Which **one** of the following is **not** automatically regarded as a related party of an entity by IAS 24 *Related party disclosures*?

A   Directors of the entity.
B   The entity's main customer, which accounts for 40% of the entity's sales volume.
C   The entity's employee pension fund.
D   A close relative of a director of the entity.   **(2 marks)**

7   QR announced a rights issue of 1 for every 6 shares currently held, at a price of $2 each.

QR currently has 2,400,000 $1 ordinary shares with a quoted market price of $3.00 each. Directly attributable issue costs will amount to $45,000.

Calculate the amount that will be credited to the share premium account in respect of the rights issue assuming all rights are taken up and all monies are paid in full.

(2 marks)

8   HX acquired 100% of SA's equity shares on 1 July 2010 for $342,000. On 1 July 2010 the property plant and equipment of SA had a fair value of $350,000 and a book value of $325,000. All other assets and liabilities had a fair value approximately equal to their book value.

SA has $200,000 $1 equity shares in issue and at 1 July 2010 its reserves comprised share premium of $40,000 and retained earnings of $62,000.

Calculate any goodwill arising on the acquisition of SA.   **(2 marks)**

9   The HY group acquired 35% of the equity share capital of SX on 1 July 2010 paying $70,000. This shareholding enabled HY group to exercise significant influence over SX.

At 1 July 2010 the equity of SX comprised:

	$
$1 equity shares	100,000
Retained earnings	50,000

SX made a profit for the year ended 30 June 2011 (prior to dividend distribution) of $130,000 and paid a dividend of $80,000 to its equity shareholders.

Calculate the value of HY's investment in SX for inclusion in its consolidated statement of financial position at 30 June 2011.   **(2 marks)**

10 HW sold goods to SD, its 100% owned subsidiary on 1 February 2011. The goods were sold to SD for $48,000. HW made a profit of 33.33% on the original cost of the goods.

At the year end, 30 June 2011, 40% of the goods had been sold by SD, the balance were still in SD's inventory and SD had not paid for any of the goods.

Which **ONE** of the following states the correct adjustments required in the HW group's consolidated statement of financial position at 30 June 2011?

A   Reduce inventory and retained earnings by $7,200 and Reduce payables and receivables by $7,200
B   Reduce inventory and retained earnings by $9,600 and Reduce payables and receivables by $9,600
C   Reduce inventory and retained earnings by $7,200 and Reduce payables and receivables by $48,000
D   Reduce inventory and retained earnings by $9,600 and Reduce payables and receivables by $48,000

(2 marks)

(Total = 20 marks)

61   Mixed objective test questions bank 6 (11/11)   36 mins

1   Which **one** of the following would **not** normally be considered a principle of a modern tax system?

A   Efficiency
B   Equity
C   Economic impact
D   Raise revenues   **(2 marks)**

2   Which **one** of the following is an example of formal incidence, but not effective incidence?

A   An entity being assessed for corporate income tax by the tax authority.
B   An individual purchasing goods in a shop, the price including VAT.
C   An employee having tax deducted from salary through the PAYE system.
D   An entity charging VAT on its sales and paying its net VAT to the tax authority.   **(2 marks)**

3   Which **one** of the following does **not** give rise to a deferred tax adjustment?

A   Entertaining expenses paid.
B   Revaluation of a property.
C   Depreciation of an asset that qualifies for tax writing down allowances.
D   Tax losses that are carried forward for relief in future periods.   **(2 marks)**

4   BCF purchased an asset for $600,000 on 1 September 2004. BCF incurred additional purchase costs of $5,000.

Indexation of the cost of BCF's asset is allowed in Country X. The relevant index increased by 60% in the period from 1 September 2004 to 31 August 2011.

BCF sold the asset on 1 September 2011 for $1,200,000. BCF incurred selling costs of $9,000

Assume all purchase and selling costs are tax allowable.

How much tax was due from BCF on disposal of its asset?

A $55,750
B $56,500
C $64,250
D $146,500   **(2 marks)**

---

5   Which **one** of the following defines the meaning of "tax gap"?

A   The difference between the tax an entity expects to pay and the amount notified by the tax authority.

B   The difference between the total amount of tax due to be paid and the amount actually collected by the tax authority.

C   The difference between the due date for tax payment and the date it is actually paid.

D   The difference between the amount of tax provided in the financial statements and the amount actually paid.   **(2 marks)**

---

6   Which **one** of the following would **not** be regarded as a related party of RST?

A   RST's chief executive officer.
B   RST's largest single shareholder holding 35% of RST's equity shares.
C   RST's biggest customer, providing 55% of RST's revenue.
D   The wife of the chief executive officer of RST.   **(2 marks)**

---

7   Which **one** of the following **cannot** be recognised as an intangible non-current asset in GHK's statement of financial position at 30 September 2011?

A   GHK spent $12,000 researching a new type of product. The research is expected to lead to a new product line in 3 years' time.

B   GHK purchased another entity, BN on 1 October 2010. Goodwill arising on the acquisition was $15,000.

C   GHK purchased a brand name from a competitor on 1 November 2010, for $65,000.

D   GHK spent $21,000 during the year on the development of a new product. The product is being launched on the market on 1 December 2011 and is expected to be profitable.   **(2 marks)**

---

8   Which **one** of the following would be classified by WDC as a non-adjusting event according to IAS 10 *Events after the reporting period?* WDC's year end is 30 September 2011.

A   WDC was notified on 5 November 2011 that one of its customers was insolvent and was unlikely to repay any of its debts. The balance outstanding at 30 September 2011 was $42,000.

B   On 30 September WDC had an outstanding court action against it. WDC had made a provision in its financial statements for the year ended 30 September 2011 for damages awarded against it of $22,000. On 29 October 2011 the court awarded damages of $18,000.

C   On 5 October 2011 a serious fire occurred in WDC's main production centre and severely damaged the production facility.

D   The year end inventory balance included $50,000 of goods from a discontinued product line. On 1 November 2011 these goods were sold for a net total of $20,000.   **(2 marks)**

9   IFRS 8 *Operating Segments* requires information about operating segments to be disclosed in the financial statements. According to IFRS 8 *Operating Segments* which **one** of the following defines an operating segment.

An operating segment is a component of an entity:

A   that is considered to be one of the entity's main products or services.
B   whose operating results are regularly reviewed by the entity's chief operating decision maker.
C   whose results contribute more than 10% of the entity's total sales revenue.
D   whose assets are more than 10% of the entity's total assets.   **(2 marks)**

10 On 28 September 2011, GY received an order from a new customer, ZZ, for products with a sales value of $750,000. ZZ enclosed a deposit with the order of $75,000.

On 30 September 2011, GY had not completed the credit referencing of ZZ and had not despatched any goods.

Which **one** of the following will correctly record this transaction in GY's financial statements for the year ended 30 September 2011 according to IAS 18 *Revenue:*

A   Debit Cash $75,000; Credit Revenue $75,000
B   Debit Cash $75,000; Debit Trade Receivables $675,000; Credit Revenue $750,000
C   Debit Cash $75,000; Credit Deferred Revenue $75,000
D   Debit Trade Receivables $750,000; Credit Revenue $750,000   **(2 marks)**

(Total = 20 marks)

62 Mixed objective test questions bank 7 (3/12)   36 mins

1   Which **one** of the following would be considered to be an example of an indirect tax?

A   An entity assessed for corporate income tax on its profit.
B   An individual purchases goods in a shop, the price includes VAT.
C   An employee has tax deducted from salary through the PAYE system.
D   An individual pays capital gains tax on a gain arising on the disposal of an investment. **(2 marks)**

2   **Define** the meaning of "a tax base".   **(2 marks)**

3   Which **one** of the following would cause a deferred tax balance to be included in the statement of financial position for an entity, as required by IAS 12 *Income taxes*?

A   An expense that is included in the statement of profit or loss and other comprehensive income but is not allowed for tax.

B   A non-current asset that does not qualify for tax depreciation.

C   Tax depreciation being allowed on a non-current asset at a different annual rate to that used for depreciation in the financial statements.

D   Impairment of goodwill that arose on the acquisition of a subsidiary entity.   **(2 marks)**

4   CFP, an entity resident in Country X, had an accounting profit for the year ended 31 December 2011 of $860,000. The accounting profit was after charging depreciation of $42,000 and amortisation of development costs of $15,000.

CFP was entitled to a tax depreciation allowance of $51,000 for the year to 31 December 2011.

CFP's tax payable for the year ended 31 December 2011 is:

A $202,250
B $206,500
C $212,750
D $216,500   **(2 marks)**

5   Which **one** of the following defines the meaning of "hypothecation"?

   A   A new tax law has to be passed each year to allow taxes to be legally collected.

   B   The difference between the total amount of tax due to be paid and the amount actually collected by the tax authority.

   C   Tax is deducted from amounts due before they are paid to the recipient.

   D   The products of certain taxes are devoted to specific types of public expenditure.   **(2 marks)**

6   Which **one** of the following would be regarded as a related party of CXZ?

   A   The wife of CXZ's finance director.
   B   CXZ's main supplier, supplying approximately 35% of CXZ's purchases.
   C   CXZ's biggest customer, providing 60% of CXZ's annual revenue.
   D   CXZ's banker providing CXZ with an overdraft facility and a short-term loan at market rates.   **(2 marks)**

7   Which **one** of the following events would result in an asset being recognised in KJH's statement of financial position at 31 January 2012?

   A   KJH spent $50,000 on an advertising campaign in January 2012. KJH expects the advertising to generate additional sales of $100,000 over the period February to April 2012.

   B   KJH is taking legal action against a contractor for faulty work. Advice from its legal team is that it is likely that KJH will receive $250,000 in settlement of its claim within the next 12 months.

   C   KJH purchased the copyright and film rights to the next book to be written by a famous author for $75,000 on 1 March 2011.

   D   KJH has developed a new brand name internally. The directors value the brand name at $150,000.   **(2 marks)**

8   Briefly **explain** how operating segments disclosed in the financial statements are determined according to IFRS 8 Operating Segments.   **(2 marks)**

9   IAS 18 *Revenue* specifies conditions that are required to be met before revenue from the sale of goods can be recognised.

   List four of the conditions specified in IAS 18.   **(4 marks)**

(Total = 20 marks)

63 Mixed objective test questions bank 8 (5/12)   36 mins

1   Complete the following sentence.

   Under the OECD model tax convention an entity will generally have residence for tax purposes in
   ....   **(2 marks)**

2   XZ sells two types of product, A and B. A is standard rated for VAT purposes and B is zero rated. All purchases have incurred VAT at standard rate.

   XZ's sales (inclusive of VAT where applicable) for the three months to 31 March 2012 were:

	$
A	63,250
B	24,150
	87,400

   XZ's purchases for the three months to 31 March 2012 were $32,333 exclusive of VAT.

   Calculate the amount of VAT that XZ is due to pay for the three months to 31 March 2012.

   (2 marks)

3   An entity earns a profit of $60,000 for the year to 31 March 2012. The entity is assessed as owing $15,000 tax for the year. Which ONE of the following types of tax would best describe the tax due?

A   Capital tax.
B   Income tax.
C   Wealth tax.
D   Consumption tax.   **(2 marks)**

4   **List two** possible powers that a tax authority may be granted to enable it to enforce tax regulations.

                                                                                            (2 marks)

5   A customer purchases goods for $115, inclusive of VAT. From the customer's point of view the VAT could be said to be:

A   a direct tax with formal incidence.
B   an indirect tax with formal incidence.
C   a direct tax with effective incidence.
D   an indirect tax with effective incidence.   **(2 marks)**

6   Which **one** of the following is **not** a fundamental ethical principle indentified in CIMA's code of ethics?

A   Professional competence.
B   Professional behaviour.
C   Integrity.
D   Independence.   **(2 marks)**

7   Which **one** of the following would **not** be regarded as a responsibility of the IASB?

A   Responsibility for all IFRS technical matters.

B   Publish IFRSs.

C   Overall supervisory body of the IFRS organisations.

D   Final approval of interpretations by the IFRS Interpretations Committee.   **(2 marks)**

8   TY is the main contractor employing sub-contractors to assist it when required.

     TY has recently completed a contract replacing a roof on the local school. Despite this, the roof has been leaking and some sections are now unsafe. The school is suing TY for $20,000 to repair the roof.

     TY used a sub-contractor to install the roof and regards the sub-contractor's work as faulty. TY has raised a court action against the sub-contractor claiming the cost of the school's action plus legal fees, a total of $22,000.

     TY has been informed by legal advisers that it will probably lose the case brought against it by the school and will probably win the case against the sub-contractor.

     How should these items be treated in TY's financial statements?

A   A provision should be made for the $20,000 liability and the case against the sub- contractor ignored.

B   A provision should be made for the $20,000 liability and the probable receipt of cash from the case against the sub-contractor disclosed as a note.

C   No provisions should be made but the $20,000 liability should be disclosed as a note.

D   A provision should be made for the $20,000 liability and the probable receipt of cash from the case against the sub-contractor recognised as a current asset.   **(2 marks)**

9   BN has an asset that was classified as held for sale at 31 March 2012. The asset had a carrying value of
     $900 and a fair value of $800. The cost of disposal was estimated to be $50.

     According to IFRS 5 *Non-current Assets Held for Sale and Discontinued Operations*, which **one** of the
     following values should be used for the asset in BN's statement of financial position as at 31 March
     2012?

     A $750
     B $800
     C $850
     D $900   **(2 marks)**

10   MN obtained a government licence to operate a mine from 1 April 2011. The licence requires that at the
     end of the mine's useful life, all buildings must be removed from the site and the site landscaped. MN
     estimates that the cost of this decommissioning work will be $1,000,000 in ten years' time (present
     value at 1 April 2011 $463,000) using a discount factor of 8%.

     According to IAS 37 *Provisions, contingent liabilities and contingent assets* how much, to the nearest
     $1,000, should MN include in provisions in its statement of financial position as at 31 March 2012?

     A $100,000
     B $463,000
     C $500,000
     D $1,000,000   **(2 marks)**

                                                                                        (Total = 20 marks)

64   Mixed objective test questions bank 9 (9/12)   36 mins

1   Which **one** of the following is **not** generally considered a source of tax rules?

     A   Precedents based on previous legislation
     B   Directives from international bodies, such as the EU
     C   Tax assessments issued by the local tax authority
     D   Double tax treaties with other countries   **(2 marks)**

2   GX sold an asset on 31 March 2012 for $10,000. The asset cost $90,000 and at 31 March 2012 had
     accumulated depreciation of $85,000.

     The asset was eligible for tax depreciation and at 31 March 2012 its accumulated tax depreciation was
     $75,760.

     What was the balancing allowance on the disposal of the asset?

     A $4,240
     B $5,000
     C $9,240
     D $14,240   **(2 marks)**

3   HY is registered for VAT in Country X.

     HY purchased a consignment of goods for $70,000 plus VAT at the standard rate and then sold the
     goods for $138,000 inclusive of VAT at the standard rate.

     How much profit should HY record in its statement of profit or loss and other comprehensive income for
     this consignment?

     A $50,000
     B $57,500
     C $68,000
     D $77,130   **(2 marks)**

4   Complete the following sentence.

        A schedular system of tax is .... **(2 marks)**

5   Assume that Countries M; N; O and P each has a double tax treaty with each other based on the OECD model tax convention.

        JZ is incorporated in Country M

        JZ earns the majority of its revenue from Country N

        JZ holds its management board meetings in Country O

        JZ raises most of its finance and operating capital in Country P

        In which country will JZ be deemed to be resident for tax purposes?

        A   Country M
        B   Country N
        C   Country O
        D   Country P   **(2 marks)**

6   Which **one** of the following is **not** a common threat identified in CIMA's code of ethics?

        A   Self interest
        B   Bias
        C   Self review
        D   Familiarity   **(2 marks)**

7   **List two** of the responsibilities of the IFRS Interpretations Committee?   **(2 marks)**

8   EH is resident in Country X. EH purchased an asset on 1 April 2005 for $420,000, incurring additional import duties of $30,000. The relevant index increased by 40% in the period from 1 April 2005 to 31 March 2012.

        EH sold the asset on 31 March 2012 for $700,000, incurring selling costs of $10,000.

        Assume all purchase and selling costs are allowable for tax purposes.

        How much tax was due from EH on disposal of its asset?   **(2 marks)**

9   CF, a contract cleaning entity, signed a contract to provide 12 months cleaning of an office block. The contract for $12,000 commenced on 1 June 2012. The terms of the contract provided for payment six monthly in advance on 1 June and 1 December 2012. CF received $6,000 and started work on 1 June 2012.

        How should CF account for the contract in its financial statements for the year ended 30 June 2012?

        A   Debit cash $6,000 and credit revenue $6,000
        B   Debit cash $6,000, credit revenue $1,000 and credit deferred income $5,000
        C   Debit cash $6,000, debit receivables $6,000 and credit revenue $12,000
        D   Debit cash $6,000 and credit deferred income $6,000   **(2 marks)**

10   According to IFRS 8 *Operating segments* which **one** of the following defines an operating segment?

        An operating segment is a component of an entity:

        A   whose results contribute more than 10% of the entity's total sales revenue.
        B   that is considered to be one of the entity's main geographical areas of operation
        C   whose operating results are regularly reviewed by the entity's chief operating decision maker.
        D   whose results contribute more than 10% of the entity's total profit.   **(2 marks)**

                                                                          (Total = 20 marks)

65   Mixed objective test questions bank 10 (11/12)   36 mins

1   Taxes commonly used by many countries include:

   (i)   import duty payable on specific types of imported goods;
   (ii)   individual income tax, usually deducted at source;
   (iii)   corporate income tax;
   (iv)   value added tax.

Which of the above would normally be defined as direct taxation?

   A   (i) and (ii)
   B   (i) and (iv)
   C   (ii) and (iii)
   D   (ii) and (iv)   **(2 marks)**

2   Which **one** of the following is **not** part of the process of **developing** a new International Financial Reporting Standard (IFRS)?

   A   Issuing a discussion paper that sets out the possible options for a new standard.
   B   Publishing clarification of an IFRS where conflicting interpretations have developed.
   C   Drafting an IFRS for public comment.
   D   Analysing the feedback received on a discussion paper.   **(2 marks)**

3   At 1 October 2011 DX had the following balances in respect of property, plant and equipment:

Cost	$220,000
Tax written down value	$82,500
Statement of financial position:	
Carrying value	$132,000

DX depreciates all property, plant and equipment over 5 years using the straight line method and no residual value. All assets were less than 5 years old at 1 October 2011.

No assets were purchased or sold during the year ended 30 September 2012.

DX's deferred tax balance (to the nearest $) in its statement of financial position at 30 September 2012 will be:

   A $5,843
   B $6,531
   C $12,375
   D $23,375   **(2 marks)**

4   The IASB's *Conceptual Framework for Financial Reporting (2010)* lists two fundamental qualitative characteristics of useful financial information, one of which is faithful representation.

Which **one** of the following lists describes the three characteristics of faithful representation?

   A   Neutrality, free from error and comparability.
   B   Free from error, materiality and relevance.
   C   Comparability, understandability and completeness.
   D   Neutrality, completeness and free from error.   **(2 marks)**

5   An external auditor gives a modified audit report that is a "disclaimer of opinion".

This means that the auditor has:

   A   Been unable to access sufficient appropriate audit evidence.

   B   Been unable to agree with the directors over an accounting treatment of a material item.

   C   Found a few immaterial errors that have no impact on the auditor's opinion.

   D   Found many errors causing material misstatements and has concluded that the financial statements do not present fairly the financial position and financial performance.   **(2 marks)**

6   E, a trainee management accountant, prepares an annual analysis of the performance of all staff, including her own. The analysis is used by the financial director to calculate staff bonuses each year.

According to the CIMA code of ethics for professional accountants which **one** of the threats listed below would apply to E?

A   Advocacy threat
B   Intimidation threat
C   Familiarity threat
D   Self-interest threat   **(2 marks)**

7   Which **one** of the following would be shown in a statement of cash flow using the direct method but not in a statement of cash flow using the indirect method of calculating cash generated from operations?

A   Cash payments to employees
B   Increase/(decrease) in receivables
C   Depreciation
D   Finance costs   **(2 marks)**

8   Accounting and information disclosure practices are influenced by a variety of factors around the world.

Identify one of these factors and **briefly explain** how it influences accounting and information disclosure.
                                                                           (2 marks)

9   IAS 10 *Events after the reporting period* distinguishes between adjusting and non-adjusting events.

Which **one** of the following is an adjusting event in XS's financial statements?

A   A dispute with workers caused all production to cease six weeks after the year end.

B   A month after the year end XS's directors decided to cease production of one of its three product lines and to close the production facility.

C   One month after the year end a court determined a case against XS and awarded damages of $50,000 to one of XS's customers. XS had expected to lose the case and had set up a provision of $30,000 at the year end.

D   Three weeks after the year end a fire destroyed XS's main warehouse facility and most of its inventory.   **(2 marks)**

10   LP received an order to supply 10,000 units of product A every month for 2 years. The customer had negotiated a low price of $200 per 1,000 units and agreed to pay $12,000 in advance every 6 months.

The customer made the first payment on 1 July 2012 and LP supplied the goods each month from 1 July 2012.

LP's year end is 30 September.

In addition to recording the cash received, how should LP record this order, in its financial statements for the year ended 30 September 2012, in accordance with IAS 18 *Revenue*?

A   Include $6,000 in revenue for the year and create a trade receivable for $36,000
B   Include $6,000 in revenue for the year and create a current liability for $6,000
C   Include $12,000 in revenue for the year and create a trade receivable for $36,000
D   Include $12,000 in revenue for the year but do not create a trade receivable or current liability
                                                                           (2 marks)

                                                                    (Total = 20 marks)

66 Mixed objective test questions bank 11 (3/13)   36 mins

1   AB made a profit of $320,000 for the year ended 31 December 2012 and paid $80,000 tax on its
     profits. AB pays a gross dividend of $150,000 to its holding company, which operates in a foreign
     country. When AB pays the dividend it deducts a 10% tax. This 10% tax is called:

     A   underlying tax.
     B   corporate income tax.
     C   foreign tax.
     D   withholding tax.   **(2 marks)**

2   Which **one** of the following is a function of the IFRS Foundation?

     A   Complete responsibility for the preparation and publication of International Financial Reporting
          Standards (IFRSs).

     B   Approving annually the budget and determining the funding of the International Accounting
          Standards Board (IASB).

     C   To inform the IASB of the views of organisations and individuals on major standard setting
          projects.

     D   To review new financial reporting issues not yet covered by an IFRS.   **(2 marks)**

3   Accounting depreciation is usually disallowed when calculating tax due by an entity and a deduction for
     tax depreciation is given instead.

     Explain one reason why accounting depreciation is replaced with tax depreciation in a tax computation?
                                                                                        (2 marks)

4   Which **one** of the following is stated as an underlying assumption according to the IASB's *Framework for
     the Preparation and Presentation of Financial Statements* (Framework)?

     A   Neutrality
     B   Accruals
     C   Relevance
     D   Prudence   **(2 marks)**

5   An external auditor gives a modified audit report that is an "adverse opinion".

     This means that the auditor:

     A   Has been unable to agree with the directors over an accounting treatment of a material but not
          pervasive item.

     B   Has been unable to access important accounting records.

     C   Was unable to attend the inventory count and is unable to agree the inventory value, which is
          material.

     D   Has found many errors causing material misstatements in the financial statements. **(2 marks)**

6   R, a trainee management accountant is employed by JH. R has prepared the draft annual financial
     statements for JH and presented them to JH's Chief Executive prior to the executive board meeting. The
     Chief Executive has told R that the profit reported in the financial statements is too low and must be
     increased by $500,000 before the financial statements can be approved by the executive board.

     Which **one** of the threats listed below would apply to R in this situation, according to the CIMA code of
     ethics for professional accountants?

     A   Advocacy threat
     B   Self-review threat
     C   Intimidation threat
     D   Self-interest threat   **(2 marks)**

7   IAS 7 Statement of cash flows sets out the three main headings to be used in a statement of cash flows. Items that may appear on a statement of cash flows include:

(i)   Tax paid
(ii)   Purchase of investments
(iii)   Loss on disposal of machinery
(iv)   Purchase of equipment

Which of the above items would be included under the heading "Cash flows from operating activities" according to IAS 7?

A   (i) and (ii)
B   (i) and (iii)
C   (ii) and (iv)
D   (iii) and (iv)   (2 marks)

8   The IASB Framework identifies several different user groups of financial statements.

List four user groups identified by the Framework.   (2 marks)

9   Which **one** of the following would be regarded as a related party transaction of the entity NV?

A   A close family member of the Chief Executive of NV purchased an asset from NV.

B   XYZ Bank lends NV $100,000 on commercial loan terms.

C   The government of Country X awarded NV a grant of $25,000 to help fund a new production facility.

D   YU supplies 60% of NV's raw materials.   (2 marks)

10   IAS 18 *Revenue* sets out criteria for the recognition of revenue from the sale of goods.

Which **one** of the following is **not** a criterion specified by IAS 18 for recognising revenue from the sale of goods?

A   The seller no longer retains any influence or control over the goods.
B   The cost to the seller can be measured reliably.
C   The buyer has paid for the goods.
D   The significant risks and rewards of ownership have been transferred to the buyer.   (2 marks)

(Total = 20 marks)

67 Mixed objective test questions bank 12 (5/13)   36 mins

1   An entity makes a taxable profit of $500,000 and pays corporate income tax at 25%. The entity pays a dividend to its shareholders. A shareholder receiving $5,000 dividend then pays the standard personal income tax rate of 15% on the dividend, paying a further $750 tax.

The tax system could be said to be:

A   A classical system
B   An Imputation system
C   A partial imputation system
D   A split rate system   (2 marks)

2   Tax authorities use various methods to reduce tax avoidance and tax evasion.

    (i)   Increase tax rates to compensate for losses due to evasion.
    (ii)   Make the tax structure as complicated as possible.
    (iii)   Increase the perceived risk by auditing tax returns.
    (iv)   Simplify the tax structure, minimising allowances and exemptions.

    Which of the above methods could be used to help reduce tax evasion and avoidance?

    A   (i) and (ii)
    B   (i) and (iv)
    C   (ii) and (iii)
    D   (iii) and (iv)   **(2 marks)**

---

3   **List two** of the main methods of giving double taxation relief.   **(2 marks)**

---

4   CG purchased an asset on 1 April 2006 for $650,000, exclusive of import duties of $25,000. CG is resident in Country X where the indexation factor increased by 50% in the period from 1 April 2006 to 31 March 2013.

    CG sold the asset on 31 March 2013 for $1,200,000 incurring transaction charges of $17,000.

    Calculate the capital gains tax due from CG on disposal of the asset.   **(2 marks)**

---

5   Which **one** of the following gives the meaning of rollover relief?

    A   Trading losses can be carried forward to future years.

    B   Inventory can be valued using current values instead of original cost.

    C   Capital losses made in a period can be carried forward to future years.

    D   Payment of tax on a capital gain can be delayed if the full proceeds from the sale of an asset are reinvested in a replacement asset.   **(2 marks)**

---

6   Countries are subject to a variety of economic, social and political factors. In some countries accounting rules are largely driven by taxation laws. The legal system in these countries is known as:

    A   Case law
    B   Common law
    C   Code law
    D   Tax law   **(2 marks)**

---

7   **List two** potential benefits of global harmonisation of accounting standards to multinational entities.   **(2 marks)**

---

8   **List two** functions of the IFRS Advisory Council.   **(2 marks)**

---

9   The IASB's *Conceptual Framework for Financial Reporting (2010)* splits qualitative characteristics of useful information into two categories, fundamental and enhancing.

    List the **two** fundamental qualitative characteristics.   **(2 marks)**

---

10   An external audit report usually has the following 5 sections:

    (i)   Title and addressee
    (ii)   Introduction
    (iii)   Scope
    (iv)   ***
    (v)   Signature and name of audit firm

    State the section marked (iv).   **(2 marks)**

                                   (Total = 20 marks)

68 Mixed section B questions bank 1 (Specimen Paper)   54 mins

(a)   ATOZ operates in several countries as follows:

- ATOZ was incorporated in country BCD many years ago. It has curtailed operations in BCD but still has its registered office in country BCD and carries out a small proportion (less than 10%) of its trade there.

- ATOZ buys most of its products and raw materials from country FGH.

- ATOZ generates most of its revenue in country NOP and all its senior management live there and hold all the management board meetings there.

Required

(i)   **Explain** why determining corporate residence is important for corporate income tax.   **(2 marks)**

(ii) **Explain** which country ATOZ will be deemed to be resident in for tax purposes   **(3 marks)**

(Total = 5 marks)

(b)   WX operates a retail business in country X and is registered for VAT purposes.

During the last VAT period WX had the following transactions:

Purchases of materials and services, all at standard VAT rate, $130,000 excluding VAT.

Purchase of new machinery, $345,000, inclusive of VAT.

Sales of goods in the period, all inclusive of VAT where applicable, were:

Sales of goods subject to VAT at standard rate	$230,000
Sales of goods subject to VAT at zero rate	$115,000

Assume you are WX's trainee management accountant and you have been asked to prepare the VAT return and calculate the net VAT due to/from the tax authorities at the end of the period.

Assume WX has no other transactions subject to VAT and that all VAT paid can be recovered.

Required

(i)   **Explain** the difference between a single stage sales tax and VAT.   **(2 marks)**

(ii) **Calculate** the net VAT due to/from WX at the end of the period.   **(3 marks)**

(Total = 5 marks)

(c)   Country K uses prescriptive accounting standards. Country K's standard on intangible assets has a list of intangible assets covered by the standard and an extensive list of items that are not allowed to be recognised as assets. RS has incurred expenditure on a new product that does not appear to be specifically listed as "not allowed" by the standard. RS's management want to classify the expenditure as an intangible non-current asset in RS's statement of financial position. They argue that the type of expenditure incurred is not listed in the accounting standard as being "not allowed" therefore it is allowed to be capitalised.

RS's auditors have pointed out that the expenditure is not listed as being "allowed" and therefore should not be capitalised.

Required

Explain the possible advantages of having accounting standards based on principles rather than being prescriptive. Use the scenario above to illustrate your answer.   **(Total = 5 marks)**

(d)   BD is a well established double glazing business, manufacturing building extensions, doors and windows in its own manufacturing facility and installing them at customer properties.

BD's financial statements for the year ended 31 March 20X7 showed the manufacturing facility and installation division as separate reportable segments.

On 1 March 20X8, BD's management decided to sell its manufacturing facility and concentrate on the more profitable selling and installation side of the business.

At BD's accounting year end, 31 March 20X8, BD had not found a buyer for its manufacturing facility and was continuing to run it as a going concern. The facility was available for immediate sale; the management were committed to the sale and were actively seeking a buyer. They were quite sure that the facility would be sold before 31 March 20X9.

The manufacturing facility's fair value at 31st March 20X8 was $2.8 million, comprising total assets with a fair value of $3.6 million and liabilities with a fair value of $0.8 million. BD's management accountant calculated that the manufacturing facility had incurred a loss for the year of $0.5 million before tax and the estimated cost of selling the manufacturing facility was $0.2 million.
Required

Explain, with reasons, how BD should treat the manufacturing facility in its financial statements for the year ended 31 March 20X8. **(Total = 5 marks)**

(e)   L leases office space and a range of office furniture and equipment to businesses. On 1 April 20X8 C acquired a lease for a fully furnished office space (office space plus office furniture and equipment) and a separate lease for a computer system from L.

The office space was a lease of part of a large building and the building had an expected life of 50 years. The lease was for 5 years with rental payable monthly. The first year was rent free. The $1,000 per month rental commenced on 1 April 20X9.

The computer system lease was for 3 years, the expected useful life of the system was 3 years. The $15,000 per year lease rental was due annually in arrears commencing with 31 March 20X9. The interest rate implicit in the lease is 12.5% and the cost of the leased asset at 1 April 20X8 was $35,720. C depreciates all equipment on the straight line basis.

Under the terms of the computer system lease agreement C is responsible for insuring, servicing and repairing the computers. However, L is responsible for insurance, maintenance and repair of the office.

C allocates the finance charge for finance leases using the actuarial method.

Required

Explain the accounting treatment, required by international financial reporting standards, in the financial statements of C in respect of the two leases for the year ended 31 March 20X9.   **(Total = 5 marks)**

(f)   PS issued 1,000,000 $1 cumulative, redeemable preferred shares on 1 April 20X8. The shares were issued at a premium of 25% and pay a dividend of 4% per year.

The issue costs incurred were $60,000. The shares are redeemable for cash of $1.50 on 31 March 20Y8. The effective interest rate is 5.18%. Ignore all tax implications.

The management accountant of PS has extracted the following amounts from the preferred shares ledger account, for the year ended 31 March 20X9:

Account – Non-current liability – Preferred shares

	$
Net amount received on issue	1,190,000
Finance cost @5.18%	61,642
Less dividend paid	(40,000)
Balance at 31 March 20X9	1,211,642

Required

(i)   **Explain** the IAS 32 *Financial instruments: presentation* and IAS 39 *Financial instruments: recognition and measurement* requirements for the presentation and measurement of an issue of preferred shares. **(3 marks)**

(ii)   Using the information provided above, **explain** the amounts that PS should include for the preferred shares in its statement of profit or loss and other comprehensive income and statement of financial position for the year ended 31 March 20X9. **(2 marks)**

(Total = 5 marks)

(Total = 30 marks)

69   Mixed section B questions bank 2 (5/10)   54 mins

(a)   Cee has reduced her tax bill by taking advice from a tax expert and investing her surplus cash in government securities. The income from government securities is free of tax.

Gee works as a night security guard for a local entity and also has a job working in a supermarket during the day. Gee has reduced his tax bill by declaring only his day job income on his annual tax return.

Required

Explain the difference between tax evasion and tax avoidance, using Cee and Gee to illustrate your answer.   **(5 marks)**

(b)   W is a business in Country X, that uses locally grown fruit and vegetables to make country wines. During 20X8 W paid $30,000 plus VAT for the ingredients and other running costs.

When the wine is bottled W pays $1 tax per bottle to the tax authority. During 20X8 W produced 10,000 bottles.

W sold all the wine to retailers for an average price of $8.05 per bottle, including VAT at standard rate.

Required

(i)   **Explain** the difference between unit taxes and ad valorem taxes, using the scenario above to illustrate your answer.   **(3 marks)**

(ii)   **Calculate** the amounts of indirect tax payable by W for the year ended 31 December 20X8.
                                                                                              (2 marks)

                                                                                     (Total = 5 marks)

(c)   H, an entity, carries out business in Country X, buying and selling goods.

The senior management of H meet regularly in the entity's offices in Country X.

H owns 100% of S, an entity that buys and sells goods in Country Y. The senior management of S meet regularly in the entity's offices in Country Y. S reported a profit of $500,000 for 20X8 and received an income tax bill from Country Y's tax authority for $100,000.

S has declared a dividend of $200,000 and is required to deduct tax at 10% before remitting cash to overseas investors, such as H.

Assume Country X and Country Y have a double tax agreement based on the Organisation for Economic Co-Operation and Development (OECD) – Model Tax Convention.

Required

Explain the terms "competent jurisdiction" and "withholding tax". Illustrate how each relates to the H group.   **(5 marks)**

(d)   B's profits have suffered due to a slow-down in the economy of the country in which it operates. AB's draft financial statements show revenue of $35 million and profit before tax of $4 million for the year ended 31 December 20X8.

AB's external auditors have identified a significant quantity of inventory that is either obsolete or seriously impaired in value. The audit senior has calculated the inventory write-down of $1 million. AB's directors have been asked by the audit senior to record this in the financial statements for the year ended 31 December 20X8.

AB's directors are refusing to write-down the inventory at 31 December 20X8, claiming that they were not aware of any problems at that date and furthermore do not agree with the auditor that there is a problem now. The directors are proposing to carry out a stock-take at 31 May 20X9 and to calculate their own inventory adjustment, if required. If necessary the newly calculated figure will be used to adjust inventory values in the year to 31 December 20X9.

Required

(i) **Explain** the objective of an external audit. **(2 marks)**

(ii) Assuming that AB's directors continue to refuse to amend the financial statements, **explain** the type of audit report that would be appropriate for the auditors to issue. **(3 marks)**

(Total = 5 marks)

(e) On 1 April 20X7 CC started work on a three year construction contract. The fixed value of the contract is $63 million.

During the year ended 31 March 20X8 CC's contract costs escalated.

The value of work done and the cash received for the two years to 31 March 20X9 are summarised below:

	Year to 31 March 20X9	*Year to 31 March 20X8*
Percentage of work completed in year	40%	35%
Cost incurred in year	$26 million	$18 million
Estimated further costs after the year end to complete project	$20 million	$36 million
Progress payments received in the year	$22 million	$15 million

Amounts recognised by CC in its statement of profit or loss and other comprehensive income for the year ended 31 March 20X8:

Revenue	$22 million
Cost of sales	$18 million

Required

Calculate the amounts to be recorded for the above contract in CC's statement of profit or loss and other comprehensive income for the year ended 31 March 20X9 and in the statement of financial position at that date.

Show all calculated figures to the nearest $ million. **(5 marks)**

(f) AD operates five factories in different locations in a country. Each factory produces a different product line and each product line is treated as a separate segment under IFRS 8 Operating Segments.

One factory, producing a range of shoes, had an increased annual loss of an estimated $2,000,000 for the year to 31 March 20X9. On 1 March 20X9 AD's management decided to close the factory and cease the sale of it's range of shoes. Closure costs, net of any gains on disposal of the assets, are estimated as $150,000.

On 31 March 20X9 AD's management is still negotiating payment terms with the shoe factory workforce and has not agreed an actual closure date. AD has not yet attempted to find a buyer for the factory or its assets.

AD's management wants to completely exclude the shoe factory results from AD's financial statements for the year ended 31 March 20X9. They argue that as the shoe factory is about to be closed or sold, it would mislead investors to include the results of the shoe factory in the results for the year.

Required

Assume that you are a trainee accountant with AD.

AD's finance director has asked you to draft a briefing note that she can use to prepare a response to AD's management.

Your briefing note should **explain** how AD should treat the shoe factory in its financial statements for the year ended 31 March 20X9.

You should make reference to any relevant International Financial Reporting Standards and to CIMA's Code of Ethics for Professional Accountants. **(5 marks)**

(Total = 30 marks)

70 Mixed section B questions bank 3 (11/10)   54 mins

(a) ZK is part of a group of entities and has traded profitably for a number of years. During the year to 31 August 20X9, ZK made a tax adjusted trading loss of $30,000 and a capital gain of $5,000. In the following year to 31 August 20Y0, ZK made a taxable trading profit of $10,000. ZK expects to increase taxable trading profits to $50,000 for the year to 31 August 20Y1. ZK does not expect any capital gains or losses in the year to 31 August 20Y1.

Required

Explain four methods that a Country can allow to relieve trading losses of an entity and **illustrate** the effect of each method on ZK for the years ended 31 August 20X9 to 20Y1.   **(5 marks)**

(b) HW, an entity resident in Country X, owns 40% of the equity shares in SV, an entity resident in a foreign country, Country Y. For the year to 31 March 20Y0 SV had taxable profits of $12,500,000 and paid corporate income tax of $1,875,000. On 31 October 20Y0 HW received a dividend of $3,375,000 from SV, the amount received is net of tax of 10%.

Country X has a double taxation treaty with Country Y. The treaty provides for a group of entities to only be taxed once on each entity's profits. Credit is given for withholding tax and underlying tax paid in other countries, but no refunds are available if a higher rate of tax has been paid.

Required

(i) **Explain** the meaning of "withholding tax" and provide an explanation as to why countries levy "withholding" taxes.   **(2 marks)**

(ii) **Calculate** the amount due to be paid by HW on receipt of this dividend in Country X. Show all workings.   **(3 marks)**

(**Total = 5 marks**)

(c) *Required*

Explain the **two** fundamental qualitative characteristics and any **two** of the enhancing qualitative characteristics of financial information specified in the IASB's *Conceptual Framework*.   **(5 marks)**

(d) HB paid $2.50 per share to acquire 100% of PN's equity shares on 1 September 20X9. At that date PN's statement of financial position showed the following balances with equity:

	$'000
Equity shares of $1 each	180
Share premium	60
Retained earnings	40

PN's net asset values were the same as their book values, except for land which was valued at $70,000 more than its book value.

HB directors estimate that any goodwill arising on the acquisition will have a useful life of 10 years.

Required

(i) **Calculate** goodwill arising on the acquisition of PN.   **(2 marks)**

(ii) **Explain** how HB should record the goodwill in its group financial statements for the year ended 31 August 20Y0, in accordance with IFRS 3 *Business combinations*.   **(3 marks)**

(**Total = 5 marks**)

(e) HI, a parent entity, is planning to acquire a shareholding in ABC. The following alternative investment strategies are being considered:

(i) HI can purchase 80,000 preferred shares in ABC
(ii) HI can purchase 40,000 equity shares and 50,000 preferred shares in ABC
(iii) HI can purchase 70,000 equity shares in ABC and no preferred shares

ABC has the following issued share capital:

	$
$1 Equity shares	100,000
$1 10% Preferred Shares	100,000

Holders of preferred shares do not have any votes at annual general meetings.

Required

Identify with **reasons** how HI would classify its investment in ABC in its consolidated financial statements for each of the alternative investment strategies. **(5 marks)**

(f) MN obtained a licence free of charge from the government to dig and operate a gold mine.

MN spent $6 million digging and preparing the mine for operation and erecting buildings on site. The mine commenced operations on 1 September 20X9.

The licence requires that at the end of the mine's useful life of 20 years, the site must be reinstated, all buildings and equipment must be removed and the site landscaped. At 31 August 20Y0 MN estimated that the cost in 19 years' time of the removal and landscaping will be $5 million and its present value is $3 million.

On the 31 October 20Y0 there was a massive earthquake in the area and MN's mine shaft was badly damaged. It is estimated that the mine will be closed for at least six months and will cost $1 million to repair.

Required

(i) **Explain** how MN should record the cost of the site reinstatement as at 31 August 20Y0 in accordance with IAS 37 *Provisions, contingent liabilities and contingent assets*. **(2 marks)**

(ii) **Explain** how MN should treat the effects of the earthquake in its financial statements for the year ended 31 August 20Y0 in accordance with IAS 10 *Events after the reporting period*. **(3 marks)**

(Total = 5 marks)

(Total = 30 marks)

71 Mixed section B questions bank 4 (5/11)   54 mins

(a) FG, an entity operating in Country X, purchased a machine costing $500,000 on 1 April 20X6, which qualified for tax depreciation allowances. All other non-current assets are leased.

FG's policy in respect of machines is to charge depreciation on a straight line basis over 5 years, with no residual value.

FG had profits of $192,000 for the year ended 31 March 20X8. These profits are after charging depreciation and before adjusting for tax allowances.

Required

Use the above information to:

(i) **Calculate** FG's corporate income tax due for the year ended 31 March 20X8. **(2 marks)**

(ii) **Calculate** the deferred tax charge to FG's statement of profit or loss and other comprehensive income for the year ended 31 March 20X8 in accordance with IAS 12 *Income taxes*. **(3 marks)**

(Total = 5 marks)

(b) JK, an entity operating in Country X, purchased land on 1 March 20X5 for $850,000. JK incurred purchase costs of surveyor's fees $5,000 and legal fees $8,000. JK spent $15,000 clearing the land and making it suitable for development. Local tax regulations classified all of JK's expenditure as capital expenditure.

JK sold the land for $1,000,000 on 1 February 20X8, incurring tax allowable costs of $6,000.

Assume JK had no temporary differences between taxable and accounting profits.

Required

(i) **Explain** the meaning of a capital gain and capital gains tax. **(2 marks)**

(ii) Use the above information to **calculate** the capital gains tax due on the disposal of JK's land. **(3 marks)**

(Total = 5 marks)

(c) HC acquired a 75% holding in SU on 1 April 20X0.

HC received a dividend from SU of $156,000, the amount received is after deduction of withholding tax of 20%. SU profit before tax was $650,000 and it paid corporate income tax of $130,000 in respect of these profits.

Required

(i) **Explain** the meaning of "underlying tax". **(2 marks)**

(ii) **Calculate** the amount of underlying tax that HC can claim for double tax relief. **(3 marks)**

(Total = 5 marks)

(d) Generally accepted accounting practice (GAAP) in a country can be based on legislation and accounting standards that are either

- very prescriptive in nature; or
- principle-based

Required

Explain the possible advantages of having principle-based accounting standards as opposed to prescriptive standards. **(5 marks)**

(e) *Required*

(i) **Explain** the objective of financial reporting according to the IASB's *Conceptual Framework for Financial Reporting (2010)*. **(3 marks)**

(ii) **Explain** the underlying assumption outlined in the *Conceptual Framework*. **(2 marks)**

(Total = 5 marks)

(f) CX, a professional accountant, is facing a dilemma. She is working on the preparation of a long term profit forecast required by the local stock market listing regulations prior to a new issue of equity shares.

At a previous management board meeting, her projections had been criticised by board members as being too pessimistic. She was asked to review her assumptions and increase the profit projections.

She revised her assumptions, but this had only marginally increased the forecast profits.

At yesterday's management board meeting the board members had discussed her assumptions and specified new values to be used to prepare a revised forecast. In her view the new values grossly overestimate the forecast profits.

The management board intends to publish the final revised forecasts.

Required

Explain the ethical problems that CX faces and **identify** her possible options. You should refer to CIMA's Code of ethics for professional accountants. **(5 marks)**

(Total = 30 marks)

72 Mixed section B questions bank 5 (9/11)   54 mins

(a)   SV is registered for value added tax (VAT) in country X. During the last VAT period, SV purchased materials and services costing $200,000, excluding VAT. All materials and services were at the standard rate of VAT.

      SV converted the materials into two products Y and Z; product Y is zero rated and product Z is standard rated for VAT purposes.

      During the same VAT period, SV made the following sales, inclusive of VAT

	$
Y	90,000
Z	207,000

      At the end of the period, SV pays the net VAT due to the tax authorities or claims a refund of the VAT paid.

      Assume SV had no other VAT-related transactions in the period.

      Required

      (i)   **Explain** the difference between a single-stage sales tax and VAT.   **(2 marks)**

      (ii)   **Calculate** the net amount of VAT due to be paid by SV or any refund to be claimed by SV at the end of the period.   **(3 marks)**

                                          (Total = 5 marks)

(b)   *Required*

      (i)   **Explain** the meaning of deferred tax as defined in IAS 12 *Income taxes*   **(2 marks)**

      (ii)   **Explain** how a deferred tax debit balance can arise in an entity and the criteria for its recognition as an asset.   **(3 marks)**

                                          (Total = 5 marks)

(c)   *Required*

      (i)   **Explain** the worldwide approach to taxing entities in a country.   **(2 marks)**

      (ii)   **Explain** the problems caused by the worldwide approach and how they can be overcome.

                                          (3 marks)

                                          (Total = 5 marks)

(d)   Accounting and disclosure practices are subject to a number of influences that vary from country to country. This leads to a variety of different accounting regulations around the world.

      Required

      Explain the factors that may influence accounting regulations in a country.

                                          (5 marks)

(e)   The International Accounting Standards Board (IASB)'s *Conceptual Framework for Financial Reporting (2010)* identifies assets and liabilities as two key elements.

      Required

      (i)   **Define** assets and liabilities in accordance with the *Conceptual Framework*

      (ii)   **Explain** the criteria that must be met for assets and liabilities to be recognised in an entity's financial statements.

                                          (5 marks)

(f)   WZ is an assistant accountant with ABC. On 31 March 2011 ABC decided to sell a property. This property was correctly classified as held for sale in accordance with IFRS 5 *Non-Current Assets Held For Sale and Discontinued Operations*.

In its draft financial statements ABC has written down the property by $3.4 million. The write down was charged to the statement of profit or loss and other comprehensive income for the year ended 31 August 2011. The draft financial statements showed a loss of $1.3 million for the year to 31 August 2011.

When the management board of ABC reviewed the draft financial statements the board members were unhappy that the draft statements showed a loss and decided that the property should continue to be shown under non-current assets at its previous carrying value.

Required

Explain the ethical problems that WZ faces AND identify his possible options. Your answer should refer to CIMA's Code of ethics for professional accountants

(5 marks)

(Total = 30 marks)

73   Mixed section B questions bank 6 (11/11)   54 mins

(a)   The following is an extract from KM's statement of profit or loss and other comprehensive income for the year ended 31 March 2011:

	$
Revenue	966,000
Cost of sales	(520,000)
Gross profit	446,000
Administrative expenses	(174,000)
Distribution costs	(40,000)
	232,000
Finance cost	(67,000)
Profit before tax	165,000

Cost of sales includes depreciation charges of $42,000 for property, plant and equipment. Distribution costs include a depreciation charge for a new vehicle (see below). Included in administrative expenses are entertainment costs of $9,800.

KM had been selling through retail outlets, but from 1 April 2010 began selling on the internet and delivering to customers as well. KM purchased its first delivery vehicle on 1 April 2010 for $18,000. The vehicle qualifies for a first year tax allowance and is depreciated on a straight line basis over six years.

The property, plant and equipment (excluding the delivery vehicle) qualified for tax depreciation allowance of $65,000 in the year ended 31 March 2011.

Required

(i)   **Calculate** the estimated amount of corporate income tax that KM is due to pay for the year ended 31 March 2011.

(ii)   **Calculate** the income tax expense charged to the statement of profit or loss and other comprehensive income for the year ended 31 March 2011.   **(5 marks)**

(b)   LM imports luxury goods in bulk. LM repackages the products and sells them to retailers. LM is registered for Value Added Tax (VAT) in Country X.

LM imported a consignment of perfume costing $50,000, paying excise duty of 20% of cost. The consignment was subject to VAT on the total (including duty). LM paid $9,775 repackaging costs, including VAT and sold the perfume for $105,800 including VAT.

LM had not paid or received any VAT payments to or from the VAT authorities for this consignment.

Required

(i)   **Calculate** the net VAT due to be paid by LM on the perfume consignment.
(ii)   **Calculate** LM's net profit on the perfume consignment.   **(5 marks)**

(c)   *Required*

Explain the meaning of "tax base" **and** give **three** examples of the different tax E; bases regularly used by governments. I   **(5 marks)**

(d)   *Required*

Explain the concepts of capital and capital maintenance as defined in the International Accounting Standards Board (IASB)'s *Conceptual Framework for Financial Reporting (2010)).*   **(5 marks)**

(e)   You are the partner in charge of the audit of LMN. The following matter has been brought to your attention in the audit working papers. During the year LMN spent $500,000 on applied research, trying to find an application for a new process it had developed. LMN's management has capitalised this expenditure. LMN management is refusing to change its accounting treatment as it does not want to reduce the year's profit. The draft financial statements show revenue of $40 million and net profit of $4.5 million.

Required

(i)   **Explain** what is meant by "materiality" AND whether the matter highlighted above is material.

(3 marks)

(ii)   **Identify** the type of audit report that would be appropriate to the above statements, assuming that LMN's management continue to refuse to change the financial statements.   **(2 marks)**

(Total = 5 marks)

(f)   RS an employee, prepares monthly management accounting information for XYZ which includes detailed performance data that is used to calculate staff bonuses. Based on information prepared by RS this year's bonuses will be lower than expected. RS has had approaches from other staff offering various incentives to make accruals for additional revenue and other reversible adjustments, to enable all staff (including RS) to receive increased or higher bonuses.

Required

Explain the requirements of the CIMA Code of Ethics for Professional Accountants in relation to the preparation and reporting of information AND the ethical problems that RS faces.

(5 marks)

(Total = 30 marks)

74   Mixed section B questions bank 7 (3/12)   54 mins

(a)   TY, an entity operating in Country X, purchased plant and equipment on 1 January 2010 for $440,000. TY claimed a first year tax allowance and thereafter annual writing down allowances.

TY is depreciating the plant and equipment over eight years using straight line depreciation, assuming no residual value.

On 1 January 2011, TY revalued the plant and equipment and increased the net book value by $70,000. The asset's useful life was not affected.

Assume there are no other temporary differences in the period.

Required

Calculate the amount of deferred tax movement in the year ended 31 December 2011 AND the deferred tax balance at 31 December 2011, in accordance with IAS 12 *Income taxes*.   **(5 marks)**

(b)   UYT is an entity supplying goods and services to other businesses. UYT is registered for Value Added Tax (VAT) in Country X.

UYT is partially exempt for VAT purposes.

During the last VAT period UYT purchased materials and services costing $400,000 excluding VAT. UYT used these goods and services to produce both standard and exempt supplies. VAT was payable at standard rate on all purchases.

UYT supplied goods and services to its customers, some of these were at standard rate VAT and some were exempt VAT.

Excluding VAT: $
Standard rate goods and services   450,000
Exempt supplies   150,000

At the end of the period UYT prepared a VAT return. Assume UYT had no other VAT related transactions.

Required

(i)   **Explain** the difference between the treatment of items that are zero rated and items that are exempted from VAT.   **(2 marks)**

(ii)   **Calculate** the net VAT balance shown on UYT's VAT return.   **(3 marks)**

    (Total = 5 marks)

(c)   LKJ, an entity resident in Country X, reported a taxable profit for the year to 31 December 2011 and declared a dividend for the year.

YT, a director and shareholder of LKJ, received a dividend payment from LKJ and is certain that the dividend he received will have been taxed twice.

Country X applies a full imputation system to corporate income taxes.

Required

Explain to YT how the imputation system of corporate income tax works AND whether his dividend will have been taxed twice.   **(5 marks)**

(d)   *Required*

Identify the four main entities that are involved in developing and implementing International Accounting Standards. Briefly describe the role of each entity.   **(5 marks)**

(e) Countries differ quite widely in their audit requirements, but most agree that large corporate entities should have an annual external audit.

Required

(i) **Explain** the objective of an external audit of the financial statements of an entity. **(2 marks)**

(ii) Briefly **explain three** key areas of content of the audit report as required by ISA 700 The Auditor's Report on Financial Statements. **(3 marks)**

(Total = 5 marks)

(f) XQ, an employee of ABC, prepares monthly management accounting information for ABC. This information includes detailed performance data that is used to evaluate managers' performance. The directors are considering the closure of some facilities and XQ's management information will be included in the review.

XQ has had approaches from a number of concerned managers offering various incentives to make adjustments to the management accounting information to improve their performance statistics.

Required

Briefly **explain** the ethical problem that XQ faces AND what XQ should do in this situation. Your answer should refer to the appropriate fundamental principles of the CIMA Code of Ethics. **(5 marks)**

(Total = 30 marks)

---

75 Mixed section B questions bank 8 (5/12) 54 mins

(a) *Required*

Explain the main benefits, to users of the accounts, of including a statement of cash flows in published financial statements. **(5 marks)**

(b) The draft financial statements for the year ended 31 March 2012 for TX include the following:

	$'000
Statement of profit or loss and other comprehensive income (extract)	
Income tax expense	850
Notes to the accounts:	
Over provision for the year to 31 March 2011	(50)
Estimate of tax due for the year to 31 March 2012	700
Increase in deferred tax provision for the year to 31 March 2012	200
	850
Statement of cash flows (extract)	
Tax paid in the year to 31 March 2012	600

Required

(i) **Explain** how deferred tax arises.

Use the information given above to:

(ii) **Identify** the most likely reason for the increase of $200,000 in the deferred tax provision for the year to 31 March 2012.

(iii) **Explain** what the over provision of $50,000 in the statement of profit or loss and other comprehensive income represents.

(5 marks)

(c)   PQ is resident in Country X. PQ's summary statement of profit or loss and other comprehensive income for the year ended 31 March 2012 was as follows:

	$'000
Revenue	567
Cost of sales and other expenses	(253)
	314
Finance income	85
Finance cost	(12)
Profit before tax	387

Other expenses include depreciation of $92,000 and amortisation of intangible assets of $14,000.

PQ's property, plant and equipment qualified for tax depreciation of $98,000 for the year.

PQ holds a number of bonds and bank deposits in Country Z. PQ received interest of $85,000 (net of withholding tax at 15%) during the year to 31 March 2012.

Country X has a double taxation treaty with Country Z that provides for double taxation relief using the tax credit method.

Required

Calculate the estimated amount of corporate income tax that PQ is due to pay for the year ended 31 March 2012.   **(5 marks)**

(d)   *Required*

(i)   **Explain** the difference between an excise duty and a single stage sales tax.   **(3 marks)**

(ii)   **Describe** the characteristics of commodities that make them most suitable, from the revenue authority's point of view, for the application of excise duty.   **(2 marks)**

(Total 5 marks)

(e)   The International Accounting Standards Board (IASB)'s *Conceptual Framework for Financial Reporting (2010)* identifies five key elements of financial statements.

Required

(i)   **Define** income and equity in accordance with the IASB *Conceptual Framework*.   **(3 marks)**

(ii)   **Explain** the criteria that must be met for income to be recognised in an entity's financial statements.   **(2 marks)**

(Total = 5 marks)

(f)   You are a trainee accountant working for ABC, which is listed on the local stock exchange. A new chief executive has recently been appointed and has queried the benefits to ABC of having an external audit carried out each year.

Required

Prepare a short briefing note that highlights the benefits of an external audit to ABC.

(5 marks)

(Total = 30 marks)

76 Mixed section B questions bank 9 (9/12)   54 mins

(a)   PY is resident in Country X. PY's statement of financial position extracts as at 31 March 2011 and 2012 are as follows:

Statement of financial position (extracts) as at:	2011 $'000	2012 $'000
Non-current Liabilities		
Deferred tax provision	540	560
Current Liabilities		
Tax payable	1,820	1,980

Statement of cash flows (extract) for year ended 31 March 2012:

	$'000
Tax paid	1,795

Required

(i)   **Calculate** the income tax charge to be included in PY's statement of profit or loss and other comprehensive income for the year ended 31 March 2012.   **(3 marks)**

(ii)   **Explain** the impact of an increase in the corporate profits tax rate to 30% from 1 April 2012 on PY's deferred tax provision at 31 March 2012.   **(2 marks)**

(Total = 5 marks)

(b)   *Required*

Explain the main methods of giving double taxation relief to entities with overseas earnings.

(Total = 5 marks)

(c)   SM is a small local corporate entity that delivers products to local businesses. The following is a summary of SM's statement of profit or loss and other comprehensive income for the year ended 31 March 2012:

	$
Revenue	200,000
Expenses	157,000
Profit before tax	43,000

Expenses include depreciation charges of $16,500 for property. These properties qualified for tax depreciation allowances of $19,300 in the year ended 31 March 2012.

On 1 April 2011 SM had to replace its only delivery vehicle. The vehicle was sold for $2,000. At the date of disposal the vehicle had a carrying value of $3,000 and a tax written down value of $2,000.

SM's replacement vehicle cost $32,000, has an expected useful life of 7 years with a residual value of $4,000. The appropriate accounting entries for these vehicles have been included in the accounts.

SM's expenses include $6,300 for entertainment costs.

Required

Calculate the amount of tax that SM is due to pay for the year ended 31 March 2012.

(Total = 5 marks)

(d)   TY has a construction contract in progress. The contract commenced on 1 April 2011 and is scheduled to run for two years. The contract has a fixed price of $9,000,000. TY uses the value of work completed method to recognise attributable profit for the year.

At 31 March 2012 the proportion of work certified as completed was 35%.

	$'000
Work in progress (cost incurred during year to 31 March 2012)	4,000
Estimated cost to complete contract	6,000
Cash received on account from contract client	3,250

Required

(i)   **Calculate** the amount of revenue and cost that TY should include in its statement of profit or loss and other comprehensive income for the year ended 31 March 2012 in respect of the construction contract.

(3 marks)

(ii)   **Calculate** the gross amount due from/to customers to be included in TY's statement of financial position as at 31 March 2012.   (2 marks)

(Total = 5 marks)

(e)   *Required*

Explain the steps in the IASB's standard setting process that most IFRSs go through during development.

(Total = 5 marks)

(f)   VB's sales revenue for the year was $2,000,000 and its profit was $300,000. VB's external audit has just been completed and there are two outstanding matters.

(i)   An inventory count did take place at the year-end but there are very few supporting records available. The inventory value stated, $90,000, cannot be verified from the available records.

(ii)   VB is facing a court case accusing it of breaching another international entity's copyright. If VB loses the case it will be unable to continue as a going concern. VB's directors have assessed the likelihood of losing the case and have disclosed the court case as a contingent liability in its financial statements. The auditors have agreed with the directors' treatment and disclosure.

Required

Explain for each of the two matters listed above:

(i)   The impact that each would have (if any) on the audit report in respect of VB.

(ii)   Whether the audit report in respect of VB requires modification and if so the type of modification required.

(Total = 5 marks)

(Total = 30 marks)

77   Mixed section B questions bank 10 (11/12)   54 mins

(a)   *Required*

Explain the powers that tax authorities may be given to enable them to enforce tax regulations.

(Total = 5 marks)

(b)   For the year ended 30 September 2012 KQ's statement of profit or loss and other comprehensive income included a profit before tax of $147,000. KQ's expenses included political donations of $9,000 and entertaining expenses of $6,000.

KQ's statement of financial position at 30 September 2012 included plant and machinery with a carrying value of $168,500. This is comprised of plant purchased on 1 October 2010 at a cost of $180,000 and machinery purchased on 1 October 2011 at a cost of $50,000.

KQ depreciates all plant and machinery on the straight line basis at 15% per year.

Required

Calculate the tax payable by KQ for the year to 30 September 2012.   (Total = 5 marks)

(c)   *Required*

Define an operating segment according to IFRS 8 *Operating segments* and **explain** when a segment is classified as a reportable segment.   (Total = 5 marks)

(d) A taxable person making a taxable supply of goods or services must register for VAT in most countries once their taxable turnover reaches a certain limit.

HJ is registered for VAT in Country X. HJ is partially exempt for VAT purposes.

During the latest VAT period HJ purchased materials and services costing $690,000 including VAT at standard rate. These goods and services were used to produce standard rated, zero rated and exempt goods.

Goods supplied to customers (excluding VAT) were:

	$
Goods at standard rate	720,000
Goods at zero rate	100,000
Exempt goods	205,000

Assume HJ had no other VAT related transactions.

Required

(i) Once registered for VAT an entity must abide by the VAT regulations.

Identify four typical requirements of VAT regulations. **(2 marks)**

(ii) **Calculate** the net VAT balance shown on HJ's VAT return for the period. **(3 marks)**

(Total = 5 marks)

(e) HC, resident in Country X for tax purposes, owns 100% of shares in a foreign entity, OC. OC operates in a country that has a double taxation treaty with Country X that provides for the use of the tax credit method of double taxation relief.

OC reported profits before tax of $600,000 with corporate income tax of $126,000 for the year ended 31 March 2012.

OC paid HC a dividend for the year ended 31 March 2012 of $200,000 gross which was subject to withholding tax of 12%.

Required

(i) **Calculate** the total foreign tax suffered on the dividend. **(2 marks)**

(ii) **Calculate** the amount of tax that HC will be liable to pay on receipt of the dividend in Country X, applying the tax credit method of double taxation relief. **(3 marks)**

(Total = 5 marks)

(f) *Required*

Explain the roles of the following in relation to International Financial Reporting Standards.

- The IFRS Interpretations Committee
- The IFRS Advisory Council **(Total = 5 marks)**

(Total = 30 marks)

78 Mixed section B questions bank 11 (3/13)   54 mins

(a) Most governments require detailed records to be kept for each type of tax to which an entity is subject.

Required:

(i) **List four** taxes that are likely to require detailed records to be maintained by an entity. **(2 marks)**

(ii) **Identify** the records that an entity would be required to keep to support its VAT or sales tax returns. **(3 marks)**

(Total = 5 marks)

(b)   HG is resident in Country X.

HG had a tax loss of $49,000 for the year ended 31 December 2011.

HG made an accounting profit of $167,000 for the year ended 31 December 2012. The profit was after charging $4,000 for entertaining and $5,000 for donations to a political party. HG's revenue includes a non-taxable government grant of $12,000 received during the year ended 31 December 2012.

HG has plant and equipment that cost $50,000 on 1 January 2011 and new equipment that cost $8,000 on 1 January 2012. HG depreciates its plant and equipment on a straight line basis over 5 years with no residual value.

Required

Calculate the tax payable by HG for the year ended 31 December 2012.   **(Total = 5 marks)**

(c)   LP is an entity that up until 30 June 2012 operated 3 divisions; division A, B and C. LP closed division C on 30 June 2012.

Division C had the following results for the period 1 January 2012 to 30 June 2012:

	$000
Revenue	95
Operating expenses	(110)
Operating loss	(15)
Tax refund	3
Loss	(12)

(excluding disposal of assets and restructuring)

The disposal of the assets of division C incurred a loss of $30,000.

LP incurred an expense of $75,000 for restructuring the remaining divisions after the closure of division C. LP regards $75,000 as material in the context of its financial statements.

Required

Explain how the closure of division C and restructuring of the other divisions will be reported in LP's Statement of comprehensive income for the year ended 31 December 2012, according to IFRS 5 *Non-current assets held for sale and discontinued operations*   **(Total = 5 marks)**

(d)   Excise duties are charged on certain types of specific goods by most governments. Excise duties are often charged in addition to VAT/sales tax.

Required

Explain three reasons why an excise duty may be imposed on certain types of goods by a government. For each reason give an example to illustrate your answer.   **(Total = 5 marks)**

(e)   OW is an international entity that has operations in two countries:

•   OW has a number of branch offices in Country Z, each office provides services to customers and sells OW's products.

•   OW's head office is in Country X, where OW's production facility and head office are located. All directors' board meetings are held in Country X.

Assume countries X and Z have double tax treaties with each other based on the OECD model tax convention.

Required

(i)   **Explain**, with reasons, which country/countries OW will be regarded as resident in for tax purposes.   **(2 marks)**

(ii)   **Explain** how the profits made by OW in Country Z will be taxed.   **(3 marks)**

(Total = 5 marks)

(f)   *Required*

      The IASB has developed a conceptual framework called *The Framework for the Preparation and Presentation of Financial Statements (Framework)*.

      Identify FIVE purposes of the *Framework*.   **(Total = 5 marks)**

(Total = 30 marks)

79   Mixed section B questions bank 12 (5/13)   54 mins

(a)   Extracts from CFQ's Statement of financial position at 31 March 2013, with comparatives appear below:

	31 March 2013	31 March 2012
	$million	$million
Property, plant and equipment	635	645
Non-current asset investments at fair value	93	107
Deferred development expenditure	29	24

      During the year to 31 March 2013, CFQ sold property, plant and equipment for $45m. It had originally cost $322m and had a carrying value of $60m at the date of disposal.

      CFQ's statement of profit or loss for the year ended 31 March 2013 included:

- depreciation of property, plant and equipment of $120m;
- amortisation of deferred development expenditure of $8m;
- revaluation loss on investments of $21m.

      Required

      Prepare the cash flows from the investing activities section of CFQ's statement of cash flows for the year ended 31 March 2013.   **(Total = 5 marks)**

(b)   Ace is a management accountant working as part of a small team that has been set up by ZY, his employer, to evaluate tenders submitted for contracts being awarded by ZY. He has just discovered that one of the other team members accepted large payments in exchange for information, from an entity at the time it was considering tendering. Ace suspects that this may have influenced the winning tender submitted by the entity.

      Required

      Explain the steps that Ace could follow to ensure that he adheres to CIMA's code of ethics for professional accountants.   **(Total = 5 marks)**

(c)   On 1 January 2012 PS issued at par, 500,000 $1 5% cumulative preferred shares, redeemable at par in four years. The issue costs were $20,000.

      PS has not issued preferred shares before and the managing director has asked you to explain how the preferred shares should be treated in the financial statements of PS.

      Required

      Explain with reasons, how PS should:

      (i)   classify the preferred shares in its financial statements for the year ended 31 December 2012, in accordance with *IAS 32 Financial Instruments: Presentation;*

      (ii)   account for the related costs in accordance with IAS 39 Financial Instruments: Recognition and Measurement.   **(Total = 5 marks)**

(d)   GH, an entity operating in Country X, purchased plant and equipment on 1 April 2011 for $260,000. GH claimed first year allowances and thereafter annual writing down allowances.

      GH depreciates plant and equipment over 6 years, using the straight line method, assuming a 10% residual value.

Required

(i)   **Define** the meaning of the tax base of an asset and its significance for deferred tax.   **(2 marks)**

(ii) **Calculate** the amount of the deferred tax provision that GH should include in its statement of financial position as at 31 March 2013 in respect of this plant and equipment.   **(3 marks)**

(Total = 5 marks)

(e)   MT's summarised statement of profit or loss for the year ended 31 March 2013 is as follows:

	$
Gross profit	187,000
Administrative expenses	(126,000)
Distribution costs	(22,000)
	39,000
Finance cost	(2,000)
Profit before tax	37,000

Administrative expenses include donations to the local ruling political party of $5,000 and depreciation of property, plant and equipment of $39,000 (inclusive of depreciation of new purchases).

MT an entity operating in Country X made a tax loss for the year ended 31 March 2012. The loss carried forward at 31 March 2012 was $12,000.

At 31 March 2012 MT's tax written down value of its property, plant and equipment was $120,000. All of these assets qualified for the annual tax depreciation allowances. MT purchased property, plant and equipment during the year to 31 March 2013 for $30,000.

Required

Calculate the amount of tax that MT is due to pay for the year ended 31 March 2013.

(Total = 5 marks)

(f)   During the last VAT period AV purchased materials and services costing $620,000 excluding VAT. $400,000 were standard rated for VAT and $220,000 were zero rated.

AV sold the following goods to its customers during the period, including VAT:

- At standard rate $828,000
- At zero rate $150,000

Assume that AV had no other VAT related transactions during the period.

Required

(i)   **Explain** the difference between a cascade sales tax and value added tax (VAT).   **(2 marks)**

(ii) **Calculate** the net profit/loss that AV should recognise AND the VAT due for the period.   **(3marks)**

(Total = 5 marks)

(Total = 30 marks)

ANSWERS

1 Objective test answers: The regulatory framework

1	C	Guidance on application and interpretation of IFRSs is provided by the IFRS Interpretations Committee.
2	A	The priority given to different user groups in different countries (eg investor groups in the US and employees in Europe) is actually a **barrier** to harmonisation.
3	D	The IFRS Interpretations Committee develops its interpretations through a due process of consultation and debate which includes making Draft Interpretations available for public comment.
4		Expenses and equity
5	C	The statement that the business is expected to continue in operation for the foreseeable future means that the business is a going concern. Going concern is an underlying assumption because the *Conceptual Framework* states that users should assume that the financial statements are prepared on the going concern basis unless there is disclosure to the contrary.
6	B	The elements of financial statements are assets, liabilities and equity in the statement of financial position and income and expenses in the statement of profit or loss and other comprehensive income. Profits and losses are not elements.
7	B	The statement of profit or loss and other comprehensive income measures **financial performance**. The entity's economic resources and claims are shown in the statement of financial position and financial adaptability is shown in the statement of cash flows
8	D	Going concern.
9		An asset is a **resource controlled** by an entity as a result of **past transactions or events** and from which **future economic benefits** are expected to flow to the entity.
10	D	Generally accepted accounting practice
11	C	The IFRS Foundation Trustees are responsible for governance and fundraising and publish an annual report on the IASB's activities. The trustees also review annually the strategy of the IASB and its effectiveness.
12	C	The IFRS Interpretations Committee reports to the IASB. The IFRS Advisory Council advises the IASB. The IFRS Foundation is the parent entity of the IASB.
13		Expenses are **decreases in economic benefits** during the accounting period in the form of outflows or depletions of assets or incurrences of liabilities that result in decreases in equity, **other than those relating to distributions to equity participants**.
14		The objective of financial reporting is to provide financial information about the reporting entity that is useful to existing and potential investors, lenders and other creditors in making decisions about providing resources to the entity.
15	C	A is the definition of a liability, B is the definition of an asset and D is the definition of income according to the *Conceptual Framework*.
16	D	The IFRS Foundation Trustees are responsible for:

- appointing members of the IASB, the IFRS Interpretations Committee and the IFRS Advisory Council
- establishing and amending the operating procedures, consultative arrangements and due process for the IASB, the Interpretations Committee and the Advisory Council
- reviewing annually the strategy of the IASB and assessing its effectiveness
- ensure the financing and approve annually the budget of the IFRS Foundation and the IASB

17		Relevance and faithful representation.
18	D	The IFRS Advisory Council is a forum for the IASB to consult with the outside world. The IASB produces IFRSs and is overseen by the IFRS Foundation.

19 The four stages are:

   1 Establishment of Advisory Committee
   2 Discussion Paper issued
   3 Exposure Draft issued
   4 IFRS issued

20 D Providing information regarding the economic resources and claims of a business and its performance are important factors for users in making decisions about providing resources to the business.

21 C For financial information to faithfully represent a business's underlying transactions it must be complete and neutral (free from bias). Note also that the information must be free from error (although this was not required for this question).

22 B Relevance is a fundamental qualitative characteristic and comparability and timeliness are enhancing qualitative characteristics. Completeness is part of faithful representation.

23 D Verifiability, understandability, comparability, timeliness.

24 C The role of the IASB is to develop and publish International Financial Reporting Standards

25 A The IFRS Advisory Council

2 Objective test answers: External audit

1 D An external audit provides reasonable assurance that the financial statements are free from material misstatements. An external audit does not **guarantee** that there are no material misstatements in the financial statements. There are inherent limitations in an audit which affect the auditor's ability to discover material misstatements that arise from the nature of financial reporting, the nature of audit procedures, time and cost limitations and the requirement for the auditor to exercise judgment.

2 B An opinion must be disclaimed when the auditor **cannot obtain sufficient appropriate audit evidence** on which to base the opinion and concludes that the **possible effects** on the financial statements of undetected misstatements, if any, **could be both material and pervasive**.

3 C No modification is needed as the directors have made full disclosure.

4 D The auditors' report covers all of these matters.

5 B The auditor cannot obtain sufficient appropriate audit evidence on which to base the opinion but concludes that the possible effects of undetected misstatements, if any, could be material but not pervasive.

6 C The auditors will be unable to give an opinion in this case.

7 C Even though the finance department may prepare the accounts, management have overall responsibility for the preparation of the financial statements. External auditors give an opinion on whether the financial statements give a true and fair view.

8 A In order to state that the financial statements show a true and fair view the auditor must satisfy himself that the other three matters are valid.

9 D The auditors will begin by trying to persuade the directors.

10 Power to require access to all books and records
Power to require information and explanations from officers of the company
Power to attend meetings and address shareholders

11 C If the auditor believes that the financial statements do not show a true and fair view this should first be discussed with management. If management refuse to adjust the accounts, the auditor would give an adverse opinion in the audit report.

12 A The external audit is carried out by external auditors who are independent of the company so that they can provide an independent opinion as to the truth and fairness of the company's financial statements.

13 A The auditor does not report on items that are not material.

14 To enable the auditor to express an opinion as to whether the financial statements give a true and fair presentation of the entity's affairs.

15 D The external auditors will issue a qualified opinion on the basis that the misstatement is material, but not pervasive to the financial statements.

3 Objective test answers: Ethics

1 B The audit of the financial statements will be carried out by an accountant in practice.

2 B Reliability, Morality and Efficiency are not fundamental principles.

3 A Self-interest. If such threats are significant (ie the interest is direct and of high value), safeguards will have to be put in place.

4 B A principles-based approach sets out principles and guidelines, rather than detailed rules to cover every specific situation. This leads to the listed advantages – but not to consistent application, since there is a high degree of discretion in applying guidelines to different cases.

5 A The principle of due care is that, having accepted an assignment, you have an obligation to carry it out to the best of your ability, in the client's best interests, and within reasonable timescales, with proper regard for the standards expected of you as a professional. In this scenario, any answer you give on the spot would risk being incomplete, inaccurate or out-of-date, with potentially serious consequences, if the client relies and acts on your reply. Integrity is honesty, fair dealing and truthfulness; professional behaviour is upholding the reputation of your profession; and confidentiality is not using or disclosing information given to you by employers or clients in the course of your work. (None of these issues applies directly here.)

6 B This raises issues of professional competence and due care. You know that you do not have the knowledge to answer these questions at this time and in this situation. For your own professional safety, you should make the client clearly aware of this and not be prepared to give any opinion, as this may be relied upon by the client despite the circumstances. The most appropriate form of action would be to make an appointment with the client to discuss the matter properly after you have done some research into these specific areas, or refer them to a colleague with experience in this area.

7 Confidentiality
Professional competence/due care.

8 C A, B and D all describe the features of a rules-based code.

9 A B describes integrity; C describes objectivity and D describes professional competence and due care.

10 B Disclosure of information to advance the interests of a new client would not be permitted under the Code.

11 D HMRC is not a source of ethical codes for accountants.

4 Section B answers: Regulation

(a) The IASB's *Conceptual Framework* lays out the elements of financial statements as follows.

(i) *Asset*

A resource controlled by an entity as a result of past events and from which future economic benefits are expected to flow to the entity.

An example of an asset is an item of machinery used in the business.

(ii)   *Liability*

A present obligation of the entity arising from past events, the settlement of which is expected to result in an outflow of resources from the entity.

An example of a liability is an amount due to a supplier for goods received.

(iii)   *Equity*

The residual interest in the assets of the entity after deducting all its liabilities.

Ordinary share capital is an example of equity.

(iv)   *Income*

Increases in economic benefits during the accounting period in the form of inflows or enhancements of assets or decreases of liabilities that result in increases in equity, other than those relating to contributions from equity participants.

An example of income is income recognised on the sale of goods.

(v)   *Expenses*

Decreases in economic benefits during the accounting period in the form of outflows or depletions of assets that result in decreases in equity, other than those relating to distributions to equity participants.

Depreciation is an example of an expense.

(b)

> **Examiner's comments.** Candidates failed to include enough detail in their answers. Many answers identified a characteristic and then the explanation added nothing to it, for example, 'Relevance – information needs to be relevant'.

The four enhancing qualitative characteristics of financial information are as follows.

Comparability

Information is more useful if it can be compared with similar information about other entities and/or other accounting periods. Consistency in the preparation of financial information helps achieve comparability. For this to be possible users must be informed of the accounting policies employed in the preparation of the financial statements and any changes to those policies and their effects. The financial statements must also show corresponding amounts for the previous period.

Verifiability

Information must be verifiable in order to give assurance to the users of financial information that the information has been prepared so that it faithfully represents the economic phenomena it purports to represent. Verification can be direct or indirect.

Timeliness

Financial information is required by users in order to make decisions based on that information. It must therefore be made available in a timely manner if it is to influence the decisions they make.

Understandability

The financial statement information should be readily understandable to users. For this purpose users are assumed to have a reasonable knowledge of business and economic activities and accounting and a willingness to study the information with reasonable diligence. The information provided should be presented in a clear and concise manner.

(c)

> **Examiner's comments.** Most candidates did well on this question, although some could not think of three alternatives. A common error was using bullet points or short notes to answer the question and as a result not providing sufficient detail for 5 marks.

C could pursue any of the following options:

(i) **Develop its own standards without reference to the IASB**. This would produce standards which reflected trading conditions in the country but, when it developed to the point of needing to attract foreign investment, investors may not be drawn to companies whose financial statements are not prepared under generally recognised standards.

(ii) **Adopt IFRS**. This would mean that C had adopted high-quality, generally recognised standards from the outset, and would have no future harmonisation process to undergo. However, it may find that time and expense has gone into implementing standards which may not be that relevant to its current economic situation.

(iii) **Adopt those IFRSs which are currently applicable**, such as IAS 41 *Agriculture*, and **develop additional standards of its own based on IFRS**. This would produce a set of standards which were theoretically high-quality and relevant to its own economy. However, the judgement and expertise required to carry this out may not be available and C will be resolving issues between local standards and IFRS on an ongoing basis.

(d)

> **Top tips.** We have only given five answers here as this is all that is required for five marks.
>
> **Examiner's comments.** The answers provided for this question were very weak. Many candidates did not know what the purpose of the *Conceptual Framework* was and tried explaining the purpose of financial statements.

The purposes of the *Conceptual Framework* are:

(i) To assist in the **review of existing IASs and IFRSs** and the **development of new IFRSs**

(ii) To promote **harmonisation** of accounting standards by reducing the number of allowed alternative accounting treatments

(iii) To **assist national standard-setting bodies** in developing national standards

(iv) To assist preparers of financial statements in **applying IFRSs** and dealing with topics not yet covered by an IFRS

(v) To **assist auditors** in determining whether financial statements comply with IFRS

> Alternative answers
>
> You would also have scored marks if you had identified any of the following purposes.
>
> • To assist users of financial statements prepared under IFRS in interpreting the information contained in them
>
> • To provide general information on the approach used in formulating IFRSs

(e) **IFRS Advisory Council**

The IFRS Advisory Council provides a forum for groups and individuals to give advice to the International Accounting Standards Board (IASB), the board responsible for setting IFRS. The committee members are from diverse geographical and functional backgrounds to allow them to gather opinions from a wide range of representatives.

The committee advises the IASB on its agenda and priorities for setting new IFRS. Consultation with the IFRS Advisory Council continues throughout the development of an IFRS. In particular, the IFRS Advisory Council advises the IASB on issues related to the practical application and implementation of new IFRS. It also advises on the advantages and disadvantages of different proposals.

International Financial Reporting Interpretations Committee

The IFRS Interpretations Committee provides timely guidance on the application and interpretation of IFRS. It normally deals with complex accounting issues that could give rise to a diversity of accounting treatments. In this way it assists the IASB in setting and improving IFRS.

IFRS Interpretations Committee produces interpretations which, once finalised, are ratified and issued by the IASB. The IASB may choose to add an item to its own agenda if an interpretation is not ratified.

5   Section B answers: External audit

(a)

> **Examiner's comments.** Common errors made by candidates in this question were:
>
> – incorrectly concluding that item 1 was material by incorrectly calculating the percentage of revenue as 500/15,000 instead of 500/15,000,000 and the percentage of profit as 500/1,500 instead of 500/1,500,000.
>
> – suggesting that item 2 (development costs) should be written off against the previous year's profit, which is incorrect as the circumstances existing at that balance sheet date met the criteria required by IAS 38.
>
> – not recognising that item 3 required immediate full provision as per IAS 37.

(i) *Item 1* – the obsolete inventory is not material as $500 is 0·003% of revenue and is 0·03% of profit, therefore management's decision is acceptable. The inventory can be written off in the current year.

Item 2 – the deferred development expenditure must be charged to profit or loss as soon as it ceases to meet the IAS 38 criteria for deferral. As the project has now been abandoned, the expenditure ceases to meet the IAS 38 criteria for deferral. Therefore the $600,000 should be charged to profit or loss in the current year.

(ii) *Item 3 – decommissioning costs*

IAS 37 *Provisions, contingent liabilities and contingent assets* requires decommissioning costs to be recognised as soon as the liability arises, which is usually when the facility starts to operate. HF should create a provision for the full $5,000,000 decommissioning costs, discounted to present value, and add it to the cost of the asset (debit asset, credit provision). This will be a material increase in the net asset value and will increase the depreciation charged to profit or loss.

Audit opinion

If the directors do not agree to change the treatment of the decommissioning costs to recognise the full provision in the financial statements, an "except for" qualified audit report will need to be issued as all matters are correct except for the treatment of the decommissioning costs.

(b) (i) **Qualified opinion** – A qualified opinion must be expressed in the auditor's report in the following two situations:

(1) The auditor concludes that misstatements are **material**, but **not pervasive**, to the financial statements.

Material misstatements could arise in respect of the appropriateness of selected accounting policies, the application of accounting policies or the adequacy of disclosures.

(2) The auditor cannot obtain **sufficient appropriate audit evidence** on which to base the opinion but concludes that the possible effects of undetected misstatements, if any, could be **material** but **not pervasive**.

This is often referred to as a 'limitation on scope' and could arise from situations including the accounting records being destroyed or management preventing the auditor reviewing certain records.

The opinion will be expressed as being 'except for' the effects of the matter to which the qualification relates.

(ii) **Disclaimer of opinion** – An opinion must be disclaimed when the auditor cannot obtain sufficient appropriate audit evidence on which to base the opinion and concludes that the possible effects on the financial statements of undetected misstatements, if any, could be **both material and pervasive**. This limitation on scope may have arisen through circumstances, or may have been imposed by the client or may have arisen due to the inadequate nature of the company's accounting records. The auditor's report should give an explanation of the nature of the limitation of scope and quantify the effects on the financial statements where possible.

(iii) **Adverse opinion** – An adverse opinion is expressed when the auditor, having obtained sufficient appropriate audit evidence, concludes that misstatements are **both material and pervasive** to the financial statements. The audit report must fully describe the circumstances leading to the adverse opinion. The opinion will state that, because of the effect of these circumstances, the financial statements do not present fairly the financial position of the company and its results.

(c)   *Right of access to records*

The auditor has a right of access at all times to the books, accounts and vouchers of the company.

Right to require information

The auditor has a right to require from the company's officers such information and explanations as he thinks necessary for the performance of his duties as auditor. It is an offence for a company's officer to make a statement to the auditor which is materially misleading, false or deceptive.

These rights make it possible for the auditor to carry out an audit. If these rights are violated, the auditor will qualify his report. If the situation is serious, for instance if the auditor believes the directors to be involved in a fraud, he has the following rights which enable him to communicate directly to the shareholders:

Right to attend/receive notice of general meetings

The directors cannot keep the auditor away from the AGMs by not informing him of when they are taking place.

Right to speak at general meetings

The auditor has a right to be heard at general meetings which he attends, on any part of the business that concerns him as auditor.

Right in relation to written resolutions

The auditor has the right to receive a copy of any written resolution proposed. This means that he must receive a copy of any resolution which is proposed to terminate his engagement.

In practice, an auditor would not expect to have to invoke these rights very often, but the fact that they exist establishes his status in relation to the directors and makes it possible for him to get the co-operation that he needs in order to carry out his engagement.

(d)

> **Examiner's comments.** Many answers to this question were of low quality. Many candidates clearly did not understand the objective of an audit and a large proportion of answers were unable to correctly identify the type of report or the information required.

(i)   **The objective of an external audit** is to enable the auditor to express an opinion on whether the financial statements give a true and fair view (or present fairly) the financial position of the company and the results of its operations and its cash flows, in accordance with applicable Accounting Standards.

(ii)   The misstatement is $2.4m which is 15% of profits for the year and is therefore material, but not pervasive (because only this balance is affected, not the rest of the accounts). EA & Co should issue a **qualified opinion** because the misstatement identified is material but not pervasive, to the financial statements.

The auditors will include in their report:

'Profit on long-term contracts has not been accounted for in accordance with IAS 11. Per the standard, a foreseeable loss on a long-term contract should be recognised immediately. In the financial statements for the year to 30 September 2006, only that portion of the loss which has been incurred to date has been included. $3.7m has been included in the statement of comprehensive income in respect of long-term contracts. This should be amended to $1.3m in order to recognise in full the expected loss.

In our opinion, except for the effect on the financial statements of the matter referred to in the preceding paragraph, the financial statements give a true and fair view...'

6   Section B answers: Ethics

(a)   The CIMA Code requires the professional accountant to comply with five fundamental principles:

- Integrity
- Objectivity
- Professional Competence and Due Care
- Confidentiality
- Professional Behaviour

Compliance with these principles is required in order for the accountant to discharge his duty to act in the public interest.

Specific threats to his compliance with these principles can arise during the course of his work. The conceptual framework requires the accountant to identify, evaluate and address threats to compliance with the fundamental principles.

The framework sets out five categories of threat:

- Self-interest threats
- Self-review threats
- Advocacy threats
- Familiarity threats
- Intimidation threats

The accountant must recognise the threat when it arises, evaluate whether or not it is significant and put in place safeguards to deal with it. The Code gives examples of how the categories of threat can arise and examples of relevant safeguards.

There are major differences between this approach and a rules-based approach. The conceptual framework approach puts the responsibility on the accountant to ensure compliance with the principles. In this way, whatever threat arises, the accountant has to consider it. A list of rules could not encompass every possible threat and could even lead to attempts to circumvent them. Any situation not explicitly covered would be deemed to be not a threat and situations would then arise which would require the rules to be continually updated. The application of a conceptual framework avoids this.

(b)   The five fundamental principles are:

Integrity – a professional accountant should be straightforward and honest in all professional and business relationships.

Objectivity – a professional accountant should not allow bias, conflict of interest or undue influence of others to override professional or business judgments.

Professional competence and due care - a professional accountant has a continuing duty to maintain professional knowledge and skill at the level required to ensure that a client or employer receives competent professional service based on current developments in practice, legislation and techniques. A professional accountant should act diligently and in accordance with applicable technical and professional standards when providing professional services.

Confidentiality – a professional accountant should respect the confidentiality of information acquired as a result of professional and business relationships and should not disclose any such information to third parties without proper and specific authority unless there is a legal or professional right or duty to disclose. Confidential information acquired as a result of professional and business relationships should not be used for the personal advantage of the professional accountant or third parties.

Professional behaviour – a professional accountant should comply with relevant laws and regulations and should avoid any action that discredits the profession.

(c)   **Advantages of a code based on principles include**:

- Having principles rather than rules places the onus on the professional to **consider actively** relevant issues in a given situation, rather than just agreeing action with a checklist of forbidden items.

- Principles rather than rules prevent professionals interpreting legalistic requirements narrowly to get around the ethical requirements.

- Principles rather than rules allow for variations that are found in every individual situation.

- A principles-based code prescribes minimum standards of behaviour that are expected.

Disadvantages of a code based on principles include:

- Principles-based codes can be difficult to enforce legally, unless the breach of the code is blatant.

- International codes (such as the IFAC Code) cannot fully capture regional variations in beliefs and practice.

- Illustrative examples given in principles-based codes can be interpreted mistakenly as rules to follow in all similar circumstances.

- As ethical codes cannot include all circumstances and dilemmas, accountants need a very good understanding of the underlying principles in order to effectively apply them.

7 Objective test answers: Presentation

1	A	Members do not inspect the accounting records – the auditors do this on their behalf.
2	A	All of these items appear in the statement of changes in equity.
3	D	Authorised share capital is disclosed in the notes to the balance sheet, the other disclosures are made in the income statement or notes.
4	C	2 is a change of accounting estimate, 4 is specifically mentioned in IAS 8 as not constituting a change of accounting policy.
5	D	Material errors are treated in the same way as changes of accounting policy, by the application of retrospective restatement.
6	B	IAS 8 requires that a change in accounting policy is accounted for by retrospective application.
7	B	A change in the method of valuing inventory is a change of accounting policy
8	A	Changing the method of depreciation is a change of estimation technique not a change of accounting policy and therefore retrospective application is not required. However the current year figures must be changed to reflect the change in estimation technique and the change must be disclosed.
9	C	Provisions are covered by IAS 37.
10	D	Revenue and finance cost
11	B	This is the most commonly seen form of the statement of comprehensive income (income statement), which includes cost of sales and distribution costs.
12	D	A is a change in accounting policy, B is specifically mentioned in IAS 8 as a change in an accounting policy to be dealt with as a revaluation in accordance with IAS 16, C is an error per IAS 8.

8 Section B answers: Presentation

(a) Companies might be expected to publish accounts using standard formats so as to ensure **complete disclosure** of material and important items and to ensure **consistency between accounting periods and comparability between companies.**

In addition, in certain European and other countries where standard formats have been in use for many years their use provides governments with **consistent information for the preparation of national accounts** and other economic statistics.

The detail shown in each of the standard statements of profit or loss would enable users of accounts to calculate certain key **ratios** such as gross margins, net margins, ratio of administration costs to sales or

profit and to identify the proportion of the net income arising from operations separately to that arising from financing transactions.

This information would be of use to **shareholders** and stockholders' analysts who will wish to assess the **profitability** of a company and compare it with possible alternative investments.

(b)

> **Examiner's comments.** Candidates scored high marks on this question. This question was the most popular part of question 2 and was generally the best answer.
>
> The most common error was to incorrectly adjust for the change in inventory value and some candidates ignored the requirement to make a provision for compensation.

CE
STATEMENT OF PROFIT OR LOSS FOR THE YEAR ENDED 31 MARCH 20X6

	$'000
Revenue	2,000
Cost of sales (W)	(688)
Gross profit	1,312
Distribution costs	(200)
Administrative expenses (260 + 500)	(760)
Finance costs	(190)
Profit before tax	162

Working: Cost of sales

Per trial balance	480
Inventory adjustment	16
Depreciation ((1,500 – 540) × 20%)	192
	688

9 Objective test answers: Statements of cash flows

1   A   It is important to know which way round the additions and subtractions go when preparing a statement of cash flows.

2   D   Profit on disposal will be included in profit, so should be deducted.

3   C   These items do not affect cash flow.

4   D   The final figure in the statement of cash flows is the increase or decrease in cash and cash equivalents.

5   A

Property, plant and equipment

	$'m
Balance b/d	30
Additions	16
	46
Depreciation	(6)
Disposals (balancing figure)	(4)
Balance c/d	36

Alternative working:

PROPERTY, PLANT & EQUIPMENT CARRYING AMOUNT

	$m		$m
Balance b/d	30	Depreciation	6
		Disposals (balancing figure)	4
Cash paid for additions	16	Balance c/d	36
	46		46
Balance b/d	36		

As the carrying value of the asset disposed of is $4m and there was a loss on disposal of $1m, the proceeds were $3m.

6   B   Equity investments do not generally fulfil the description of cash equivalents

7   A   All of these items involve movements of cash

8   C   Depreciation and losses on disposal are added back.

9   A

	$'000
Cash from sales	
$3,600 + $600 – $700	3,500
Cash paid for purchases	
$2,400 + $300 – $450	(2,250)
Payments for expenses	(760)
	490

10   Property, plant and equipment purchases = $105,000

Property, plant and equipment working

	$'000
Balance b/d	180
Revaluation	20
Additions (balancing figure)	105
	305
Depreciation	(40)
Disposals	(5)
Balance c/d	260

Alternative working:

PROPERTY, PLANT & EQUIPMENT CARRYING AMOUNT

	$'000		$'000
Balance b/d	180	Depreciation	40
Revaluation	20	Disposals	5
Cash paid for additions (bal figure)	105	Balance c/d	260
	305		305
Balance b/d	260		

11   A   Interest paid = $38,000

Interest payable working

	$
Balance b/d	12,000
Finance charge per SPLOCI	41,000
	53,000
Cash paid (balancing figure)	(38,000)
Balance c/d	15,000

Alternative working:

INTEREST PAYABLE

	$		$
Cash paid (bal figure)	38,000	Balance b/d	12,000
Balance c/d	15,000	SPLOCI	41,000
	53,000		53,000

10   Section B answer: Statements of cash flows

(a)

Examiner's comments. A very large proportion of candidates prepared a statement of cash flows according to IAS 7 indirect method rather than the direct method, thereby losing most of the marks.

STATEMENT OF CASH FLOWS FOR THE YEAR ENDED 31 MARCH 20X8

	$'000	$'000
Cash flows from operating activities		
Cash received from customers (W1)	440	
Rents received	45	
Cash paid to suppliers (W2)	(225)	
Cash paid to and on behalf of employees	(70)	
Other operating expenses	(15)	
Cash generated from operations		175

Workings

1   *Cash received from customers*

	$'000
Opening trade receivables	45
Revenue	445
Closing trade receivables	(50)
Cash received from customers	440

2   *Cash paid to suppliers*

	$'000
Cost of sales	220
Opening inventory	(25)
Closing inventory	40
Purchases	235
Opening payables	20
Closing payables	(30)
Cash paid to suppliers	225

11   Dickson

> **Text references.** Statements of cash flows are covered in Chapter 9.
>
> **Top tips.** This is a really great question to practice preparing statements of cash flows. The calculation of interest paid and income tax paid should have been fairly straightforward. It was easy to miss the amortisation on development expenditure and instead just include the cash spent during the year – be on the lookout for this in your exam. The new finance lease was tricky – make sure you understand how it affected the PPE and finance liability workings. Remember that no cash changes hands in a bonus issue of shares!

DICKSON CO

STATEMENT OF CASH FLOWS FOR THE YEAR ENDED 31 MARCH 20X6

	$'000	$'000
Cash flows from operating activities		
Profit before taxation	342	
Adjustments for:		
Depreciation	57	
Amortisation (W3)	60	
Interest expense	15	
Profit on disposal of assets	(7)	
	467	
Decrease in trade receivables (W1)	50	
Increase in inventories (W1)	(133)	
Decrease in trade payables (W1)	(78)	
Cash generated from operations	306	
Interest paid (15 – 5)	(10)	
Income taxes paid (W4)	(256)	
Net cash from operating activities		40

Cash flows from investing activities

Development expenditure	(190)	
Purchase of property, plant & equipment (W2)	(192)	
Proceeds from sale of property, plant & equipment	110	
Net cash used in investing activities		(272)

Cash flows from financing activities

Issue of shares (850 – 500 – (400 × 1/8)]	300	
Issue of loan notes	50	
Payment of finance lease liabilities (W5)	(31)	
Dividends paid (W6)	(156)	
Net cash from financing activities		163
Net decrease in cash and cash equivalents		(69)
Cash and cash equivalents at beginning of period		109
Cash and cash equivalents at end of period		40

NOTES TO THE STATEMENT OF CASH FLOWS

1   *Property, plant and equipment*

During the period, the company acquired property, plant and equipment with an aggregate cost of $248,000 of which $56,000 was purchased by means of finance leases. Cash payments of $192,000 were made to acquire property, plant and equipment.

2   *Cash and cash equivalents*

Cash and cash equivalents consist of cash on hand and balances with banks, and investments in government bonds. Cash and cash equivalents included in the cash flow statement comprise the following balance sheet amounts.

	20X6	20X5
	$'000	$'000
Cash on hand and balances with banks	(103)	63
Short-term investments	143	46
Cash and cash equivalents	40	109

Workings

1   *Inventories, trade receivables and trade payables*

	Inventories	Trade receivables	Trade payables
	$'000	$'000	$'000
Balance b/d	227	324	352
Increase/(decrease) (balancing figure)	133	(50)	(78)
Balance c/d	360	274	274

2   *Property, plant and equipment*

	$'000
Balance b/d	637
Revaluations (160 – 60)	100
Finance leases	56
Additions (balancing figure)	192
	985
Depreciation	(57)
Disposals	(103)
Balance c/d	825

3   *Development expenditure*

	$'000
Balance b/d	160
Expenditure	190
	350
Amortisation (balancing figure)	(60)
Balance c/d	290

4   *Income tax payable*

	$'000
Balance b/d - current	45
Balance b/d - deferred	153
SPLOCI	162
	360
Paid (balancing figure)	(256)
Balance c/d – current (56) & deferred (48)	104

5   *Finance lease liability*

	$'000
Balance b/d - > 1 year	80
Balance b/d - < 1 year	12
New finance lease	56
	148
Paid (balancing figure)	(31)
Bal c/d – > 1 year (100) & < 1 year (17)	117

6   *Dividends payable*

	$'000
Balance b/d	103
Retained earnings	131
	234
Paid (balancing figure)	(156)
Balance c/d	78

Alternative layout for workings 2 to 6 using T accounts

PROPERTY, PLANT AND EQUIPMENT

	$		$
Balance b/d	637	Depreciation	57
Revaluations (160 – 60)	100	Disposals	103
Finance leases	56	Balance c/d	825
∴ Additions	192		
	985		985

DEVELOPMENT EXPENDITURE

	$		$
Balance b/d	160		
Expenditure	190	∴ Amortisation	60
		Balance c/d	290
	350		350

INCOME TAX PAYABLE

	$		$
		Balance b/d – current	45
		– deferred	153
∴ Paid	256	SPLOCI	162
Balance c/d – current	56		
– deferred	48		
	360		360

FINANCE LEASE LIABILITY

	$		$
		Balance b/d – > 1 year	80
		– < 1 year	12
∴ Paid	31		
Balance c/d – > 1 year	100	New finance lease	56
– < 1 year	17		
	148		148

DIVDENDS PAYABLE

	$		$
		Balance b/d	103
∴ Paid	156	Retained earnings	131
Balance c/d	78		
	234		234

12 UV (9/11)

Text references. Statements of cash flows are covered in Chapter 9. Tangible non-current assets are covered in Chapter 6.

Top tips. A question like this requires you to manage your time well. Preparing a property, plant and equipment note for 6 marks was a nice start to the question, although you may have struggled with the disclosure for the revaluation because of the twist with deferred tax. Time management is important here – if you don't know what to do with one part of a question (eg the deferred tax/revaluation twist) then leave it and move on as there are more easy marks to gain elsewhere. The deferred tax on revalued property only had an effect on the tax working, not on the PPE note.

Following a logical approach to a statement of cash flow question is an absolute must if you are to get the easy marks. Lay out your proforma and then work through the SPLOCI and SOFP, transferring the figures to your proforma or to workings as you go.

This question was unusual in that it gave you cash balances for some things (eg development expenditure and restructuring) and expected you to calculate the non-cash charges in the SPLOCI. Don't be put off with this, just use the standard workings to calculate the required amounts.

Easy errors to make were:

- Getting the signs mixed up on the working capital adjustments
- Incorrect treatment of the legal provision/restructuring provision
- Not including the dividend paid

Easy marks. Part (a) is should have been relatively straightforward to complete – most of the numbers didn't involve any calculations and could be inserted straight from the question. In part (b), as with most statement of cash flow questions, there were some easy marks are those available for working through the SOFP and the SPLOCI and transferring the numbers to your proforma – eg SPLOCI: profit before tax, finance cost, loss on disposal, and SOFP: year end cash balances, working capital changes (though watch the signs!), share issue and the loan repayment. Even the additional notes gave you a couple of figures that could go straight into your proforma – the cash spent on restructuring and on development expenditure.

Examiner's comments. "There were some very good answers to this question, some candidates scoring full marks on part (b), but it also produced some very poor answers scoring just a few marks. Candidates either new how to do cash flows and scored fairly high marks or didn't really know what they were doing."

Marking scheme

		Marks
(a)	**PPE note**	
	B/f and c/f figures	1
	Disposal	1
	Revaluation	1½
	Additions	½
	Depreciation charge	1
	Carrying amount	1
		6
(b)	**Statement of cash flows**	
	Cash flows from operating activities	
	Profit before tax	½
	Finance cost	½
	Depreciation	½
	Loss on disposal	1
	Amortisation of development expenditure	1
	Restructuring provision/expenses	2
	Legal provision	1
	Working capital adjustments - 1 each	3
	Interest paid	1
	Income taxes paid	1
		11½
	Cash flows from investing activities	
	Purchase of PPE	½
	Proceeds of sale of PPE	1
	Development expenditure	1
		2½
	Cash flows from financing activities	
	Proceeds from issue of share capital	1
	Repayment of borrowings	1
	Dividends paid	1½
		3 ½
	Cash and cash equivalents	½
	Presentation	1
	Total	19
	Total marks for question	25

(a) Property, plant and equipment

	Property $'000	Plant $'000	Equipment $'000	Total $'000
Carrying amount at 1 July 2010	3,700	1,000	85	4,785
Additions		215	275	490
Disposals		(30)		(30)
Revaluation	800			800
Charge for the year	(50)	(280)	(40)	(370)
Carrying amount at 30 June 2011	4,450	905	329	5,675

As at 30 June 2011

Cost/valuation	4,500	2,475	1,260	8,235
Accumulated depreciation	(50)	(1,570)	(940)	(2,560)
Carrying amount	4,450	905	320	5,675

As at 30 June 2010

Cost/valuation	4,150	2,350	985	7,485
Accumulated depreciation	(450)	(1,350)	(900)	(2,700)
Carrying amount	3,700	1,000	85	4,785

(b)   UV
        STATEMENT OF CASH FLOWS FOR THE YEAR ENDED 30 JUNE 2011

	$'000	$'000
Cash flows from operating activities		
Profit before taxation	1,540	
Finance cost (W4)	95	
Depreciation (part (a))	370	
Loss on disposal	15	
Amortisation of development expenditure (W1)	13	
Increase in restructuring provision (W6)	60	
Restructuring expenses (W6)	(160)	
Increase in legal provision (105 – 75)	30	
Operating profit before working capital changes	1,963	
Increase in inventories (W1)	(15)	
Increase in receivables (W1)	(45)	
Decrease in payables (W1)	(25)	
Cash generated from operations	1,878	
Interest paid (W4)	(122)	
Income taxes paid (W3)	(229)	
Net cash from operating activities		1,527
Cash flows from investing activities		
Purchase of property, plant and equipment (part (a))	(490)	
Proceeds of sale of property, plant and equipment (30 – 15)	15	
Development expenditure (W2)	(114)	
Net cash used in investing activities		(589)
Cash flows from financing activities		
Dividend paid (W4)	(168)	
Proceeds from issue of equity shares (910 – 760) + (665 – 400)	415	
Repayment of long term borrowings (1,500 – 250)	(1,250)	
Net cash used in financing activities		(1,003)
Net decrease in cash and cash equivalents		(65)
Cash and cash equivalents at 30 June 2010		160
Cash and cash equivalents at 30 June 2011		95

Workings

1   *Inventories, trade receivables and trade payables*

	Inventories	Trade receivables	Trade payables
	$'000	$'000	$'000
Balance b/d	80	145	85
Increase/(decrease) (balancing figure)	15	45	(25)
Balance c/d	95	190	60

2   *Development expenditure*

	$'000
Balance b/d	69
Additions during year	114
	183
Amortisation (balancing figure)	(13)
Balance c/d	170

3   *Income taxes*

	$'000
Balance b/d - current	305
Balance b/d - deferred	0
Deferred tax on revalued property	200
Tax charge per SPLOCI	455
	960
Income taxes paid (balancing figure)	(229)
Balance c/d – current (321) & deferred (410)	731

4 *Interest paid*

	$'000
Balance b/d	32
Finance cost per SPLOCI	95
	127
Interest paid (balancing figure)	(122)
Balance c/d	5

5 *Dividend paid*

	$'000
Balance b/d	1,982
Profit for the year	1,085
	3,067
Dividend paid (balancing figure)	(168)
Bal c/d	2,899

6 *Restructuring provision*

	$'000
Balance b/d	100
Charge per SPLOCI (balancing figure)	60
	160
Restructuring cash spend	(160)
Balance c/d	0

Alternative layout for workings 2 to 6 using T accounts

DEVELOPMENT EXPENDITURE

	$'000		$'000
Balance b/f	69	Amortisation (bal fig)	13
Additions during year	114	Balance c/f	170
	183		183

INCOME TAXES

	$'000		$'000
Income taxes paid (bal fig)	229	Balance b/f current	305
		Balance b/f deferred	0
Balance c/f current	321	Deferred tax on revalued property	200
Balance c/f deferred	410	Tax charge per SPLOCI	455
	960		960

INTEREST PAYABLE

	$'000		$'000
Interest paid (bal fig)	122	Balance b/f	32
Balance c/f	5	Finance cost per SPLOCI	95
	127		127

RETAINED EARNINGS

	$'000		$'000
Dividend paid (bal fig)	168	Balance b/f	1,982
Balance c/f	2,899	Profit for year	1,085
	3,067		3,067

RESTRUCTURING PROVISION

	$'000		$'000
Restructuring cash spend	160	Balance b/f	100
Balance c/f	0	Charge per SPLOCI (bal fig)	60
	160		160

BPP
LEARNING MEDIA

13 OP (5/11)

Text references. Statements of cash flows are covered in Chapter 9. Finance leases are covered in Chapter 8.

Top tips. As with many statement of cash flow questions, this is question is time pressured and you need to make sure you leave adequate time to address part (b) which is worth 6 marks. You must be logical in your approach to answering part (a) – set up the proforma, and insert the numbers that don't require adjustment first. Most of the adjustments (interest, tax development expenditure) were pretty straightforward if you had practiced a few SOCF questions, though the PPE working was a bit more involved than it can be in other questions and the downwards valuation may have put you off. Remember to work logically through the information you have. This isn't the first time the examiner has included a provision in a statement of cash flows question, so it may appear in the real exam. Make sure you know how to deal with it.

Easy errors to make were:

- Getting the signs mixed up on the working capital adjustments
- Incorrect treatment of the legal provision
- Not including the downward valuation of PPE in the PPE working

Part (b) was a finance lease using the actuarial method. If you struggled with this part of the question, make sure you go back and revise how to do the workings. Easy errors to make were accounting for the repayments as if they were paid in advance instead of in arrears and missing out the depreciation and finance charge from the financial statement extracts.

Easy marks. In part (a), the question gave you lots of figures that could be plugged straight into you proforma for some easy marks: finance cost, amortisation, depreciation and loss on disposal of PPE. In part (b), if you couldn't remember the workings for finance leases, you could still have picked up some marks by including the figures from the extracts from the financial statements that didn't involve any (or very little) calculation – eg the cost of the non-current asset, the depreciation charge and the finance lease payments.

Marking scheme

		Marks
(a)	**Statement of cash flows**	
	Cash flows from operating activities	
	Profit before tax	½
	Finance cost	½
	Depreciation	½
	Loss on disposal	1
	Amortisation of development expenditure	½
	Impairment of brand name	½
	Legal provision	1
	Working capital adjustments - 1 each	3
	Interest paid	1
	Income taxes paid	1
		9½
	Cash flows from investing activities	
	Purchase of PPE	2
	Proceeds of sale of PPE	1
	Development expenditure	1½
		4½
	Cash flows from financing activities	
	Proceeds from issue of share capital	1½
	Repayment of borrowings	1
	Dividends paid	1½
		4
	Cash and cash equivalents	½
	Presentation	½
	Total	19
	Cash flows from operating activities	

(b) **Finance lease**
Statement of financial position extracts 2
Statement of profit or loss and other comprehensive income extracts 2
Statement of cash flows extracts 2
6

Total marks for question 25

(a) OP
STATEMENT OF CASH FLOWS FOR THE YEAR ENDED 31 MARCH 20X1

	$'000	$'000
Cash flows from operating activities		
Profit before taxation	1,089	
Finance cost	15	
Depreciation (17 + 25)	42	
Loss on disposal	6	
Amortisation of development expenditure	15	
Impairment of brand name	10	
Legal provision	40	
Operating profit before working capital changes	1,217	
Decrease in inventories (W1)	4	
Increase in receivables (W1)	(70)	
Increase in payables (W1)	55	
Cash generated from operations	1,206	
Interest paid (W6)	(25)	
Income taxes paid (W5)	(280)	
Net cash from operating activities		901
Cash flows from investing activities		
Purchase of property, plant and equipment (W2)	(432)	
Proceeds of sale of property, plant and equipment (11 – 6)	5	
Development expenditure (W3)	(10)	
Net cash used in investing activities		(437)
Cash flows from financing activities		
Dividend paid (W7)	(580)	
Proceeds from issue of equity shares (400 – 200) + (200 -100)	300	
Repayment of long term borrowings (250 – 100)	(150)	
Net cash used in financing activities		(430)
Net increase in cash and cash equivalents		34
Cash and cash equivalents at 1 April 20X0		35
Cash and cash equivalents at 31 March 20X1		69

Workings

1 *Inventories, trade receivables and trade payables*

	Inventories	Trade receivables	Trade payables
	$'000	$'000	$'000
Balance b/d	450	310	95
Increase/(decrease) (balancing figure)	(4)	70	55
Balance c/d	446	380	150

2   *Property, plant and equipment*

Total PPE additions in year: 171 + 230 + 31 = $432,000

Land – cost/valuation	$'000
Balance b/d	320
Additions in year (balancing figure)	<u>171</u>
	491
Downwards valuation	(65)
Bal c/d	<u>426</u>

Buildings - cost	$'000
Balance b/d	610
Additions in year (balancing figure)	<u>230</u>
Bal c/d	<u>840</u>

Plant and equipment - cost	$'000
Balance b/d	180
Additions in year (balancing figure)	<u>31</u>
	211
Disposals	(45)
Bal c/d	<u>166</u>

3   *Development expenditure*

	$'000
Balance b/d	65
Additions during year	<u>10</u>
	75
Amortisation	(15)
Balance c/d	<u>60</u>

4   *Brand name*

	$'000
Balance b/d	<u>40</u>
	40
Impairment	(10)
Balance c/d	<u>30</u>

5   *Income taxes paid*

	$'000
Balance b/d - current	260
Balance b/d - deferred	120
Tax charge per SPLOCI	<u>280</u>
	660
Income taxes paid (balancing figure)	(280)
Balance c/d – current (260) & deferred (120)	<u>380</u>

6   *Interest paid*

	$'000
Balance b/d	20
Finance costs per SPLOCI	<u>15</u>
	35
Interest paid	(25)
Balance c/d	<u>10</u>

7   *Dividend paid*

	$'000
Balance b/d	423
Profit for the year	<u>809</u>
	1,232
Dividend paid	(580)
Balance c/d	<u>652</u>

Alternative layout for workings 2 to 7 using T accounts

LAND – COST/VALUATION

	$'000		$'000
Balance b/d	320	Downwards valuation	65
Additions in year (balance)	171	Balance c/d	426
	491		491

BUILDINGS - COST

	$'000		$'000
Balance b/d	610		
Additions in year (balance)	230	Balance c/d	840
	840		840

PLANT & EQUIPMENT - COST

	$'000		$'000
Balance b/d	180	Disposals	45
Additions in year (balance)	31	Balance c/d	166
	211		211

DEVELOPMENT EXPENDITURE

	$'000		$'000
Balance b/d	65	Amortisation	15
Additions during year	10	Balance c/d	60
	75		75

BRAND NAME

	$'000		$'000
Balance b/d	40	Impairment	10
		Balance c/d	30
	40		40

INCOME TAXES

	$'000		$'000
Income taxes paid	280	Balance b/d current	260
Balance c/d current	250	Balance b/d deferred	120
Balance c/d deferred	130	Tax charge per SPLOCI	280
	660		660

INTEREST PAYABLE

	$'000		$'000
Interest paid	25	Balance b/d	20
Balance c/d	10	Finance cost per SPLOCI	15
	35		35

RETAINED EARNINGS

	$'000		$'000
Dividend paid	580	Balance b/d	423
Balance c/d	652	Profit for year	809
	1,232		1,232

(b)

Financial statement extracts

Statement of financial position $
Non-current assets
Property, plant and equipment
Held under finance lease   248,610
Depreciation (1/10)   (24,861)
                                                                                                           223,749

Non-current liabilities
    Amounts due under finance leases   218,576

Current liabilities
    Amounts due under finance leases (234,443 – 218,576)   15,867

Statement of profit or loss and other comprehensive income
Depreciation charge   24,861
Finance cost   29,833

Statement of cash flows
Cash flows from operating activities
Add back: Depreciation   24,861
Add back: Finance cost   29,833
Interest paid   (29,833)

Cash flows from financing activities
Finance lease payments (44,000 – 29,833)   (14,167)

Working

                                                                                                           $
1.4.X1 Fair value of asset   248,610
Finance charge @ 12%   29,833
Repayment   (44,000)
Balance 31.3.X2   234,443
Finance charge @ 12%   28,133
Repayment   (44,000)
Balance 31.3.X3   218,576

14 YG (11/10)

Text references. Statements of cash flows are covered in Chapter 9. Ethics is covered in Chapter 3.

Top tips. This is question is very time pressured and you will probably have struggled to get all the figures into the statement of cash flows in the time allowed. However remember that you need to leave some time to address part (b) as you can pick up an easy 5 marks there. You must be logical in your approach to answering part (a) – set up the proforma, and insert the numbers that don't require adjustment first. Most of the adjustments (PPE, interest, tax, development) were pretty straightforward if you had practiced a few SOCF questions. The redundancy provision was a bit unusual, but if you keep in mind that you are showing cash movements, it wasn't too tricky to work out the extra amount to include in cash from operating activities.

Easy errors to make were:

*   Getting the signs mixed up on the working capital adjustments
*   Incorrect treatment of the redundancy provision
*   Missing out the dividend paid
*   Not including the revaluation of PPE in the PPE working

Easy marks. The question gave you amortisation, depreciation and cash received on disposal of PPE, you should have inserted these straight into your proforma to get some quick easy marks. Writing sensible comments in part (b) would get you 5 easy marks.

Marking scheme

	Marks	

(a)   **Statement of cash flows**

Cash flows from operating activities

	Marks	
Profit before tax	1	
Finance cost	1	
Depreciation	1	
Loss on disposal	1	
Working capital adjustments - 1 each	3	
Interest paid	1	
Income taxes paid	1	
		9

Cash flows from investing activities

Purchase of PPE	2	
Proceeds of sale of PPE	1	
Development expenditure	2	
		5

Cash flows from financing activities

Proceeds from issue of share capital	1½	
Repayment of borrowings	1	
Dividends paid	1½	4

Cash and cash equivalents		1
Presentation		1
Total		20

Cash flows from operating activities

(b)   ½ mark per valid point for each strategy, up to a maximum of   5

Total marks for question   25

(a)   YG STATEMENT OF CASH FLOWS FOR THE YEAR ENDED 31 OCTOBER 20X9

	$'000	$'000
Cash flows from operating activities		
Profit before taxation	266	
Finance cost	16	
Depreciation	250	
Loss on disposal of PPE (66 - 70)	4	
Amortisation of capitalised development expenditure	145	
Decrease in redundancy provision	(150)	
Operating profit before working capital changes	531	
Increase in inventory (W1)	(97)	
Increase in receivables (W1)	(84)	
Increase in payables (W1)	115	
Cash generated from operations	465	
Interest paid (W2)	(14)	
Income taxes paid (W3)	(180)	
Net cash from operating activities		271
Cash flows from investing activities		
Purchase of property, plant and equipment (W4)	(448)	
Proceeds of sale of property, plant and equipment	66	
Development expenditure (W5)	(68)	
Net cash used in investing activities		(450)

	$'000	$'000
Cash flows from financing activities		
Dividend paid (W6)	(82)	
Repayment of long term borrowings (715 – 360)	(355)	
Proceeds from issue of shares (1,600 + 800)	2,400	
Net cash from financing activities		1,963
Net increase in cash and cash equivalents (1,989 – 205)		1,784
Cash and cash equivalents at 31 October 20X8		205
Cash and cash equivalents at 31 October 20X9		1,989

Workings

1 *Inventories, trade receivables and trade payables*

	Inventories $'000	Trade receivables $'000	Trade payables $'000
Balance b/d	509	372	310
Increase (balancing figure)	97	84	115
Balance c/d	606	456	425

2 *Interest paid*

	$'000
Balance b/d	3
Finance costs per SPLOCI	16
	19
Interest paid	(14)
Balance c/d	5

3 *Income tax payable*

	$'000
Balance b/d - current	170
Balance b/d - deferred	170
Tax charge per SPLOCI	120
	460
Income taxes paid (balancing figure)	(180)
Balance c/d – current (70) & deferred (210)	280

4 *Property, plant and equipment*

	$'000
Balance b/d	4,248
Revaluation	300
Additions (balancing figure)	448
	4,996
Depreciation	(250)
Disposal	(70)
Balance c/d	4,676

5 *Development expenditure*

	$'000
Balance b/d	494
Cash paid (balancing figure)	68
	562
Amortisation	(145)
Bal c/d	417

6 *Dividend paid*

	$'000
Balance b/d	1,250
Profit for the year	146
	1,396
Dividend paid	(82)
Balance c/d	1,314

Alternative layout for workings 2 to 6 using T accounts

INTEREST PAYABLE

	$'000		$'000
Interest paid	14	Balance b/d	3
Balance c/d	5	Finance cost per SPLOCI	16
	19		19

INCOME TAXES

	$'000		$'000
Income taxes paid (bal fig)	180	Balance b/d current tax	170
		Balance b/d deferred tax	170
Balance c/d current tax	70		
Balance c/d deferred tax	210	Tax charge per SPOCI	120
	460		460

PROPERTY, PLANT AND EQUIPMENT

	$'000		$'000
Balance b/d	4,248	Depreciation	250
Revaluation	300	Disposal	70
Additions (balancing figure)	448	Balance c/d	4,676
	4,996		4,996

DEVELOPMENT EXPENDITURE

	$'000		$'000
Balance b/d	494	Amortisation	145
Cash paid (balancing figure)	68	Balance c/d	417
	562		562

RETAINED EARNINGS

	$'000		$'000
Dividend paid	82	Balance b/d	1,250
Balance c/d	1,314	Profit for year	146
	1,396		1,396

(b)   *Ethical issues*

I should not accept the dinner invitation as this may cause me issues with **objectivity** as I will feel pressure to reveal information that I should not disclose about the proposed takeover.

Revealing information about the proposed takeover before it is made public would be unethical. It would give my friend 'insider information' about the proposed takeover, which he could then use to his advantage to make money on buying or selling shares in either entity, which is illegal.

Giving this information to my friend would breach the fundamental principle of **confidentiality** in the CIMA Code of Ethics. The information I have obtained in my role as a professional accountant at YG should not be shared with third parties unless there is a legal or professional right or duty to disclose, there is neither in this case. The information I have obtained should also not be used for the personal advantage of myself or third parties, there is a risk it might be in this case.

If my friend used this 'insider information' to make a personal gain, which is illegal, this would breach the fundamental principle of **professional behaviour** in the CIMA Code of Ethics which requires that a professional accountant should comply with the law.

15 Objective test answers: Non-current assets, inventories and construction contracts I

1   C $780 + 117 + 30 + 28 + 100 = 1,055$

2   D   They are all correct

3   D   Neither internally generated goodwill nor internally developed brands can be capitalised.

4   A   Goodwill on acquisition is retained in the statement of financial position and reviewed annually for impairment.

5   A   Carriage outwards is charged to distribution, abnormal costs are not included in inventory.

6   D   1   Production overheads should be included in cost on the basis of a company's normal level of activity.

              2   Trade discounts should be deducted but not settlement discounts.

              3   IAS 2 does not allow the use of LIFO.

7   C

	$
Contract revenue recognised (900 × 60%)	540,000
Costs	(840,000)
Expected loss (900 – 1,200)	(300,000)
Costs incurred	720,000
Recognised loss	(300,000)
Progress billings	(400,000)
Due from customer	20,000

8   C   Recoverable amount is the higher of value in use and net realisable value.

9   Revenue = $40m × 45% = $18m
        Profit   = $6m × 45% = $2.7m

	$m
Contract price	40
Total costs (16 + 18)	(34)
Anticipated profit	6

10

	$
Carrying value (100,000 × 0.75^4)	31,640
Recoverable amount	28,000
Impairment loss	3,640

11   The contract is 70% complete. Revenue earned = $90m × 70% = $63m.

12   CN should recognise a loss of $20m (90m – 77m – 33m).

13   D   An allocation of EW's administration costs would not be included as these do not relate specifically to the non-current asset.

16 Objective test answers: Non current-assets, inventories and construction contracts II

1   C

	$
Original purchase price	50,000
Depreciation 20X1: (50,000 – 5,000)/5	(9,000)
Depreciation 20X2	(9,000)
Upgrade	15,000
	47,000
Depreciation 20X3: (47,000 – 5,000)/5	(8,400)
Carrying amount 1 January 20X4	38,600
Disposal proceeds	(7,000)
Loss on disposal	31,600

2   B   The impairment loss is applied first against the goodwill and then against the other non-current assets on a pro-rata basis. It will be allocated as follows:

	$m
Building	10
Plant and equipment	5
Goodwill	5
	20

The carrying amount of the building will then become $10m (20 – 10)

3   A fall in the value of an asset, so that its recoverable amount is now less than its carrying amount in the statement of financial position.

4   B   Low production or idle plant does *not* lead to a higher fixed overhead allocation to each unit.

5   The amount for which an asset could be exchanged between knowledgeable, willing parties in an arm's length transaction.

6   The publishing rights cannot be recognised as they have no reliable monetary value as they were a gift and had no cost. The expected future value cannot be recognised as an asset as the event has not yet occurred.

7   Value of goodwill = $130,000

	$'000	$'000
Fair value of consideration – shares (10,000 × $20)		200,000
Cash		20,000
		220,000
Fair value of net assets acquired:		
Tangible non-current assets	25,000	
Patents	15,000	
Brand name	50,000	
		(90,000)
Goodwill		130,000

8

Year ended:	Cost/valuation	Depreciation	Acc depreciation	Carrying Amount
March 20X2	100,000	10,000	10,000	90,000
March 20X3	100,000	10,000	20,000	80,000
March 20X4	95,000	–	(20,000)	95,000
March 20X4	95,000	11,875 (95,000/8)	11,875	83,125
March 20X5	**95,000**	**16,625** (83,125/5)	**28,500**	**66,500**

9   Depreciable amount is asset cost or valuation less residual value.

10   A   This is replacement of a significant part of the asset. The carrying amount of the existing furnace lining must be derecognised. B, C and D refer to repairs and maintenance.

11   Carrying amount of machine at 30 September 20X5 = 10,500

Remaining useful life = 2 years

Depreciation for year ended 30 September 20X6 (10,500/2) = 5,250

12   This question appears to refer to the criteria for recognising development expenditure, which are:

1   Technical feasibility of completing the intangible asset
2   Intention to complete and use or sell the asset
3   Ability to use or sell the asset
4   The asset will generate future economic benefits
5   Adequate resources exist to complete the project
6   Expenditure on the asset can be reliably measured

The answer only requires four of these.

13

	$'000
Total contract value	3,000
Total costs (1,500 + 250 + 400)	(2,150)
Expected total profit	850

Percentage completed = 1,500/2,150 % = 70%

Statement of profit or loss and other comprehensive income amounts:

	$'000
Revenue (3,000 × 70%)	2,100
Costs	(1,500)
Profit	600

17   Section B answers: Non-current assets, inventories and construction contracts

(a)   (i)   **Research costs**

IAS 38 does not allow the capitalisation of research costs.

Development costs

IAS 38 lays down strict **criteria** to determine when carry forward of development costs is permissible.

* The expenditure attributable to the intangible asset during its development must be measurable.

* The technical feasibility of completing the product or process so that it will be available for sale or use can be demonstrated.

* The entity intends to complete the intangible asset and use or sell it.

* It must be able to use or sell the intangible asset.

* There must be a market for the output of the intangible asset or, if it is to be used internally rather than sold, its usefulness to the entity, can be demonstrated.

* Adequate technical, financial and other resources must exist, or their availability must be demonstrated, to complete the development and use or sell the intangible asset.

(ii)   IAS 1 has three basic accounting assumptions: going concern, accruals and consistency.

Each of these concepts is relevant in considering the criteria discussed above for carrying forward development expenditure.

Going concern. The business must be in a position to continue its operations at least to the extent of generating resources sufficient to complete the development project and therefore to market the end product.

Accruals. The purpose of deferring development expenditure at all is to comply with the accruals concept by matching such expenditure with the income expected to arise from it.

Consistency. IAS 38 states that the criteria for deferral of expenditure should be consistently applied.

(b) The general principle underlying IAS 2 is that inventories should be shown in financial statements at the **lower of cost and net realisable value**. This principle accords with both the matching concept, which requires costs to be matched with the relevant revenues, and the prudence concept, which requires that profits are not anticipated and any probable losses are provided for.

The **cost** of an item of manufactured inventory can include both external and internal costs and it is important that only correctly attributable costs are included. These are direct acquisition costs, direct inventory holding costs and production overheads based on a **normal** level of activity. General overheads are excluded.

Production overheads are usually incurred on a time basis and not in relation to the quantities of inventory produced. Most businesses, however, are assumed to continue to exist in the medium term and production overheads are part of the inevitable cost of providing production facilities in the medium term. Thus, so long as the scale of the overheads is not distorted by unusual levels of activity, it is reasonable to include them in the 'cost' of inventory produced in the period to which they relate. Identifying a 'normal' level of activity is more difficult where business is seasonal.

The establishment of NRV also poses a number of practical problems. For many intermediate products, and even for finished items, there may be a limited market and the inventory volumes may represent a significant proportion of the market especially if disposed of under distress conditions. Where a well-developed and liquid market does not exist, it is usually appropriate to base NRV on an orderly disposal after allowing for the reasonable additional costs of marketing and distribution.

(c)

MEMO

To: Transport manager
From: Trainee management accountant
Subject: Useful life

IAS 16 *Property, plant and equipment* requires that the useful lives of non-current assets should be regularly reviewed and changed if appropriate.

By 31 March 20X2 the delivery vehicle will have been depreciated for two years out of the original estimate of its useful life of four years:

	$
Cost	20,000
Depreciation ($20,000 × $^2/_4$)	(10,000)
Carrying amount at 31 March 20X2	10,000

The carrying amount at the start of the year ending 31 March 20X3 should now be written off over the remaining, revised useful life of four years giving an annual depreciation charge of $2,500 ($10,000/4).

In the statement of profit or loss and other comprehensive income for the year ended 31 March 20X3 therefore the depreciation charge will be $2,500. In the statement of financial position the delivery vehicle will appear at its carrying amount of $7,500 ($10,000 – 2,500).

(d)

> **Examiner's comments**. Most candidates made a better attempt at the buildings part of the question then the brand name. Some candidates did not depreciate the buildings for enough years before revaluating. Despite the question saying that the brand name had been acquired for $500,000, many candidates treated it as internally generated.

Building

The building has previously been revalued upwards and the gain on revaluation taken to the revaluation surplus). Therefore IAS 36 *Impairment of assets* states that the impairment loss of $200,000 ($1.7m – 1.5m) should be charged against the previous revaluation surplus of $900,000 leaving a revaluation surplus of $700,000 and a carrying amount for the building of $1,500,000. The building is reported under property, plant and equipment.

Revaluation surplus at 30 Sept 20X4 = $1.8m – ($1.0 – ($1.0 × 2/20))
= $900,000

Carrying amount of building at 30 Sept 20X5 = $1.8m – ($1.8m/18)
= $1.7m

Market value at 30 Sept 20X5 = $1.5m

Brand name

IAS 36 requires the brand to be written down to its recoverable amount, which is the higher of its fair value less costs to sell and value in use. Therefore the recoverable amount is the market value of $200,000 as this is higher than its value in use of $150,000.

The impairment loss of $50,000 (250,000 – 200,000) is recognised immediately in the statement of profit or loss and other comprehensive income. The brand is measured at $200,000 in the statement of financial position and reported as an intangible asset.

Carrying amount = $500,000 – ($500,000 × 5/10)
= $250,000

Recoverable amount = higher of fair value and value in use
= $200,000

Impairment = $50,000 ($250,000 – 200,000) charged to the statement of profit of loss and other comprehensive income

Brand in statement of financial position = $200,000

(e)

> **Examiner's comments**. The most common error made by those who understood the concept of revaluing non-current assets was to miscount the number of years' depreciation, either using 4 or 6 years before the first revaluation in 2007.

Building A

	$
Cost	200,000
Depreciation to 31.8.01 (200,000/20 × 5)	(50,000)
Carrying amount	150,000
Revaluation 31.8.01 to revaluation surplus	30,000
Carrying amount	180,000
Depreciation to 31.8.06 (180,000/15 × 5)	(60,000)
	120,000
Valuation 31.8.06 – impairment loss	(20,000)
Carrying amount	100,000

Building A has suffered an impairment loss of $20,000 at 31 August 2006 which can be debited to revaluation surplus reversing the previous revaluation gain.

Building B

	$
Cost	120,000
Depreciation to 31.8.01 (120,000/15 × 5)	(40,000)
Carrying amount	80,000
Valuation 31.8.01 – impairment loss	(5,000)
Carrying amount	75,000
Depreciation to 31.8.06 (75,000/10 × 5)	(37,500)
	37,500
Valuation 31.8.06 – impairment loss	(7,500)
Carrying amount	30,000

Building B has suffered impairment losses totalling $7,500 at 31 August 2006, which will be charged to the statement of profit or loss and other comprehensive income.

(f)

> **Examiner's comments.** This question caused problems for some candidates who ignored the details given and calculated the percentage complete using costs instead of using the value of work completed as specified in the question. Other common errors were not identifying clearly what each result represented and not identifying the amount due on the contract as an asset or a liability.

HS Construction contract

	$'000
Total revenue	300
Total costs to complete (170 + 100)	(270)
Total profit	30

State of completion of contract = 165/300 × 100% = 55%

<u>Amounts recognised in the statement of profit or loss and other comprehensive income for the year ended 31 March 20X9</u>

	$'000
Revenue (value of work completed)	165.0
Profit (30 × 55%)	16.5

<u>Amounts recognised in the statement of financial position at 31 March 20X9</u>

	$'000
Costs incurred	170.0
Profit recognised	16.5
	186.5
Less progress billings	(130.0)
Amount recognised as an asset/(liability)	56.5

Recognise an asset in statement of financial position under current assets:

Gross amount due from customer	$56,500

(g)

> **Examiner's comments.** This question was very badly answered. Those candidates that did identify the correct IAS and the correct accounting treatment often omitted to explain why the items should be treated that way, as a consequence only partial marks could be awarded.

In order to decide how to treat these items of expenditure in its financial statements, EK must decide whether the expenditure gives rise to an asset or intangible asset which can be recognised in the statement of financial position. Asset recognition criteria are dealt with in the IASB's *Conceptual Framework*. Intangible assets are covered by IAS 38 *Intangible assets*.

The IASB's *Conceptual Framework* defines an asset as **a resource controlled by an entity as a result of past events** and from which **further economic benefits are expected to flow** to the entity.

Both assets and intangible assets can only be recognised if both the following apply.

- It is probable that future economic benefits will flow to the entity.
- The cost of the asset can be measured reliably.

(i) *Book publishing and film rights*

These rights give access to future economic benefits and could even be resold, so the $1m cost can be recognised as an intangible asset. No amortisation is necessary until the book is actually published.

(ii) *Trade fair*

Since no new orders were taken as a direct result of the event and no estimate can be made of additional revenue, the cost of the trade fair cannot be recognised as an asset. Future economic benefits may not be probable. The cost of the trade fair does not meet the

recognition criteria for an asset and should therefore be treated as an expense in the year incurred.

(iii)   *Consultant*

Although the cost of the consultancy itself is known, it is virtually impossible to quantify any change in the value of the image of EK. Since the cost of the corporate image cannot be measured reliably, the consultancy fees should not be recognised as an asset and should be expensed in the year incurred.

18 Geneva

Top tips. Begin by working out for each contract whether a profit or a loss is forecast. If it is a profit, calculate how much can be recognised. If it is a loss, it is all recognised immediately.

Easy marks. Note that all of these contacts started in the current year – so any attributable profit to date belongs to the current year. This makes the calculations easier.

Treatment of construction contracts in the statement of financial position

	$'000
Contract Lausanne	
Asset (1,000 + 240 – 1,080)	
Gross amount due from customers for contract work	160
Contract Bern	
Liability (1,100 – 200 – 950)	
Gross amount due to customers for contract work	50
Contract Zurich	
Liability (640 + 70 – 800)	
Gross amount due to customers for contract work	90

Treatment of construction contracts in the statement of profit or loss and other comprehensive income

	Lausanne	Bern	Zurich
	$'000	$'000	$'000
Revenue	1,200	1,000	700
Cost of sales	960	1,200	630
Gross profit/(loss)	240	(200)	70

19 Objective test answers: Capital transactions and financial instruments

1	C	The premium is transferred from share capital to share premium
2	C	$500,000 + $11,000 (990,000 × 50c + 10,000 × $1.60)

Note that the forfeited shares each brought in a total of $2.60

3	D	Share capital $500,000 + $250,000 + $300,000 + $350,000 = $1,400,000
		Share premium $800,000 – $250,000 + $900,000 + $910,000 = $2,360,000

4   D   If a shareholder fails to pay a call his shares are forfeited and the company is not obliged to return his money.

5   C   Cumulative and redeemable preference shares are classified as financial liabilities under IAS 32.

6   B   As a deduction from equity.

7    $3.8m

	$m
Receipt from issue ($10m - $0.5m)	9.5
Dividend payable over 4 years ($10m × 7% × 4)	(2.8)
Payable on redemption ($10m + 5%)	(10.5)
Total finance charge	(3.8)

8    $10.025m

	$m
Receipt from issue	9.5
Finance charge 10%	0.95
Dividend paid	(0.7)
Balance at 31 December 20X8	9.75
Finance charge 10%	0.975
Dividend paid	(0.7)
Balance at 31 December 20X9	10.025

9   B   Treasury shares are an entity's own shares which it has repurchased and holds in 'treasury'. Treasury shares can be re-issued or issued as part of employee share schemes in the future.

10   B

	$
Ordinary shares at start of year	50,000
Add: bonus issue 50,000 × 50c	25,000
Add: new issue 60,000 × 50c	30,000
	105,000
Share premium at start of year	180,000
Less: bonus issue 50,000 × 50c	(25,000)
Add: new issue 60,000 × 30c	18,000
	173,000

11   $248,800

Share premium

		$
Opening balance		100,000
Rights issue	250,000 × 75c	187,500
Share issue costs		(1,200)
Bonus issue	150,000 × 25c	(37,500)
		248,800

20 Objective test answers: Accounting standards I

1   A $^3/_{10}$ × $3,000

2   D $^2/_6$ × $3,000

3   A   (1) describes an adjusting event which should be adjusted for in the financial statements.

4   C $1,800,000 – $116,000 – $20,000 = $1,664,000

5   B   Discovery of fraud, error or impairment, which will have existed at the end of the reporting period.

6   D   These have all occurred after the reporting period.

7   C   1   Contingent liability that is possible, therefore disclose.
          2   Contingent liability but remote, therefore no disclosure.
          3   Non-adjusting event after the reporting period, material therefore disclose.

8   B   IAS 37 excludes retraining and relocation of continuing staff from restructuring provisions.

9   A   All three criteria must be present.

10   D   This does not affect the position as at the year end.

11   D   The dividend will not be shown in the statement of profit or loss and other comprehensive income or appear as a liability in the statement of financial position.

12	1	An entity has a present obligation as a result of a past event.
	2	It is probable that an outflow of resources embodying economic benefits will be required to settle the obligation.
	3	A reliable estimate can be made of the amount of the obligation.
13	C	
14		An **operating segment** is a component of an entity:
	(a)	that engages in business activities from which it may earn revenues and incur expenses
	(b)	whose operating results are regularly reviewed by the entity's chief operating decision maker to make decisions about resources to be allocated to the segment and assess its performance, and
	(c)	for which discrete financial information is available
15	B	Revenue must be 10% or more of the total revenue of all segments.
16	B	This does not affect the position as at the year end.
17	D	

21 Objective test answers: Accounting standards II

1	C	Item 1 is not correct – if it is probable and the amount can be estimated reliably, then it must be provided for.
2	C	Customers, suppliers and providers of finance are not related parties.
3	C	In a finance lease, the risks and rewards of ownership are transferred.

4   A

	$
Deposit	30,000
Instalments (8 × $20,000)	160,000
	190,000
Fair value	154,000
Interest	36,000

$$\text{Sum-of-the-digits} = \frac{8 \times 9}{2} = 36$$

6 months to	June X1	$^{8}/_{36} \times \$36,000$		
	Dec X1	$^{7}/_{36} \times \$36,000$		
	June X2	$^{6}/_{36} \times \$36,000$		
	Dec X2	$^{5}/_{36} \times \$36,000$		
	June X3	$^{4}/_{36} \times \$36,000$	=	$4,000
	Dec X3	$^{3}/_{36} \times \$36,000$	=	$3,000
				$7,000

5	D	The fire is non-adjusting as it does not clarify the 31 December value of the building. It is therefore only disclosed if it threatens the company's going concern status.
		Again the customer is assumed to be insolvent at 31 December. We simply did not know this and therefore it is an adjusting event and it should be adjusted for.
		The answer would be B if the customer had become insolvent after the year end.
6	C	1 As the board decision had not been communicated to customers and employees there is assumed to be no legal or constructive obligation therefore no provision should be made.
		2 As refunds have been made in the past to all customers there is a valid expectation from customers that the refunds will be made therefore the amount should be provided for.
		3 There is no present obligation to carry out the refurbishment therefore no provision should be made under IAS 37.
7	B	Members of the close family of any key management of an entity are presumed to be related parties.

8   An entity has a present obligation (legal or constructive) as a result of a past event.

It is probable that an outflow of resources embodying economic benefits will be required to settle the obligation.

A reliable estimate can be made of the amount of the obligation.

9   C   A provision should be made for the claim against AP.

10   B   Customers, suppliers and bankers are not normally related parties.

11   Finance cost = $2,160

		$
Total finance cost		
Total payments 12,000 × 5		60,000
Fair value		51,900
Finance cost		8,100

Payments being made over five year period:

To 30 Sept 20X4   5/15 × 8,100
To 30 Sept 20X5   4/15 × 8,100 $2,160

12   C   BW must provide for customer refunds.

13   Any four of the following:

- the seller has transferred to the buyer the significant risks and rewards of ownership

- the seller retains neither continuing managerial involvement to the degree usually associated with ownership nor effective control over the goods sold

- the amount of revenue can be measured reliably

- it is probable that the economic benefits associated with the transaction will flow to the seller

- the costs incurred or to be incurred in respect of the transaction can be measured reliably

14

	$
Cost 1.1.X4	80,000
Interest 7.93%	6,344
Instalment	(20,000)
Balance 31.12.X4	66,344
Interest 7.93%	5,261
Instalment	(20,000)
Balance 31.12.X5	51,605
Interest 7.93%	4,092
Instalment	(20,000)
Balance 31.12.X6	35,697
Current liability (51,605 – 35,697) =	15,908
Non-current liability	35,697
Total balance at 31.12.X5	51,605

15

	$
Original cost	80,000
Depreciation 2004/2005 (80,000/12,000 × (2,600 + 2,350))	(33,000)
Carrying amount	47,000

16   D   No sale has taken place, so DT must show that it is holding $90,000 which belongs to XX.

17   D   Fair value less costs to sell ($740,000 - $10,000) is lower than carrying value ($750,000).

Note that non-current assets held for sale are not depreciated.

18   B   Non-current assets held for sale are shown separately under the 'current assets' heading.

19   C   Share transactions after the reporting period do not require adjustment.

20   A   Large customers are *not necessarily* related parties of the entity.

21   Operating lease – spread the rent-free period over the term of the lease

Total rent payable = 4 × $12,000 = $48,000

Over five years = $48,000/5 = $9,600 per annum

$9,600 charged to profit or loss in each of 30 April 20X8 and 30 April 20X9.

22   Section B answers: Accounting standards I

(a)   Asset

IAS 17 is an example of economic substance triumphing over legal form. In legal terms, with a finance lease, the lessor may be the owner of the asset, but the lessee enjoys all the **risks and rewards** which ownership of the asset would convey. This is the key element to IAS 17. The lessee is deemed to have an asset as they must maintain and run the asset through its useful life.

Liability

The lessee enjoys the future economic benefits of the asset as a result of entering into the lease. There is a corresponding liability which is the obligation to pay the instalments on the lease until it expires. Assets and liabilities cannot be netted off. If finance leases were treated in a similar manner to the existing treatment of operating leases then no asset would be recognised and lease payments would be expensed through the statement of comprehensive income as they were incurred. This is '**off balance sheet finance**'. The company has assets in use and liabilities to lessors which are not recorded in the financial statements. This would be misleading to the user of the accounts and make it appear as though the assets which were recorded were more efficient in producing returns than was actually the case.

(b)   **MEMO**

To: Production manager
From: Trainee management accountant
Subject: De-commissioning costs

Provision

The accounting question regarding the de-commissioning costs is whether or not a provision should now be set up in the accounts for the eventual costs. According to IAS 37 any future obligations arising out of past events should be recognised immediately. The de-commissioning costs are a future obligation and the past event is the granting of the licence and the drilling of the site.

Therefore a provision should be recognised immediately in the financial statements for the year ended 31 March 20X3. This will be $20million discounted to present value.

Discounting

As this cost gives access to future economic benefits in terms of oil reserves for the next 20 years then the discounted present value of the de-commissioning costs can be capitalised and treated as part of the cost of the oil well in the statement of financial position. However this total cost, including the discounted de-commissioning costs should be reviewed to ensure that the carrying amount does not exceed the recoverable amount. If there is no impairment then the total cost of the oil well and discounted de-commissioning costs should be depreciated for the next 20 years and a charge made to the statement of profit or loss and other comprehensive income.

(c)   Because the airline operation was sold before the year end and was a distinguishable component of the entity it is a **discontinued operation** as defined by IFRS 5 *Non-current assets held for sale and discontinued operations.* A separate line in the statement of profit or loss and other comprehensive income for discontinued operations should be included after the profit after tax for continuing operations. IFRS 5 states that this should be made up of the post-tax profit or loss of the discontinued operation and the post-tax gain or loss on disposal of the airline assets. The loss on sale of the fleet of aircraft of $250m and the provision for severance payments of $20m will both be reported in this line.

	$m
Discontinued operations	(270)

IFRS 5 also requires an **analysis** of the amount into:

(i)   the revenue, expenses and pre-tax profit of discontinued operations (to include the loss made by the airline for the year and the provision for the $20m severance payments); and

(ii)   the gain or loss recognised on the disposal of the assets (the $250m loss on the sale of the fleet of aircraft).

This can be presented either on the face of the statement of profit or loss and other comprehensive income or in the notes.

The **cash flows** attributable to the operating, investing and financing activities of the airline should also be disclosed, either in the notes to the financial statements or in the statement of cash flows itself.

As the restructuring has been agreed and active steps have been taken to implement it a **provision** is required for $10m (because the entity has a constructive obligation to carry out the plan). This will be reported as part of the continuing activities, probably as part of administrative expenses.

(d)

> **Examiner's comments.** Most candidates correctly identified that the customer was not a related party. Most candidates correctly identified that George was a related party but did not give sufficient explanation.
>
> Some candidates correctly identified the provider of finance as not being a related party, but did not go on to identify that Arnold was a related party.

XC

XC is not a related party of CB. The discount represents no more than a normal commercial arrangement with a favoured customer.

Property

George is one of the key management personnel of the company and thus a related party, and the sale of the property to him at a discount of $250,000 must be disclosed in the financial statements.

FC

As a provider of finance, FC is not itself a related party. However, Arnold is close family of George and therefore a related party to CB, and the loan does not appear to have been advanced at normal commercial terms. The loan and the involvement of Arnold will need to be disclosed.

(e)

> **Examiner's comments.** Few candidates did well on this question. Most candidates failed to include all three elements of the finance cost in the total cost. Some candidates used the straight line or sum of digits method to allocate the finance cost instead of the actuarial method, despite the discount rate of 10% being given.

(i)

	$
Receipt (2,000,000 – 192,800)	1,807,200
Costs:	
Dividends (100,000 × 5)	500,000
Redemption	2,300,000
	(2,800,000)
Finance cost	(992,800)

(ii)

	Balance	Interest 10%	Dividend	Balance
20X6	1,807,200	180,720	(100,000)	1,887,920
20X7	1,887,920	188,792	(100,000)	1,976,712
20X8	1,976,712	197,671	(100,000)	2,074,383
20X9	2,074,383	207,438	(100,000)	2,181,821
20Y0	2,181,821	218,179	(100,000)	2,300,000

The balance at 31 March 20Y0 is $2,300,000, which is the amount needed to redeem the shares.

(f)

Fraud

The discovery of the fraud in April 20X6 would be an adjusting event after the reporting period if it had occurred before the financial statements were authorised for issue. If the accounts were approved on 1 March, they would probably have been issued by April. So it is unlikely that this can be accounted for in the September 20X5 financial statements.

In the September 20X6 financial statements the overstatement of profit for the year ended 30 September 20X5 must be accounted for as a prior year adjustment. This will be shown in the Statement of Changes in Equity. The profit for the year ended 30 September will be reduced to $555,000. This will affect the retained earnings for the current year but not the current year profit.

Payment from new customer

The payment received in advance in September 20X6 cannot be treated as income because DF has not yet done anything to earn that income. It should be posted to current liabilities as 'deferred income' and released to the statement of profit or loss and other comprehensive income when the goods are despatched.

(g)

The factory will be treated as a *discontinued operation* under IFRS 5 at 31 March 20X7, as all operations have ceased and sale of the land and buildings is 'highly probable'.

In the statement of profit or loss and other comprehensive income **one figure** will be shown under *discontinued operations*, being the trading loss for the period from the discontinued operation (we are not told what this is), plus the loss on disposal of the plant and equipment ($70,000), plus the closure costs ($620,000), less any tax allowances. This single figure should then be analysed in the notes.

In the statement of financial position, the carrying amount of the land and buildings ($750,000) should be moved out of non-current assets and shown under current assets as 'non-current assets held for sale'. The fair value less costs to sell would be higher, so the property is left at its carrying amount. It is not depreciated.

(h)   (i)

EK can treat the sale of its retailing division as a discontinued operation under IFRS 5 for the following reasons:

- It is classified as held for sale.
- It represents a separate major line of business, with clearly distinguishable cash flows.

The retailing division can be classified as 'held for sale' because it is available for immediate sale, the company expects to dispose of it within one year and negotiations are already proceeding with a buyer.

(ii)   Statement of profit or loss and other comprehensive income

EK should disclose a single amount on the face of the statement of profit or loss and other comprehensive income comprising:

(a)   The post-tax profit or loss of the retailing division up to 31 October 20X7; and

(b)   The post tax gain or loss on measurement to fair value less costs to sell. A disposal group held for sale should be measured at the lower of its carrying amount and fair value less costs to sell. For EK this is the lower of $443,000 and $398,000 ($423,000 – $25,000). The impairment loss of $45,000 should be recognised.

Statement of financial position

The assets of the retailing division should be removed from non-current assets and shown at their fair value under current assets, classified as 'non-current assets held for sale'. The impairment should all be deducted from the goodwill balance.

23   Section B answers: Accounting standards II

(a)   IAS 37 defines a provision as a liability of uncertain timing or amount. It goes on further to state that a provision should only be recognised when:

(a)   There is a present obligation, either legal or constructive, arising as a result of a past event.

(b)   It is probable that an outflow of resources embodying economic benefits will be required in order to settle the obligation.

(c)   A reliable estimate of the amount of the obligation can be made.

This can be compared to the IASB's definition of a liability in its *Conceptual Framework for Financial Reporting*:

A liability is a present obligation of the entity arising from past events, the settlement of which is expected to result in an outflow of resources from the entity.

The key elements from the liability definition are all encompassed in the rules for recognising a provision.

(a)   **Obligation**. A liability is a present obligation and a provision is only recognised if there is an obligation. This obligation can either be a legal or a constructive obligation. A constructive obligation arises out of past practice or as a result of actions which have previously taken place which have created an expectation that the organisation will act in such a way.

(b)   **Past event.** A provision must arise out of a past event so the event must already have happened at the balance sheet date. If the event has not yet occurred then there is no provision as the entity may be able to avoid it.

(c)   **Outflow of resources.** A provision will only be recognised if it is probably that there will be an outflow of resources to settle the obligation which ties in with the IASB's definition of a liability.

(b)   STATEMENT OF PROFIT OR LOSS AND OTHER COMPREHENSIVE INCOME (EXTRACTS)

	Year 1 $'000	Year 2 $'000
Finance charge (W1)	5,567	4,453
Depreciation charge (W3)	17,660	17,660

STATEMENT OF FINANCIAL POSITION (EXTRACTS)

	Year 1 $'000	Year 2 $'000
Non– current assets		
Property, plant and equipment (W3)	70,640	52,980
Non-current liabilities		
Amounts due under leases (W2)	56,320	38,660
Current liabilities		
Amounts due under leases		
(72,867 – 56,320) (W2)	16,547	
(56,320 – 38,660) (W2)		17,660

Workings

1   *Finance charge*

		$'000
Total lease payments (5 × $21,000)		105,000
Fair value of asset		(88,300)
Total finance charge		16,700

Finance charge allocation

		$
Year 1	5/15 × 16,700	5,567
Year 2	4/15 × 16,700	4,453
Year 3	3/15 × 16,700	3,340
Year 4	2/15 × 16,700	2,227
Year 5	1/15 × 16,700	1,113
		16,700

2   *Lease liabilities*

	$
Fair trade value	88,300
Finance charge	5,567
Repayment	(21,000)
Balance end year one	72,867
Finance charge	4,453
Repayment	(21,000)
Balance end year two	56,320
Finance charge	3,340
Repayment	(21,000)
Balance end year three	38,660

3   *Non-current assets*

Annual depreciation charge $= \dfrac{\$88,300}{5} = \$17,660$

	$
Year 1	
Cost	88,300
Depreciation	(17,660)
Carrying amount	70,640
Year 2	
Depreciation	(17,660)
Carrying amount	52,980

(c)

> **Examiner's comments**. Few candidate were able to produce a correct answer. Errors included:
> - Not calculating overall profitability of the contract
> - Ignoring the work in progress inventory

STATEMENT OF PROFIT OR LOSS AND OTHER COMPREHENSIVE INCOME

	$'000
Sales revenue (W)	30,000
Cost of sales (balancing figure)	21,500
Recognised profit (W)	8,500

STATEMENT OF FINANCIAL POSITION	$,000
Total costs to date	24,000
Recognised profit	8,500
Progress billings	(25,000)
Gross amount due from customer	7,500

Working

Revenue	60,000
Costs to date	(24,000)
Costs to completion	(19,000)
Total expected profit	17,000
Profit to date: 17,000 × 50%	8,500
Revenue to date: 60,000 × 50%	30,000

(d)

> **Examiner's comments.** Most candidates were able to calculate the finance cost and the outstanding balances at each year end, but many were unable to produce correct statement of profit or loss and other comprehensive income and statement of financial position extracts.
>
> Common errors included:
> - Basing the calculation on 4 years instead of 5
> - Applying the digit weightings in reverse order
> - Applying the sum of the digits to the annual repayment instead of the finance charge

(i)   The amount of finance cost charged to the statement of profit of loss and other comprehensive income for the year ended 31 March 20X5 is $9,067.

Working

	$
Total lease payments	150,000
Fair value of asset	116,000
Finance charge	34,000

Using sum of the digits:

31.3.X4	34,000 × 5/15 =	11,333
31.3.X5	34,000 × 4/15 =	9,067
31.3.X6	34,000 × 3/15 =	6,800
31.3.X7	34,000 × 2/15 =	4,533
31.3.X8	34,000 × 1/15 =	2,267
		34,000

(ii)   *Statement of financial position extracts*

	$
Property, plant and equipment	
Held under finance lease	116,000
Depreciation (2/5)	46,400
	69,600
Non-current liabilities	
Amounts due under finance leases	53,200
Current liabilities	
Amounts due under finance leases (76,400 – 53,200)	23,200

Working

	$
1.4.X3 Fair value of asset	116,000
Finance charge	11,333
Repayment	(30,000)
Balance 31.3.X4	97,333
Finance charge	9,067
Repayment	(30,000)
Balance 31.3.X5	76,400
Finance charge	6,800
Repayment	(30,000)
Balance 31.3.X6	53,200

(e)

> **Examiner's comment.** Most candidates were able to score good marks on this question. Many had learnt a mnemonic to aid their recall of the six criteria. In Part (ii) some candidates failed to explain why the development costs should be treated as recommended.

(i)   Under IAS 38 development costs will normally be recognised as an expense in the accounting period in which they are incurred. However, they may be capitalised if they meet *all* of the following criteria:

- It is **technically feasible** to complete the asset so that it is available for use or sale.

- The **intention** is to **complete** the asset so that it can be used or sold.

- The business is able to **use** or **sell** the asset

- It can be demonstrated that the asset will **generate future economic benefits**. For instance, a market must exist for the product.

- Adequate technical, financial and other resources exist to complete the development.

- The development expenditure can be **reliably measured**.

(ii)   CD's development costs meet all of the above criteria. The development is complete, testing has confirmed the future economic benefits and the costs involved have been reliably measured. CD should capitalise $180,000 development costs at 30 April 20X6. Amortisation should begin on 1 May 20X6 and continue over the expected life of the process.

(f)

> **Examiner's comments.** Most candidates were able to correctly calculate the finance charges and balances for each of the three years, but many candidates could not select the correct figures from their workings to answer the question.

(i)   Finance charge for the year ended 31 March 20X7: $72,000

(ii)   Current liability: $228,000
       Non-current liability: $378,000

Working

	$'000
Purchase price	900
Payment 1 April 20X5	(228)
	672
Interest 13.44%	90
Payment 1 April 20X6	(228)
	534
Interest 13.44%	72
Balance at 31 March 20X7	606
Payment due 1 April 20X7 (current liability)	228
Balance due (non-current liability)	378
	606

Note. As payments are made in advance, the payment due on 1 April 20X7 includes no interest relating to future periods.

(g) **Related party** – under the terms of IAS 24 a party is related to an entity if:

  (i) Directly or indirectly the party:

  - Controls, is controlled by, or is under common control with, the entity
  - Has an interest in the entity that gives it significant interest over the entity; or
  - Has joint control over the entity

  (ii) The party is a member of the key management personnel of the entity or its parent, such as a director

  (iii) The party is a close member of the family of any individual referred to in (i) or (ii) above

  (iv) The party is an entity that is controlled, jointly controlled or significantly influenced by, or a significant proportion of whose voting rights are held by, any individual referred to in (ii) or (iii)

Related party transaction – a transfer of resources, services or obligations between related parties, regardless of whether a price is charged.

(h)

> **Examiner's comments**. Most candidates were able to give most of the IAS 18 criteria but few were able to apply the criteria correctly to the scenario.

  (i) The criteria in IAS 18 for income recognition are as follows.

  - The **risks** and **rewards** of ownership of the goods have been **transferred to the buyer**.
  - The entity **retains neither managerial involvement nor effective control** over the goods.
  - The amount of **revenue** can be **measured reliably**.
  - It is **probable** that the **economic benefits** associated with the transaction will **flow** to the entity.
  - The **costs** incurred in respect of the transaction can be measured reliably.
  - The **stage of completion** of the transaction at the balance sheet date can be measured reliably (rendering of services).

  (ii) The $150,000 received on 1 September 20X7 cannot be recognised as income at that point because the risks and rewards of ownership have not yet been transferred.

  The $150,000 should be credited to deferred income in the statement of financial position and $25,000 should be released to income each month as the magazines are supplied. The estimated $20,000 each month cost of making the supply will be recognised as it arises – at which point it can be measured reliably.

Therefore at 31 October two months revenue can be taken into account and two months costs will be set against that as follows:

	$
Revenue	50,000
Cost of sales	(40,000)
Gross profit	10,000

24 SA (5/13)

(a) The criteria that must be met before an operation can be classified as "held for sale" under IFRS 5 *Non-current assets held for sale and discontinued operations* are:

- It must be available for immediate sale in its present condition

- The sale must be highly probable, management must be committed to selling the assets and have an active programme to locate a buyer

- It must be being offered at a reasonable price

- The sale is expected within the next year

(b) **SA – Statement of profit or loss for the year ended 31 March 2013**

Continuing Operations		$000	$000
Revenue			2,784
Cost of sales			(1,900)
Gross Profit			884
Administrative expenses	W3	(368)	
Distribution costs	W3	(20)	(388)
Profit from operations			496
Finance cost	W4		(27)
Profit before tax			469
Income tax	W5		(87)
Profit for the period from Continuing operations			382
Discontinued Operations			
Loss from discontinued operations	W6		(284)
Profit for the period			98

SA Statement of financial position as at 31 March 2013

	$000	$000
Non-current assets		
Property, plant and equipment		983
Current Assets		
Inventory	68	
Trade receivables	56	
Cash and cash equivalents	202	
		326
Non-current assets held for sale		431
Total Assets		1,740
Equity and liabilities		
Equity		
Share capital	800	
Revaluation reserve	80	
Retained earnings	226	
Total equity		1,106
Non-current Liabilities		
Long term borrowings	450	
Deferred tax (W5)	69	
Total non-current liabilities		519

	$000	$000
Current liabilities		
Trade payables	51	
Interest payable (W4)	14	
Tax payable (W5)	50	
Total current liabilities		115
Total equity and liabilities		1,740

SA Statement of changes in equity for the year ended 31 March 2013

	Equity Shares $000	Revaluation reserve $000	Retained earnings $000	Total $000
Balance at 1 April 2012	800	80	183	1,063
Profit for period			98	98
Dividend paid			(55)	(55)
Balance at 31 March 2013	800	80	226	1,106

Workings - All figures in $000

(W1) *Tangible Non-current Assets (continuing operations)*

	$000
Plant & Equipment	
Cost balance 1/4/12	1,010
Less discontinued operations	(180)
	830
Depreciation balance 1/4/12	360
Less discontinued operations	(140)
	220
Charge for year ([830-220] × 20%)	122
	342
Carrying amount at 31/3/13	488
Buildings	
Cost 1/4/12	995
Less discontinued operations	(460)
	535
Depreciation balance 1/4/12	50
Less discontinued operations	(23)
Depreciation balance 1/4/12	27
Charge for year (535x2.5%)	13
	40
Carrying amount at 31/3/13	495
	983

(W2) *Non-current Assets - Discontinued Operations*

Buildings	
Cost	460
Depreciation b/f	(23)
Depreciation – year (460 × 2.5%)	(12)
	425
Plant and equipment	
Cost	180
Depreciation b/f	(140)
Depreciation – year (40x20%)	(8)
	32
	457
Fair Value	431
Loss on adjustment in value to fair value	(26)

(W3)

	Administration	Distribution
Per trial balance	263	145
Less discontinued	(30)	(125)
Depreciation (W1) (122+13)	135	
	368	20

(W4) *Finance charge*

Years loan interest (450 × 6%)	27
Paid	(13)
Accrued	14

(W5) *Tax*

Continuing Operations

Current year (50+40)	90
Decrease in deferred tax	(3)
Charge for year	87

Deferred tax

Per trial balance	72
Decrease in year	(3)
	69

(W6) **Discontinued Operations**

Revenue		185
Cost of sales		(230)
		(45)
Administration (W3+W2)(30+20)	(50)	
Distribution (W3)	(125)	(175)
		(220)
Closure costs		(78)
		(298)
Tax refund		40
		(258)
Loss on adjustment in value to fair value (W2)		(26)
		(284)

25   CQ (3/13)

CQ - Statement of comprehensive income for the year ended 31 December 2012

		$000	$000
Revenue			1,992
Cost of sales	W2		(1,107)
Gross Profit			885
Administrative expenses	W3	(407)	
Distribution costs	W3	(140)	(547)
Profit from operations			338
Finance cost	W4		(35)
Profit before tax			303
Income tax expense	W5		(67)
Profit for the period			236

CQ Statement of financial position as at 31 December 2012

	$000	$000
Non-current assets		
Property, plant and equipment (W1)		1,472
Intangible assets – Patent (W7)		65
		1,537
Current Assets		
Inventory (W8)	170	
Trade receivables	249	
Cash and cash equivalents	192	
		611
Total Assets		2,148

Equity and liabilities

Equity

Share capital	750	
Share premium	225	
Retained earnings	374	
Total equity		1,349

Non-current Liabilities

Bank loan	375	
Deferred tax (W5)	168	
Finance lease (W6)	27	
Total non-current liabilities		570

Current liabilities

Trade payables	140	
Tax payable (W5)	77	
Finance lease (W6)	12	
Total current liabilities		229
Total equity and liabilities		2,148

CQ Statement of changes in equity for the year ended 31 December 2012

	Equity Shares $000	Share Premium $000	Retained earnings $000	Total $000
Balance at 1 January 2012	500	150	168	818
Shares issued during year	250	75		325
Profit for period			236	236
Dividend paid			(30)	(30)
Balance at	750	225	374	1,349

Workings - All figures in $000

(W1) Tangible Non-current Assets

Cost/Valuation	Land $000	Buildings $000	Plant & Equip. $000	Vehicle $000	Total $000
Balance 1/1/12	1,015	400	482	0	1,897
Finance lease				46	46
Depreciation					
Balance 1/1/12		(120)	(279)	0	(399)
Charge for year		(12)	(51)	(9)	(72)
Carrying amount at 31/12/12	1,015	268	152	37	1,472

$$\frac{\text{Depreciation}}{\text{Buildings}} 400 \times 3\% = 12$$

Plant and equipment

Reducing balance = $482 - 279 = 203 \times 25\% = 51$

Vehicle – over lease period

$46 \times 1/5 = 9$

(W2)

	Administration	Distribution
Per trial balance	395	140
Buildings depreciation (W1)	12	0
	407	140

(W4) Finance charge

Years loan interest (375 × 8%)	30
Finance lease (W6)	5
	35

(W5) *Tax*

Last Year b/f	32
Current year	77
	109
Decrease in deferred tax	(42)
	67

Deferred tax

Per trial balance	210
Decrease in year	(42)
	168

(W6) *Lease*

	Opening balance	Paid	Sub-total	Interest @ 15%	Closing balance
Year to 31/12/12	46	(12)	34	5	39
Year to 31/12/13	39	(12)	27	4	31

(W7) *Patent*

Cost	180
Amortisation – year	(18)
– b/f	(90)
Carrying value	72
Fair value	65
Impairment	7
Amortisation	18
	25

(W8) *Inventory*

Balance 31/12/12	183
Obsolete items	(13)
	170

26 YZ (11/12)

Text references. Preparation of single company financial accounts is covered in Chapters 4 to 12 of the Study Text. Operating leases are covered in Chapter 8. Intangible non-current assets, including patents and research and development, are covered in Chapter 7.

Top tips. This was a fairly standard question on accounts preparation, the main complication being the treatment of the operating lease. Under the accruals concept this should be accounted for over the 4-year period of the lease. Standard workings were required, for example for non-current assets and expenses.

Potential areas for mistakes include:

–   failing to take the research costs out of the patent and writing them off against profit

–   incorrect calculation of deferred tax

–   accounting for the lease over three years instead of four

–   failing to realise that the share issue has already been accounted for in the trial balance

Easy marks. As with most accounts preparation questions, easy marks can be gained by making full use of the information given in the question and inserting figures into the proformas. These easy marks can only be gained, however, by adopting a methodical approach and laying out clear and accurate proformas.

YZ STATEMENT OF PROFIT OR LOSS AND OTHER COMPREHENSIVE INCOME

FOR THE YEAR ENDING 30 SEPTEMBER 2012

	$'000
Revenue	9,820
Cost of sales (W2)	(4,287)
Gross profit	5,533
Administrative expenses (W2)	(978)
Distribution costs (W2)	(515)
Finance costs	(210)
Profit before tax	3,830
Tax expense (W6)	(698)
Profit for the year	3,132
Other comprehensive income:	
Revaluation gain on land (W4)	500
Total comprehensive income for the year	3,632

YZ STATEMENT OF FINANCIAL POSITION AS AT 30 SEPTEMBER 2012

	$'000	$'000
Assets		
Non-current assets		
Property, plan and equipment (W3)		13,247
Intangible asset - patent		294
		13,541
Current assets		
Inventory (W2)	422	
Trade receivables	1,130	
Cash and cash equivalents	130	
		1,682
Total assets		15,223
Equity and liabilities		
Equity		
Share capital	1,700	
Share premium	100	
Retained earnings (3,117 – 170 + 3,132)	6,079	
Revaluation reserve (1,800 + 500)	2,300	
		10,179
Non-current liabilities		
Loan	3,000	
Deferred tax provision (430 – 47)	383	
		3,383
Current liabilities		
Trade and other payables (940 + 6)	946	
Current tax payable	715	
		1,661
Total equity and liabilities		15,223

YZ STATEMENT OF CHANGES IN EQUITY FOR THE YEAR ENDING 30 SEPTEMBER 2012

	Share capital $'000	Share premium $'000	Retained earnings $'000	Revaluation reserve $'000	Total $'000
Balance at 1 October 2011	1,500	-	3,117	1,800	6,417
Issue of shares (W8)	200	100	-	-	300
Dividends	-	-	(170)	-	(170)
Total comprehensive income for the year	-	-	3,132	500	3,632
Balance at 30 September 2012	1,700	100	6,079	2,300	10,179

W1 *Disposal of machinery*

	$
Cost	35,000
Accumulated depreciation	(32,000)
Carrying amount	3,000
Proceeds of disposal	8,000
Gain on disposal	5,000

Note that this amount is not significant enough to disclose separately on the face of the statement of profit or loss and other comprehensive income, so it will be included in cost of sales as a deduction. This is consistent with the treatment of depreciation on plant and equipment, which also goes through cost of sales.

W2 *Expenses*

	Cost of sales $'000	Administrative $'000	Distribution $'000
Per question		910	515
Gain on disposal (W1)	(5)		
Depreciation – buildings (W3)		68	
Depreciation – P&E (W3)	411		
Amortisation – patent (W5)	42		
Research costs	190		
Closing inventory (242 + 180)	(422)		
Operating lease (W7)	6		
Cost of raw materials	2,220		
Direct labour	670		
Opening inventory (190 + 275)	465		
Production overheads	710		
	4,287	978	515

W3 *Non-current assets*

	Plant and equipment $'000	Land $'000	Buildings $'000	Total $'000
Cost/valuation at 1 October 2011	3,900	9,000	3,400	16,300
Less: disposal (i)	(35)	-	-	(35)
Revaluation (W4)	-	500	-	500
Cost/valuation at 30 September 2012	3,865	9,500	3,400	16,765

	Plant and equipment $'000	Land $'000	Buildings $'000	Total $'000
Accum dep'n at 1 October 2011	2,255	-	816	3,071
Less: disposal (i)	(32)	-	-	(32)
Depreciation charge – buildings (2% × 3,400)	-	-	68	68
Depreciation charge – P&E (25% × [3,900 – 35] – [2,255 – 32])	411	-	-	411
Accum dep'n at 30 September 2012	2,634	-	884	3,518
Carrying amount 30 September 2012	1,231	9,500	2,516	13,247

W4 *Land revaluation*

	$'000	
Land value at 30 September 2011	9,000	
Land value at 30 September 2012	9,500	
Revaluation gain	500	Shown in other comprehensive income and transferred to revaluation reserve

W5 *Patent*

	$'000
Cost at 1 October 2011	420
Amortisation as 1 October 2011	(84)
	336
Amortisation for the year ending 30 September 2012 (420 / 10 years)	(42)
	294

Show as an expense under cost of sales.

W6 *Tax expense*

	$'000
Corporation tax	715
Underprovision re: prior year	30
Less: reduction in deferred tax provision (ix)	(47)
	698

W7 *Operating lease*

4-year lease, total payable 3 × $8,000 = $24,000
Spread over 4 years = $6,000 p.a.
Nothing is paid in the first year, so accrue both the expense and the liability.
The lease relates to machinery therefore assume that the rental is charged to cost of sales.

W8 *Share issue*

200,000 × $1 shares issued at a 50% (ie 50c) premium. This transaction is already reflected in the trial balance (xi). The double entry to record this was:

		$'000	$'000
DR	Cash (200,000 × $1.50)	300	
	CR Share capital		200
	CR Share premium		100

27 QWE (9/12)

Text references. Single entity financial statements are covered in Chapters 4 to 12 of the Study Text.

Top tips. You should be familiar with the common adjustments required, such as depreciation, irrecoverable debts, and interest. Make sure that you account for the debit and the credit side for each adjustment that you make.

Easy marks. A good grasp of the principles of double entry should make for an easy three marks for part (a). In part (b) a methodical approach to the working for cost of sales, administration and distribution costs can save time and provides many of the figures for the first part of the answer. There are also generous presentation marks for this question so make sure your answer is set out clearly and neatly.

Examiner's comments. 'Question 3 produced some very good answers with some candidates scoring full marks. However a considerable number of candidates were unable to prepare the journal entries to clear the suspense account in part (a) or prepare correct calculations for the deferred development expenditure and deprecation of property, plant and equipment.

Marking scheme

			Marks
(a)	Journal entries to clear suspense account		3
(b)	SPLOCI up to gross profit	3.5	
	SPLOCI – expenses and tax	5.0	
	Statement of financial position - assets	5.5	
	Statement of financial position – equity and liabilities	4.0	
	Statement of changes in equity	1.5	
	Format and presentation	2.5	
			22
Total marks for question			25

(a)

QWE

Journal entries to clear suspense:

	Debit $'000	Credit $'000
Suspense account	15	
Plant and equipment disposal account		15
Cash received on disposal of some plant and equipment		
Research expense account	20	
Suspense account		20
Research cost to be treated as an expense		

(b)

QWE - Statement of profit of loss and other comprehensive income for the year ended 31 March 2012

		$'000	$'000
Revenue			2,220
Cost of sales	W3		(1,675)
Gross Profit			545
Administrative expenses	W3	(295)	
Distribution costs	W3	(72)	(367)
Profit from operations			178
Finance cost	W4		(20)
Profit before tax			158
Income tax expense	W5		(116)
Profit for the period			42

	Equity Shares $'000	Share Premium $'000	Retained Earnings $'000	Total $'000
Balance at 1 April 2011	930	310	621	1,861
SPLOCI for year			42	42
Dividend paid			(62)	(62)
Balance at 31 March 2012	930	310	601	1,841

QWE - Statement of Financial Position at 31 March 2012

		$'000	$'000
Non-current assets			
Property, plant and equipment	W1		2,301
Deferred development expenditure	W2		105
Current assets			
Inventory		214	
Trade receivables		98	
Cash and cash equivalents		42	
			354
			2,760

Total assets
Equity and liabilities
Equity

Share capital	930	
Share premium	310	
Retained earnings	601	
Total equity		1,841
Non-current liabilities		
Long term borrowings	500	
Deferred tax	111	
Total non-current liabilities		611
Current liabilities		
Trade payables	190	
Tax payable	83	
Provision legal claim	25	
Interest payable	10	
Total current liabilities		308
Total equity and liabilities		2,760

Workings (All figures in $'000)

(W1) Non-current assets

Cost	Land	Buildings	Plant and equipment
Balance b/fwd	800	1,610	560
Disposal (W6)			(82)
Balance c/fwd	800	1,610	478
Depreciation			
Balance b/fwd	0	386	185
Disposal (W6)			(79)
	0	386	106
Year (1610x3%)		48	
Year [(478 – 106) × 12.5%)]			47
Balance c/f	0	434	153
Carrying amount	800	1,176	325
Total PPE c/f			2,301

(W2) Deferred Development Expenditure

Balance b/f	150
Years amortisation – 10%	(15)
Amortisation b/f	(30)
Balance c/f	105

(W3)

	Cost of sales	Administration	Distribution
Trial balance	1,605	190	72
Amortisation development expenditure W2	15		
Research (from part (a)	20		
Depreciation – buildings W1		48	
Depreciation – plant and equipment W1	47		
Gain on disposal PPE W6	(12)		
Irrecoverable debt		32	
Legal claim		25	
Totals	1,675	295	72

(W4) Interest

Years loan interest (500 × 4%)	20
Paid	10
Accrued	10

(W5) **Tax**

Last Year b/f	8
Current year	83
	91
Increase in deferred tax	25
	116

(W6) **Disposal of plant and equipment**

Cost	82
Less depreciation	(79)
Carrying amount	3
Proceeds	(15)
Gain on disposal	(12)

28 DFG (5/12)

Text references. Financial statements for single entities are covered in Chapter 4 to Chapter 12 of the Study Text.

Top tips. Do not ignore the narrative parts of longer questions like this one (see easy marks below!). Read the requirements carefully; here you need to produce three financial statements.

Easy marks. A good knowledge of accounting standards would have enabled a well-prepared candidate to score well on part (a) without using up too much time allocation.

Marking scheme

	Marks
Treatment of items (vi) and (vii)	6.0
Statement of profit or loss and other comprehensive income	6.5
SFP - assets	5.0
SFP – equity and liabilities	5.5
Maximum marks	**25**

(a) **Item (vi) revenue recognition:**

IAS 18 specifies five conditions that must be met before revenue can be recognised. The first two conditions:

- that significant risks and rewards of ownership of the goods have transferred to the buyer

- the entity selling does not retain any influence or control over the goods are not satisfied by this customer order as no goods have been despatched.

DFG should not recognise any revenue in its financial statements for the year ended 31 March 2012 and should record the deposit received as a current liability.

Item (vii) impairment of intangible non-current assets:

An asset should be reviewed for impairment whenever circumstances indicate that an impairment may have occurred. Due to recent economic circumstances a review has been carried out of the patent. An impairment occurs where the asset's carrying value is more than the higher of its value in use and its fair value less cost to sell. The patent's carrying value at 31 March 2012, $54,000 (after annual amortisation of $9,000) is more than the higher of its value in use of $50,000 and its fair value $47,000. Therefore an impairment has occurred and the patent must be written down by $4,000 to $50,000.

(b)

DFG Statement of profit or loss and other comprehensive income for the year ended 31 March 2012

		$'000
Revenue (1,200 – 15)		1,185
Cost of sales (W3)		(642)
Gross Profit		543
Administrative expenses (W3)	(236)	
Distribution costs (W3)	(90)	(326)
Profit from operations		217
Finance cost (W4)		(14)
Profit before tax		203
Income tax expense (W5)		(77)
Profit for the period		126

DFG Statement of Changes in Equity for the year ended 31 March 2012

	Equity shares $'000	Share premium $'000	Retained earnings $'000	Total $'000
Balance at 1 April 2011	550	110	121	781
Profit for period			126	126
Dividend paid			(55)	(55)
Balance at 31 March 2012	550	110	192	852

DFG Statement of Financial Position at 31 March 2012

Non-current assets		
Patent (W2)		50
Property, plant and equipment		
Buildings (W1)	906	
Plant and equipment (W1)	171	1,077
		1,127
Current assets		
Inventory	186	
Trade receivables	135	321
Total assets		1,448
Equity and liabilities		
Equity		
Share capital		550
Share premium		110
Retained earnings		192
Total equity		852
Non-current liabilities		
5% Loan notes	280	
Deferred tax (W6)	90	
Total non-current liabilities		370
Current liabilities		
Trade payables	61	
Cash and cash equivalents	56	
Tax payable	52	
Interest payable	7	
Pre-paid deposit	15	
Provisions	35	
Total current liabilities		226
Total equity and liabilities		1,448

Workings (All figures in $'000)

(W1) **Depreciation**

Buildings

Charge for year	$960 - 260 = 700 \times 3\% = 21$
Balance b/fwd	33
Balance c/fwd	54
Carrying amount	$960 - 33 - 21 = 906$

Plant and equipment

Cost balance b/fwd	$480 - 120 = 360$
Year's depreciation	$360 \times 12.5\% = 45$
Other P&E cost	120
Depreciation already charged	$120 \times 12.5\% \times 4 = 60$
Carrying amount at 1/4/2011	60
Annual depreciation (over two years)	30
Year's depreciation P&E	$45 + 30 = 75$
Carrying amount at year end	$(480 - 234 - 45 - 30) = 171$

(W2) **Patent**

Balance b/fwd – cost	90
– amortisation	27
	63
Annual amortisation to 31/03/12	9
Carrying amount 31/03/12	54
Value in use	50
Impairment	4

(W3)

	Cost of sales	Administrative expenses	Distribution Costs
Trial balance:	554	180	90
Provision		35	
Depreciation – buildings (W1)		21	
Depreciation – plant and equipment (W1) (45 + 30)	75		
Patent amortisation/impairment (W2) (9 + 4)	13		
	642	236	90

(W4) **Interest**

Paid in year	7
Due for year (280 × 5%)	14
Accrued	7

(W5) **Tax**

Last year adjustment	10
Current year	52
Increase in deferred tax	15
	77

(W6) **Deferred Tax**

Balance b/f	75
Current year	15
	90

29 RTY (3/12)   45 mins

Text references. Preparation of single company financial accounts is covered in Chapters 4 to 12. Accounting for non-currents assets specifically is in Chapter 6.

Top tips. Make sure that you are comfortable with accounting for non-current assets, including depreciation, revaluations, disposals and gains and losses on disposals. This is an easy area to examine and in this question is worth a considerable proportion of the marks.

Easy marks. Familiarity with the layout of the principal financial statements will enable you to slot in the figures quickly; some of the figures given need no or minimal workings.

Marking scheme

	Marks
Prepare the SPLOCI – to gross profit	5.5
Prepare the SPLOCI – expenses and tax	3.5
Prepare the SPLOCI – other comprehensive income and presentation	1.5
Prepare SOFP - assets	6.5
Prepare SOFP – equity and liabilities	4.0
Prepare statement of changes in equity	4.0
Maximum marks	**25**

RTY - Statement of profit or loss and other comprehensive income for the year ended 31 January 2012

	$'000	$'000
Revenue		9,320
Cost of sales		(6,059)
Gross Profit		3,261
Administrative expenses		(1,225)
Distribution costs		(679)
Profit from operations		1,357
Finance cost		(137)
Profit before tax		1,220
Income tax expense		(755)
Profit for the period		465
Other Comprehensive Income		
Revaluation of property (W7)		1,240
		1,705

RTY - Statement of Financial Position at 31 January 2012

	$'000	$'000
Non-current assets		
Property, plant and equipment		14,877
Deferred development expenditure		272
		15,149
Current assets		
Inventory	330	
Trade receivables	1,428	
Cash and cash equivalents	142	
Total assets		1,900
		17,049
Equity and liabilities		
Equity		
Share capital	1,375	
Share premium	2,750	
Retained earnings	3,912	
Revaluation reserve	3,340	
Total equity		11,377

Non-current liabilities

Long term borrowings	2,740	
Deferred tax	1,019	
Total non-current liabilities		3,759

Current liabilities

Trade payables	1,080	
Tax payable	765	
Interest payable	68	
Total current liabilities		1,913
Total equity and liabilities		17,049

RTY Statement of changes in equity for year ended 31 January 2012

	Equity Shares $'000	Share Premium $'000	Retained Earnings $'000	Revaluation Reserve $'000	Total $'000
Balance at 1 February 2011	1,375	2,750	2,785	2,900	9,810
SPLOCI for year			465	1,240	1,705
Disposal of revalued property (W4)			800	(800)	0
Dividend paid			(138)		(138)
Balance at 31 January 2012	1,375	2,750	3,912	3,340	11,377

Workings (All figures in $'000)

(W1) **Depreciation**

Cost/revalued amount	Land	Buildings	Plant & equipment	Total
Balance b/f	6,220	10,900	5,750	22,870
Revaluation adjustment	630	(2,000)		(1,370)
	6,850	8,900	5,750	21,500
Assets sold	(1,800)		(820)	(2,620)
	5,050	8,900	4,930	18,880
Depreciation				
Balance b/f		2,610	3,900	6,510
Assets sold			(800)	(800)
		2,610	3,100	5,710
Revaluation adjustment		(2,610)		(2,610)
Depreciation for year		445	458	903
		445	3,558	4,003
Carrying amount 31 Jan 2012	5,050	8,455	1,372	14,877

(W2) **Deferred development expenditure**

Balance b/f	455
Expenditure in year	71
	526
Year's amortisation	(254)
	272
Year's amortisation:	
Capitalised in previous years	1,199
Expenditure in 2011	71
	1,270
Amortised at 20%	254

(W3)

	Cost of sales	Administration	Distribution
Trial balance	4,939	1,225	679
Depreciation – (W1)	903		
Research	163		
Irrecoverable debt	48		
Development amortisation (W2)	254		
Gain on disposal of non-current assets	(248)		
Totals	6,059	1,225	679

(W4) **Disposal of non-current assets**

	Land	Plant and equipment	Land	
Carrying value	1,800	(820-800)= 20	Revalued amount	1,800
Selling price	2,060	8	Cost	1,000
Profit/(loss)	260	(12)	Reversal of revaluation	800

(W5) **Interest**

Years loan interest	(2740 × 5%)	137
Paid		69
Current liability		68

(W6) **Tax**

Balance b/f	35
Year	765
	800
Decrease in deferred tax	(45)
SPLOCI	755

Statement of financial position
Current liability – tax	765
Provision deferred tax	1,019

(W7) **Revaluation of Land and buildings**

Land (W1)	630
Buildings (W1) (2,610 – 2,000)	610
	1,240

30 ABC (11/11)

Text references. Preparation of single company financial accounts is covered in Chapters 4 to 12. Construction contracts are covered in Chapter 11.

Top tips. This was a pretty standard accounts preparation question, however the inclusion of the construction contracts may have put you off. Exam technique is important here. You must get the proformas on to your paper and fill in the easy numbers first. Then tackle the areas you are comfortable with. In our answer, we have left the construction contract until last as it is definitely the most tricky part.

These errors were easy to make:

* Calculating the plant and equipment depreciation on a straight line basis instead of the reducing balance basis.

* Not recording the accrued interest payable on the long term loan in both the SPLOCI and the SOFP or recording the accrued interest as $58,000 instead of $57,000.

* Incorrectly including the underprovision of tax in the tax payable balance in the SOFP or forgetting to include it in the SPLOCI tax charge.

Easy marks. There were plenty of easy marks to be gained in this question by inserting all the numbers that didn't require calculation into the proformas.

ABC STATEMENT OF PROFIT OR LOSS AND OTHER COMPREHENSIVE INCOME FOR THE YEAR ENDING 30 SEPTEMBER 2011

	$'000
Revenue (9,500 + 6,400(W4))	15,900
Cost of sales (W1)	(10,936)
Gross profit	4,964
Distribution costs	(590)
Administrative expenses (W1)	(1,045)
Profit on disposal (15 – (75 - 65)))	5
Profit from operations	3,334
Interest payable (2,300 × 5%)	(115)
Profit before tax	3,219
Income tax expense (W3)	(944)
Profit for the year	2,275
Total comprehensive income for the year	2,275

ABC STATEMENT OF FINANCIAL POSITION AS AT 30 SEPTEMBER 2011

	$'000	$'000
Assets		
Non-current assets		
Property (W2)	6,875	
Plant and equipment (W2)	2,073	
		8,948
Current assets		
Inventory	310	
Trade receivables (810 - 25)	785	
Construction contract – amount due from customer (W4)	490	
Cash and cash equivalents	440	
		2,025
Total assets		10,973
Equity and liabilities		
Equity		
Share capital	2,500	
Share premium	1,500	
Retained earnings	2,652	
		6,652
Non-current liabilities		
Long-term borrowings		2,300
Deferred tax (250 + 19)		269
Current liabilities		
Trade payables	235	
Tax payable	910	
Construction contract – gross amounts due to customer (W4)	550	
Interest payable (115 – 58)	57	
		1,752
Total liabilities and equity		10,973

ABC STATEMENT OF CHANGES IN EQUITY FOR THE YEAR ENDING 30 SEPTEMBER 2011

	Share capital $'000	*Share premium* $'000	*Retained earnings* $'000	*Total* $'000
Balance at 1.10.10	2,500	1,500	627	4,627
Dividends	–	–	(250)	(250)
Total comprehensive income for the year	–	–	2,275	2,275
Balance at 30.09.11	2,500	1,500	2,652	6,652

Workings

1   *Expenses*

	Cost of sales $'000	Administrative $'000	Distribution $'000
Per question	3,210	1,020	590
Depreciation charge (W2)	1,066		
Construction contracts (W4)	6,660		
Irrecoverable debt write off		25	
	10,936	1,045	590

2   *Non-current assets*

	Plant and equipment $'000	Land $'000	Buildings $'000	Total $'000
Cost at 30.09.10	4,930	3,500	7,500	15,930
Disposal	(75)			
Cost at 30.09.11	4,855	3,500	7,500	15,930
Accumulated dep'n at 30.09.10	2,156	-	3,750	5,906
Disposal	(65)	-	-	-
Depreciation charge	691*	-	375	1,066
Accumulated depn' at 30.09.11	2,782		4,125	6,907
Carrying amount at 30.09.11	2,073	3,500	3,375	8,948

* (4,855 – 2156 + 65) × 25% = 691

3   *Tax*

Current tax	$'000
Estimated tax charge for the year	910
Plus underprovision from previous year	15
Increase in deferred tax provision	19
	944

4   *Construction contracts*

	Contract 1 $'000	Contract 2 $'000	Total $'000
Overall profitability of contract			
Contract value	11,000	8,000	
Costs to date	3,750	2,250	
Costs to complete	5,400	6,750	
Expected profit/loss	1,850	(1,000)	
		Recognise loss immediately	
Percentage complete	40%	25%	

	$'000	$'000	$'000
Amounts to include in financial statements			
Revenue (11,000 × 40%)/(8,000 × 25%)	4,400	2,000	6,400
Cost of sales (balancing figure)	3,660	3,000	6,660
Profit/expected loss (1,850 × 40%)	740	(1,000)	(360)

	Contract 1 $'000	Contract 2 $'000
Gross amounts due to/from customers		
Costs incurred	3,750	2,250
Recognised profits less recognised losses	740	(1,000)
	4,490	1,250
Less progress billings to date	(4,000)	(1,800)
Amount recognised as asset/(liability)	490	(550)

31 ZY (9/11)

Text references. Preparation of single company financial accounts is covered in Chapters 4 to 12. Finance leases are covered in Chapter 8. Redeemable preference shares are covered in Chapter 12.

Top tips. This was a pretty standard accounts preparation question, but with some very tricky adjustments to put through. As with all accounts preparation questions, you should set out your proformas and insert the easy numbers first.

The finance lease added an extra dimension to the PPE working – but all you had to do for the PPE working was to insert the cost of the new leased assets into the standard workings. If you are not comfortable with the standard workings for finance leases, go back to Chapter 8 to revise as it seems to be a popular topic with the examiner.

There were a couple of adjustments required to inventory. The write down was not too difficult, but it was easy to forget to adjust sales/receivables as well as inventories for the returned goods, watch out for this in your real exam.

The finance charge was a really tricky number to get right as you had to include the preference share dividend, the full year's worth of interest on the borrowings and the finance lease interest charge. Don't forget that redeemable preference shares are classified as liabilities and not as equity.

Easy marks. There were easy marks to be gained in this question by inserting all the numbers that didn't require calculation into the proformas, for example, share capital, share premium, dividends paid, long term loans etc.

Examiner's comments. "This question produced some very good answers with some candidates scoring full marks. However a considerable number of candidates lost marks on the finance lease, the cumulative redeemable preferred shares and inventory adjustments."

Marking scheme

	Marks
Statement of profit or loss and other comprehensive income	
Sales revenue	1
Cost of sales	2
Distribution costs	½
Administration expenses	1
Profit on disposal	1
Finance cost	2½
Income tax expense	2
	10
Statement of financial position	
Property, plant and equipment	1½
Inventory	1½
Trade receivables	1½
Cash	½
Equity and reserves	1
Deferred tax	1
Long-term borrowings	½
Finance lease	2
Preferred shares	1
Trade payables	½
Tax payable	1
Interest payable	1
	11

Statement of changes in equity

Share capital	½
Share premium	½
Revaluation reserve	½
Retained earnings	<u>1½</u>
	3
Presentation	1
Total marks for question	<u>25</u>

(a)   ZY STATEMENT OF PROFIT OR LOSS AND OTHER COMPREHENSIVE INCOME
        FOR THE YEAR ENDING 30 JUNE 2011

	$'000
Revenue (2,084 - 30)	2,054
Cost of sales (W1)	(1,146)
Gross profit	908
Administrative expenses (W1)	(386)
Distribution costs (W1)	(221)
Profit on disposal of vehicle (W3)	10
Finance costs (W5)	(29)
Profit before tax	282
Income tax expense (W4)	(64)
Profit for the year	218
Total comprehensive income for the year	218

(b)   ZY STATEMENT OF FINANCIAL POSITION AS AT 30 JUNE 2011

	$'000	$'000
Assets		
Non-current assets		
Property (W3)	828	
Plant and equipment (W3)	<u>557</u>	
		1,385
Current assets		
Inventory (W2)	385	
Trade receivables (280 – 48 – 30)	202	
Cash	<u>229</u>	
		816
Total assets		2,201
Equity and liabilities		
Equity		
Share capital	500	
Share premium	270	
Revaluation reserve	220	
Retained earnings	<u>416</u>	
		1,406
Non-current liabilities		
Long-term borrowings		320
Preferred shares		150
Deferred tax (W4)		38
Finance lease liability (W6)		78
Current liabilities		
Trade payables	120	
Finance lease liability (W6)	22	
Tax payable (W4)	56	
Interest payable (W5)	<u>11</u>	
		209
Total liabilities and equity		2,201

BPP
LEARNING MEDIA

ZY STATEMENT OF CHANGES IN EQUITY FOR THE YEAR ENDING 30 JUNE 2011

	Share capital $'000	Share premium $'000	Revaluation Reserve $'000	Retained earnings $'000	Total $'000
Balance at 1.07.10	500	270	220	288	1,278
Total comprehensive income for the year	–	–	–	218	218
Dividends	–	–	–	(90)	(90)
Balance at 30.06.11	500	270	220	416	1,406

Workings

1   *Expenses*

	Cost of sales $'000	Administrative $'000	Distribution $'000
Per question		338	221
Opening inventory	358		
Purchases	987		
Closing inventory (W2)	(385)		
Depreciation	186		
Irrecoverable debt write off		48	
	1,146	386	221

2   *Closing inventories*

	$'000
Per question	390
Less write down of inventory*	(20)
Add returned goods	15
	385

* Inventory should be valued at the lower of cost and NRV:

	$'000
Cost	100
NRV (110 – 30)	80
Write down required	20

3   *Non-current assets*

PROPERTY – CARRYING AMOUNT

	$'000		$'000
Balance b/f (844 – 8)	836	Depreciation charge (844 × 1%)	8
		Balance c/f	828
	836		836

PLANT AND EQUIPMENT – CARRYING AMOUNT

	$'000		$'000
Balance b/f (864 – 249)	615	Disposal (95 – 95)	0
Additions (finance lease)	120	Dep'n charge (864 + 120 (finance lease) – 95 (disposal) × 20%)	178
		Balance c/f	557
	735		735

Profit on disposal of vehicle = 10 (proceeds) – 0 (carrying value) = $10,000

4   *Tax*

	$'000
Deferred tax	
Deferred tax provision required	38
B/f deferred tax provision	(45)
Decrease required – credit to profit or loss	(7)

Current tax

Estimated tax charge for the year	56
Plus underprovision from previous year	15
	71

Total charge to profit or loss	64

5 *Finance charges*

	$'000
Redeemable preference share dividends (150 × 4% × 6/12)	3
Long term borrowings interest (320 × 5%)	16
Finance lease interest (W6)	10
	29

Accrued interest

Long term borrowings (320 × 5% × 6/12)	8
Redeemable preference share dividends	3
	11

6 *Finance lease*

	$'000
1.7.10 Fair value of asset	120
Finance charge @ 7.93%	10
Repayment	(30)
Balance 30.6.11	100
Finance charge @ 7.93%	8
Repayment	(30)
Balance 30.6.12	78
Non-current liability	78
Current liability (100 – 78)	22

32 MN (5/11)

Text references. Preparation of single company financial accounts is covered in Chapters 4 to 12. Discontinued operations is covered in Chapter 5. Calculation of provisions is covered in Chapter 10.

Top tips. This was a tricky question with lots of twists! The discontinued operation may have thrown you, but remember that by following the recommended step-by-step approach covered in the Text, you would have had a good chance of scoring many of the easy marks before attempting to tackle the discontinued operation.

The tax charge on continuing operations required quite a few adjustments: a credit to the SPLOCI for the reduced deferred tax provision, plus a charge for the tax for the year, plus an increase of $10,000 because the discontinued operation was due to receive a tax credit. Don't worry if you didn't get all of these, just remember to set out your workings clearly and you will get marks for the items you *did* include.

Accounting for the discontinued operation and the assets held for sale was quite involved as there were a few things to remember to do in the financial statements. This isn't the first time discontinued operations have been examined, so if you struggled with this question, go back to the Study Text Chapter 5 to revise and then attempt some more questions from the Kit.

These errors were easy to make, look out for them in your exam:

- Including the bank overdraft as cash at bank in current assets
- Not recording the accrued interest payable on the long term loan in both the SPLOCI and the SOFP
- Not including the impairment on assets held for sale in the loss from discontinued operations for the year
- Forgetting to include the charge for the increase in the warranty provision in the SPLOCI.

Easy marks. There were still easy marks to be gained in this question by inserting all the numbers that didn't require calculation into the proformas, for example, share capital, share premium, dividends paid, long term loans etc. Calculating the depreciation charge for the year was pretty standard and you should have been able to do this. If you remembered the expected value approach for provisions, then the warranty provision was also fairly straightforward.

Marking scheme

Statement of profit or loss and other comprehensive income		Marks
Sales revenue	1	
Cost of sales	3	
Distribution costs	1	
Administration expenses	1	
Finance cost	1	
Income tax expense	1	
Discontinued operation	2½	
		10½

Statement of financial position		
Property, plant and equipment	1	
NCA held for sale	1	
Current assets	1	
Share capital	½	
Share premium	½	
Retained earnings	½	
Deferred tax	1	
Long-term borrowings	½	
Overdraft	½	
Trade payables	½	
Tax payable	1	
Interest payable	1	
		9

Statement of changes in equity		
Share capital	½	
Share premium	½	
Retained earnings	1½	
		3½

Presentation		2
Total marks for question		25

(a)   MN STATEMENT OF PROFIT OR LOSS AND OTHER COMPREHENSIVE INCOME
FOR THE YEAR ENDING 31 MARCH 20X1

	$'000
Revenue (1,120 – 80*)	1,040
Cost of sales (W2)	(553)
Gross profit	487
Administrative expenses (W3)	(120)
Distribution costs (W2)	(80)
Finance costs (300 × 4%)	(12)
Profit before tax	275
Income tax expense (W4)	(72)
Profit for the year from continuing operations	203
Discontinued operations	
Loss for the year from discontinued operations (W5)	(189)
Profit for the year	14
Total comprehensive income for the year	14

* To remove the discontinued operation's results

(b) MN STATEMENT OF FINANCIAL POSITION AS AT 31 MARCH 20X1

	$'000	$'000
Assets		
Non-current assets		
Property, plant and equipment (W1)		1,823
Current assets		
Inventory	65	
Trade receivables	101	
		166
Non-current assets held for sale		176
Total assets		2,165
Equity and liabilities		
Equity		
Share capital	600	
Share premium	200	
Retained earnings	761	
		1,561
Non-current liabilities		
Long-term borrowings		300
Deferred tax (W4)		78
Current liabilities		
Overdraft	14	
Trade payables	51	
Interest payable (300 × 4%)	12	
Tax payable (W4)	67	
Provision (W3)	82	
		226
Total liabilities and equity		2,165

MN STATEMENT OF CHANGES IN EQUITY FOR THE YEAR ENDING 31 MARCH 20X1

	Share capital $'000	Share premium $'000	Retained earnings $'000	Total $'000
Balance at 1.04.X1	600	200	777	1,577
Dividends	–	–	(30)	(30)
Total comprehensive income for the year	–	–	14	14
Balance at 31.03.X2	600	200	761	1,561

Workings

1 *Non-current assets*

Continuing operations

Asset type	Cost – continuing activities $'000	Accumulated depreciation – continuing activities $'000	CA at 31 March 20X0 $'000	Dep'n charge for year $'000	CA at 31 March 20X1 $'000
Land	1,220	0	1,220	0	1,220
Buildings	700	140	560	35	525
Plant & equipment	240	142	98	20	78
	2,160	282	1,878	55	1,823

Discontinued operations

Asset type	Cost – discontinued operations	Accumulated depreciation – discontinued operations	CA at 31 March 20X0	Dep'n charge for year	CA at 31 March 20X1
	$'000	$'000	$'000	$'000	$'000
Land	150	0	150	0	150
Buildings	40	20	20	2	18
Plant & equipment	60	35	25	5	20
	250	55	195	7	188

Assets held for sale

Impairment on reclassification as held for sale = 188 – 176 = $12,000

2 *Expenses*

	Cost of sales	Administrative	Distribution
	$'000	$'000	$'000
Per question	622	160	170
Depreciation continuing activities (W1)	55		
Depreciation discontinued activities (W1)	7		
Increase in warranty provision (W3)	6		
Less discontinued operation	(137)	(40)	(90)
	553	120	80

3 *Warranty provision*

	$'000
Provision required ($0.1 \times 190 + 0.15 \times 20 + 0.75 \times 8$)	82
B/f provision	(76)
Increase required – charge to profit or loss	6

4 *Tax*

Deferred tax	$'000
Provision required	78
B/f provision	(83)
Decrease required – credit to profit or loss	(5)

Tax charge in SPLOCI	$'000
Estimated income tax charge per question	67
Add back tax credit applicable to discontinued operation	10
Less credit for decrease in deferred tax provision	(5)
Charge in SPLOCI	72

5 *Discontinued operation*

	$'000
Revenue	80
Cost of sales (130 + 7 (W1))	(137)
Administration expenses	(40)
Distribution costs	(90)
	(187)
Income tax credit	10
	(177)
Less impairment loss on assets held for sale	(12)
	(189)

33 XB (11/10)

Text references. Preparation of single company financial accounts is covered in Chapters 4 to 12. Calculation of income tax on company profits is covered in Chapter 18 and deferred tax is covered in Chapter 19.

Top tips. The question specified that 8 marks out of 14 were available for the tax calculations, so this should have highlighted to you that tax was a major issue in part (a). Don't let this put you off though, you should still lay out your statement of comprehensive income proforma and work through the TB and the adjustments plugging in the figures to your proforma. This will give you the accounting profit figure required to then work out the income tax charge. Part (b) was a pretty straightforward preparation of a statement of financial position and a statement of changes in equity.

These errors were easy to make:

- Charging all tax depreciation at 25% instead of 50% for the new additions and 25% for the remaining balance

- Not recording the accrued interest payable on the long term loan in both the SPLOCI and the SOFP

- Incorrectly including the underprovision of tax in the tax payable balance in the SOFP or forgetting to include it in the SPLOCI tax charge

Easy marks. There were plenty of easy marks to be gained in this question by inserting all the numbers that didn't require calculation into the proformas, particularly in part (b). The time pressure may have got to you in this question though as there was a lot to do.

Marking scheme

	Marks
Statement of profit or loss and other comprehensive income	
Sales revenue	½
Cost of sales	1
Distribution costs	½
Administration expenses	½
Other costs	½
Finance cost	1
Income tax expense	1½
Presentation	½
	6
Tax computation	
Accounting profit	½
Add back: entertaining expenses	1
political donation	1
accounting depreciation	1½
Less: tax depreciation	2
Deferred tax	2
	8
Total	14

Statement of financial position

Property, plant and equipment	½
Land	½
Current assets	1½
Share capital	½
Share premium	½
Retained earnings	½
Deferred tax	½
Long-term borrowings	½
Trade payables	½
Tax payable	1
Interest payable	1
Maximum of	7

Statement of changes in equity

Share capital	1
Share premium	1
Retained earnings	1½
Maximum of	3
Presentation	1
	11
Total marks for question	25

(a) XB STATEMENT OF PROFIT OR LOSS AND OTHER COMPREHENSIVE INCOME
FOR THE YEAR ENDING 31 OCTOBER 20Y0

	$'000
Revenue	690
Cost of sales (237 + 86 (W))	(323)
Gross profit	367
Distribution costs	(62)
Administrative expenses	(185)
Other costs (12 + 5)	(17)
Profit from operations	103
Finance cost (3 + 3% × 200 × 6/12)	(6)
Profit before tax	97
Income tax expense (31(W) - 2(W) + 6)	(35)
Profit for the year	62
Total comprehensive income for the year	62

Working

Taxation

	$'000	$'000
Accounting profit		97
Add back: entertaining expenses	5	
political donation	12	
accounting depreciation (W2)	86	
		103
Less: tax depreciation (W2)		(78)
Taxable profit		122
Tax charge @ 25%		31

	Carrying value $'000	Tax base $'000
Cost	320	–
Depreciation 25%	(192)	–
Balance 31.10.X9	128	90
Additions	110	110
	238	200
Depreciation (20% × (320 + 110))	(86)	–
Tax depreciation ((110 × 50%) + (90 × 25%))	–	(78)
Balance 31.10.Y0	152	122

*Deferred tax at 31.10.Y0 = (152 − 122) × 25% = $7,500, round to **$8,000***

Decrease in deferred tax balance = $8,000 - $10,000 = $2,000

Note. The question specifies working to the nearest $'000.

(b)   XB STATEMENT OF FINANCIAL POSITION AS AT 31 OCTOBER 20Y0

	$'000	$'000
Assets		
Non-current assets		
Land	730	
Property, plant and equipment (a)	152	
		882
Current assets		
Inventory	18	
Trade receivables	109	
Cash and cash equivalents	216	
		343
Total assets		1,225
Equity and liabilities		
Equity		
Share capital	630	
Share premium	99	
Retained earnings	180	
		909
Non-current liabilities		
Long-term borrowings		200
Deferred tax (a)		8
Current liabilities		
Trade payables (77 − 3)	74	
Tax payable (a)	31	
Interest payable (3% × 200 × 6/12)	3	
		108
Total liabilities and equity		1,225

XB STATEMENT OF CHANGES IN EQUITY FOR THE YEAR ENDING 31 OCTOBER 20Y0

	Share capital $'000	Share premium $'000	Retained earnings $'000	Total $'000
Balance at 1.09.X9	300 (bal.fig)	0 (bal.fig)	168	468
Issue of share capital	330	99	–	429
Dividends	–	–	(50)	(50)
Total comprehensive income for the year	–	–	62	62
Balance at 31.10.Y0	630	99	180	909

34 EZ (5/10)

Text references. Preparation of single company financial accounts is covered in Chapters 4 to 12.

Top tips. This question is relatively straightforward if you know your proformas – the best way to get to grips with the proformas is through question practice. These errors were easy to make:

- Incorrectly accounting for the land revaluation
- Not recording interest payable on the long term loan in both the SPLOCI and the SOFP
- Incorrectly accounting for the operating lease charge and forgetting to include the operating lease payable.

Easy marks. There were plenty of easy marks to be gained in this question by inserting all the numbers that didn't require calculation into the proformas. The property, plant and equipment calculation was also fairly straightforward. Don't be put off by the mention of deferred tax – all you had to do was deduct 10 from the deferred tax provision and from the income statement tax charge!

EZ STATEMENT OF PROFIT OR LOSS AND OTHER COMPREHENSIVE INCOME
FOR THE YEAR ENDING 31 MARCH 20X9

	$'000
Revenue	720
Cost of sales (418 + 44 (W1))	(462)
Gross profit	258
Loss on disposal of non-current assets (2 – 7)	(5)
Distribution costs	(69)
Administrative expenses (86 + 125)	(211)
Impairment of land (675 – 700 + 10)	(15)
Operating lease (W2)	(24)
Loss from operations	(66)
Finance cost (4% × 250)	(10)
Loss before tax	(76)
Income tax expense (18 – 10)	(8)
Loss for the year	(84)
Other comprehensive income:	
Loss on revaluation of land	(10)
Total comprehensive loss for the year	(94)

EZ STATEMENT OF FINANCIAL POSITION AS AT 31 MARCH 20X9

	$'000	$'000
Assets		
Non-current assets		
Land	675	
Property, plant and equipment (W1)	285	
		960
Current assets		
Inventory	112	
Trade receivables	150	
Cash and cash equivalents	22	
		284
Total assets		1,244

	$'000	$'000
Equity and liabilities		
Equity		
Share capital	600	
Share premium	300	
Retained earnings	5	
		905
Non-current liabilities		
Long-term borrowings		250
Deferred tax		20
Current liabilities		
Trade payables	32	
Operating lease payable	9	
Tax payable	18	
Interest payable	10	
		69
Total liabilities and equity		1,244

EZ STATEMENT OF CHANGES IN EQUITY FOR THE YEAR ENDING 31 MARCH 20X9

	Share capital $'000	Share premium $'000	Revaluation surplus $'000	Retained earnings $'000	Total $'000
Balance at 1 April 20X8	400 (bal.fig)	200 (bal.fig)	10	181	791
Issue of share capital	200	100	–	–	300
Dividends	–	–	–	(92)	(92)
Total comprehensive income for the year	–	–	(10)	(84)	(94)
Balance at 31 March 20X9	600	300	0	5	905

Workings

1   *Property, plant and equipment*

	$'000
Cost at 31 March 20X8	480
Less disposal	(37)
Cost at 31 March 20X9	443
Accumulated depreciation at 31 March 20X8	(144)
Disposal	30
Charge for year (443 × 10%)	(44)
	(158)

Depreciation charged to administrative expenses

2   *Operating lease*

	$'000
Total charge over 30 months (2.5 × 24)	60
Charge per month (60/30)	2
Charge for year (2 × 12)	24

35   XY (Specimen paper)

Text references. Deferred tax is covered in Chapter 19. Preparation of single company financial accounts is covered in Chapters 4 to 12.

Top tips. Don't be put off by part (a), the deferred tax is not too difficult to calculate. Don't forget that you need to calculate the movement on the deferred tax provision for the statement of comprehensive income. For part (b) the key to success is familiarity with the format of the statements. The best way to achieve this is through practising your question technique. Easy errors to make are:

- Not accounting for the impairment of the land
- Not recording interest payable on the long term loan in both the SPLOCI and the SOFP
- Ignoring the underprovision for tax in the previous year
- Not including the gain on available-for-sale investments in the revaluation reserve.

Easy marks. There were easy marks to be gained by inserting all the numbers that didn't require calculation into the proformas – eg revenue, trade payables, trade receivables, cash, share capital, share premium.

(a)   *Deferred tax at 31 March 20X9*

	$'000
Accounting value	
Cost (630 – 378)	252
Accounting depreciation (630 × 20%)	(126)
Carrying amount	126
Tax WDV	
Cost (630 – 453)	177
Tax depreciation @ 25%	(44)
Tax written down value	133
Temporary difference	(7)
Deferred tax @ 25%	(2)

Change in deferred tax balance

	$'000
Deferred tax liability at 31.03.X8	(19)
Less deferred tax asset at 31.08.X9	(2)
Credit to income tax expense	(21)

XY STATEMENT OF PROFIT OR LOSS AND OTHER COMPREHENSIVE INCOME FOR YEAR ENDING 31 MARCH 20X9 (extract)

	$'000
Income tax expense – reduction in deferred tax	21

XY STATEMENT OF FINANCIAL POSITION AT 31 MARCH 20X9 (extract)

	$'000
Non-current assets	
Deferred tax asset	2

(b) XY STATEMENT OF PROFIT OR LOSS AND OTHER COMPREHENSIVE INCOME FOR THE YEAR ENDING 31 MARCH 20X9

	$'000
Revenue	1,770
Cost of sales (908 + 126 (part a))	(1,034)
Gross profit	736
Profit on disposal of non-current assets (W2)	9
Distribution costs	(176)
Administrative expenses (303 + 14 (W1))	(317)
Profit from operations	252
Finance cost (5% × 280)	(14)
Profit before tax	238
Income tax expense (W3)	(87)
Profit for the year	151
Other comprehensive income:	
Gain on available for sale investments	44
Total comprehensive income for the year	195

XY STATEMENT OF FINANCIAL POSITION AS AT 31 MARCH 20X9

	$'000	$'000
Assets		
Non-current assets		
Land	729	
Property, plant and equipment	126	
Available for sale investments	608	
Deferred tax asset	2	
		1,465
Current assets		
Inventory	76	
Trade receivables	210	
Cash and cash equivalents	21	
		307
Total assets		1,772
Equity and liabilities		
Equity		
Share capital	500	
Share premium	200	
Revaluation surplus (160 + 44)	204	
Retained earnings	422	
		1,326
Non-current liabilities		
Long-term borrowings		280
Current liabilities		
Trade payables	56	
Tax payable	96	
Interest payable	14	
		166
Total liabilities and equity		1,772

XY STATEMENT OF CHANGES IN EQUITY FOR THE YEAR ENDING 31 MARCH 20X9

	Share capital $'000	Share premium $'000	Revaluation surplus $'000	Retained earnings $'000	Total $'000
Balance at 1 April 20X8	400 (bal.fig)	150 (bal.fig)	160	321	1,031
Issue of share capital	100	50	–	–	150
Dividends	–	–	–	(50)	(50)
Total comprehensive income for the year	–	–	44	151	195
Balance at 31 March 20X9	500	200	204	422	1,326

Workings

1   *Impairment of land*

	$'000
Cost at 31 March 20X8	782
Less disposal	(39)
Cost at 31 March 20X9	743
Fair value at 31 March 20X9	729
Impairment of land	(14)

Charge to administrative expenses

2   *Profit on disposal of land*

	$'000
Proceeds	48
Carrying amount of land	(39)
Profit on disposal	9

3   *Income tax expense*

	$'000
Under provision from prior year	12
Current year charge	96
Reduction in deferred tax	(21)
	87

36 Objective test answers: Group financial statements

1   D

	$'000
Fair value of net assets acquired:	
Ordinary shares	400
Retained earnings at 1 January 20X7	100
Retained for 9 months to acquisition date (80 × 9/12)	60
	560
Add goodwill	30
	590

2   D

	$
Consolidated retained earnings	560,000
Less Mercedes plc	(450,000)
Add back unrealised profit (50,000 × 25/125)	10,000
	120,000

3   C

	$
Cost of investment	50,000
Share of post-acquisition retained earnings (20 × 35%)	7,000
Less dividend received (10 × 35%)	(3,500)
Less impairment	(6,000)
	47,500

4   B

	$'000
Profit on sale (160,000/4)	40,000
Unrealised profit (40,000 × 25%)	10,000
Group share (10,000 × 30%)	3,000

5   A

	Colossal plc	Enormous Ltd
	$	$
Retained earnings per question	275,000	177,000
Less pre-acquisition		(156,000)
Depreciation on FV adjustment (20,000/4)		(5,000)
		16,000
Goodwill impairment (W)	(12,000)	
Enormous Ltd	16,000	
Group retained earnings	279,000	

Working

	$	$
Consideration transferred		300,000
Share capital	100,000	
Retained earnings	156,000	
Fair value adjustment	20,000	
		(276,000)
Goodwill at acquisition		24,000
Impairment (50%)		12,000

6   C

	$
Consideration transferred	120,000
Share of post-acquisition retained earnings ((140 – 80) × 40%)	24,000
Unrealised profit (30,000 × 25% × 40%)	(3,000)
	141,000

7   C

	$	$
Consideration transferred		210,000
Fair value of net assets acquired:		
Share capital	100,000	
Retained earnings	90,000	
		(190,000)
Goodwill at acquisition		20,000
Impairment		(10,000)
Goodwill at 31 December 20X9		10,000

8   A

	A	B
	$	$
Retained earnings at 31 December 20X9	210,000	160,000
Less: pre-acquisition retained earnings		(90,000)
		70,000
Group share of B post-acquisition retained earnings		
($70,000 × 100%)		
Goodwill impairment	(10,000)	
Group retained earnings	270,000	

9   B

	$	$
Consideration transferred		350,000
Fair value of net assets acquired:		
Share capital	140,000	
Share premium	50,000	
Retained earnings	60,000	
		(250,000)
Goodwill at 31 December 20X9		100,000

10   A $140,000 + $80,000 + $40,000 = $260,000

37 Club, Green and Tee (5/13)

(a) If an impairment review indicates that goodwill has increased in value, the increase is deemed to be internally generated goodwill. Internally generated goodwill is not allowed to be recognised in the financial statements.

Club will therefore not recognise the increase in goodwill and will include goodwill in its statement of financial position at its original value.

(b)

CLUB GROUP CONSOLIDATED STATEMENT OF FINANCIAL POSITION AS AT 31 MARCH 2013

	$'000	$'000
Assets		
Non-current assets		
PPE (50,050 + 30,450 + 1,000 (W5) – 20 (W7))		81,480
Intangible asset: goodwill (W2)		10,570
Investment in associate (W3)		8,573
		100,623
Current assets		
Inventory (34,910 + 9,310 – 192 PUP (W6))	44,028	
Trade receivables (38,790 + 16,530 – 960 (W6) – 115 (W8))	54,245	
Cash and cash equivalents (5,010 + 1,480 + 115 (W8))	6,605	
		104,878
Total assets		205,501
Equity and liabilities		
Equity		
Share capital	112,620	
Share premium	0	
Retained earnings (W4)	23,441	
		136,061
Non-current liabilities		
Long term borrowings (32,000 + 15,000)		47,000
Current liabilities		
Trade payables (11,320 + 10,830 – 960 (W6))	21,190	
Loan interest payable (800 + 450)	1,250	
		22,440
Total equity and liabilities		205,501

Workings

W1 Group structure

Club

100% — Green

Retained earnings 1 April 2011 (i)
$3,000,000

3,980/15,920 = 25% — Tee

But there is significant influence (iv)

Retained earnings 1 April 2012	$1,300,000
RE 31 March 13 (SOFP)	3,590,000
Less profit for the year (per SPL)	(2,290,000)
RE at acquisition	1,300,000

W2 Goodwill on acquisition of Green

	$'000	$'000
Consideration transferred		35,610
Less: fair value of identifiable net assets acquired		
Share capital	17,370	
Share premium	3,470	
Retained earnings	3,000	
Fair value adjustment (W5)	1,200	
		(25,040)
Goodwill at end of reporting period		10,570

W3 Investment in associate

	$'000
Cost of associate	8,000
Share of post-acquisition retained reserves (W4)	573
Less: group impairment losses on associate to date	-
	8,573

W4 Retained earnings

	Club	Green	Tee
	$'000	$'000	$'000
Retained earnings per SOFP	15,630	10,650	3,590
Less: retained earnings at acquisition (W1)		(3,000)	(1,300)
Fair value adjustment movement (W5)		(200)	
Less: PUP adjustment (W6)	(192)		
Less: PUP adjustment re: sale of machinery (W7)	(20)		
		7,450	2,290
Green post acquisition retained earnings (7,450 × 100%)	7,450		
Tee share of post acquisition retained earnings (2,290 × 25%)	573		
Less: group share of impairment losses to date	-		
	23,441		

W5 Fair value adjustment (acquisition 1 April 2011)

	At acquisition date	Movement	At end of reporting period	
	$'000	$'000	$'000	
Buildings	1,200	(200)	1,000	Note 1
	1,200	(200)	1,000	
	Goodwill (W2)	Retained earnings (W4)	Consolidated SOFP	

Note 1: Two years' post-acquisition = 1,200 / 12 years × 2 years = 200

W6 Inter-group trading

Club (parent) sold goods to Green (subsidiary)

Sale price	960,000	= 133⅓%
Cost of sales	720,000	= 100%
Profit	240,000	= 33⅓%

20% of the goods remain in Green's closing inventory so 80% of the profit is unrealised, therefore reduce consolidated inventory by $192,000 and reduce Club's retained earnings by $192,000.

The goods have not been paid for so in Club's books there is an inter-group receivable due of $960,000 and Green has a payable of $960,000. These must be eliminated on consolidation.

W7 Sale of machinery

Club (parent) sold machinery to Green (subsidiary)

Proceeds	115,000
Carrying amount	(90,000)
Profit on disposal	25,000
Less: proportion realised through excess depreciation	
(1/5 × 25,000)	(5,000)
	20,000 Note

Note: Remove from Club's retained earnings as unrealised profit (see W4) and reduce group PPE.

W8 Cash in transit

Cash in transit of $115,000 paid by Green to Club:

DR	Cash and cash equivalents	$115,000	
CR	Receivables (intra-group)		$115,000

38   TX, SX and LW (3/13)

(a)   IAS 27 *Consolidated and separate financial statements* states that the key concept that determines whether an entity is a subsidiary of another entity is that of control. Any situation that gives an entity control of another creates a parent/subsidiary relationship.

IAS 27 provides the following instances where control can be achieved with fewer than 50% of equity shares:

- Power over more than 50% of voting rights by virtue of an agreement with other investors

- Power to govern the financial and operating policies of the entity under a statute or agreement

- Power to appoint or remove the majority of the members of the board of directors or equivalent governing body and control of the entity is by that board or body

- Power to cast the majority of votes at meetings of the board of directors or equivalent governing body and control of the entity is by that board or body

(b)

TX GROUP CONSOLIDATED STATEMENT OF FINANCIAL POSITION AS AT 31 MARCH 2013

	$'000	$'000
Assets		
Non-current assets		
PPE (545 + 480 + 68 (W5))		1,093
Intangible asset: goodwill (W2)		0
Investment in associate (W3)		205
		1,298
Current assets		
Inventory (221 + 55 – 11 PUP (W6))	265	
Trade receivables (98 + 75 – 44 (W6) – 15 (W7))	114	
Cash and cash equivalents (72 + 0 + 15 (W7))	87	
		466
Total assets		1,764
Equity and liabilities		
Equity		
Share capital	800	
Share premium	400	
Retained earnings (W4)	342	
		1,542
Current liabilities		
Trade payables (156 + 47 – 44 (W6))	159	
Bank overdraft (0 + 63)	63	
		222
Total equity and liabilities		1,764

Workings

W1 Group structure

```
                              TX
        100%                 ╱    ╲          150/500
                            ╱      ╲         = 30%
           SX ↙                     ↘  LW
Retained earnings 1 Jan 2012 (i)    Retained earnings 1 Jan 2012
         $110,000                            $70,000
```

W2 Goodwill on acquisition of SX

	$'000	$'000
Consideration transferred		530
Less: fair value of identifiable net assets acquired		
Share capital	360	
Share premium	0	
Retained earnings	110	
Fair value adjustment (W5)	72	
		(542)
Negative goodwill (credit to retained earnings)		(12)

W3 Investment in associate

	$'000
Cost of associate	190
Share of post-acquisition retained reserves (W4)	15
Less: group impairment losses on associate to date	-
	205

W4 Retained earnings

	TX	SX	LW
	$'000	$'000	$'000
Retained earnings per SOFP	300	140	120
Less: retained earnings at acquisition (W1)		(110)	(70)
Fair value adjustment movement (W5)		(4)	
Less: PUP adjustment (W6)	(11)		
Add: negative goodwill (W2)	12		
		26	50
SX post acquisition retained earnings (26 × 100%)	26		
LW share of post acquisition retained earnings (50 × 30%)	15		
Less: group share of impairment losses to date	-		
	342		

W5 Fair value adjustment (acquisition 1 Jan 2012)

	At acquisition date	Movement	At end of reporting period	
	$'000	$'000	$'000	
Buildings	72	(4)	68	Note 1
	72	(4)	68	
	Goodwill (W2)	Retained earnings (W4)	Consolidated SOFP	

Note 1: One year post-acquisition = 72 / 18 years × 1 year = 4

W6 Inter-group trading

TX (parent) sold goods to SX (subsidiary)

Sale price	44,000	= 133⅓%
Cost of sales	33,000	= 100%
Profit	11,000	= 33⅓%

All of the goods remain in SX's closing inventory so all of the profit is unrealised, therefore reduce consolidated inventory by $11,000 and reduce TX's retained earnings by $11,000.

The goods have not been paid for so in TX's books there is an inter-group receivable due of $44,000 and SX has a payable of $44,000. These must be eliminated on consolidation.

W7 Cash in transit
Cash in transit of $15,000 paid by SX to TX:

DR	Cash and cash equivalents	$15,000
	CR Receivables (intra-group)		$15,000

39 AZ, PQ and SY (11/12)

> **Text references.** Group financial statements are covered in Chapters 13 to 16 of the Study Text. Fair values are covered in Chapter 14 and revaluation of non-current assets in Chapter 6.
>
> **Top tips.** Consolidation questions require excellent time management skills if they are to be tackled successfully, and they also require good exam techniques, particularly when it comes to setting out and producing the workings you need to fill out the proforma.
>
> Part (a) of this question has a small narrative element and a calculation, for four marks in total; it is important that you do not spend any more than your strict time allocation on this part.
>
> In part (b) of this question it is not explicitly stated whether PQ's share premium and revaluation reserve are pre- or post-acquisition; in the answer they have been treated as pre-acquisition. If you need to make an assumption in the exam make it clear to the examiner what that assumption is, and stick with it throughout your answer.
>
> **Easy marks.** Some figures can be found in the question and put into the proforma without resorting to workings, but as with most consolidation questions the process is what is being examined and this is what needs to be shown clearly to the examiner.

(a) (i) IAS 27 allows an investment in a subsidiary to be recorded in the parent's individual financial statements at cost or at fair value.

If fair value is used, the investment is valued at the number of shares held multiplied by the market price of the share. This is because the investment represents shares held in another entity and the fair value of those shares is the amount at which they can be bought or sold in an active market. The fair value of each share is therefore its market price.

(ii) The fair value of PQ's net assets acquired by AZ on 1 October 2010 was:

	$'000
Share capital	100
Share premium	50
Retained earnings (i)	38
Revaluation reserve	60
Fair value adjustment – property (300 – 200)	100
Fair value adjustment – plant and equipment (117 – 97)	20
	368

(b)

AZ GROUP CONSOLIDATED STATEMENT OF FINANCIAL POSITION AS AT 30 SEPTEMBER 2012

	$'000	$'000
Assets		
Non-current assets		
PPE (400 + 297 + 112 (W5) – 18 (W7))		791
Intangible asset: goodwill (W2)		112
Investment in associate (W3)		136
		1,039
Current assets		
Inventory (190 + 60 – 13 PUP (W6))	237	
Trade receivables (144 + 63 – 52 (W6) – 60 (W8))	95	
Cash and cash equivalents (48 + 21 + 60 (W8))	129	
		461
Total assets		1,500
Equity and liabilities		
Equity		
Share capital	900	
Share premium	300	
Retained earnings (W4)	137	
Revaluation reserve	-	
		1,337
Current liabilities		
Trade payables (96 + 119 – 52 (W6))		163
Total equity and liabilities		1,500

Workings

W1 Group structure

AZ

100%	80/400 = 20%	But there is significant influence (iv)

PQ	SY
Retained earnings 1 Oct 2010 (i)	Retained earnings 1 Oct 2011
$38,000	$40,000

RE 30 Sep 12 (SOFP)	95,000
Less profit for the year (v)	(55,000)
RE at acquisition	40,000

W2 Goodwill on acquisition of PQ

	$'000
Consideration transferred	500
Less: fair value of identifiable net assets acquired (a) (ii)	(368)
	132
Less: impairment losses to date (iii)	(20)
Goodwill at end of reporting period	112

W3 Investment in associate

	$'000
Cost of associate	125
Share of post-acquisition retained reserves (W4)	11
Less: group impairment losses on associate to date	-
	136

W4 Retained earnings

	AZ $'000	PQ $'000	SY $'000
Retained earnings per SOFP	111	112	95
Less: retained earnings at acquisition (W1)		(38)	(40)
Fair value adjustment movement (W5)		(8)	
Less: PUP adjustment (W6)		(13)	
Less: PUP adjustment re: sale of machinery (W7)	(18)		
	93	53	55
PQ post acquisition retained earnings (53 × 100%)	53		
SY share of post acquisition retained earnings (55 × 20%)	11		
Less: group share of impairment losses to date (iii)	(20)		
	137		

W5 Fair value adjustment (acquisition 1 October 2010)

	At acquisition date $'000	Movement $'000	At end of reporting period $'000	
Property (300 – 200)	100	-	100	Note 1
Plant and equipment (117 – 97)	20	(8)	12	Note 2
	120	(8)	112	
	Goodwill (W2)	Retained earnings (W4)	Consolidated SOFP	

Note 1: Assume no movement as depreciation policy is given for plant and equipment only.

Note 2: Two years' post-acquisition = 20 / 5 years × 2 years = 8

W6 Inter-group trading

PQ (subsidiary) sold goods to AZ (parent)

Sale price	52,000	= 133 1/3%
Cost of sales	39,000	= 100%
Profit	13,000	= 33 1/3%

All of the goods remain in AZ's closing inventory so all the profit is unrealised, therefore reduce consolidated inventory by $13,000 and reduce PQ's retained earnings by $13,000.

The goods have not been paid for so in PQ's books there is an inter-group receivable due of $52,000 and AZ has a payable of $52,000. These must be eliminated on consolidation.

W7 Sale of machinery

AZ (parent) sold machinery to PQ (subsidiary)

Proceeds	74,000	
Carrying value	(50,000)	
Profit on disposal	24,000	
Less: proportion realised through excess depreciation (1/4 × 24,000)	(6,000)	
	18,000	Note

Note: Remove from AZ's retained earnings as unrealised profit (see W4) and reduce group PPE.

W8 Cash in transit

Cash in transit of $60,000 paid by AZ to PQ:

DR	Cash and cash equivalents	$60,000	
	CR Receivables (intra-group)		$60,000

40 Wood, Plank and Bush (9/12)

Text references. Group financial statements are covered in Chapters 13 to 16 of the Study Text.

Top tips. Consolidation questions require a planned, methodical approach if they are to be completed in the time available. Sufficient practice on the common adjustments/calculations such as goodwill and intra-group trading will enable you to tackle these confidently and get some figures into your answer at the outset.

Easy marks. There were marks available for a mainly narrative answer in part (a).

Examiner's comments. 'The answer to part (a), explanation of the treatment of an inter-group transfer of a piece of machinery at a profit to the holding entity, was very poor with many candidates not attempting an answer and a large proportion of the rest explaining that the profit should be increased to record the transfer gain. A number of the answers to part (b) simply added the holding entity's and subsidiary's figures together, making no attempt at consolidation adjustments other than a goodwill calculation. There were notable fewer candidates using proportional consolidation in this examination.

Marking scheme

		Marks
(a)	Explanation of treatment of assets sold	3
(b)	Calculation of goodwill on acquisition of Plank	2.5
	Calculation of investment in Bush	1.5
	Calculation of consolidated retained earnings	3.5
	Consolidated statement of profit or loss and other comprehensive income	6.5
	Consolidated statement of financial position	8.0
		22
Total marks for question		25

(a) The sale to Plank must be recognised in the group consolidated accounts at carrying amount, with no profit or loss recognised. Therefore the following adjustments need to be made:

- Cancel the profit on the sale - reduce consolidated profit for the year/consolidated retained earnings by $20,000.

- Cancel the increase in depreciation [($95,000-$75,000)/10], $2,000 - increase consolidated profit for the year/consolidated retained earnings by $2,000.

- Reduce consolidated non-current assets – property, plant and equipment in the statement of financial position by $20,000-$2,000 = $18,000.

(b) <u>Investment of Wood in Plank</u>

Wood purchased all 6,000,000 shares in Plank on 1 April 2011.

100% shares purchased therefore treat Plank as wholly owned subsidiary of Wood from 1 April 2011.

Investment of Wood in Bush

Wood purchased 1,540,000 of Bush's 5,500,000 shares on 1 April 2011.

This gave Wood 28% of Bush's equity.

As Wood has in excess of 20% of Bush's equity and can exercise significant influence over all aspects of Bush's strategic and operational decisions Wood will treat Bush as an associated entity from 1 April 2011.

Workings (All workings in $'000)

(i) <u>Fair value of net assets of Plank at acquisition</u>

Equity shares	6,000
Retained earnings	1,280
Fair value adjustment	1,350
	8,630

(ii) <u>Goodwill - Plank</u>

Cost	9,200
Fair value of net assets acquired:	8,630
Goodwill	570
Impairment	(80)
Balance at 31 March 2012	490

(iii) <u>Investment in associate – Bush</u>

Cost 2,420
Add group share of post acquisition profits

$(1,240 - 410) = 830 \times 28\% =$	232
Investment at 31 March 2012	2,652

(iv) <u>Intra-group trading</u>

Mark up on cost 100% = 100/200 or 50% margin on selling price.

Selling price 520; unrealised profit = $520 \times 50\% = 260$

All goods remain in inventory – 260

	Dr.	Cr.
Consolidated cost of sales	260	
Consolidated current assets – inventory		260
Consolidated revenue	520	
Consolidated cost of sales		520
Loan interest		

	Dr	Cr
Accrue interest receivable by Wood:		
Receivables – interest	155	
Interest receivable – SPLOCI		155
Receivables – interest		155
Loan interest payable	155	
Interest payable – SPLOCI		155
Interest receivable –SPLOCI	155	

Consolidated interest payable = $(810+440 - 155) = 1,095$
Consolidated receivables – interest $(155 - 155) = 0$

Consolidated trade receivables

Wood	13,400
Plank	5,710
Less intra-group sales	(520)
Less cheque in transit	(210)
	18,380

Consolidated trade payables

Wood	3,910
Plank	3,740
Less intra-group sales	(520)
	7,130

(v) Excess depreciation

Fair value adjustment – 1,350
Economic life 15 years, straight line basis
Excess depreciation = 1,350/15 = 90

(vi) <u>Consolidated Retained Earnings</u>

Balance – Wood at 1 April 2011 (5,400 – 3,490)	1,910
Add consolidated profit for year	5,829
Balance 31 Jan 2012	7,739

(vii) <u>Consolidated Property, plant and equipment</u>

Wood	11,820
Plank	7,240
Adjustment for sale of asset, net (see (a))	(18)
Fair value adjustment	1,350
Excess depreciation	(90)
	20,302

Wood Group – Consolidated statement of profit of loss and other comprehensive income for year ended 31 March 2012

	$'000
Revenue(15,500+6,900 – 520)	21,880
Cost of sales (8,700+3,080-520+260+90+20 – 2)	(11,628)
Gross profit	10,252
Expenses (1,250+750+80)	(2,080)
Profit from operations	8,172
Share of profit of associated entity	232
Finance cost	(1,095)
Profit before tax	7,309
Tax (1,250+230)	(1,480)
Profit for the year	5,829

Wood Group - Consolidated statement of financial position as at 31 March 2012

	$'000	$'000
Non-current assets		
Property, plant and equipment (vii)	20,302	
Goodwill (ii)	490	
Investment in associate (iii)	2,652	
		23,444
Current assets		
Inventory (12,060 + 3,215 – 260)	15,015	
Trade receivables (iv)	18,380	
Cash and cash equivalents (1,730+510+210)	2,450	
		35,845
		59,289
Total assets		
Equity and liabilities		
Equity shares	38,900	
Share premium	5,520	
Retained earnings (vi)	7,739	
		52,159
Current liabilities		7,130
Trade payables (iv)		59,289

41 Loch, River and Stream (5/12)

Text references. Consolidated financial statements are covered in Chapter 13 to Chapter 16 of the Study Text.

Top tips. As with all questions involving groups, a methodical approach is essential. See the step-by-step guide in Chapter 14 of the Study Text.

Easy marks. An accurate journal in part (a) could have scored 3 easy marks

Marking scheme

	Marks
Journal	3.0
Goodwill	3.0
Investment in associate	1.5
Intra-group transactions - workings	2.0
Consolidated retained earnings	3.5
Statement of profit or loss and other comprehensive income	6.0
SOFP	6.0
Maximum marks	**25**

(a) Consideration for River paid in shares:

Cost $950,000; share market value $2. Therefore Loch issued 475,000 shares at a premium of $475,000.

Journal

	Dr	Cr
	$'000	**$'000**
Investment in River	950	
Equity shares		475
Share premium		475

(b) <u>Investment of Loch in River</u>

Loch purchased all 600,000 shares in River on 1 April 2011.

100% shares purchased therefore treat River as wholly owned subsidiary of Loch from 1 April 2011.

<u>Investment of Loch in Stream</u>

Loch purchased 156,000 of Stream's 520,000 shares on 1 April 2011.

This gave Loch 30% of Stream's equity.

As Loch has in excess of 20% of Stream's equity and can exercise significant influence over all aspects of Stream's financial and operating policies Loch will treat Stream as an associated entity from 1 April 2011.

Loch Group – Consolidated Statement of Profit or Loss for year ended 31 March 2012

	$'000
Revenue (1,500 + 693 – 220 (W6))	1,973
Cost of sales (865 + 308 + 12 (W5) – 220 (W6) + 73 (W6))	(1,038)
Gross profit	935
Expenses (124 + 70 + 20 (GW imp))	(214)
Profit from operations	721
Finance cost (80 + 40 – 15 (inter-co))	(105)
Share of profit of associate (30% × 80)	24
Profit before tax	640
Tax (118 + 20)	(138)
Profit for the year	502

Loch Group - Consolidated Statement of Financial Position as at 31 March 2012:

	$'000	$'000
Non-Current Assets		
Property, plant and equipment		2,092
(1,193 + 767 + 132 (W5))		
Goodwill (W2)		56
Investment in associate (W3)		247
		2,395
Current Assets		
Inventory (1,107 + 320 – 73 (W6))	1,354	
Trade receivables (1,320 + 570)	1,890	
Cash and cash equivalents (62 + 58 + 26 (W7))	146	
		3,390
Total assets		5,785
Equity and Liabilities		
Equity Shares (3,500 + 475)		3,975
Share premium		475
Retained Earnings (W4)		602
Current Liabilities		
Trade payables (393 + 340)		733
		5,785

Workings

W1 Group structure

Loch

100%   156/520
= 30%

River   Stream

Retained earnings 1 April 2011   Retained earnings 1 April 2011

$130,000 $45,000

W2 Goodwill on acquisition of River

	$'000	$'000
Consideration transferred		950
Less: fair value of identifiable net assets acquired		
Share capital	600	
Retained earnings	130	
Fair value adjustment (W5)	144	
		(874)
Goodwill at acquisition		76
Less: impairment losses to date		(20)
Goodwill at end of reporting period		56

W3 Investment in associate

	$'000
Cost of associate	223
Share of post-acquisition retained earnings (125,000 – 45,000)	
× 30% (W4)	24
	247

W4 Retained earnings

	Loch $'000	River $'000	Stream $'000
Retained earnings per SOFP	413	385	125
Less: retained earnings at acquisition		(130)	(45)
Fair value adjustment movement (W5)		(12)	
Less: PUP adjustment (W6)	(73)		
Finance income not recorded by Loch	15		
		243	80

Share of River post acquisition retained earnings (100% × 243)	243
Share of Stream post acquisition retained earnings (30% × 80)	24
Less: group share of impairment losses to date	(20)
	602

W5 Fair value adjustment

	At acquisition date $'000	Movement $'000	At end of reporting period $'000
Building (Note 1)	144	(12)	132
	144	(12)	132
	Goodwill (W2)	Retained earnings (W4)	Consolidated SOFP

Note 1: One year post-acquisition = 144 / 12 years × 1 year = 12

W6 Provision for unrealised profit

Sale price	150%	220
Cost of sales	100%	(147)
Profit	50%	73

Step 1: Remove intra-group trading:

Dr Revenue   220

Cr Cost of sales   220

Step 2: Remove unrealised profit (note all inventory still held):

Dr Loch retained earnings (& increase cost of sales)   73

Cr Inventory   73

W7 Cash in transit
Cash in transit of $26,000 paid by River to Loch:

DR   Cash and cash equivalents $26,000

   CR   Receivables (intra-group) $26,000

42 Tree, Branch and Leaf (3/12)

Text references. Group financial statements (including Associates) are dealt with in Chapters 13 to 16 of the Study Text.

Top tips. Exam technique is crucial when dealing with groups as there is a lot to think about. Getting the group structure right at the beginning is essential if your subsequent calculations are to be accurate so it is worth spending enough time on this. Don't make the common mistake of consolidating associates. Look carefully at the information you are given on intra-group trading and set out your workings clearly.

Marking scheme

	Marks
Goodwill	2.5
Investment in associate	2.0
Consolidated retained earnings	5.0
Consolidated SPLOCI	7.0
Consolidated SOFP	8.5
Maximum marks	**25**

Workings (All workings in $'000)

(i) Fair value of net assets of Branch at acquisition

Equity Shares	790
Retained earnings	380
Fair value adjustment	240
	1,410

(ii) Goodwill - Branch

Cost	1,500
Fair value of net assets acquired:	1,410
Goodwill	90

(iii) Investment in associate - Leaf

Cost	550
Add group share of post acquisition profits	
$(220 - 70) = 150 \times 40\% =$	60
Investment at 31 January 2012	610

(iv) Intra-group trading

Mark up on cost 50% = 50/150 or 33.3% margin on selling price.
Selling price 180; profit = $180 \times 33.3\% = 60$
2/3 remain in inventory - unrealised profit $60 \times 2/3 = 40$

	Dr	Cr
Consolidated cost of sales	40	
Consolidated current assets – inventory		40
Consolidated revenue	180	
Consolidated cost of sales		180

Current accounts:

Tree current account with Branch	123	
Less cheque in transit	28	
	95	Cancels
Branch current account with Tree	95	Cancels

Loan interest
Accrue interest receivable by Tree 30

	Dr	Cr
Interest payable	30	
Interest receivable		30

Consolidated interest payable = $(102 + 59 - 30) = 131$
Consolidated interest receivable $(30 - 30) = 0$

(v) Excess depreciation

Fair value adjustment – 240
Economic life 10 years, straight line basis
Excess depreciation = 240/10 = 24

(vi)   Consolidated Retained Earnings

      Balance – Tree at 1 Feb 2011 (665 – 620)   45
      Add consolidated profit for year   <u>761</u>
      Balance 31 Jan 2012   <u>806</u>

Alternative calculation:

(vi)   Consolidated Retained Earnings

      Balance - Tree (665 + 30)   695
      Branch - group share of post acquisition profits (495 – 380) = 115
      Associate - Leaf, group share of post acquisition profits (iii)   60
      Excess depreciation   (24)
      Cancel unrealised profit in inventory (iv)   <u>(40)</u>
                                                <u>806</u>

(vii)   Consolidated Property, plant and equipment

      Tree   1,535
      Branch   1,155
      Fair value adjustment   240
      Excess depreciation   <u>(24)</u>
                            <u>2,906</u>

Tree Group – Consolidated Statement of Comprehensive Income for year ended 31

January 2012	$'000
Revenue(2,200 + 777 –180)	2,797
Cost of sales (1,112 + 456 – 180 + 24 + 40)	(1,452)
Gross profit	1,345
Expenses (221 + 115)	(336)
Profit from operations	1,009
Share of profit of associated entity	60
Finance cost	(131)
Profit before tax	938
Tax (145 + 32)	(177)
Profit for the year	761

Tree Group - Consolidated Statement of Financial Position as at 31 January 2012

	$'000	$'000
Non-Current Assets		
Property, plant and equipment (vii)	2,906	
Goodwill (ii)	90	
Investment in associate (iii)	610	
		3,606
Current Assets		
Inventory (1,360 + 411 – 40)	1,731	
Trade receivables (1,540 + 734)	2,274	
Cash and cash equivalents (47 + 75 + 28)	150	
		4,155
Total assets		7,761
Equity and Liabilities		
Equity Shares	3,900	
Retained Earnings (vi)	806	
		4,706
Current Liabilities		
Trade payables (2,690 + 365)		3,055
		7,761

43 PH, SU and AJ (11/11)

Text references. Preparation of the consolidated statement of financial position is covered in Chapter 14. Accounting for associates is covered in Chapter 16.

Top tips. Don't get carried away with part (a), stick to the time allocation and then move on to part (b). If you couldn't remember these definitions, go back to your Study Text and revise as you could pick up some easy marks with a question like this in your real exam.

The consolidated statement of financial position was a reasonable consolidation on which you should have comfortably passed. There were a lot of marks available for going through the mechanics of consolidating the parent and subsidiary, make sure you stick to your exam technique to get these first. There were a couple of tricky parts that you may have not known what to do with: the cash in transit and the additional depreciation on the fair value adjustment. Easy errors to make are:

- Not including the fair value uplift in your goodwill calculation

- Not including the depreciation on the fair value uplift in your retained earnings working

- Including the parent's loan to the subsidiary as part of the group's long-term loans.

Easy marks. There were easy marks to be gained in part (a) for explaining control. In part (b), there were easy for inserting the figures for PH's share capital and long-term borrowings straight from the question onto your answer, and then for going through the mechanics of consolidation and showed your workings, even if you didn't get it all right!

(a) Control is defined by IFRS 10 as follows: 'An investor controls an investee when the investor is exposed, or has rights, to variable returns from its involvement with the investee and has the ability to affect those returns through power over the investee'.

Control can usually be assumed to exist when the parent **owns more than half (ie over 50%) of the voting power** of an entity *unless* it can be clearly shown that **such ownership does not constitute control**, which is rare.

IFRS 10 states that an investor controls an investee only if all three of the following apply; the investor has:

(i) Power over the investee;
(ii) Exposure to, or rights to, variable returns from its involvement with the investee; and
(iii) The ability to use its power over the investee to affect the amount of the investor's returns.

Power may be obtained from direct ownership of voting rights or may be derived from other rights, such as the right to appoint and remove key personnel.

(b) PH GROUP
CONSOLIDATED STATEMENT OF FINANCIAL POSITION AS AT 31 SEPTEMBER 2011

	$'000	$'000
Non-current assets		
Intangible: goodwill (W2)		18,610
Property, plant and equipment (50,390 ǀ 57,590 +1,235 (W5))		109,215
Investment in associate (W3)		17,670
		115,300
Current assets		
Inventory (10,160 + 14,410 – 1,200(W6))	23,370	
Receivables (21,400 + 13,200 – 90)	34,510	
Bank (1,260 + 3,600 + 2,800)	7,660	
		65,540
Total assets		211,035

	$'000	$'000
Equity and liabilities		
Share capital (PH only)		126,000
Retained earnings (W4)		34,425
		160,425
Non-current liabilities		
Long-term loan		32,700
Current liabilities		
Payables (12,600 + 5,400 – 90)		17,910
Total equity and liabilities		211,035

Workings

1   *Group structure*

```
                      PH
        100%         /  \        33⅓%
                    /    \
                  SU      AJ
```

2   *Goodwill*

	$'000	$'000
Consideration transferred		75,590
Net assets acquired as represented by:		
Ordinary share capital	48,000	
Retained earnings on acquisition	7,680	
Fair value adjustment on PPE (W5)	1,300	
		(56,980)
Goodwill		18,610

3   *Investment in associate*

	$'000
Cost of associate	16,400
Share of post-acquisition retained reserves (W4)	1,270
	17,670

4   *Retained earnings*

	PH	SU	AJ
	$'000	$'000	$'000
Per Question	26,500	15,600	28,800
Less pre-acquisition		(7,680)	(24,990)
Unrealised profit (W6)	(1,200)		
Depreciation on FV adjustment (W5)	–	(65)	–
	25,300	7,855	3,810
Group share of SU post acquisition RE (7,855 × 100%)	7,855		
Group share of AJ post acquisition RE (3,810 × 33⅓%)	1,270		
	34,425		

5   *Fair value adjustments*

	At acquisition date	Movement	At year end
	$'000	$'000	$'000
Buildings	1,300	(65)*	1,235
	Goodwill (W2)	Retained Earnings (W4)	Consolidated PPE

*1,300/20 years = 65

6   *Intra-group trading*

		$'000
Revenue	133⅓%	4,800
Cost	100%	(3,600)
Profit	33⅓%	1,200
Unrealised profit		1,200

44 AX (5/10)

Text references. Accounting for associates is covered in Chapter 16. Preparation of a consolidated statement of financial position is covered in Chapter 14.

Top tips. This is a pretty straightforward consolidation question. Though you might have been pushed for time because you had to do both the consolidated statement of financial position and the consolidated statement of comprehensive income. The question tried to throw you off course with a negative retained earnings balance in the subsidiary – but don't worry about it, just put it into your calculations! Part (a) was a basic corporate tax calculation that you should have found easy – the question even supplied the tax depreciation amount to use. Calculating the change in the deferred tax provision required a bit more thought.

Working methodically through part (b) using our recommended approach is the best way to make sure you have included all the balances and get the most marks.

Easy errors to make were:

*   Not adjusting retained earnings for the tax calculated in part (a)
*   Not including the fair value uplift in your goodwill calculation
*   Incorrectly calculating goodwill due to the negative retained earnings figure
*   Forgetting to remove the intra-group sales figures from revenue and cost of sales

Easy marks. There were easy marks to be gained in part (a) for calculating the corporate income tax. In part (b), there were easy marks for doing the basic adding across procedure for consolidation, filling in your proforma as you go.

(a)   AX CORPORATE INCOME TAX FOR YEAR ENDED 31 MARCH 20X9

	$'000	$'000
Accounting profit		264
Add back: entertaining expenses	4	
Accounting depreciation	31	
		35
Less: tax depreciation		(49)
Taxable profit		250
Tax charge @ 25%		63

Deferred tax provision

Difference between carrying amount and tax base increased by 49,000 – 31,000 = $18,000

Increase in deferred tax provision = 25% × 18,000 = $4,500 (round to $5,000)

(b) AX CONSOLIDATED STATEMENT OF PROFIT OR LOSS AND OTHER COMPREHENSIVE INCOME FOR THE YEAR ENDED 31 MARCH 20X9

	$'000
Revenue (820 + 285 – 55)	1,050
Cost of sales (406 + 119 – 55 +5 (W2))	(475)
Gross profit	575
Administrative expenses (84 + 36)	(120)
Distribution costs (48 + 22)	(70)
	385
Income from associate (51 × 22%)	11
Finance cost (18 + 5)	(23)
Profit before tax	373
Taxation (16 + 63 + 5)	(84)
Profit for the year/Total consolidated income for the year	289

AX CONSOLIDATED STATEMENT OF FINANCIAL POSITION AS AT 31 MARCH 20X9

	$'000	$'000
Assets		
Non-current assets		
Property, plant and equipment (1,120 + 700 + 75)	1,895	
Goodwill (W3)	137	
Investment in associate (W4)	156	
		2,188
Current assets		
Inventory (205 + 30 – 5(W2))	230	
Trade receivables (350 + 46)	396	
Cash and cash equivalents	30	
		656
Total assets		2,844
Equity and liabilities		
Equity attributable to owners of the parent		
Share capital	1,500	
Retained earnings (W5)	543	
Total equity		2,043
Non-current liabilities		
Long-term borrowings		440
Deferred tax (120 + 16 +5)		141
Current liabilities		
Trade payables (92 + 29)	121	
Tax payable (16 + 63)	79	
Bank overdraft	20	
		220
Total liabilities and equity		2,844

Workings

1   *Group structure*

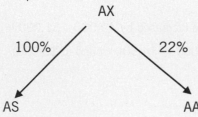

2   *Unrealised profit/Intra-group sales*

	$'000
Sale price (125%)	25
Cost price (100%)	(20)
Unrealised profit	5

			$
DR	Group retained earnings	$5,000	
CR	Group inventory	$5,000	
DR	Revenue	$55,000	
CR	Cost of sales	$55,000	

3   *Goodwill*

	$'000	$'000
Consideration transferred		740
Net assets acquired as represented by:		
Ordinary share capital	600	
Retained earnings on acquisition	(72)	
Fair value adjustment on land	75	
		(603)
Goodwill		137

4   *Investment in associate*

	$'000
Cost	145
Share of profit for the year (22% × 51)	11
	156

5   *Retained earnings*

	AX $'000	AS $'000	AA $'000
Per Question	518	15	100
Less pre-acquisition retained earnings	–	72	(49)
Less current tax charge (a)	(63)	–	–
Less increase in DT provision (a)	(5)	–	–
Less unrealised profit (PUP) adjustment (W2)		(5)	
	450	82	51
Group share of AS post acquisition retained earnings (82 x 100%)	82		
Group share of AA post acquisition retained earnings (51 x 22%)	11		
	543		

45   PSA (Specimen paper)

Text references. Accounting for associates is covered in Chapter 16. Preparation of the consolidated statement of financial position is covered in Chapter 14.

Top tips. Don't get carried away with part (a), stick to the time allocation and then move on to part (b). Don't forget to include a short discussion on the relevant ethical issues in your answer to part (a).

The consolidated statement of financial position was fairly straightforward, but did contain a couple of tricky parts. Easy errors to make are:

- Not including the fair value uplift in your goodwill calculation

- Not including the depreciation on the fair value uplift in your retained earnings working

- Incorrectly calculating the investment in associate balance due to the loss made by the associate in the year

Easy marks. There were easy marks to be gained in part (a) for explaining equity accounting. In part (b), there were easy marks for calculating trade payables and receivables and cash, and for inserting the figures for P's share capital and long-term borrowings straight from the question onto your answer.

(a) DRAFT MEMO

To: The Directors of P

From: A Management Accountant

Treatment of A in the consolidated financial statements

A is classified as an **associate** under IAS 28 because P can exercise **significant influence** (but not control) over A's strategic and operating decisions.

IAS 28 requires associates to be accounted for in the consolidated financial statements using the **equity method**.

Under the equity method, P will take account of its **share of the earnings** of A, whether or not A distributes the earnings as dividends. This is achieved by adding P's share of A's profit after tax to the consolidated profit of P. In the statement of financial position, the investment in A is recorded initially at cost and then each year will increase (or decrease) by the amount of P's share of A's change in retained reserves.

A will not be consolidated as a subsidiary as P does not exercise control over it.

It would not be in line with IAS 28 to include A as a simple investment of $13,000 in the consolidated financial statements. Including A as a simple investment would suggest that P did not have influence over the strategic and operating decisions of A. This would be potentially misleading to users of the financial statements.

The CIMA code of Ethics states that professional accountants should behave with integrity. Producing potentially misleading information is a breach of integrity and therefore is unethical.

(b) P CONSOLIDATED STATEMENT OF FINANCIAL POSITION AS AT 31 MARCH 20X9

	$'000	$'000
Assets		
Non-current assets		
Property, plant and equipment (W2)	88,950	
Goodwill (W4)	12,600	
Investment in associate (W5)	7,720	
		109,270
Current assets		
Inventory (8,000 + 12,000 – 1,000)	19,000	
Trade receivables (17,000 + 11,000 – 250 – 4000)	23,750	
Cash and cash equivalents (1,000 + 3,000 + 2,000)	6,000	
		48,750
Total assets		158,020
Equity and liabilities		
Equity attributable to owners of the parent		
Share capital	100,000	
Retained earnings (W6)	21,270	
Total equity		121,270
Non-current liabilities		
Long-term borrowings		26,000
Current liabilities		
Trade payables (10,000 + 5,000 – 250 – 4,000)		10,750
Total liabilities and equity		158,020

Workings

1 *Group structure*

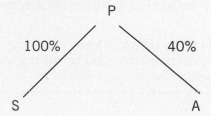

2   *Property, plant and equipment*

	$'000
P carrying value of PPE	40,000
S carrying value of PPE	48,000
Fair value uplift	1,000
Less additional depreciation*	(50)
	88,950

* Additional depreciation for fair value uplift = 1,000,000/20 = $50,000 per annum

3   *Unrealised profit*

	$'000
Sale price (cost plus 1/3)	4,000
Cost price (sales price × 3/4)	(3,000)
Unrealised profit	1,000

DR   Group retained earnings
CR   Group inventory

4   *Goodwill*

	$'000	$'000
Consideration transferred		60,000
Net assets acquired as represented by:		
Ordinary share capital	40,000	
Retained earnings on acquisition	6,400	
Fair value adjustment on buildings	1,000	
		(47,400)
Goodwill		12,600

5   *Investment in associate*

	$'000
Cost	13,000
Share of loss for the year (40% × (7,800 – 21,000))	(5,280)
	7,720

6   *Retained earnings*

	P	S	A
	$'000	$'000	$'000
Per Question	21,000	13,000	7,800
Less pre-acquisition	–	(6,400)	(21,000)
Unrealised profit (W3)	(1,000)	–	–
Depreciation on FV adjustment	–	(50)	–
	20,000	6,550	(13,200)
S × 100%	6,550		
A × 40%	(5,280)		
	21,270		

46   Parsley

Text references. Consolidated financial statements are covered in Chapters 13-16.

Top tips. Points to watch in this question are:

(a)   Correct consolidation technique – not proportionate consolidation
(b)   Elimination of intra-group transactions
(c)   Adjustments to inventory, receivables and cash

(a) *Goodwill arising on acquisition of Sage*

	$'000	$'000
Consideration transferred		30,000
Net assets acquired:		
Share capital	25,000	
Retained earnings	2,000	
		27,000
Goodwill		3,000

(b) (i) PARSLEY
CONSOLIDATED STATEMENT OF PROFIT OF LOSS AND OTHER COMPREHENSIVE INCOME
FOR THE YEAR ENDED 31 DECEMBER 20X9

	$'000
Revenue (135m + 74m – 12m)	197,000
Cost of sales (W1)	(89,000)
Gross profit	108,000
Distribution costs	(13,700)
Administrative expenses	(26,784)
Impairment of goodwill (3,000 – 2,250)	(750)
Finance charges (W2)	(12)
Profit before taxation	66,754
Taxation	(19,000)
Profit for the year	47,754

(ii) PARSLEY
CONSOLIDATED STATEMENT OF FINANCIAL POSITION AS AT 31 DECEMBER 20X9

	$'000	$'000
Non-current assets		
Intangible: goodwill		2,250
Property, plant and equipment (net book value):		
$(74,000,000 + 39,050,000)		113,050
		115,300
Current assets		
Inventory (10,630,000 + 4,498,000 – 1,000,000 (W1))	14,128	
Receivables (W3)	20,886	
Bank	14,744	
		49,758
		165,058
Equity and liabilities		
Share capital		80,000
Retained earnings (W5)		48,790
		128,790
Non-current liabilities		
8% loan notes		150
Current liabilities		
Payables (W4)	6,118	
Taxation	18,000	
Dividends: Parsley	12,000	
		36,118
		165,058

Workings

1   *Cost of sales*

	$'000
Parsley	70,000
Sage	30,000
	100,000
Less intra-group	(12,000)
	88,000
Add back unrealised profit in inventory $(12m − 8m) × 25\%$	1,000
	89,000

2   *Finance charges*

	$'000
Per question – Sage	16
Less loan interest payable to Parsley: $50,000 × 8\%$	(4)
	12

3   *Receivables*

	$'000	$'000
Parsley		18,460
Sage		12,230
Dividends	8,000	
Loan interest	4	
Intra-group	1,800	
		(9,804)
		20,886

4   *Payables*

	$'000	$'000
Parsley		6,000
Sage		1,922
Loan interest (W2)	4	
Intra-group	1,800	
		(1,804)
		6,118

5   *Retained earnings*

	Parsley	Sage
	$'000	$'000
Per question	37,540	15,000
Less provision for unrealised profit (W1)	(1,000)	
Pre-acquisition		(2,000)
		13,000
Goodwill impairment (W6)	(750)	
	35,790	
Share of Sage	13,000	
	48,790	

6   *Impairment of goodwill*

	$'000
Goodwill at acquisition (part (a))	3,000
Goodwill at 31 December 20X9	2,250
Impairment	750

(c)   The purpose of consolidated accounts is to present the financial position of connected companies as that of a **single entity, the group.** This means that, **in the consolidated statement of financial position, the only profits recognised should be those earned by the group in providing services to outsiders.** Similarly, inventory should be valued at the cost to the group.

When a company sells goods to another company in the same group, it will recognised revenue and profit in its own books. However, **from the point of view of the group, no sale has taken place,** because the goods have not been sold outside the group. The sale must therefore be eliminated from revenue and **the unrealised profit** (that is profit on inventory not sold outside the group) **must be eliminated from inventory.**

47 Tom, Dick and Harry

Text references. The consolidated statement of financial position is covered in Chapter 14. Associates are covered in Chapter 16.

Top tips. Calculating the goodwill value in part (a) is tricky, however, you should be able to explain the treatment of negative goodwill under IFRS 3 to gain some easy marks. Watch out for the extra depreciation charge created when the fair value exceeds the book value of non-current assets. In this question you have been given the extra depreciation charge, but in your exam you might be asked to calculate it. Remember that to calculate the extra depreciation charge, you need to divide the fair value adjustment by the remaining useful life.

In part (b), don't forget to set out your proforma and insert the easy numbers first.

(a)   (i)   *Goodwill on acquisition of Dick*

	$
Consideration paid	200,000
Less net assets acquired represented by:	
Share capital	(100,000)
Retained earnings	(90,000)
Plus fair value adjustment	(50,000)
	(240,000)
Goodwill	(40,000)

(ii)   *Treatment of negative goodwill under IFRS 3*

If goodwill calculated is negative it means that the aggregate value of the net assets acquired may exceed what the parent company paid for them. Under IFRS 3, this is referred to as a 'bargain purchase'. In this situation, IFRS 3 requires that:

(a)   The group should first re-assess the amounts at which it has measured both the cost of the combination and the acquired net assets. This is to identify any errors in the calculation and to check that a 'bargain purchase' really has occurred.

(b)   Any negative goodwill remaining after this exercise should be recognised immediately in profit or loss.

(b)   TOM GROUP
CONSOLIDATED STATEMENT OF FINANCIAL POSITION AS AT 31 OCTOBER 20X1

	$'000	$'000
Non-current assets		
Property, plant and equipment (W2)		373
Investment in associate (W5)		117
		490
Current assets		
Inventory (100 + 70 – 2 (W3))	168	
Receivables (170 + 40)	210	
Bank (190 + 30)	220	
		598
		1,088

Equity and liabilities

Share capital	500
Retained earnings (W6)	448
	948
Current liabilities (110 + 30)	140
	1,088

Workings

1   *Group structure*

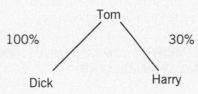

                                    Tom

100%   30%

       Dick   Harry

2   *Property, plant and equipment*

	$'000
Tom	205
Dick	120
Fair value adjustment	50
Depreciation adjustment	(2)
	373

3   *Unrealised Profit*

Total profit – 25,000/5 = 5,000

Profit on goods left in stock = 5,000 × 40% = 2,000

DR Retained earnings, CR Group inventory

4   *Investment in associate*

	$'000
Cost of investment	115
Share of post-acquisition retained earnings ((150 – 130) × 30%)	6
Impairment	(4)
	117

5   *Retained earnings*

	Tom $'000	Dick $'000	Harry $'000
Per individual statements	370	130	150
Less pre-acquisition		(90)	(130)
		40	20
Unrealised profit (W2)	(2)		
Negative goodwill (part (a))	40		
Depreciation adjustment	(2)		
Impairment of investment in associate	(4)		
Dick (40 × 100%)	40		
Harry (20 × 30%)	6		
	448		

48 ZA

Text references. The consolidated statement of financial position is covered in Chapter 14 and the consolidated statement of comprehensive income is covered in Chapter 15. Associates are covered in Chapter 16.

Top Tips. Note that you are specifically asked for a working for retained earnings. The adjustments for intra-group trading may be on the face of the consolidated statement of financial position or in a separate working.

(a) *Calculation of goodwill on the acquisition of ZB*

	$'000	$'000
Consideration transferred		4,545
Share of net assets acquired		
Share capital	4,000	
Retained earnings	60	
		4,060
Goodwill		485

NOTE. Goodwill is fully written off and will not appear in the statement of financial position. The impairment will be deducted from retained earnings.

(b) ZA GROUP
CONSOLIDATED STATEMENT OF COMPREHENSIVE INCOME
FOR THE YEAR ENDING 31 MARCH 20X9

	$'000
Revenue (870 + 285 – 240*)	915
Cost of sales (540 + 119 – 240* + 20(W2))	(439)
Gross profit	476
Distribution costs (54 + 36)	(90)
Administrative expenses (78 + 22)	(100)
Profit from operations	286
Interest payable	(10)
Share of profit of associate (40 × 30%)	12
Profit before tax	288
Income tax expense (40 + 25)	(65)
Profit for the year	223
Total comprehensive income for the year	223

* To remove intra-group revenue

ZA GROUP
CONSOLIDATED STATEMENT OF FINANCIAL POSITION AS AT 31 OCTOBER 20X7

	$'000	$'000
Non-current assets		
Property, plant and equipment (3,000 + 3,300)		6,300
Investment in associate (W4)		712
Current assets		
Inventory (1,500 + 800 – 20(W3))	2,280	
Receivables (1,800 + 750 – 30)	2,520	
Bank (600 + 350)	950	
		5,750
		12,762
Equity and liabilities		
Equity		
$1 Ordinary shares		9,000
Retained earnings (W2)		872
		9,872
Current liabilities		
Payables (1,220 + 200 – 30)	1,390	
Tax (700 + 800)	1,500	
		2,890
Total equity and liabilities		12,762

Workings

1   *Group structure*

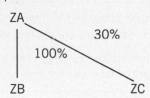

2 *Unrealised profit on intra-group sale*

Profit on intra-group sale is $\$240,000 \times \dfrac{20}{120} = \$40,000$

∴ Unrealised profit is $\$40,000 \times 50\% = \$20,000$

Dr retained earnings, Cr group closing inventory

3 *Investment in associate*

	$'000
Cost of investment	800
Share of post-acquisition retained earnings ((340-300) × 30%)	12
Less impairment	(100)
	712

4 *Retained earnings*

	ZA $'000	ZB $'000	ZC $'000
Per question	1,325	200	340
Unrealised profit (W3)	(20)		
Less pre-acquisition		(60)	(300)
		140	40
Impairment of goodwill/investment in associate (485+100)	(585)		
ZB	140		
ZC (40 × 30%)	12		
	872		

(c) **Significant influence** can usually be determined by the holding of **voting rights** in the entity, generally in the form of shares.

Significant influence may take various forms:

(i) Participation in the policy making process
(ii) Material transactions between investee and investor
(iii) Board representation
(iv) Provision of technical advice
(v) An interchange of personnel between the companies

49 Objective test answers: General principles of taxation

1 B The tax authorities do not have the power to detain company officials. Their powers relate to documents and information (eg information held on computer).

2 Direct taxation is charged directly on the **person** or **entity** that is intended to pay the tax.

3 C Equity

4 Tax evasion is manipulation of the tax system by illegal means to avoid paying taxes.

5 • Domestic legislation and legal decisions
 • Tax authority practice
 • International treaties
 • Supranational bodies

6 B The person or entity that finally bears the cost of the tax.

7 The tax authority whose tax laws apply to an entity or person.

8 A Power of arrest.

9 C Effective incidence

10   Any three of the following:

    (1)   To give a date from which penalties and/or interest can accrue

    (2)   To get funds in as quickly as possible for use by central government

    (3)   To reduce backlogs and extra work for the tax department

    (4)   To prevent entities deducting tax at source, eg employers collecting payroll tax, from spending it before it reaches the tax authority

11   A   An example of hypothecation is the 'congestion charge' levied on London motorists that can only be spent on London transport.

12   **Equity**: the tax burden should be fairly distributed

    Efficiency: tax should be easy and cheap to collect

    Economic effects: the government must consider the effect of taxation policy on various sectors of the economy

13   A

14   A   Formal incidence

15   C   Naturally, tax authorities like to minimise the tax gap.

16   C   International tax treaties (eg double taxation treaties) are a source of tax rules.

    The other options are all sources of accounting rules.

50   Objective test answers: Types of taxation I

1   (a)   Tax is deducted at source, so non-payment is not an issue
    (b)   The costs of collection are borne by employers
    (c)   The funds are received at the same time each month, which helps financial planning

2   C   The company acts as a tax collector on behalf of the tax authority. Therefore any tax deducted is put in a payable account until the money is actually paid to the tax authority. The balance on the payable account represents the amount collected but not yet paid over.

3   Accounting profit + disallowable expenditure – non-taxable income – tax allowable expenditure = taxable profit

4   C   Tax deducted at source before payment of interest or dividends.

5   A   A progressive tax

6   (a)   Under group loss relief, it is possible to set the losses of a group member against the profits of another group member. If the profit-making group member pays tax at a higher rate than the one making the loss, the total tax liability of the group for the year can be reduced.

    (b)   Claiming group loss relief can help improve group cash flows as the loss is relieved more quickly.

7   A   The classical system

	$'000
Company income tax (400,000 × 25%)	100
Personal income tax (250,000 × 30%)	75
	175

8   B   The company income tax that has already been paid on the distribution is **imputed** to the shareholder as a tax credit.

9   D   The head office is located, and all board meetings take place in, the Cayman Islands. Therefore the place of management is in the Cayman Islands.

10   The EU issues rules on sales taxes, which must be applied by all member states.

11
- Interest payments
- Dividends
- Royalties
- Capital gains accruing to non-residents

12
- Full deduction
- Exemption
- Credit

13 B Double taxable treaties deal with **overseas** income.

14 D The country where most of the entity's products are sold.

15 B

	$
50,000 × 12%	6,000
Less already paid	(5,000)
Balance due:	1,000

16 B Corporate income tax is due on all profits of the branch, not just those remitted.

17 C EA will be deemed resident in Country C, which is its place of management.

18 D A construction project is only a permanent establishment if it lasts more than 12 months.

19 Net assets and consumption

20 C Under the OECD model, an entity is considered to have residence in the country in which it has a permanent establishment, which includes a place of management.

21 $20,000

	$
Net dividend	90,000
Withholding tax	10,000
Gross dividend	100,000
Underlying tax (100,000 × 200,000/1,000,000)	$20,000

22

	$	$
Proceeds of sale		425,000
Less costs of sale		(8,000)
		417,000
Cost:		
Purchase price	155,000	
Refurbishment of building	50,000	
		(205,000)
Indexation allowance on building and refurbishment costs (100 + 50) × 35%		(52,500)
Capital gain		159,500
Tax at 25%		39,875

Note: no indexation is allowed on land.

51 Objective test answers: Types of taxation II

1 A suitable commodity would have the following characteristics:

- A limited number of large producers
- Products that are easily defined
- A commodity produced in large volume

2 C Sales tax is an indirect tax, all the others are direct taxes.

3 B As long as they are registered for sales tax, options A, C and D merely act as tax collectors, it is the end consumer who suffers the tax.

BPP LEARNING MEDIA

4

			$
DA	Input tax (200 × 15%)		(30)
	Output tax (500 × 15%)		75
	Total due		45
DB	Input tax		(75)
	Output tax (1,000 × 15%)		150
	Total due		75
	Total		120

5

	$
Sale by ZA (500 × 15%)	75
Sale by ZB (1,000 × 15%)	150
Total paid	225

6　　D　　Sales taxes such as VAT are indirect

7　　B　　$1,450

	$
VAT output tax (200 × 50 × 15%)	1,500
VAT input tax (200 × 35 × 15%)	(1,050)
VAT payable	450
Excise duty payable (200 × 5)	1,000
Total payable	1,450

8　　Amount paid = $3,000

	$
Output VAT 120,000 × 15%	18,000
Input VAT 100,000 × 15%	(15,000)
Amount paid	3,000

9

		$			$
CU:	Output tax (250 × 15%)	37.5	CZ:	Output tax (690 × 15/115)	90.0
	Input tax (115 × 15/115)	(15.0)		Input tax (250 × 15%)	(37.5)
	Payable	22.5		Payable	52.5

10　　VAT paid $15,000

Gross profit $170,000

	$
Output VAT (253,000 × 15/115)	33,000
Input VAT (138,000 × 15/115)	(18,000)
Amount paid	15,000
Revenue (253,000 × 100/115) + 70,000	290,000
Cost of sales (138,000 × 100/115)	(120,000)
Gross profit	170,000

11　　C　　$5,550

Workings	$
Cost	14,000
Excise duty	3,000
	17,000
VAT @ 15%	2,550
	19,550

Taxes paid = $3,000 + $2,550 = $5,550

12

	$'000
Output tax (18,400 × 15/115)	2,400
Input tax (10,000 + 4,000 × 15%)	(2,100)
VAT due from FE	300

Note that VAT is deductible on purchases relating to zero-rated outputs, but not on purchases relating to exempt outputs

			$	$
13	B	Accounting profit		350,000
		Add: depreciation	30,000	
		disallowed expenses	15,000	
				45,000
				395,000
		Less: non-taxable income	25,000	
		tax allowable depreciation	32,000	
				(57,000)
		Taxable profit		338,000

			$	$
14	D	Taxable profit		350,000
		Less: depreciation	30,000	
		disallowed expenses	15,000	
				(45,000)
				305,000
		Add: non-taxable income	25,000	
		tax allowable depreciation	32,000	
				57,000
		Accounting profit		362,000

			$	$
15	A	Accounting loss		(350,000)
		Add: depreciation	30,000	
		disallowed expenses	400,000	
				430,000
				80,000
		Less: non-taxable income	25,000	
		tax allowable depreciation	32,000	
				(57,000)
		Taxable profit		23,000

			$m	$m
16	B	Taxable profit		50
		Less: depreciation	15	
		disallowed expenses	1	
				(16)
				34
		Add: non-taxable income	3	
		tax allowable depreciation	4	
				7
		Accounting profit		41

			$	$
17	D	Accounting profit		250,000
		Add: depreciation	45,000	
		disallowed expenses	20,000	
				65,000
				315,000
		Less: tax allowable depreciation		(30,000)
		Taxable profit		285,000

Tax payable = $285,000 × 25% = $71,250.

18	C			$	$
		Accounting profit			360,000
		Add: depreciation		40,000	
		disallowed expenses		10,000	
					50,000
					410,000
		Less: non-taxable income		35,000	
		tax allowable depreciation		30,000	
					(65,000)
		Taxable profit			345,000

Tax payable = $345,000 × 25% = $86,250.

19	B			$	$
		Accounting profit			500,000
		Add: depreciation		50,000	
		disallowed expenses		5,000	
					55,000
					555,000
		Less: non-taxable income		25,000	
		tax allowable depreciation		60,000	
					(85,000)
		Taxable profit			470,000

Tax payable = $470,000 × 25% = $117,500.

20	D			$	$
		Accounting profit			250,000
		Add: depreciation		40,000	
		disallowed expenses		2,000	
					42,000
					292,000
		Less: tax allowable depreciation			(30,000)
		Taxable profit			262,000

Tax payable = $262,000 × 25% = $65,500.

21 Tax due = $22,500

	$
Accounting profit	95,000
Less non-taxable income	(15,000)
Add non–allowable expenditure	10,000
Taxable profit	90,000

Tax = $90,000 × 25%
    = $22,500

22 $2,000

	$'000
Revenue	45
Operating costs	(23)
Finance costs	(4)
Taxable allowance (20 × 50%)	(10)
Taxable amount	8
Tax @ 25%	2

23

		$
30 September 20X3	Tax on trading profits = 200 × 25%=	50,000
30 September 20X4	No tax to pay	
30 September 20X5	Tax on trading profit = (150 – 120) × 25% =	7,500
	Tax on capital gains = (130 – 100) × 25% =	7,500
		15,000

24 A $320,000 less prior year over-provision ($290,000 – $280,000)

52 Objective test answers: Deferred tax

1   A

	$
Over provision for prior period	(2,000)
Provision for current period	50,000
Increase in deferred tax charge	5,000
Charge to income statement	53,000

2   C

	$
Under provision for prior period	200
Provision for current period	30,000
Decrease in deferred tax charge	(5,000)
Charge to income statement	25,200

3   A   Item 2 consists of permanent differences, all the rest are temporary differences.

4   D   All four items have a carrying amount equal to their tax base.

5   B   IAS 12 states that deferred tax assets and liabilities should not be discounted.

6    $287,500

	$
Taxable temporary differences b/f	850,000
Depreciation for tax purposes	500,000
Depreciation charged in the financial statements	(450,000)
Revaluation surplus	250,000
Taxable temporary differences c/f	1,150,000
Deferred tax at 25%	287,500

7   D

	$
Over-provision for prior period	(27,500)
Provision for current period	30,000
Decrease in deferred tax charge	(10,000)
Credit to income statement	(7,500)

8   D

	$
Under-provision for prior period	2,800
Provision for current period	28,000
Increase in deferred tax charge	5,000
Charge to income statement	35,800

9   Deferred tax balance = $55,625

Tax written down value:

	$
1 Oct 20X3 cost	900,000
20X4 tax allowance – 50% × 900,000	(450,000)
30 Sept 20X4 tax written down value	450,000
20X5 tax allowance – 25% × 450,000	(112,500)
30 Sept 20X5 tax written down value	337,500

Accounting carrying value:

	$
Cost	900,000
Depreciation 2 × (900-50)/5	(340,000)
30 Sept 20X5 accounting carrying value	560,000

Temporary difference = $560,000 – 337,500
                     = $222,500

Deferred tax balance = $222,500 × 25%
                    = $55,625

10

	$
Taxable profit for the year	946,000
Tax at 25%	236,500
Prior year over-provision	(31,000)
Increase in deferred tax provision	117,000
Charge to income statement	322,500

11 Deferred tax balance at 31 March 20X7 = $34
Deferred tax balance at 31 March 20X8 = $(2)

Tax written down value:

	$ '000
1 Apr 20X5 cost	600
20X6 tax allowance (50% × 600,000)	(300)
31 Mar 20X6 tax written down value	300
20X7 tax allowance (25% × 300,000)	(75)
31 Mar 20X7 tax written down value	225
20X8 tax allowance (25% × 225,000)	(56)
31 Mar 20X8 tax written down value	169

Accounting carrying value:

	$'000
Cost	600
Depreciation (2 × (600/5))	(240)
31 Mar 20X7 carrying value	360
1 Apr 20X7 impairment review	(120)
1 Apr 20X7 carrying value	240
Depreciation X7/X8 (240/3)	(80)
31 Mar 20X8 carrying value	160

31 March 20X7
Temporary difference = $360 – $225 = $135,000
Deferred tax balance = $135 × 25% = $34,000

31 March 20X8
Temporary difference = $160 – $169 = $(9,000)
Deferred tax balance = $(9) × 25% = $(2,000)

Note. The question specifies working to the nearest $1,000.

12 $200,250

	$
Accounting profits	822,000
Entertaining expenses	32,000
Political donation	50,000
	904,000
Government grant	(103,000)
Taxable profit	801,000
Tax at 25%	200,250

13 $18,750

	Carrying value	Tax base
	$	$
1 October 20X5	400,000	400,000
Depreciation 25%	(100,000)	–
Tax depreciation 50%	–	(200,000)
Balance 30 Sept 20X6	300,000	–
Depreciation 25%	(75,000)	–
Balance 30 Sept 20X7	225,000	150,000

Difference between carrying value and tax base = $225,000 – 150,000 = $75,000

Deferred tax at 25% = $18,750

14

	Carrying value $	Tax base $	Difference $
1 April 20X7	220,000	220,000	
Depreciation (220,000/8)	(27,500)	–	
Tax depreciation 50%	–	(110,000)	
Balance 30 March 20X8	192,500	110,000	82,500
Revaluation	50,000	–	
	242,500	110,000	
Depreciation (242,500/7)	(34,643)	–	
Tax depreciation 25%	–	(27,500)	
Balance 30 March 20X9	207,857	82,500	125,357

Deferred tax balance at 30 March 20X9 = 125,357 × 25% = $31,339

Deferred tax balance at 30 March 20X8 = 82,500 × 25% = $20,625

Movement on deferred tax balance at 30 March 20X9 = 31,339 – 20,625 = $10,714

15

	Temporary difference
B/f (12,500 – 5,000)	7,500
20X3 (2,120 – 1,630)	490
20X4 (1,860 – 1,590)	270
20X5 (1,320 – 1,530)	(210)
Balance at 31 December 20X5	8,050 × 25% = 2,012.50

16

	Accounting book value $	Tax basis $	Difference $	Deferred tax Balance (25%) $
Cost 1.4.X4	500,000	500,000		
Depreciation to 31.3.X5	(100,000)			
Tax depreciation 50%	-	(250,000)	-	-
	400,000	250,000	150,000	37,500
Depreciation to 31.3.X6	(100,000)			
Tax depreciation 25%	-	(62,500)	-	-
Balance at 31.3.X6	300,000	187,500	112,500	28,125
Revaluation 1.4.X6	120,000			
	420,000			
Depreciation (420,000/3)	(140,000)			
Tax depreciation 25%	-	46,875	-	-
Balance at 31.3.X7	280,000	140,625	139,375	34,844

Deferred tax balance 31.3.X6	28,125
Deferred tax balance 31.3.X7	34,844
Income statement charge X6/X7	6,719

53 Section B answers: Taxation I

(a) (i) Jurisdiction relates to the power of a tax authority to charge and collect tax. Competent jurisdiction refers to the authority whose tax laws apply to an entity or person.

(ii) Hypothecation is the ring-fencing of revenue from certain types of tax for certain types of expenditure only, eg revenue raised from road taxes can only be spent on road improvements.

(iii) A taxable person is a person liable to pay tax. In this context, person refers to individuals but also to companies and other entities that are liable to pay tax.

(iv) Regressive tax structure – a tax structure whereby the rate of tax falls as income rises.

(v) The tax gap is the gap between the tax theoretically collectable and the amount actually collected.

(b) (i) **Indirect taxation** is charged indirectly on the final consumer of the goods or services and is a tax on consumption or expenditure. An example is a sales tax (eg VAT in the UK; TVA in France). As value is added, the tax increases cumulatively.

Indirect taxes are not actually paid by the business. Instead, the business acts as a tax collector on behalf of the tax authorities. For example, a business charges sales tax on its sales (output tax) and it pays sales tax on its purchases (input tax). The difference between output tax and input tax is paid over to the tax authorities.

(ii) **Unit taxes** are based on the number or weight of items, eg excise duties on the number of cigarettes or on the weight of tobacco.

Ad valorem taxes are based on the value of the items, eg a sales tax or value added tax.

(c)

	$'000
INCOME STATEMENT (EXTRACT)	
Income tax expense (W1)	1,145
STATEMENT OF FINANCIAL POSITION (EXTRACT)	
Non-current liabilities	
Deferred tax (W2)	1,750
Current liabilities	
Income tax	1,000

Workings

1   *Income statement*

	$
Income tax for year	1,000,000
Over-provision in previous year	(5,000)
Increase in deferred tax	150,000
Income tax expense	1,145,000

2   *Deferred tax*

	$
Opening balance	1,600,000
Increase in year	150,000
Closing balance	1,750,000

(d)

> **Examiner's comments.** Most candidates could define withholding tax whilst many candidates found difficulty defining underlying tax. A common error Part (ii) was not grossing up the amount received before calculating withholding tax. As many candidates did not know what underlying tax was they could not calculate it.

(i) **Withholding tax** is deducted at source by the tax authority before a payment is made. This occurs most commonly when dividends are paid to non-residents. The tax authority has no power to tax the non-resident, so it taxes the dividend at source.

Underlying tax is the tax which has already been suffered by the profits from which a dividend is paid. When the recipient pays tax on his dividend income, this means that the dividend has effectively been taxed twice. To mitigate this, some tax authorities operate an imputation system, by which the recipient obtains relief for the underlying tax.

(ii) $45,000 represents 9/10 of the amount prior to withholding tax, so withholding tax is therefore $45,000/9 = $5,000.

(iii) The amount of dividend prior to withholding tax was $50,000. This has already been taxed at 20% (100/500). Therefore $50,000 is 80% and the other 20% is the underlying tax - $12,500.

(e)

> **Examiner's comments.** It was surprising how many candidates could not correctly calculate VAT when the figure inclusive of VAT was given.

(i)

		$
Revenue (40,250 × 100/115)		35,000
Cost of sales:		
Purchases plus excise duty	12,000	
Repackaging (6,900 × 100/115)	6,000	
		(18,000)
Net profit		17,000

(ii)

	$
VAT output tax (35,000 × 15%)	5,250
VAT input tax (18,000 × 15%)	(2,700)
Due to VAT authorities	2,550

54 Section B answers: Taxation II

(a) (i) Governments might apply specific excise duties:

– To discourage people from consuming too much of a substance which is harmful to health – such as alcohol and tobacco

– To raise funds to pay for the consequences of the consumption of these harmful substances – for example, the additional health care required for patients with smoking-related illnesses

– To discourage the excessive use of products which damage the environment, such as the use of petrol or diesel in vehicles and aircraft

– To raise maximum revenue by targeting goods which are widely used and relatively expensive.

(ii) A single stage sales tax is chargeable once in the supply chain, usually at the point of sale to the end customer. The tax paid is not recoverable. An example of a single stage sales tax is the retail sales tax applied in the USA.

A multi stage sales tax is chargeable and deductible at different points in the supply chain, such as VAT in the UK. As value is added the tax increases cumulatively. Tax paid by an entity at one point in the supply chain is usually recoverable by deducting it from the tax charged at the next point in the supply chain. The end consumer therefore bears all the VAT. A multi-stage sales tax can also be cumulative, where no credit is received for tax paid in the previous stage.

(b) *Power to review and query filed returns*

The tax authorities usually have the power to ask for further information if they are not satisfied with a filed return. These queries must be answered or there may be legal penalties.

Power to request special reports or returns

The special report may take the form of asking for details of pay and tax deducted from an individual employee, where there are indications that the tax rules have been broken. There have been instances of casual employees having a number of jobs but using a number of false names, so that the tax authority has been defrauded.

Power to examine records

Most tax authorities have the power to inspect business records to ensure compliance. If mistakes in returns have been made, the tax authority may be able to re-open earlier years and collect back taxes owed.

Powers of entry and search

Where the tax authority believes fraud has occurred, it can obtain warrants to enter a business's premises and seize the records.

Exchange of information with tax authorities in other jurisdictions

This has become very important as a counter-terrorism measure in recent years. One tax authority may become aware of funds being moved to another country in suspicious circumstances. It will then warn the tax authority in that other jurisdiction. Exchange of information is also useful in dealing with drug smuggling and money laundering.

(c)   If a company makes payments to an individual or another company resident in a different tax jurisdiction, it may have to pay **withholding tax** to the tax authority of its own jurisdiction.

The reason for this is to stop companies paying all their earnings abroad and then stopping trading without paying any tax to the tax authorities of the country where they are resident. Therefore the local tax authority will take a payment on account of the final tax liability by deducting at source a withholding tax from all payments sent abroad. The withholding tax can be as low as 5% or as high as 40%.

Payments affected are usually interest payments or dividends.

> **Alternative answers**. You would also have scored marks for stating royalties or capital gains accruing to non-residents.

(d)   *Double taxation agreements*

A company is taxed in the country it is resident in for tax purposes. Tax residency can be determined in different ways in different jurisdictions, so that a company may find itself deemed to be resident in two different countries. For example if a company is legally incorporated in one country, but has its place of effective management in another country, it may be deemed resident in both countries and its income may be taxed in both countries – ie it may suffer double taxation.

Countries need double taxation agreements to determine which country such tax a company's income in this kind of situation. Double taxation agreements also specify what kind of reliefs are available to companies who have a taxable presence in more than one country.

Methods of giving relief

One way is to give full **deduction** for foreign taxes paid. However this is not always appropriate, particularly if the country where the tax is paid has a high tax rate and the other has a low rate.

Relief may be given by **exemption**. In this case, if income is taxed in Country A, then it will not be taxed in Country B.

Another way of giving relief is by **credit**. This usually occurs where the tax rate in Country A is higher than that in Country B. Instead of deducting the full amount of tax paid in Country A, Country B credits the amount it would have paid in Country B. For example, the income is $10,000 and the tax rate in Country A is 30%, while that in Country B is 20%. The tax paid in Country A will be $3,000 but the double tax relief allowed in Country B will be $2,000 (20% × $10,000).

(e)

> **Examiner's comments.** Most candidates were able to explain the meaning of avoidance and evasion, with fewer highlighting the difference between them. Some candidates gave odd examples of tax avoidance, such as 'claiming capital allowances' or 'claiming loss relief'. These are not examples of tax avoidance, they are proper application of the tax legislation and are not 'loopholes'.
>
> Several candidates stated that giving double taxation relief on overseas profits was a means of preventing tax avoidance, which is incorrect.
>
> Many candidates did not give enough examples or sufficient detail within the examples to earn full marks.

(i)   **Tax avoidance** is successful tax planning. It is arranging the financial affairs of an individual or an entity in such a manner as to minimise tax liability. It is perfectly legal.

Tax evasion is the use of illegal means to avoid paying tax, such as not declaring income, claiming deduction for non-deductible expense, or contravening tax legislation.

(ii)   Although only evasion is illegal, avoidance is just as much of a problem for government. Methods that governments can use to reduce avoidance and evasion are:

- Anti-avoidance legislation. This outlaws specific avoidance schemes.
- Deducting tax at source such as the PAYE system in the UK.
- Keeping the tax system as simple as possible to minimise the number of factors that can be manipulated.
- Making sure that penalties for evasion are high enough to act as a deterrent.
- Increasing the efficiency of the tax collection and investigation machinery.
- Having a tax system which is not generally perceived as unfair. An unfair system makes people feel justified in avoiding tax.

55 Section B answers: Taxation III

(a) **Deferred tax – disclosure and note**

	$m
Deferred tax provision	0.50
Provision at 30 April 20X3	0.58
Deferred tax credit in income statement	(0.08)
Provision at 30 April 20X4	0.50

Working

Deferred tax

	$m
Temporary difference at 30 April 20X3	2.30
Temporary difference at 30 April 20X4	2.00
Deferred tax at 30 April 20X3 (2.30 × 25%)	0.58
Deferred tax at 30 April 20X4 (2.00 × 25%)	0.50
Reduction in deferred tax provision	0.08

Alternative approach

The reduction in provision can also be calculated as follows:

	$m
Reversal of temporary differences ((2.30 – 2.00) × 25%)	0.08

(b) **Tax on profit on ordinary activities – note to income statement**

	$m
Tax on profit for the period	1.40
Overprovision for previous period ($750,000 – $720,000)	(0.03)
Increase in deferred tax liability ($300,000 – $250,000)	0.05
Total tax charge	1.42

Statement of financial position

	$m
Non-current liabilities	
Deferred tax (0.25 + 0.05)	0.30
Current liabilities	
Current tax	1.40

(c)

Examiner's comments. Part (i) was fairly well done; most candidates seem to be getting the idea of temporary differences and deferred tax balances. However, some had trouble with the dates. The asset had been owned for three years but many candidates calculated four or even five years before working out the temporary difference.

	Accounting value $	Tax value $
Cost	200,000	200,000
Depreciation/Allowance year to 30 September 20X3	(40,000)	(100,000)*
Balance at 30 September 20X4	160,000	100,000
Depreciation/Allowance year to 30 September 20X4	(40,000)	(25,000)**
Balance at 30 September 20X5	120,000	75,000
Depreciation/Allowance year to 30 September 20X5	(40,000)	(18,750)***
Balance 30 September 20X5	80,000	56,250
Disposal proceeds	(60,000)	(60,000)
Loss/balancing charge	20,000	(3,750)

* (200,000 × 50%)

** 20X4: (100,000 × 25%) = $25,000

*** 20X5: (100,000 – 25,000) = 75,000 × 25% = $18,750

(i) Timing difference at 30 September 20X5 (80,000 – 56,250) = 23,750

Tax at 25% = $5,938

(ii) The carrying value of the asset at 30 September 20X6 is $80,000. Disposal at $60,000 will give rise to an accounting loss of $20,000.

(iii) At the date of disposal the tax WDV of the asset is $56,250. Disposal at $60,000 gives rise to a balancing charge of $3,750.

(d)

> **Examiner's comments**. Very few candidates provided a fully correct answer to this question, and some demonstrated very little knowledge of deferred tax.
>
> Some candidates used the wrong periods, some failed to apply the tax rate to the year end balances and some described the credit to the income statement as a charge.

Year ended	Cost $	Depreciation	Tax allowance
31.3.X4	250,000	50,000	125,000
31.3.X5	250,000	50,000	31,250
		100,000	156,250

(i) Deferred tax balance: 31.3.X4: (125,000 – 50,000) × 25% = $18,750
(ii) Deferred tax balance: 31.3.X5: (156,250 – 100,000) × 25% = $14,063
(iii) Income statement credit: year ended 31.3.X5 = (18,750 – 14,063) = $4,687

(e)

> **Examiner's comments**. Some candidates filled a page or more with calculations but did not show how the results would be used. You must answer the question asked, in this case the question asked for tax payable so the answer must state the taxable profits and tax payable otherwise the question has not been answered.

	$
Profit before tax	29,800
Gain on disposal of plant and equipment	(4,000)
Depreciation (5,000 + 3,200 + 6,000)	14,200
	40,000
Tax depreciation:	
Buildings (30,000 × 25%)	(7,500)
Plant and equipment – first year (30,000 × 50%)	(15,000)
– disposal balancing allowance (7,875 – 5,000)	(2,875)
Fixtures and fittings (5,625 × 25%)	(1,406)
Taxable profit	13,219
Tax due for year ended 30 April 20X8 at 25%	3,305

56 Mixed objective test answers bank 1 (Specimen paper)

1   D   Tax evasion is a way of paying less tax by illegal methods

Tax avoidance is a way of arranging your affairs to take advantage of the tax rules to pay as little tax as possible, and is legal.

2   D

	$
Accounting profit	72,000
Add: disallowable expenditure: entertaining	15,000
book depreciation	12,000
	99,000
Less: tax allowable depreciation (40,000 × 25%)	(10,000)
	89,000

Tax at 25% × $89,000 = $22,250

3   B   The effective incidence is on B's customers.

4   C   This is a classical system of taxation as company income tax is charged on all the profits of the entity, whether distributed or not. This leads to double taxation of dividends as dividends are paid out of taxed profits and are then chargeable to personal income tax in the hands of the shareholder. Under an imputation system the shareholder would receive a tax credit for some or all of the underlying tax.

5   Understandability and Comparability

6   Any two of: Confidentiality, Integrity, Professional behaviour

7   B   The purpose of an external audit is to enable the auditor to express an opinion on whether the financial statements are prepared, in all material respects, in accordance with an identified financial reporting framework. The auditor will express this opinion using the phrases 'give a true and fair view' or 'present fairly, in all material respects'.

8   A   In accordance with IFRS 3, goodwill arising on acquisition is recognised at cost and then reviewed annually for impairment.

9   A   Per IAS 2, inventories should be measured at the lower of cost and net realisable value.

	$
Cost	2.20
Net realisable value:	
Selling price	3.50
Less additional costs for repair and sale	(1.50)
	2.00

Therefore, inventories held at $2.00 each

Total value 300 × $2.00 = $600

10   C   ST is a related party of Z as he is a member of key management personnel of Z

JT is related part of Z as he is a close family member of ST.

57 Mixed objective test answers bank 2 (5/10)

1 C A 'good tax' should be **convenient**, **equitable**, **certain** and **efficient** according to Adam Smith's canons of taxation.

2 D In a progressive tax structure, the rate of tax rises as income rises.

3 B $3,461

	Carrying amount $	Tax base $
Cost	60,000	60,000
Depreciation/Tax-depreciation	(12,000)	(30,000)
Balance at 31.3.X7	48,000	30,000
Depreciation/Tax-depreciation	(9,600)	(7,500)
Balance at 31.3.X8	38,400	22,500
Depreciation/Tax-depreciation	(7,680)	(5,625)
Balance at 31.3.X9	30,720	16,875

Deferred tax = 25% × (30,720 – 16,875) = $3,461

4 A IAS 1 deals with the format of financial statements.

5 A Timeliness is an enhancing qualitative characteristic.

6 B (500 × 12) – (300 × 12) = 2400 × 6/12 = $1,200 profit

7 D A: project is not yet viable, costs are therefore research costs and cannot be capitalised

B: payment is for research and therefore cannot be capitalised

C: project is not expected to generate future economic benefits therefore costs cannot be capitalised

8 B Interest = (24 × 6) – 106 = $38k

Sum-of-the-digits = 6(6+1)/2 = 21

	$
Fair value	106.00
Interest (6/21 × 38)	10.86
Repayment	(24.00)
Capital balance at end of year 1	92.86
Interest (5/21 × 38)	9.05
Repayment	(24.00)
Capital balance at end of year 2	77.91

9 C The costs of restructuring the head office do not form part of the post-tax profit or loss of the discontinued operation, or of the post-tax gain or loss recognised on the measurement to fair value less costs to sell or on the disposal of the foreign operations.

10 A $98,000

DEFERRED TAX

	$'000		$'000
Bal c/f	38	Bal b/f	27
		I/S (bal fig)	11
	38		38

CURRENT TAX

	$'000		$'000
Cash paid (bal fig)	**98**	Bal b/f	106
Bal c/f	119	I/S (122-11)	111
	217		217

58 Mixed objective test answers bank 3 (11/10)

1   B   The imputation system

	Classical $	Imputation $
Tax on profits (25% × 750)	187,500	187,500
Shareholder:		
Dividend received		350,000
Tax at 30%	105,000	105,000
Less tax credit (350 × 25%)		(87,500)
Tax on dividend (30%)		17,500
Total tax due	292,500	205,000

2   C   The tax payable is the same if it is collected by PAYE or in one lump sum.

3   A   The **formal incidence** of a tax is on the person or organisation who has direct contact with the tax authorities.

4   D   A deadline will not help ensure the correct amount of tax is paid.

5   Net VAT due = output VAT – input VAT

	UF $	ZF $
Output VAT		
Standard rate		
($2,875 × 15/115)/($6,900 × 15/115)	375	900
Input VAT		
Purchases		
($1,000 × 15 %)/($2,875 × 15/115)	(150)	(375)
VAT due	225	525

6   B   The auditor should issue an audit report with a qualified opinion on the basis that the misstatement identified is material, but not pervasive to the financial statements. The audit opinion should be modified to include the phrase "In our opinion, **except for** the effects of the matter described in the Basis for Qualified Opinion paragraph, the financial statements present fairly, in all material respects ...."

7   D   Treasury shares are shown in the statement of financial position as a deduction from equity.

8   C   Regulatory bodies is not a topic discussed by the *Conceptual Framework*.

9   C   MN is a related party of Z as MN is a member of the key management personnel of Z (marketing director), and also owns 20% of the equity of Z which is presumed to give MN significant influence over Z.

          Note that IAS 24 states that the following are not necessarily related parties: a customer, supplier, franchisor, distributor or general agent with whom the entity transacts a significant volume of business, merely by virtue of the resulting economic dependence.

10   A   External revenue is only considered when determining **reportable** operating segments as at least 75% of total external revenue must be reported by operating segments.

59 Mixed objective test answers bank 4 (5/11)

1   C   Progressive tax

          A is paying tax at a rate of 17/75 = 23%

          B is paying tax at a rate of 4.8/44 = 11%

          Therefore the tax rate appears to increase as profits increase, which indicates a progressive tax system.

2   B   (ii) and (iii) are potential disadvantages of PAYE.

3   Under the OECD model an entity will have residence in the country of its effective management.

4   D $11,400

	$
Excise duty (2,000 × $3)	6,000
VAT ((15 + 3) × 2,000) × 15%	5,400
Tax due	11,400

VAT is calculated on the total of the cost plus excise duty.

5   C   High tax rates mean high tax bills for individuals and companies, and therefore may increase the incentive to avoid or evade paying tax in order to reduce costs. Imprecise and vague tax laws mean that individuals or companies may consider it easier to try to find tax loopholes, and therefore the incidence of tax evasion and avoidance may increase.

6   A   A change in the presentation of the depreciation expense from administration expenses to cost of sales is considered to be a change accounting policy. The change will reduce gross profit and will have an effect on the financial ratios of the company.

A change in depreciation method and a change in the level of warranty provision are both changes in accounting estimates. The creation of a provision is not a change in accounting policy. In accordance with IAS 37, a provision should only be made when three criteria are satisfied (past event, probably outflow of economic benefits and obligation) and it appears from the question that those conditions where not satisfied until the current accounting period, even though the incident happened in the previous year.

7   D   A reportable segment is an operating segment which exceeds the thresholds set out in IFRS 8. An operating segment is a component of an entity that generates revenues and incurs expenses, whose operating results are reviewed by the entity's chief operating decision maker to make decisions about resources allocation and assess its performance, and for which discrete financial information is available.

There is no requirement in IFRS 8 for the segment's results to be prepared using the same accounting policies as the financial statements. The segment information instead should be presented in the way that it is viewed by management along with a reconciliation to the reported figures.

Geographical disclosures are required on a country by country basis only if they are material.

8    $32,000

	$'000
Consideration	185
Less fair value of net assets acquired:	
Share capital	(150)
Share premium	(15)
Retained earnings	22
Fair value adjustment on acquisition	(10)
Goodwill	32

9    $25,900

	$
Cost of investment	25,000
Share of post-acquisition reserves (30% × (6,500 – 3,500))	900
	25,900

10    $3,300

	$
Sales (125%)	33,000
Cost of sales (100%)	(26,400)
Profit (25%)	6,600

PURP = 50% × 6,600 = $3,300

60 Mixed objective test answers bank 5 (9/11)

1   D   Corporate income tax and individual income tax are direct taxes. VAT and import duty are indirect taxes.

2   B   When an asset is disposed of for more than its original cost, a **capital gain** arises.

3   C   This is a specific unit tax as it is a charge on each unit (litre) of a specific product (imported petroleum products). The answer cannot be a general consumption tax because the tax applies to a particular product only, and is therefore not 'general'. Ad valorem taxes are based on the value of the items, eg a sales tax or value added tax, therefore B and D are also incorrect.

4   Tax evasion is a way of paying less tax by illegal methods, for example by not declaring income or claiming fictitious expenses.

5   C   Corporate residence is usually determined on the basis of place of incorporation, place of effective management and control or place of permanent establishment.

6   B   IAS 24 specifically excludes an entity's main customer or supplier from being a related party merely because of the resulting economic dependence.

7   $355,000

Number of shares issued (2,400,000/6)	400,000
	$
Share premium on issue (400,000 × (2 – 1))	400,000
Less share issue costs offset against share premium	(45,000)
Credit to share premium account	355,000

8   $15,000

	$'000
Consideration	342
Less fair value of net assets acquired:	
Share capital	(200)
Share premium	(40)
Retained earnings	(62)
Fair value adjustment on acquisition (350 – 325)	(25)
Goodwill	15

9   $87,500

	$
Cost of investment	70,000
Share of post-acquisition reserves (35% × (130 - 80))	17,500
	87,500

10   C

	$
Sales (133.33%)	48,000
Cost of sales (100%)	(36,000)
Profit (33.33%)	12,000

PURP = 60% × 12,000 = $7,200

Adjustment required in consolidated financial statements is:

1   Remove intragroup balances: Dr payables $48,000, Cr receivables $48,000

2   Remove PURP in inventory: Dr retained earnings $7,200, Cr inventory $7,200

61   Mixed objective test answers bank 6 (11/11)

1   D   The principles of a modern tax system are efficiency, equity and economic effects.

2   D   The formal incidence of a tax is on the person or organisation who has direct contact with the tax authorities.

3   A   Deferred tax arises on temporary differences. Entertaining expenses are not deductible for tax purposes and are therefore a permanent difference and will not give rise to deferred tax.

4   A $55,750

	$'000	$'000
Proceeds of sale		1,200
Less costs of sale		(9)
		1,191
Cost:		
Purchase price	600	
Purchase costs	5	
		(605)
Indexation allowance (605 × 60%)		(363)
Capital gain		223
Tax at 25%		55.75

5   B   The tax gap is the gap between the tax theoretically collectable and the amount actually collected.

6   C   IAS 24 states that a significant customer is not necessarily a related party merely by virtue of the resulting economic dependence.

7   A   Research expenditure can never be capitalised and must be expensed in accordance with IAS 38.

8   C   Adjusting events are events that provide further evidence of conditions that already existed at the reporting date. Only C is non-adjusting.

9   B   IFRS 8 specifies that an operating segment is a component of an entity whose operating results are regularly reviewed by the entity's chief operating decision maker. The '10% test' is the test used to determine whether an operating segment is *reportable*.

10   C   Revenue can only be recognised when all of the conditions laid down in IAS 18 are satisfied, including the condition that the entity has transferred the significant risks and rewards of ownership of the goods to the buyer. As GY still has the goods, the risks and rewards of owning those goods are still with GY and have not been transferred to ZZ. Therefore no revenue can be recognised. The cash received should be classified as a liability.

62   Mixed objective test answers bank 7 (3/12)

1   B   VAT is collected by the shop and passed on to the tax authorities via its VAT return. The other options are all direct taxes.

2   The tax base of an asset or a liability is the value of that item for tax purposes.

3   C   Deferred tax arises in this case because the accounting treatment is different from the tax treatment.

4   D

	$'000
Accounting profit	860
Add depreciation	42
Add amortisation	15
	917
Less tax depreciation	(51)
Taxable profit	866
Tax @ 25%	216.5

5   D   This is sometimes referred to as 'ring-fencing'.

6   A   Under IAS 24 the finance director is key management personnel and his wife a close family member.

7   C   IAS 38 *Intangible assets* allows recognition if:

- future economic benefits will flow to the entity and
- the asset can be reliably measured

Option A would be advertising costs, B a provision, and D is internally generated and may not therefore be recognised as an asset.

8   According to IFRS 8 an operating segment is a component of an entity that engages in business activity and whose operating results are regularly reviewed by the entity's chief operating decision maker to make decisions about resources to be allocated to the segment and assess its performance.

9   Any four from the following:

- the entity has transferred the significant risks and rewards of ownership of the goods to the buyer
- the entity retains neither continuing managerial involvement nor effective control over the goods sold
- the amount of revenue can be measured reliably
- it is probable that the economic benefits associated with the transaction will flow to the entity
- The costs incurred to the seller can be measured reliably

63 Mixed objective test answers bank 8 (5/12)

1   Under the OECD model tax convention an entity will generally have residence for tax purposes in the *country of its effective management*.

2

	$
Input tax 32,333 × 15% =	(4,850)
Output tax 63,250 × 15/115 =	8,250
VAT due to be paid	3,400

Answer $3,400

3   B   The profit is taxed as the income of the entity for the year.

4   Any two from

- Power to review and query filed returns
- Power to request special reports or returns
- Power to examine records
- Powers of entry and search
- Power to exchange information with tax authorities in other jurisdictions
- Power to impose penalties

5   D   An indirect tax is a tax on expenditure (or 'consumption') rather than income and it is effective on the customer (or 'consumer').

6   D   Independence is a state of mind that is essential for accountants but it is not formally stated as a principle in the Code.

7   C   The overall supervising body is the IFRS Foundation.

8   B   In accordance with IAS 37 a provision of $20,000 should be recognised in because there is a probable outflow relating to the case brought by the school. The probability of winning the case against the subcontractor is a contingent asset that should not be recognised, but is should be disclosed by way of a note.

9   A   The asset should be valued at fair value less the cost of disposal ($800 − $50 = $750).

10   C $1,000,000 × discount rate 0.500 = $500,000 (or $463,000 plus 8%)

64 Mixed objective test answers bank 9 (9/12)

1   C   Tax assessments issued by the local tax authority are part of the tax administration system, not a source of tax rules.

2   A   Over the life of an asset, the tax depreciation should equal the purchase price of the asset less any amount realised on disposal. When disposal takes place there is often a balancing allowance to account for any difference.

	$
Purchase price of asset	90,000
Tax depreciation	(75,760)
Carrying amount for tax purposes	14,240
Proceeds on disposal	(10,000)
Balancing allowance	4,240

3   A

	$
Sales excluding VAT (138,000 × 100/115)	120,000
Cost of goods	(70,000)
Profit	50,000)

4   Tax jurisdictions often differentiate between different types of income and apply different rules to how each type of income is taxed. This is known as a schedular system.

5   C   Under the OECD model JZ will be deemed to be resident in the country of its effective management. Management board meetings take place in Country O, so this will be the country of effective management.

6   B   Bias is not a threat identified in the CIMA code; the other two are: advocacy and intimidation.

7   The two main responsibilities are:

- To review, on a timely basis, newly identified financial reporting issues not specifically addressed in IFRSs

- To clarify issues where unsatisfactory or conflicting interpretations have developed, with a view to reaching a consensus on the appropriate treatment

8

	$
Purchase price of asset	420,000
Add: import duties	30,000
	450,000
Indexation allowance (450,000 × 40%)	180,000
	630,000
Selling price less selling costs (700,000 – 10,000)	(690,000)
Gain on disposal	60,000
Tax payable @ 25%	15,000

9   B   Revenue for the month of June (one-sixth of the $6,000 received) will be recognised in the statement of profit or loss and other comprehensive income, and the remainder will be credited to deferred income.

10   C   IFRS 8 requires entities to adopt the 'management approach' to identifying operating segments, which means that if a segment is separately identified for internal management accounting, it should be recognised as such in the published financial statements.

65 Mixed objective test answers bank 10 (11/12)

1   C   Direct taxes are imposed on the income of individuals and the profits made by companies. Items (i) and (iv) are examples of indirect taxes.

2   B   Clarification is sometimes required after an IFRS has been published and is effective. Options A, C and D are part of the development process.

3   B

	SOFP CA $	Tax WDV $	Difference $
1 October 2011	132,000	82,500	
Depreciation (220,000 × 1/5)	(44,000)		
Tax depreciation (82,500 × 25%)		(20,625)	
	88,000	61,875	26,125
Deferred tax @ 25%			6,531

4   D   Neutrality, completeness and free from error.

5   A   A disclaimer of opinion is issued where the auditor has been unable to obtain sufficient, appropriate audit evidence and the item(s) about which the auditor lacks sufficient, appropriate audit evidence is/are believed to be material and pervasive. Without this evidence the auditor is unable to come to a conclusion regarding the financial statements and must therefore issue a disclaimer of opinion.

6   D   Since the analysis prepared by E is used to calculate her own staff bonus, there is clearly a self-interest threat.

7   A   The direct method extracts the information for the statement of cash flows directly from the accounting records. The indirect method uses information contained in the financial statements.

8   Factors that influence accounting and disclosure practices include:

- National company law
- National accounting standards
- Tax laws sources of finance and capital markets
- Cultural differences

Local and national factors in particular countries may specify formats for the presentation of financial information (eg UK Companies Act) or may specify items that must be disclosed (eg directors' emoluments).

9   C   An adjusting event is one which provides evidence of conditions that existed at the end of the reporting period. The court case was known about at the year end because a provision had been recognised in the financial statements.

10   B

	$
1 July 2012	12,000
Receive cash in advance for six months July 2012 to December 2012	
Liability at year end 12,000 × 3/6	6,000

	$
Supply goods 10,000 units @ $200 per 100 units	
July	2,000
August	2,000
September	2,000
Revenue for the year to 30 September 2012	6,000

66 Mixed objective test answers bank 11 (3/13)

1   D

2   B

3   To ensure that for similar investments all entities are allowed the same rates of depreciation for tax purposes.

    Entities can use any rate for accounting depreciation, so to ensure that all entities are taxed equally the tax authority sets rates for tax depreciation for all entities. The tax depreciation rates then replace accounting depreciation in the tax computations.

4   B

5   D

6   C

7   B

8   Any four from:

    - Investors
    - Lenders
    - Employees
    - Business contacts – customers, suppliers, competitors
    - General public
    - Government

9   A

10 C

67 Mixed objective test answers bank 12 (5/13)

1   A

2   D

3   Two from:

    - Exemption
    - Tax credit
    - Deduction

4

Cost	$650,000
Duties	$25,000
$675,000	
Indexation	$337,500
	$1,012,500
Sales price	$1,200,000
Less charges	$17,000
	$1,183,000

    Profit $1,183,000 – $1,012,500 = $170,500
    Tax @ 25% = $42,625

    Answer: $42,625

5   D

6   C

7   Any two from:

- Multinational entities could benefit from access to a wider range of international finance opportunities. This could have the effect of reducing financing costs;

- Multinational entities could benefit from improved management control as all parts of the entity would be reporting using one consistent basis;

- Multinational entities could benefit from greater efficiency in accounting departments as they would not have to spend time converting data from one accounting basis to another;

- Multinational entities could benefit from easier consolidation of overseas subsidiaries' results when preparing group accounts.

8 Any two from:

- To give advice to the IASB on agenda decisions;

- To give advice to the IASB on the priorities in its work;

- In relation to major standard setting projects to inform the IASB of the views of organisations and individuals on the Council;

- To give any other advice to the IASB or the Trustees.

9 Relevance and faithful representation

10 Opinion

68 Mixed section B answers bank 1 (Specimen paper)

(a) (i) Determining corporate residence is important as corporate income tax is usually **residency-based**.

If an entity is deemed to be resident in a country, it will usually have to pay corporate income tax in that country.

(ii) Determining the corporate residence of ATOZ will depend on the tax rules of the countries ATOZ is connected with. For example, if a company is incorporated in the UK, it is usually deemed to be resident in the UK for tax purposes. However, if a company is incorporated overseas but its main place of management is the UK, it could also be deemed to be resident in the UK.

If a company has a presence in more than one country, it could be deemed by local law to be resident in all of those countries, and therefore it could be taxed more than once on the same income.

Where this is the case, the OECD's model tax convention suggests that the company will be deemed to be resident in the country in which it has its place of effective management.

Therefore ATOZ will be deemed to be resident in NOP according to the OECD's model.

(b) (i) A single stage sales tax is chargeable once in the supply chain, usually at the point of sale to the end customer. The tax paid is not recoverable.

However, VAT is chargeable and deductible at different points in the supply chain. Tax paid by an entity at one point in the supply chain is usually recoverable by deducting it from the tax charged at the next point in the supply chain. The end consumer therefore bears all the VAT.

(ii) Net VAT due = output VAT – input VAT

	$'000
Output VAT	
Standard rate ($230k × 15/115)	30
Zero rate ($115k @ 0%)	0
	30
Input VAT	
Purchases ($130 × 15%)	(19.5)
Equipment ($345k × 15/115)	(45.0)
	(64.5)
Net VAT due to WX	(34.5)

(c) The possible advantages of having accounting standards based on principles are as follows.

- Standards based on principles **don't go out of date** in the same way as those based on rules. For instance, the expenditure RS is concerned with may be a new type of expenditure that wasn't often incurred when the prescriptive standard was originally drafted, and therefore wasn't included. In a principles based standard, this wouldn't be a problem as the spirit of the standard would need to be applied to see if the expenditure should be recognised as an asset.

- It is more difficult for a company to **manipulate information** to avoid applying a standard based on principles than it is for a standard based on rules. For example, if the standard included a specific value that had to be reached in order to be recognised as an asset, then the company could manipulate its expenditure to fall just below this value to avoid recognition.

- Standards based on principles have **broader application** than those based on rules. For example RS's expenditure was not included in the list of items in the rules-based standard and so it is not clear whether the item should be capitalised or not. This would not be the case in principles-based standards as professional judgment would be applied to determine how the expenditure should be treated.

- Standards based on principles are **less likely to contradict each other** than those based on rules as they are all based on the same basic principles. For example, a rules-based standard may require revenues and expenditures to be matched in an entirely different manner depending on which industry they were generated in.

- Standards based on rules require that many detailed standards covering all possible situations have to be produced. This can result in **complexity in financial reporting** as there are a considerable number of standards to be followed. Having standards based on principles avoids this.

(d) *Held for sale*

Provided that the manufacturing facility is being marketed for a reasonable price and it is unlikely that the plan to sell should change, the manufacturing facility should be classified as **'held for sale'** in the financial statements because it meets the criteria detailed in IFRS 5:

(i) The facility is available for immediate sale

(ii) The sale is highly probable (ie management are committed to the plan, are actively engaged in finding a purchaser and expect the sale to take place within one year)

In the statement of financial position, the manufacturing facility should be **measured at the lower of its carrying value and fair value less costs to sell**.

It should be presented **separately from other assets**, and the assets and liabilities should not be offset:

	$m
Non-current assets held for sale ($3.6m – $0.2m)	3.4
Liabilities associated with non-current assets held for sale	0.8

Discontinued Operation

As the manufacturing facility is held for sale and represents a separate major line of business (apparent as it is classified as a reportable segment per IFRS 8), it should be classified as a **discontinued operation** per IFRS 5.

BD should disclose a **single amount in the statement of comprehensive income** for the discontinued operation, which is the total of:

(i) The loss for the year of ($0.5m)

(ii) The post-tax gain or loss recognised on the measurement to fair value less costs to sell of the manufacturing facility.

BD should give detailed analysis of this figure either in the notes to the accounts or on the face of the statement of comprehensive income.

Additionally, net operating, investing and financing cash flows associated with the manufacturing facility should be disclosed separately in the statement of cash flows or in the notes.

(e) *Office lease*

The office lease should be treated as an **operating lease** under IAS 17 because substantially all the risks and rewards of ownership are not passed to C under the lease. For example, the length of the lease is

significantly less than the useful life of the office, and the minimum lease payments are significantly less than the fair value of the office at the inception of the lease.

The lease rentals should be recognised on a **straight line basis** over the lease term. The rent free period should be recognised as a discount over the whole lease term.

Expense at 31 March 20X9:   (4 × 12,000)/5 = $9,600

No asset is recognised for the office.

Computer system lease

The computer system lease should be treated as a **finance lease** under IAS 17 because substantially all the risks and rewards of ownership are passed to C under the lease. For example, the computer system is leased for the whole of its useful life and the minimum lease payments are equivalent to the cost of the assets on inception of the lease.

The finance costs associated with the lease will be accounted for under the actuarial method:

		$
1.4.X8	Cost	35,720
	Interest at 12.5%	4,465
	Lease payment	(15,000)
31.3.X9		25,185
	Interest at 12.5%	3,148
	Lease payment	(15,000)
31.3.Y0		13,333
	Interest at 12.5%	1,666
	Lease payment	(15,000)
31.3.Y1		0

At 31 March 20X9, C will have the following entries in its financial statements:

STATEMENT OF COMPREHENSIVE INCOME (extract)	$
Administrative expenses	
Office lease rental	9,600
Depreciation – computer system (35,720/3)	11,907
Finance costs	
Interest on finance lease	4,465

STATEMENT OF FINANCIAL POSITION (extract)	$
Assets	
Computer systems (35,720 – 35,720/3)	23,813
Non-current liabilities	
Finance lease	13,333
Current liabilities	
Finance lease (25,185 – 13,333)	11,852
Rent payable	9,600

(f) (i) The treatment of preference shares under IAS 32 and IAS 39 depends on the contractual terms of the preference share.

If the terms of the preference share mean that the issuer has an **obligation** to deliver cash or other financial assets in the future, the preference share is classified as a **financial liability** under IAS 32. Under IAS 39, the finance cost of the preference shares, which includes any dividends payable and any redemption amount payable, should be calculated and then allocated over the life of the preference shares using the effective interest method.

If the terms of the preference share mean that the issuer does not have an obligation to deliver cash or other financial assets in the future, the preference share is classified as equity under IAS 32.

(ii) The preference shares are redeemable and cumulative so PS has an **obligation** to deliver cash in the future. Therefore the preference shares should be classified as a **financial liability**. The finance cost associated with the preference shares (ie the outstanding balance multiplied by the effective interest rate) should be shown in the statement of comprehensive income.

STATEMENT OF FINANCIAL POSITION AS AT 31 MARCH 20X9

	$
Non-current liabilities	
Preference shares	1,211,642

STATEMENT OF COMPREHENSIVE INCOME FOR YEAR ENDED 31 MARCH 20X9

	$
Finance cost	61,642

69 Mixed section B answers bank 2 (5/10)

(a) Tax avoidance is a way of arranging your affairs to take advantage of the tax rules to pay as little tax as possible. It is perfectly legal. Cee has avoided tax by taking expert tax advice and investing her money in a tax efficient way in order to pay less tax.

Tax evasion is a way of paying less tax by illegal methods, eg not declaring the income or money laundering. Gee has evaded tax by not declaring all the income he earns on his annual tax return and so reducing his tax bill.

(b) (i) Unit taxes are taxes based on the number or weight of items, eg excise duties on cigarettes or tobacco. W pays a unit tax of $1 per bottle when the wine is bottled.

Ad valorem taxes are taxes based on the value of the items, eg a sales tax or value added tax and are usually expressed as a percentage of the value. For example, W charges VAT at 15% on each bottle of wine sold for $8.05, therefore each bottle costs $7 plus VAT at 15% = $1.05.

(ii) Net VAT due = output VAT − input VAT

	$'000
Output VAT	
Standard rate ($1.05 × 10,000)	10.5
Input VAT	
Purchases ($30,000 × 15%)	(4.5)
	6.0
Unit tax (10,000 × $1)	10.0
Total indirect tax due	16.0

(c) **Jurisdiction** relates to the power of a tax authority to charge and collect tax. **Competent jurisdiction** is the authority whose tax laws apply to an entity or person. The competent jurisdiction is usually the tax authority in the country where the entity is deemed to be resident for tax purposes.

The OCED Model Tax Convention suggests that a company is deemed resident in the place of its effective management. As the senior management of H meet regularly in Country X, H will be deemed to be resident in Country X and will be subject to the tax laws of the tax authority in Country X. Similarly, S will be deemed resident in Country Y and will be subject to the tax laws of the tax authority in Country Y.

A **withholding tax** is a tax that is deducted by the local tax authorities when an entity resident in that country pays funds overseas, for example when a subsidiary pays a dividend to a foreign parent. The 10% tax charged by Country Y on the dividend declared by S is a withholding tax.

The dividend will be taxed twice because it will be included in the worldwide income of H and so taxed in Country X. However, because Country Y and Country X have a **double taxation agreement**, it is likely that H will be able to get **tax relief** for the withholding tax suffered.

(d) (i) The objective of an audit of financial statements is to enable the auditor to express an opinion on whether the financial statements are prepared, in all material respects, in accordance with an identified financial reporting framework.

(ii) Inventory is overstated by $1m. The required adjustment is:

DR	Profit before tax	$1m
CR	Inventory (SOFP)	$1m

The adjustment represents 25% of profit and therefore is a material misstatement.

If the directors refuse to amend the financial statements for this misstatement, then the auditors should issue a **qualified opinion**. An adverse opinion is not required as the misstatement is not pervasive.

The qualified opinion paragraph should state that the financial statements give a true and fair view except for the identified misstatement relating to the overstatement of closing inventory.

(e) **Year to 31.3.X8 – 35% complete**

Expected profit/(loss) on contract:

	As at 31.03.X8	*As at 31.03.X9*
	$m	$m
Total revenue	63	63
Costs to date	(18)	(44)
Costs to complete	(36)	(20)
Expected profit/(loss)	9	(1)

As at 31.03.X9, 75% (35% + 40%) complete:

	Total to 31.03.X9
	$m
Revenue (63 × 75%)	47
Costs (64 × 75%)	(48)
Profit/(loss)	(1)

Amounts to be included in statement of comprehensive income for year to 31.03.X9:

	Year to 31.03.X9
	$m
Revenue (47 – 22)	25
Costs (48 – 18)	(30)
Profit/(loss) ((1) – 4)	(5)

Amounts to be included in statement of financial position at 31.03.X9:

Current assets

Gross amount due from customer	*31.03.X9*
	$m
Costs incurred to date (26 + 18)	44
Less: recognised profits less recognised losses (4 – (5))	(1)
	43
Less: progress billings to date (22 + 15)	(37)
Amount due from customer	6

(f) **Briefing note – treatment of shoe factory**

Exclusion of factory results

It would not be in line with IFRSs to completely exclude from the financials statements the results of the factory for the year. To do so would distort the overall results of the company, making it look more profitable than it currently is and thereby **misleading** users of the accounts. This would be **unethical**. Completely excluding the results of the factory would breach the fundamental principles of the CIMA Code of Ethics for accountants to demonstrate **professional behaviour** in complying with the relevant laws and standards, and also to act with **integrity** (ie honesty) in their work.

Appropriate treatment of the factory

If the factory is classified as a discontinued operation per IFRS 5, then the loss made by the factory in the year is separately disclosed in the statement of comprehensive income, after profit from continuing operations. This would make it clear to users that the factory, although loss making, will not be part of future operations.

To be classified as a discontinued operation, the factory must firstly have either been disposed of or classified as **held for sale** under IFRS 5. To be classified as held for sale, the factory must be available for sale in its present condition and the sale must be **highly probable**. Because management have not yet committed to a plan to find a buyer for the factory, the sale is not highly probable. Therefore, the factory cannot be classified as held for sale or as a discontinued operation.

As such, management must disclose the full loss made by the factory within **continuing operations** in the statement of comprehensive income.

70 Mixed section B answers bank 3 (11/10)

Marking scheme

		Marks
(a)	1½ marks available for each method plus illustration, up to a maximum of	<u>5</u>

Four methods for relieving **trading losses** are:

1   *Carry the loss forward against future trading profits*

	31.08.X9	31.08.Y0	31.08.Y1
	$	$	$
Trading profit/(loss)	(30,000)	10,000	50,000
Offset previous trading loss	–	(10,000)	(20,000)
Capital gain/(loss)	5,000	–	–
Taxable profit	5,000	–	30,000
Tax at 25%	1,250	–	7,500
Trading loss carried fwd	(30,000)	(20,000)	–

2   *Offset the loss against other income or capital gains of the same period*

The trading losses can be offset against the capital gains made by ZK in 20X9. In the illustration below, the trading losses remaining in 20X9 have also been carried forward to be offset against the trading profits of the following years. Some countries may not allow the remaining losses to be carried forward.

	31.08.X9	31.08.Y0	31.08.Y1
	$	$	$
Trading profit/(loss)	(30,000)	10,000	50,000
Capital gain/(loss)	5,000	–	–
Offset trading loss against	(5,000)	(10,000)	(15,000)
capital gain/trading profit			
Taxable profit	–	–	35,000
Tax at 25%	–	–	8,750
Trading loss carried fwd	(25,000)	(15,000)	–

3   *Carry the loss back against profits of previous periods*

Some countries, including the UK, allow trading losses to be carried back against the taxable profits of previous periods. If we assume that ZK made a taxable profit of $40,000 in 20X8, we can illustrate this method of relief as follows.

	31.08.X8	31.08.X9	31.08.Y0	31.08.Y1
	$	$	$	$
Trading profit/(loss)	40,000	(30,000)	10,000	50,000
Capital gain/(loss)	–	5,000	–	–
Carry back trading loss against	(30,000)	–	–	–
profits				
Taxable profit	10,000	5,000	10,000	50,000
Tax at 25%	2,500	1,250	2,500	17,500

4   *Offset the loss against the profits of another group company ('group loss relief')*

If ZK is part of a group of companies, then the trading loss made by ZK in 20X9 could be transferred to another company in that group and offset against the taxable profits of that company instead. For example, assume that ZK is the parent of ZL and ZL makes a trading profit of $40,000 in 20X9, the trading loss made by ZK could be offset as follows.

	ZK 31.08.X9 $	ZL 31.08.X9 $
Trading profit/(loss)	(30,000)	40,000
Transfer trading loss	–	(30,000)
Capital gain/(loss)	5,000	–
Taxable profit	5,000	10,000
Tax at 25%	1,250	2,500
Trading loss carried fwd	–	–

Marking scheme

			Marks
(b)	(i)	Explaining the meaning of withholding tax	1
		Explanation of why countries levy withholding tax	1
			2
	(ii)	Calculation – underlying tax	1
		Calculation – withholding tax	1
		Calculation – tax due	1
			3
		Total	5

(i)   A withholding tax is a tax levied on payments, such as interest payments, dividends and royalties, made by a company to another company or individual resident in another country.

Withholding taxes are levied because countries have no power to tax non-resident companies, so they charge withholding tax to ensure that they gain some income from the payments made by non-resident companies with operations in their country to overseas companies or individuals.

(ii)   Tax paid by SV on dividend

	$'000
Net dividend received	3,375
Withholding tax (3,375 × 10/90)	375
Gross dividend	3,750
Underlying tax (3,750 × 1,875/(12,500 – 1,875)	662
Total tax paid by SV on dividend	1,037

Tax due by HW

	$'000
Dividend received	3,750
Add on underlying tax	662
Total	4,412
Tax @ 25%	1,103
Less: WHT	(375)
Less: ULT	(662)
Tax payable in Country X	66l

Tutorial note: Underlying tax is calculated as follows:

$$\text{Underlying tax} = \text{gross dividend} \times \frac{\text{tax actually paid by foreign company}}{\text{foreign company's profit after tax}}$$

Marking scheme

		Marks
(c)	1½ marks available for each explanation, up to a maximum of	5

The TWO fundamental qualitative characteristics of financial information are as follows.

Relevance

Information is said to be relevant if it is capable of making a difference to the decisions made by users of that information. To be relevant therefore information must have a predictive value and/or a confirmatory value. This will help users evaluate past, present and future events, or confirm or correct their past evaluations. So relevant information has both a predictive and confirmatory role. The relevance of information is affected by its materiality.

Faithful representation

To be useful to its users, financial information must represent faithfully that which it either purports to represent or could reasonably be expected to represent. Faithful representation requires financial information to be complete, neutral and free from error.

The FOUR enhancing qualitative characteristics of financial information are as follows:

Comparability

Information is more useful if it can be compared with similar information about other entities and/or other accounting periods. Consistency in the preparation of financial information helps achieve comparability. For this to be possible users must be informed of the accounting policies employed in the preparation of the financial statements and any changes to those policies and their effect. The financial statements must also show corresponding amounts for the previous period.

Verifiability

Information must be verifiable in order to give assurance to the users of financial information that the information has been prepared so that it faithfully represents the economic phenomena it purports to represent. Verification can be direct or indirect.

Timeliness

Financial information is required by users in order to make decisions based on that information. It must therefore be made available to users in a timely manner if it is to be capable of influencing the decisions they make.

Understandability

Financial statement information should be readily understandable to users. For this purpose users are assumed to have a reasonable knowledge of business and economic activities and accounting, and a willingness to study the information with reasonable diligence. The information provided should be presented in a clear and concise manner.

Tutorial note: the requirement specified that you explain only TWO of the FOUR enhancing qualitative characteristics. The others are provided for learning purposes.

Marking scheme

			Marks
(d)	(i)	Goodwill calculation	2
	(ii)	Explanation of how goodwill is recorded, including IFRS 3 treatment	3
			5

(i)   Goodwill arising on acquisition of PN

	$'000	$'000
Consideration transferred (2.5 × 180)		450
Share of net assets acquired		
Share capital	180	
Share premium	60	
Retained earnings	40	
Fair value adjustment	70	
		350
Goodwill		100

(ii)   Treatment of goodwill in HB's group financial statements at 31 August 20Y0

- HB should record the goodwill in its consolidated statement of financial position under the caption 'Intangible non-current assets: goodwill arising on consolidation'.

- The goodwill should be initially recognised as the difference between the fair value of the purchase consideration and the fair value of the identifiable assets and liabilities, as calculated above.

- IFRS 3 does not permit amortisation of goodwill. Instead it should be tested for impairment at least annually. After initial recognition, goodwill is measured at the original amount less any accumulated impairment losses.

- Assuming there is no impairment at 31 August 20Y0, the goodwill should be included in the statement of financial position at the original amount calculated on acquisition of $100,000.

Marking scheme

		Marks
(c)	½ mark per valid point, up to a maximum of	5

(i)   *80,000 preferred shares in ABC*

The preference shares in ABC do not have any voting rights attached to them so if HI purchased these shares, it would not have the power to control or exercise significant influence over the financial and operating policies of ABC. The investment should be classified as a simple non-current asset investment in the consolidated financial statements and should be accounted for in accordance with IAS 39.

(ii)   *40,000 equity shares and 50,000 preference shares in ABC*

An investment in 40,000 equity shares would give HI a shareholding of 40%. As this is more than 20% of the voting power of ABC, it should be assumed that HI will have significant influence over ABC. ABC should be classified as an associate of HI and accounted for using the equity method in the consolidated financial statements of HI. The preference shares should be accounted for as a simple investment as per (i) above.

(iii)   *70,000 equity shares*

An investment in 70,000 equity shares would give HI a shareholding of 70%, as this is more than 50% of the voting power of ABC, it should be assumed that HI will have the power to control ABC unless it can be clearly shown otherwise, however this is rare. ABC should be classified as a subsidiary of HI and consolidated on a line by line basis in the consolidated financial statements of HI.

Marking scheme

				Marks
(f)	(i)	Site reinstatement	– explanation of why provision required	1
			– inclusion of provision present value	$\frac{1}{2}$
				2
	(ii)	Earthquake	– explanation of why non-adjusting event	$1\frac{1}{2}$
			– treatment in financial statements	$1\frac{1}{2}$
				3
		Total		5

(i) *Site reinstatement*

IAS 37 requires that a provision for the costs of reinstating this site is set up immediately when the licence is obtained. This is because a legal obligation exists to reinstate the site at the date the licence is obtained. The provision should be the present value of the estimated costs to reinstate the site, so at 31 August 20Y0 this is $3m. The income statement should also include the unwinding of the discount on the fair value of the provision when it was first recorded in the accounts at 1 September 20X9 to 31 August 20Y0.

The costs of reinstating the site should be capitalised along with the costs of the buildings and equipment used in the mine.

(ii) *Earthquake*

Assuming that the financial statements have not yet been authorised for issue, the earthquake is a non-adjusting event in accordance with IAS 10. This is because it is indicative of conditions that arose after the end of the reporting period.

No adjustments should be made to the financial statements at 31 August 20Y0 for this event and no provision for the repair costs should be included in the accounts at this date. The closure of the mine for six months and the repair costs of $1m means that the earthquake is likely to be a material event and as such should be disclosed in a note to the accounts at 31 August 20Y0.

71 Mixed section B answers bank 4 (5/11)

Marking scheme

			Marks
(a)	(i)	Accounting profit	$\frac{1}{2}$
		Add back accounting depreciation	$\frac{1}{2}$
		Less tax depreciation	$\frac{1}{2}$
		Tax due	$\frac{1}{2}$
		Total	2
	(ii)	Temporary differences	1
		Deferred tax	1
		Income statement credit	1
			3
		Total	5

(i) $57,375

	$
Accounting profit	192,000
Add back accounting depreciation (500/5)	100,000
Less tax depreciation (500 × 50% × 25%)	(62,500)
Taxable profit	229,500
Tax due at 25%	57,375

(ii)   Deferred tax credit for year ended 31 March 20X8 = $9,375

	31.03.X7	*31.03.X8*
	$	
Book value	400,000	300,000
Tax WDV	250,000	187,500
Temporary difference	150,000	112,500
Deferred tax liability at 25%	37,500	28,125
Credit to income statement (28,125 – 37,500)		9,375

Marking scheme

			Marks
(b)	(i)	½ mark for each valid point, up to a maximum of	2
	(ii)	Sales price	½
		Deductible selling expenses	½
		Cost of asset	½
		Capital gain	½
		Tax due	1
		Total	5

(i)   A capital gain arises when an asset is disposed of for more than its original cost. Most tax regimes have separate rules covering the tax of capital gains and the tax of trading profits.

A capital gain is usually calculated as the disposal proceeds less the tax written down value of the asset being disposed of (ie original cost less tax depreciation allowed). Some countries allow the cost of improvements or the costs incurred to sell the asset to be deducted from the sales proceeds. Some countries also allow the original cost of the asset to be adjusted up to current prices by the use of an index, such as the Retail Price Index, before calculating the capital gain. This prevents the taxpayer from having to pay tax on a gain which is simply the result of inflation.

Capital gains tax is calculated as: capital gain × capital gains tax rate.

(ii) $29,000

	$
Sale price	1,000,000
Less allowable costs	(6,000)
Less cost of asset (850 + 5 + 8 + 15)	(878,000)
Capital gain	116,000
Capital gains tax at 25%	29,000

Marking scheme

			Marks
(c)	(i)	½ mark for each valid point, up to a maximum of	2
	(ii)	Gross dividend	1
		ULT	2
			3
		Total	5

(i)   Underlying tax (ULT) is the tax which has already been suffered by the profits from which a dividend is paid. This happens when an entity receives a dividend from a foreign entity when the dividend has been paid out of taxed profits.

Underlying tax is calculated as :

Underlying tax = gross dividend × $\dfrac{\text{tax actually paid by foreign company}}{\text{foreign company's profit after tax}}$

The gross dividend is the dividend paid by the foreign entity before withholding tax.

(ii) $48,750

	$'000
Net dividend received	156
Withholding tax (156 × 20/80)	39
Gross dividend	195

Underlying tax = (195 × 130/(650 – 130)) = $48,750

Marking scheme

	Marks
(d) 1 mark per well explained point, up to a maximum of	5

The possible advantages of having principle-based accounting standards as opposed to prescriptive standards are as follows.

- Standards based on principles **don't go out of date** in the same way as those based on rules. For example if a prescriptive standard includes a list of common items that would qualify for specific treatment, the list may go out of date as economies progress and develop.

- It is more difficult for a company to **manipulate information** to avoid applying a standard based on principles than it is for a standard based on rules. For example, if the standard included a specific value that had to be reached in order to be recognised as an asset, then the company could manipulate its expenditure to fall just below this value to avoid recognition.

- Standards based on principles make it harder for entities to **avoid** applying a standard as the terms of reference are broader.

- Standards based on principles are **less likely to contradict each other** than those based on rules as they are all based on the same basic principles. For example, a rules-based standard may require revenues and expenditures to be matched in an entirely different manner depending on which industry they were generated in.

- Standards based on rules require that many detailed standards covering all possible situations have to be produced. This can result in **complexity in financial reporting** as there are a considerable number of standards to be followed. Having standards based on principles avoids this.

Marking scheme

			Marks
(e)	(i)	Objective of financial reporting	3
	(ii)	Underlying assumption: going concern	2
			5

(i) The *Conceptual Framework* states that: 'The objective of general purpose financial reporting is to provide financial information about the reporting entity that is useful to existing and potential investors, lenders and other creditors in making decisions about providing resources to the entity. These decisions involve buying, selling or holding equity and debt instruments, and providing or settling loans and other forms of credit.'

Financial reporting provides information about a reporting entity's economic resources, claims against those resources and changes in resources and claims.

(ii) The underlying assumption outlined in the *Conceptual Framework* is going concern.

Going concern

Financial statements are usually prepared under the assumption that the business is a going concern. This means that it will **continue to operate** in approximately the same manner for the foreseeable future (at least the next 12 months). In particular, the entity will not go into liquidation or scale down its operations in a material way.

If the entity is not considered to be a going concern, the financial statements should be prepared on another basis, usually the 'break-up basis', where the assets of entity are included in the accounts at their 'break-up' value.

Marking scheme

		Marks
(f)	1 mark per well explained point, up to a maximum of	5

As a professional accountant, CX has an obligation to act in accordance with the fundamental principles in the CIMA Code of Ethics. These include objectivity and integrity. CX is in a position where she may be compromising these principles.

Objectivity requires that a professional accountant should not allow bias, conflict of interest or undue influence of others to override professional or business judgements.

CX's objectivity is being threatened because the board members are pressurising CX to use assumptions which she believes will grossly overestimate the forecast profits, which overrides her professional judgement on what those assumptions should be.

Integrity requires a professional accountant to be straightforward and honest in all professional and business relationships.

CX's integrity is being threatened because she is being asked to be dishonest and use assumptions which she believes are not reflective of the true situation.

The possible options CX could take are

- In the first instance, CX could inform her direct line manager (possibly a board member) that she is very unhappy with the forecasts and try to persuade them that the figures are inappropriate and should not be used.

- If the board insist on using these figures, CX should try and distance herself from the forecasts and refuse to have her name documented on them.

- CX could consider calling the CIMA ethics helpline to ask for advice

- If the situation is not appropriately resolved, CX should consider resigning her position and seeking employment elsewhere.

72 Mixed section B answers bank 5 (9/11)

			Marks
(a)	(i)	1 mark per well made point	2
	(ii)	Output VAT	1½
		Input VAT	1
		VAT refund	½
			3
		Total	5

(i) A single stage sales tax is chargeable once in the supply chain, usually at the point of sale to the end customer. The tax paid is not recoverable.

However, VAT is chargeable and deductible at different points in the supply chain. Tax paid by an entity at one point in the supply chain is usually recoverable by deducting it from the tax charged at the next point in the supply chain. The end consumer therefore bears all the VAT.

(ii) Net VAT due = output VAT – input VAT

	$'000
Output VAT	
Z - Standard rate ($207k × 15/115)	27
Y - Zero rate ($90k @ 0%)	0
	27
Input VAT	
Purchases ($200 × 15%)	(30)
Net VAT refund due to SV	**(3)**

			Marks
(b)	(i)	1 mark per well made point, up to a maximum of	2
	(ii)	1 mark per well made point, up to a maximum of	3
		Total	5

(i) Deferred tax arises because the accounting treatment of a transaction is different to the tax treatment of the transaction, resulting in **temporary differences**. Deferred tax is the tax attributable to temporary differences.

Temporary differences arise because of **timing differences** between the tax treatment and the accounting treatment, for example, items are accounted for on an accruals basis in the financial statements, but may be treated on a cash basis when calculating the tax due.

(ii) A deferred tax debit balance is called a **deferred tax asset**.

Deferred tax assets are the amounts of income taxes **recoverable in future periods** relating to:

- tax deductible temporary differences
- unused tax losses or unused tax credits that have been carried forward from previous periods.

Deferred tax assets should only be recognised in so far as it is probable that taxable profits will be available against which they can be utilised.

So if a business is loss making, and it is not probable that it will make a profit, then the deferred tax asset should not be recognised.

Marking scheme

			Marks
(c)	(i)	1 mark per well made point, up to a maximum of	2
	(ii)	1 mark per well made point, up to a maximum of	3
		Total	5

(i)   Under the worldwide approach to taxing entities, entities pay income tax on their **worldwide income** in the country they are deemed to be **resident** in for tax purposes.

Their worldwide income includes income generated in the country they are deemed resident for tax purposes, as well as income that has been generated in other countries, for example, income arising because the entity has a factory in that country or has investments in that country.

(ii)   The worldwide approach can lead to income being **taxed twice**, once in the country in which it is earned, and again in the country where the entity earning the income is deemed resident.

Double tax relief is often available to reduce the amount of tax payable in this situation. Double tax agreements between countries specify the relief available for double tax between those countries.

Because there are different methods of determining tax residency, an entity may be deemed resident in two countries and its worldwide income taxed twice.

Double tax agreements can help reduce the tax payable in this situation by clarifying which country a company is deemed to be resident in. The **OECD's model tax agreement** suggests that a company should be deemed to be resident in its place of effective management.

Marking scheme

			Marks
(d)	(i)	1 mark per well made point, up to a maximum of	5

Accounting regulations in a country are influenced by many different sources.

The main influences come from:

- **National company law** such as the UK Companies Act. Accounting regulations can be codified in law and companies must comply with the legal requirements.

- **National accounting standards.** Many countries have now adopted IFRSs as their accounting standards, but may have their own local standards for smaller entities. In the UK, entities which are not listed can apply UK GAAP.

- **Tax laws.** Some countries accounting requirements are driven by what is required for tax purposes, so accounting profit largely mirrors taxable profit.

Other influences include:

- **Sources of finance and capital markets.** There is a greater demand for information and disclosure when finance is raised from external sources such as shareholders. Local stock exchange regulations may also specify certain information that has to be disclosed.

- **Cultural differences.** The culture of a country and the values that society has can have an influence on accounting regulations and disclosures required by entities.

			Marks
(e)	(i)	1 mark per definition, up to a maximum of	2
	(ii)	1 mark per point, up to a maximum of	3
		Total	5

(i) An **asset** is a **resource controlled** by an entity as a result of **past events** and from which **future economic benefits** are expected to flow to the entity.

A **liability** is a **present obligation** of the entity arising from **past events**, the settlement of which is expected to result in an **outflow of resources** from the entity.

(ii) An asset or a liability can only be recognised in the financial statements if it **meets the definition** of an asset or a liability and it also satisfies the following **recognition criteria** specified in the IASB's *Conceptual Framework*:

(a) It is probable that any future economic benefit associated with the item will flow to or from the entity.

(b) The item has a cost or value that can be measured with reliability.

			Marks
(f)	(i)	1 mark per well explained point, up to a maximum of	5

IFRS 5 requires that assets held for sale are carried at the lower of their carrying amount and fair value less costs to sell. Management's decision to re-classify the property as a non-current asset at its previous carrying amount ignores the requirements of IFRS 5 and is therefore wrong.

As a professional accountant, WZ has an obligation to act in accordance with the fundamental principles in the CIMA Code of Ethics. These include **integrity** and **objectivity**.

Integrity requires a professional accountant to be straightforward and honest in all professional and business relationships.

WZ's integrity is under threat because he is being asked to agree to an accounting treatment which is knows is incorrect. If he agrees, then he is being dishonest.

Objectivity requires that a professional accountant should not allow bias, conflict of interest or undue influence of others to override professional or business judgements.

WZ's objectivity is under threat because management are pressurising WZ to agree to using an accounting treatment which he knows is wrong. If he agrees, he will have allowed undue influence of others to override his professional judgement.

The possible options WZ could take are:

- WZ should inform management of the correct accounting treatment in accordance with IFRS 5 and recommend that they do not reclassify the property as a non-current asset at carrying value.

- If management insist on ignoring IFRS 5, WZ should try and distance himself from the financial statements.

- WZ could consider calling the CIMA ethics helpline to ask for advice

- If the situation is not appropriately resolved, WZ should consider resigning his position and seeking employment elsewhere.

73 Mixed section B answers bank 6 (11/11)

(a)

(i)

	$	$
Accounting profit per financial statements		165,000
Add back items of expense that are not tax allowable:		
Entertaining	9,800	
Depreciation – property, plant and equipment	42,000	
Depreciation – vehicles (18/6)	3,000	
		54,800
		219,800
Deduct items of income that are not taxable or tax allowances given:		
Tax depreciation – property, plant and equipment	65,000	
Tax depreciation – vehicles (18 × 50%)	9,000	
		(74,000)
Taxable profit		145,800

Tax due = 145,800 × 25% = **$36,450**

(ii) Income tax expense charged to the statement of profit or loss: **$43,700**

	$
Current tax expense	36,450
Increase in deferred tax provision (W)	7,250
	43,700

Working – deferred tax

	$
Increase in deferred tax provision for PPE ((65 – 42) × 25%)	5,750
Increase in deferred tax provision for vehicles ((9 – 3) × 25%)	1,500
	7,250

(b) (i)

	$
Output VAT	
Sales (105,800 × 15/115)	13,800
Input VAT	
Perfume (50,000 × 1.2*) × 15%	(9,000)
Repackaging (9,775 × 15/115)	(1,275)
VAT due to tax authorities	3,525

* VAT is payable on the cost plus excise duty

(ii)

	$	$
Revenue (105,800 × 100/115)		92,000
Cost of sales:		
Purchases plus excise duty (50,000 × 1.2)	60,000	
Repackaging (9,775 × 100/115)	8,500	
		(68,500)
Net profit		23,500

(c) A 'tax base' is the thing that is subject to tax. Taxes can be classified according to their tax base (ie what is being taxed).

Three examples of a tax base are:

- Income or profits (personal income tax and company income tax)
- Assets (tax on capital gains, wealth and inheritance taxes)
- Consumption (or expenditure, eg taxes on alcohol, cigarettes or fuel and sales taxes).

BPP LEARNING MEDIA

(d) An entity has **maintained its capital** if it has as much capital at the end of the period as it had at the beginning of the period. Any amount over and above that required to maintain the capital at the beginning of the period is **profit**. It is important to know which concept of capital is being adopted as this determines how profit is calculated.

There are two concepts of capital:

Under a **financial concept** of capital, such as invested money or invested purchasing power, **capital** is the net assets or equity of the entity. The financial concept of capital is adopted by most entities.

Under a **physical concept** of capital, such as operating capability, **capital** is the productive capacity of the entity based on, for example, units of output per day.

There are therefore two concepts of capital maintenance:

(a) **Financial capital maintenance**. Under this concept, a profit is only earned if the money amount of the next assets at the end of the period is greater than the money amount of the net assets a the beginning of the period.

(b) **Physical capital maintenance**. Under this concept, a profit is only earned if the physical productive capacity of the entity at the end of the period is greater than at the beginning of the period.

(e) (i) **Materiality** - A matter is **material** if its omission or misstatement could influence the economic decisions of users taken on the basis of the financial statements.

Materiality is a judgment and there are no rules as to what makes an item material. Some items are material by nature and some items are material due to their size. A good rule of thumb for determining if an item is material by size is to consider items that are 5% or more of net profit or 1% or more of revenue to be material.

The capitalised research expenses are approximately 11% (500/4,500) of net profit and are therefore likely to be material.

(ii) The research expenditure should not be capitalised, instead it should be expensed in accordance with IAS 38. Assuming management refuse to change the financial statements, then the financial statements will contain a material error.

However, this error is restricted to the research expenses and is not pervasive to the financial statements. Therefore a **modified opinion** should be issued. The opinion should be **qualified** on the grounds that the misstatement is material, but not pervasive, to the financial statements. The opinion will contain the phrase 'true and fair view, except for...' and then a description of the issue.

(f) Section 320 of the 2010 CIMA Code (previously Section 220 of the 2007 Code) deals with the preparation and reporting of information.

It specifies that a professional accountant in business should maintain information for which they are responsible so that it describes the **true nature** of transactions, assets and liabilities, and is **timely**, **accurate** and **complete**.

The fundamental principles of the CIMA Code of ethics require RS to act with both **integrity** and **objectivity**. Integrity requires RS to act honestly and objectivity requires RS to not allow bias or conflict of interest or undue influence from others to override his professional judgment.

RS is being pressurised to present information that does not reflect the true nature of the transactions and is not accurate.

Therefore RS's integrity is under threat as he is being asked to be dishonest.

RS's objectivity is under threat as he may be unduly influenced by others to change the information or may give in to the self-interest he has in the figures due to his bonus being affected.

74 Mixed section B answers bank 7 (3/12)

(a) Deferred tax balance at 31 December 2011:

	Carrying Value	Tax base
	$'000	$'000
Cost 1 January 2010	440	440
Year to 31 December 2010	(55)	(220)
	385	220
Revaluation 1 Jan 2011	70	0
	455	220
Year to 31 December 2011	(65)	(55)
	390	165

At 31 December 2010: $385,000 − $220,000 = $165,000
At 31 December 2011: $390,000 − $165,000 = $225,000
Change (Increase) $60,000
Tax at 25% = $15,000

Deferred tax movement in year to 31 December 2011:
Debit to income statement of $15,000

Deferred tax balance at 31 December 2011:
Credit balance $225,000 × 25% = $56,250

(b) (i) Zero rated means that no VAT is charged on sales but UYT can reclaim VAT paid on its inputs.

Exemption from VAT means that the revenue earned is exempt from VAT, so no VAT is charged but UYT cannot reclaim the portion of input VAT that relates to the exempt goods. If an actual figure cannot be calculated it will be on a proportional basis.

	Excl VAT	VAT 15%
	$	$
Inputs:		
Cost	400,000	60,000
Input VAT claim limited to 450/600		45,000
Outputs:		
Standard rate	450,000	67,500
Exempt	150,000	0
	600,000	67,500
Net		22,500

(ii) Net Vat due to be paid is $22,500

(c) Under the classical system of taxation, company income tax is charged on all of the profits of the entity, whether distributed or not. Dividends are paid out of taxed profits and are then chargeable to personal income tax in the hands of the shareholder. In this case the dividends have been taxed twice.

Under the imputation system, the underlying company income tax that has already been paid is imputed to the shareholder as a tax credit. The shareholder pays income tax on the dividend but deducts the tax credit, therefore avoiding the problem of double taxation of dividends.

If the personal income tax rate of the shareholder is higher than the rate of tax credit the shareholder may have to apply additional tax on the dividend, however it will still only have been taxed once.

With systems using the full imputation system all of the underlying corporate income tax is passed to the shareholder as a tax credit. If a partial imputation system is used only part of the tax paid by the entity will be passed to the shareholder.

YT has received a dividend from LKJ and will have received a tax credit for the proportion of tax paid by LKJ on the underlying profit. As LKJ is an entity resident in Country X it will have paid corporate income tax at 25% on its taxable profit for the year. This will be passed on to its shareholders as a tax credit as Country X uses the full imputation system..

YT will receive a tax credit and will be able to set this tax credit against any tax due on the dividend leaving additional tax to be paid if YT's personal tax rate is higher than 25%.

YT is therefore incorrect in thinking that his dividend has been taxed twice.

(d)   The four main entities involved in developing and implementing IFRS are:

- IFRS Foundation (formerly known as the International Accounting Standards Committee Foundation (IASCF).

  Role – a broad range of responsibilities including strategy, governance and fund raising

- International Accounting Standards Board (IASB)

  Role – responsibility for all technical matters including the preparation and publication of international financial reporting standards

- IFRS Advisory Council (formerly known as the Standards Advisory Council)

  Role – to provide a forum for consultation with the outside world. Provides strategic advice to the IASB and informs the IASB of public views on major standard setting projects.

- IFRS Interpretations Committee (formerly known as the International Financial Reporting Interpretations Committee IFRIC)

  Role – to review newly identified financial reporting issues and to provide guidance and clarification on the application and interpretation of IFRSs

(e)   (i)   ISA 200 *Overall objectives of the independent auditor and the conduct of an audit in accordance with international standards on auditing* states that the objective of an audit is to enable the auditor to express an opinion as to whether the financial statements are prepared, in all material respects, in accordance with an identified financial reporting framework and as to whether they give a true and fair view of the affairs of the entity.

        (ii)   Any three from:

- Management's responsibility for the financial statements

  Report should state that management is responsible for the preparation and fair presentation of the financial statements.

- Auditor's responsibility

  Report should state that the responsibility of the auditor is to express an opinion on the financial statements based on the audit.

- Scope of the audit of the financial statements

  Report should give an overview of the type of work done during the audit, such as obtaining audit evidence, risk assessment, procedures selected and the evaluation of the accounting policies used.

- Auditor's opinion

  Report should give the auditor's opinion on whether the financial statements give a true and fair view or are presented fairly in all material respects, in accordance with the applicable financial reporting framework.

(f)   The ethical problem that XQ faces is that a professional accountant in business should prepare or present information fairly, honestly and in accordance with relevant professional standards so that the information will be understood in its context. A professional accountant is expected to act with integrity and objectivity and not allow any undue influence from others to override his professional judgement.

XQ is facing pressure from others to change the results and therefore break the CIMA Code.

XQ is being asked to misrepresent the facts of the actual situation which would be contrary to the CIMA Code's fundamental principles of integrity and objectivity. XQ would also be breaking the due care requirement of the CIMA Code.

XQ should apply safeguards to eliminate the threats or reduce them to an acceptable level. As other staff are offering incentives XQ will need to decline these and refuse to alter the accounting information.

XQ should also consult with his line manager. XQ may also wish to get advice from the CIMA helpline.

The situation is unlikely to require XQ to seek legal advice or resign.

75 Mixed section B answers bank 8 (5/12)

(a) The use of statements of cash flows is very much in conjunction with the rest of the financial statements. Users can gain further appreciation of the change in net assets, of the entity's financial position (liquidity and solvency) and the entity's ability to adapt to changing circumstances by affecting the amount and timing of cash flows.

Statements of cash flows enhance comparability as they are not affected by differing accounting policies used for the same types of transactions or events.

Cash flow information of a historical nature can be used as an indicator of the amount, timing and certainty of future cash flows. Past forecast cash flow information can be checked for accuracy as actual figures emerge. The relationship between profit and cash flows can be analysed as can changes in prices over time.

(b) Deferred tax and provisions for income tax

(i) Deferred tax is the estimated future tax consequences of transactions and events that have been recognised in the financial statements of the current and previous periods. Deferred tax arises due to the temporary differences between the accounting profit and the taxable profit. The temporary differences cause the carrying value of some items in the statement of financial position to be different from their tax base (the amount recognised for tax calculation).

(ii) TX's statement of comprehensive income shows an increase in deferred tax, this suggests that temporary differences increased by $800,000 in the year to 31/3/2012. The main reason was probably an increase in non-current assets causing the tax depreciation to be $800,000 more than the accounting depreciation for the year to 31/3/2012, thus causing the increase of $200,000 in deferred tax provision.

(iii) Current tax is the estimated amount of corporate income tax payable on the taxable profits of the entity for the period. The amount of current tax is accrued in the financial statements and carried forward as a current liability to the next accounting period when it will be paid. When the tax is paid there will usually be a difference between the amount paid and the amount accrued. If the amount paid is less than the amount accrued there will be an over provision of income tax. The amount over provided will be an adjustment to the income tax expense in the following period. In TX the current tax estimate for year to 31 March 2011 was $650,000, the statement of cash flows shows that $600,000 was paid in the following period leaving a balance of $50,000 over provided.

(c) **PQ Tax Calculation for the year ended 31 March 2012**

	$'000
Accounting profits before tax	387
Less finance income after tax	(85)
Add gross finance income	100
Add back:	
Depreciation	92
Amortisation	14
	508
Less tax depreciation	98
Taxable profits	410
Tax at 25%	102.5
Less tax suffered on foreign interest received:	
Gross interest 85 × 15 / 85 =	(15)
Tax due	87.5

(d) **Indirect tax**

(i) Excise Duty is a selective commodity tax, levied on certain types of goods. It is a unit tax based on the weight or size of the tax base. E.g. Petroleum products, tobacco products alcoholic drinks and motor vehicles.

Single stage sales tax is a more general consumption tax. It is applied at one level of the production/distribution chain only. It can be applied to any level but when it is used in practice it is most often applied at the retail sales level. Single stage sales taxes are levied as a percentage of value, e.g. retail sales value.

(ii) From the revenue authority's point of view, the characteristics of commodities that make them most suitable for excise duty to be applied are:

- Few large producers
- Inelastic demand with no close substitutes
- Large sales volumes
- Easy to define products covered by the duty

(e) Income and equity

(i) **Income**: Increases in economic benefits during the accounting period in the form of inflows or enhancements of assets or decreases of liabilities that result in increases in equity, other than those relating to combinations from equity participants;

Equity: Residual interest in the assets of the entity after deducting all its liabilities.

(ii) **Income** is recognised if:

- It meets the definition of income in (i) above.
- The increase has a cost or value that can be measured reliably.

Income is recognised in the statement of comprehensive income with due regard to materiality.

(f) Benefits of an audit

Briefing Note
To: Chief Executive

The benefits of having an external audit carried out each year:

- The external audit should give an independent opinion on the truth and fairness of the accounts and therefore the shareholders should have comfort that there is no material error or misrepresentation of the financial position of the entity in the statements presented

- Whilst the auditors are conducting the audit they will consider the controls in place and may be able to give constructive advice to management

- Whilst the purpose of the audit is not to find fraud, the fact that an external review is taking place is likely to act as a fraud deterrent

- Applications to third parties for finance may be enhanced

- Avoids breaking the law, for some entities an audit is not an option. Local legislation relating to entities may require an annual independent audit to be carried out. Local stock exchange regulations will usually require an annual audit.

76 Mixed section B answers bank 9 (9/12)

			Marks
(a)	(i)	Calculation of income tax charge	3
	(ii)	Explanation of effect	1
		Calculation of effect	$\frac{1}{5}$
		Total	

(i) In the statement of profit or loss and other comprehensive income for the year ended 31 March 2012 PV will report an income tax charge of $1,975,000. This is calculated as follows:

	$'000
Overprovision for the year to 31 March 2011	
(1,820 – 1,795)	(25)
Income tax charge for the year	1,980
Increase in deferred tax	20
Taxation charge for the year	1,975

(ii) If the likely future rate of tax is known, then this can be used in calculating the deferred tax provision; if not the current rate is used. Using a rate of 30% gives an increase in deferred tax to 672 (560/0.25 × 0.30) so we would need to increase the deferred tax provision by $112,000.

		Marks
(b)	2 marks per well made point, up to a maximum of	5
	Total	5

Double tax relief can be provided by one of the following methods:

Exemption – an agreement between two countries that income will be exempt in one country and taxable in another.

Deduction   foreign tax is deducted from foreign income and the remaining income it taxed in the country of residence.

Tax credit – tax paid in one country is treated as a tax credit at the lower tax rate of the other country.

		Marks
(c)	Correct treatment of expenses and depreciation	2
	Correct treatment of disposal and new vehicle	2
	Calculation of tax	1
	Total	5

		$
Profit for the year before tax		43,000
Add back:	Entertaining expense	6,300
	Loss on disposal	1,000
	Depreciation charge on property	16,500
	Depreciation charge on new vehicle	4,000
Deduct:	Allowable tax depreciation	(19,300)
	Tax depreciation on new vehicle	(16,000)
Adjusted profit chargeable to tax		35,500
Tax charge @ 25%		8,875

Marking scheme

		Marks
(d)	Amounts to be included in statement of profit or loss and other comprehensive income	3
	Amount to be included in statement of financial position	2
	Total	5

	$'000
Revenue	9,000
Total cost	10,000
Predicted loss	(1,000)
Year to 31 March 2012:	
Revenue (9000 × 35%)	3,150
Cost of sales in year (10000 × 35%)	3,500
Loss in year	(350)
Additional expected loss	(650)
	(1,000):
Amount due to client	
Cost to date (WIP)	4,000
Total loss	(1,000)
Less cash received	(3,250)
Due to client	(250)

TY should include the following in its statement of profit or loss and other comprehensive income for the year to 31 March 2012:

Revenue (9000 × 35%)		3,150
Cost of sales		
Cost to date (10000 × 35%)	3,500	
Additional expected loss	650	
		4,150

TY should include the following in its statement of financial position as at 31 March 2012:

Under current liabilities:

Amount due to client	(250)

Marking scheme

		Marks
		5
(e)	1 mark per step, up to a maximum of	
	Total	5

The IASB standard setting process can involve the following steps:

- The IASB establishes an advisory committee to advise on the issues arising from the project. The IASB consults with this committee and the IFRS advisory council throughout the development process.

- IASB develops and publishes a Discussion Paper for public comment.

- The IASB reviews the comments on the Discussion Paper and prepares and publishes an Exposure Draft for public comment.

- The comments on the Exposure Draft are reviewed by the IASB and if necessary the Exposure Draft is amended before being issued as a final standard.

- On occasion where there are significant changes to the exposure draft it may be reissued for further public comment before being issued as a final standard.

Marking scheme

		Marks
(f)	(i) 1 mark per point on the impact, up to a maximum of	2
	(ii) 1 mark per point on the report, up to a maximum of	3
	Total	5

(i) Impact on the audit report

The inventory value is material, 30% of profit and 4.5% of revenue and there is a lack of evidence to support the inventory valuation it will impact on the audit report opinion.

As the auditors have agreed with VB's directors on the treatment of the court case it will not affect the audit report opinion.

(ii) Modification of audit report

The auditors will have to issue a modified report for the inventory valuation as it is due to a material misstatement caused by insufficient appropriate evidence. The modification required is a qualified opinion expressed as showing a true and fair view 'except for' the inventory valuation.

The auditors can issue an unqualified opinion for the court case. However there is material inherent uncertainty over the outcome of the court case so the unqualified report would have to include a "fundamental uncertainty" emphasis of matter.

77 Mixed section B answers bank 10 (11/12)

(a) Tax authorities have the following powers to enforce compliance with tax rules:

- Power to review and query filed returns (in order to resolve queries)

- Power to request special reports, forms or returns (if they believe that full information has not been provided)

- Power to examine records (generally going back some years)

- Powers of entry and search (especially where fraud is suspected)

- Exchange of information with tax authorities in other jurisdictions

(b) The tax payable by KQ for the year to 30 September 2012 is $37,250

	$	$
Profit before tax		147,000
Add back expenses that are not tax deductible:		
Political donations	9,000	
Entertaining	6,000	
		15,000
Add back accounting depreciation:		
Plant (180,000 × 15%)	27,000	
Machinery (50,000 × 15%)	7,500	
		34,500
		196,500
Less: tax allowances:		
Plant (W1)	22,500	
Machinery (50,000 × 50%)	25,000	
		(47,500)
Taxable profit		149,000
Tax at 25%		37,250

W1   *Plant*

	$
Cost 1 Oct 2010	180,000
Tax depreciation y/e 30 Sep 2011 @ 50%	(90,000)
	90,000
Tax depreciation y/e 30 Sep 2012 @ 25% × 90,000	(22,500)

(c) According to IFRS 8 an operating segment is a component of an entity:

- That engages in business activities from which it may earn revenues and incur expenses

- Whose operating results are regularly reviewed by the entity's chief operating decision maker to make decisions about resources to be allocated to the segment and assess its performance, and

- For which discrete financial information is available.

An entity must report separate information about each operating segment that:

- Has been identified as meeting the definition of an operating segment; and

- Exceeds any of the following thresholds:

    - segment revenue (internal and external) is 10% or more of total revenue, or

    - segment profit or loss is 10% or more of all segments in profit (or all segments in loss if greater)

    - segment assets are 10% or more of total assets

At least 75% of total external revenue must be reported by operating segments.

(d) (i) Once an entity is registered for VAT, it must:

- Charge VAT on all its sales

- Reclaim VAT on its purchases

- Keep records relating to VAT

- Complete a quarterly VAT return and pay any VAT owed to the tax authorities.

(ii) VAT balance due to the tax authorities is $36,000

	$
VAT due to tax authorities (W1)	108,000
VAT reclaimed (W2) 90,000 × 80%	(72,000)
Net VAT balance	36,000

W1

VAT due on sale of standard rated goods is 720,000 × 15% = 108,000

W2

VAT to reclaim

Total VAT suffered 690,000 / 115 × 15 = 90,000

Total sales = 1,025,000 (720,000 + 100,000 + 205,000) of which 20% (205,000 / 1,025,000) relate to exempt goods, so only 80% of the VAT suffered can be reclaimed.

(e) (i) Total foreign tax suffered on the dividend is $77,165

	$	$
HC gross dividend		200,000
WHT @ 12%	24,000	
Underlying tax (200,000/474,000 × 126,000)	53,165	
Total foreign tax	77,165	

(ii) Tax HC is liable to pay is nil.

	$
HC gross dividend received	200,000
Add on ULT	53,165
Total:	253,165
Tax @ 25%	63,291

The $63,291 is less than the $77,165 foreign tax therefore no tax due in Country X

W1

Underlying tax = gross dividend × $\dfrac{\text{tax paid by foreign company}}{\text{foreign company PAT}}$

Double tax relief is awarded applying the tax credit method so HC can receive full relief for the tax paid by OC. However it cannot receive a refund where the tax paid by OC is greater than the tax due by HC

(f) The IFRS Interpretations Committee has two main responsibilities:

- Review, on a timely basis, newly identified financial reporting issues not specifically addressed in IFRSs

- Clarify issues where unsatisfactory or conflicting interpretations have developed, or seem likely to develop in the absence of authoritative guidance, with a view to reaching a consensus on the appropriate treatment

The IFRS Interpretations Committee also helps the IASB move towards international harmonisation by working with its equivalent national level bodies.

The IFRS Advisory Council is essentially a forum used by the IASB to consult with the outside world; it consults with national standard setters, academics, user groups and a host of other interested parties and informs the IASB of their views on a range of issues.

The IASB consults the IFRS Advisory Council on:

- Its technical agenda

- Its project priorities

- Project issues related to application and implementation of IFRSs

- Possible benefits and costs of particular proposals

78 Mixed section B answers bank 11 (3/13)

(a)

(i) Corporate income tax
VAT or sales tax
PAYE or similar employee tax
Capital gains tax

(ii) An entity would normally be required to keep the following records to support its VAT or sales tax returns:

- Orders and delivery notes
- Purchase and sales invoices
- Credit and debit notes
- Purchase and sales books
- Cashbooks and receipts
- Bank statements
- Import and export documents
- VAT account

(b)

	$
Accounting profit	167,000
Add disallowed expenses (4,000+5,000)	9,000
Less non-taxable income	(12,000)
Add depreciation	11,600
Less tax depreciation	(10,250)
Taxable profit for year	165,350
Less brought forward losses	(49,000)
	116,350
Tax due at 25%	29,088

Depreciation:

$50,000 + 8,000 = 58,000 \times 1/5 = 11,600$

Tax depreciation:

	1/1/11	1/1/12
Cost	50,000	
First year allowance 2011	25,000	
	25,000	8,000
Allowances 2012		
First year allowance	4,000	
Annual allowance	6,250	
Total allowance			10,250

(c)

A single figure should be shown on the statement of comprehensive income, comprising the loss after tax and loss incurred on the disposal of assets. Therefore a separate section "Discontinued operations" will be shown after the section of the statement of comprehensive income headed "Continuing operations". The heading will be loss for the period from discontinued operations and the amount shown will be ($42,000). The notes to the statement of comprehensive income will need to disclose each of the amounts included in the loss after tax, i.e.

	$000
Revenue	95
Operating expenses	(110)
Operating loss	(15)
Loss on disposal of assets	(30)
Tax refund	3
Loss	(42)

Comparative information for prior periods must be restated using the current classification, that is division C results for prior periods will be shown as discontinued operations.

The restructuring expense is not included in discontinued operations as according to IFRS 5 *Non-current assets held for sale and discontinued operations* this is an expense that relates to ongoing operations and should be included under continuing operations. As the $75,000 restructuring is a material item in the context of continuing operations, it will need to be shown as a separate item on the statement of comprehensive income as required by IAS 1 Presentation of financial statements.

(d)

An excise duty may be imposed on certain types of goods by a government:

- to discourage over-consumption of products which may harm the consumer or others for example alcohol;

- to alter the distribution of income by taxing 'luxuries', for example, in the USA there are excise duties on fishing equipment, firearms and airplane tickets;

- to seek to allow for externalities and to place the burden of paying the tax on the consumer of the product/service. For example the social and environmental cost of consuming the product is paid for by the consumer of products such as tobacco to help pay for the increased cost of healthcare of smokers.

- to improve infrastructure and other facilities. For example excise duty on petrol and diesel is used by some governments to build and maintain roads, bridges and mass transit systems.

- to protect or promote growth of home industries by increasing the price of imports with taxes, for example car manufacturing.

- to raise revenue for government by taxing goods with inelastic demand, thus enabling revenue to be raised without distorting consumption, for example luxury goods .

(e)

(i) OW's production facility and head office are located in Country X and all the directors' board meetings are held in Country X so OW's effective management is in Country X.

Both countries have double tax treaties with each other based on the OECD model tax convention so the OECD model tax convention will apply to OW. Where an entity is deemed to be taxable in several countries, the OECD model suggests that the entity is resident in the country of its effective management. OW will therefore be regarded as resident in Country X for tax purposes and will be taxable in Country X.

(ii) The OECD model tax convention states that an entity's profits will only be taxed in a country if the entity has a permanent establishment in the country.

OW has a number of branch offices in Country Z, each office provides services to customers and sells OW's products. – The OECD model tax convention states that a branch office is a permanent establishment, so OW will have a permanent establishment in Country Z. Profits made by OW's branch offices in Country Z will be taxable in Country Z.

As OW is resident in Country X its worldwide profits will be taxed in Country X, irrespective of where they arise.

As both countries have double tax treaties with each other based on the OECD model tax convention any tax paid in Country Z will be able to be relieved under the double taxation agreement.

(f)

According to the *Framework*, its purpose is to:

- assist the IASB in the development of future IFRSs and in its review of existing IFRSs;

- assist the IASB in promoting harmonisation of regulations, accounting standards and procedures by providing a basis for reducing the number of alternative treatments permitted by IFRSs;

- assist national standard-setting bodies in developing national standards;

- assist preparers of financial statements in applying IFRSs and in dealing with topics that have yet to be covered in an IFRS;

- assist auditors in forming an opinion as to whether financial statements comply with IFRSs;

- assist users in interpreting the information contained in a set of financial statements that are prepared using IFRSs;

- provide information about how the IASB has formulated its approach to the development of IFRSs.

(Any 5 of the above)

79 Mixed section B answers bank 12 (5/13)

(a)

Workings

	$million
Property, plant and equipment	
Balance at 31 March 2012	645
Sold in year	(60)
Annual depreciation	(120)
	465
Balance at 31 March 2013	635
Purchased	170
Non-current asset investments	
Balance at 31 March 2012	107
Revaluation loss	(21)
	86
Balance at 31 March 2013	93
Purchased	7
Deferred development expenditure	
Balance at 31 March 2012	24
Amortisation	(8)
	16
Balance at 31 March 2013	29
Purchased	13

CFQ Statement of Cash Flows for year ended 31 March 2013 (Extract)

	$million
Cash flows from Investing Activities:	
Purchase of Property, plant and equipment	(170)
Purchase of Non-current asset investments	(7)
Purchase of Deferred development expenditure	(13)
Proceeds from disposal of property, plant and equipment	45
Net cash outflow from investing activities	(145)

(b)

He should start by gathering all relevant information so that he can be sure of the facts and decide if there really is an ethical problem. All steps taken should be fully documented.

Initially he should raise his concern internally, possibly with the team's manager or a trusted colleague.

If this is not a realistic option, for example because of the relationship of the manager and the team member that Ace is concerned about, he may have to consider escalating the issue and speak to the manager's boss, a board member or a non-executive director. If there is an internal whistle blowing procedure or internal grievance procedure he should use that.

If after raising the matter internally nothing is done and he still has concerns he should take it further, for example if the other team member is an accountant Ace could consider reporting the team member to his professional body.

Ace could also distance himself from the problem and ask to be moved to a different department or to a different team.

(c)

(i) IAS 32 *Financial Instruments: Presentation* requires shares to be classified as debt (financial liability) or equity according to their substance rather than legal form.

A financial liability is defined as a contractual obligation to deliver cash or other financial asset to another entity.

Cumulative redeemable preferred shares meet the definition of financial liability and therefore must be classified as debt and included in the statement of financial position under non-current liabilities.

(ii) *IAS 39 Financial Instruments: Recognition and Measurement:* The cumulative redeemable preferred shares will initially be measured at the fair value of the consideration received. That is issue price less issue costs, ($500,000-$20,000 = $480,000).

The charge to profit or loss will be based on the effective interest rate which includes any issue costs, dividends paid and redemption costs.

(d)

(i) The tax base of an asset is the tax written down value of the asset. i.e. its cost less accumulated tax depreciation. Deferred tax arises as a result of temporary differences caused by a difference between an asset's tax base and its accounting carrying value.

(ii) Accounting carrying value:

	$000
Cost	260
Less residual value	(26)
	234
Annual depreciation 1/6	(39)
Cost	260
Depreciation 2011/12	(39)
Depreciation 2012/13	(39)
Carrying value 31 March 2013	182
Tax Base:	
Cost	260
First year allowance (50%)	(130)
Second year allowance (25%)	(32.5)
	97.5

Difference 182 – 97.5 = 84.5
Deferred tax = $84,500 × 25% = $21,125

(e)

MT Taxable profits:

	$
Profit before tax	37,000
Add back donations	5,000
Add back depreciation	39,000
	81,000
Less tax depreciation allowances:	
First year allowance (30000 × 50%)	(15,000)
Annual writing down allowance	
(120000 × 25%)	(30,000)
Taxable profits for year	36,000
Less loss b/f	(12,000)
Taxable profit	24,000
Tax due @ 25%	6,000

(f)

   (i) Cascade tax – tax is taken at each stage of production and is treated as a business cost. No refunds are provided by local government.

       VAT – charged each time a component or product is sold but government allows businesses to claim back all the tax they have paid. The entire tax burden is passed to the final consumer.

   (ii)

	$000	$000
Sales at standard rate	828	VAT
Less VAT (828x15/115)	(108)	108
	720	
Zero rated sales	150	
	870	
Purchases	(620)	(60)
	250	48
Profit for period	$250,000	
VAT due for period	$48,000	

MOCK EXAMS

314

CIMA
Financial Pillar
F1 – Financial Operations

Mock Exam 1

Question Paper
You are allowed three hours to answer this question paper.
You are allowed 20 minutes reading time *before the examination begins* during which you should read the question paper and, if you wish, highlight and/or make notes on the question paper.
You are strongly advised to carefully read ALL the question requirements before attempting the question concerned (that is all parts and/or sub-questions).
You should show all working as marks are available for the method you use.
ALL QUESTIONS ARE COMPULSORY
Section A comprises of 10 sub-questions.
Section B comprises of 6 sub-questions.
Section C comprises of 2 questions.
The country 'Tax Regime' for the paper is provided on the next page.

DO NOT OPEN THIS PAPER UNTIL YOU ARE READY TO START UNDER EXAMINATION CONDITIONS

316

COUNTRY X – TAX REGIME FOR USE THROUGHOUT THE EXAMINATION PAPER

Relevant tax rules

Corporate Profits

Unless otherwise specified, only the following rules for taxation of corporate profits will be relevant, other taxes can be ignored:

(a)   Accounting rules on recognition and measurement are followed for tax purposes.

(b)   All expenses other than depreciation, amortisation, entertaining, taxes paid to other public bodies and donations to political parties are tax deductible.

(c)   Tax depreciation is deductible as follows:

- 50% of additions to property, plant and equipment in the accounting period in which they are recorded

- 25% per year of the written-down value (i.e. cost minus previous allowances) in subsequent accounting periods except that in which the asset is disposed of

- No tax depreciation is allowed on land

(d)   The corporate tax on profits is at a rate of 25%.

(e)   No indexation is allowable on the sale of land.

(f)   Tax losses can be carried forward to offset against future taxable profits from the same business.

Value Added Tax

Country X has a VAT system which allows entities to reclaim input tax paid. In country X the VAT rates are:

Zero rated   0%

Standard rated   15%

SECTION A – 20 marks

Answer ALL sub-questions in this section

Question 1

1 A has a taxable profit of $100,000. The book depreciation was $10,000 and the tax allowable depreciation was $25,000. What was the accounting profit? **(2 marks)**

2 Company W is resident in country X and makes an accounting profit of $300,000 during the year. This includes non-taxable income of $10,000 and depreciation of $35,000. In addition, $5,000 of the expenses are for entertaining. If the tax allowable depreciation totals $30,000, what is the taxable profit?

    A $290,000
    B $295,000
    C $300,000
    D $310,000   **(2 marks)**

3 The directors of an entity are refusing to amend the financial statements to take account of a customer who went bankrupt after the year-end and who owed the entity $10,000 at the year-end. This amount is material. What type of audit opinion should be issued as a result?

    A   Qualified opinion
    B   Adverse opinion
    C   Unmodified opinion with emphasis of matter paragraph
    D   Disclaimer of opinion   **(2 marks)**

4 Company E is resident in Country X and has sales of $230,000, excluding sales tax, in a period. Its purchases total $113,000, including sales tax. Purchases of $10,000 are zero rated. What is the sales tax payable for the period?

    A $14,550
    B $17,550
    C $19,050
    D $21,065   **(2 marks)**

5 When an entity is resident for tax purposes in more than one country, the OCED model tax convention states that an entity will be deemed to be resident only in its:

    A   Place of permanent establishment
    B   Place of effective management
    C   Place of incorporation
    D   Place of main business activity   **(2 marks)**

6 IAS 10 *Events after the reporting period* distinguishes between adjusting and non-adjusting events.

Which of the following is an adjusting event?

    A   One month after the year end, a customer lodged a claim for $1,000,000 compensation. The customer claimed to have suffered permanent mental damage as a result of the fright she had when one of the entity's products malfunctioned and exploded. The outcome of the court case cannot be predicted at this stage.

    B   There was a dispute with the workers and all production ceased one week after the year end.

    C   A fire destroyed all of the entity's inventory in its furnished goods warehouse two weeks after the year end.

    D   Inventory valued at the year end at $20,000 was sold one month later for $15,000.   **(2 marks)**

7   X signed a finance lease agreement on 1 October 20X2. The lease provided for five annual payments, in arrears, of $20,000. The fair value of the asset was agreed at $80,000.

     Using the sum of digits method, how much should be charged to the statement of profit or loss and other comprehensive income for the finance cost in the year to 30 September 20X3?

     A $4,000
     B $6,667
     C $8,000
     D $20,000   **(2 marks)**

8   D purchased an item of plant on 1 April 20X0 for $200,000. The plant attracted writing down tax allowances and depreciation was 10% on the straight-line basis.

     The deferred tax balance for this item of plant at 31 March 20X3 is:

     A $7,500
     B $20,938
     C $22,500
     D $83,750   **(2 marks)**

9   C started work on a contract to build a dam for a hydro-electric scheme. The work commenced on 24 October 20X1 and is scheduled to take four years to complete. C recognises profit on the basis of the certified percentage of work completed. The contract price is $10 million.

     An analysis of C's records provided the following information:

Year to 30 September	20X2	20X3
Percentage of work completed and certified in year	30%	55%
	$'000	$'000
Total cost incurred during the year	2,900	1,700
Estimated cost of remaining work to complete contract	6,000	3,900
Total payments made for the cost incurred during the year	2,500	2,000

     How much profit should C recognise in its statement of profit or loss and other comprehensive income for the years ended:

	30 September 20X2	30 September 20X3
	$'000	$'000
A	100	375
B	330	375
C	330	495
D	500	825

                                                                                                    (2 marks)

10   S announced a rights issue of 1 for every 5 shares currently held, at a price of $2 each. S currently has 2,000,000 $1 ordinary shares with a quoted market price of $2.50 each. Directly attributable issue costs amounted to $25,000.

     Assuming all rights are taken up and all money paid in full, how much will be credited to the share premium account for the rights issue?

     A $200,000
     B $308,333
     C $375,000
     D $400,000   **(2 marks)**

                                                                          (Total for Section A = 20 marks)

SECTION B – 30 marks

Answer ALL six sub-questions

Question 2

(a)   At the beginning of the accounting period, D had a credit balance of $40,000 on its current tax account, which was paid during the period. The opening balance on the deferred tax account was $250,000 credit.

The provision for tax for the current period is $50,000 and the balance on the deferred tax account is to be reduced to $225,000.

Required

Prepare extracts from the statement of profit or loss and other comprehensive income, statement of financial position and notes to the accounts showing these tax related items.   **(Total = 5 marks)**

(b)   IAS 12 *Income taxes* requires entities to publish an explanation of the relationship between taxable income and accounting profit. This can take the form of a numerical reconciliation between the tax expense and the product of the accounting profit and the applicable tax rate.

Required

Explain why this explanation is helpful to the readers of financial statements   **(Total = 5 marks)**

(c)   Jedders Co has three long leasehold properties in different parts of the region each of which had an original life of 50 years. As at 1 January 20X0, their original cost, accumulated depreciation to date and carrying (book) values were as follows.

	Cost $'000	Depreciation $'000	Carrying value 1.1.20X0 $'000
Property in North	3,000	1,800	1,200
Property in Central	6,000	1,200	4,800
Property in South	3,750	1,500	2,250

On 1 January an independent surveyor provided valuation information to suggest that the value of the South property was the same as book value, the North property had fallen against carrying value by 20% and the Central property had risen by 40% in value against the carrying value.

The directors wish to show all their properties at a revalued amount in the accounts as at 31 December 20X0.

Required

Calculate the charges to the statement of profit or loss and other comprehensive income and the non-current asset extracts in the statement of financial position for all the properties for the year ended 31 December 20X0. You should follow the requirements of IAS 16 *Property, plant and equipment*. **(Total = 5 marks)**

The following data are to be used to answer questions (d) and (e)

The financial statements of GK for the year to 31 October 20X8 were as follows:

STATEMENT OF FINANCIAL POSITION AT	31 October 20X8		31 October 20X7	
	$'000	$'000	$'000	$'000
Assets				
Non-current tangible assets	10,000		10,500	
Property	5,000	15,000	4,550	15,050
Plant and equipment				
Current assets				
Inventory	1,750		1,500	
Trade receivables	1,050		900	
Cash and cash equivalents	310		150	
		3,110		2,550
Total assets		18,110		17,600
Equity and liabilities				
Ordinary shares @ $.050 each	6,000		3,000	
Share premium	2,500		1,000	
Revaluation reserve	3,000		3,000	
Retained earnings	1,701		1,000	
		13,201		8,000
Non-current liabilities				
Interest-bearing borrowings	2,400		7,000	
Deferred tax	540	2,940	450	7,450
Current liabilities				
Trade and other payables	1,060		1,400	
Tax payable	909		750	
		1,969		2,150
		18,110		17,600

STATEMENT OF PROFIT OR LOSS AND OTHER COMPREHENSIVE INCOME

FOR THE YEAR 31 OCTOBER 20X8

	$'000	$'000
Revenue		16,000
Cost of sales		10,000
Gross profit		6,000
Administrative expenses	(2,000)	
Distribution costs	(1,200)	(3,200)
		2,800
Finance cost		(600)
Profit		2,200
Income tax expense		(999)
Profit for the year		(1,201)

Additional information:

1   Trade and other payables comprise:

	31 October 20X8	31 October 20X7
	$'000	$'000
Trade payables	730	800
Interest payable	330	600
	1,060	1,400

2   Plant disposed of in the year had a net book value of $35,000; cash received on disposal was $60,000.

3   GK's statement of profit or loss and other comprehensive income includes depreciation for the year of $1,110,000 for properties and $882,000 for plant and equipment.

4   Dividends paid during the year were $500,000.

(d)   *Required*

Using the data relating to GK above, **calculate** the cash generated from operations that would appear in GK's statement of cash flows, using the indirect method, for the year ended 31 October 20X8, in accordance with IAS 7 *Statement of cash flows*.   **(Total = 5 marks)**

(e)   *Required*

Using the data relating to GK above, **calculate** the cash flow from investing activities and cash flows from financing activities sections of GK's statement of cash flows for the year ended 31 October 20X8, in accordance with IAS 7 *Statement of cash flows*.   **(Total = 5 marks)**

(f)   The definition of a liability forms an important element of the International Accounting Standards Board's *Conceptual Framework for Financial Reporting* which, in turn, forms the basis for IAS 37 *Provisions, Contingent Liabilities and Contingent Assets*.

Required

Define a liability and **describe** the circumstances under which provisions should be recognised. Give two examples of how the definition of liabilities enhances the reliability of financial statements.
                    (Total = 5 marks)

(Total for Section B = 30 marks)

SECTION C – 50 marks

Answer BOTH of these questions

Question 3

HI, listed on its local stock exchange, is a retail organisation operating several retail outlets. A reorganisation of the entity was started in 20X2 because of a significant reduction in profits. This reorganisation was completed during the current financial year.

The trial balance for HI at 30 September 20X3 was as follows:

	$'000	$'000
Retained earnings at 30 September 20X2		1,890
Administrative expenses	715	
Bank and cash	1,409	
Buildings	11,200	
Cash received on disposal of equipment		11
Cost of goods sold	3,591	
Distribution costs	314	
Equipment and fixtures	2,625	
Interim ordinary dividend paid	800	
Inventory at 30 September 20X3	822	
Investment income received		37
Available-for-sale investments at market value 30 September 20X2	492	
Ordinary shares of $1 each, fully paid		5,000
Provision for deferred tax		256
Provision for reorganisation expenses at 30 September 20X2		1,010
Allowances for depreciation at 30 September 20X2		
Buildings		1,404
Equipment and fixtures		1,741
Reorganisation expenses	900	
Revaluation surplus		172
Sales revenue		9,415
Share premium		2,388
Trade payables		396
Trade receivables	852	
	23,720	23,720

Additional information provided

(a)   The reorganisation expenses relate to a comprehensive restructuring and reorganisation of the entity that began in 20X2. HI's financial statements for 20X2 included a provision for reorganisation expenses of $1,010,000. All costs had been incurred by the year end, but an invoice for $65,000, received on 2 October 20X3, remained unpaid and is not included in the trial balance figures. No further restructuring and reorganisation costs are expected to occur and the provision is no longer required.

(b)   Available-for-sale investments are carried in the financial statements at market value. The market value of the available-for-sale investments at 30 September 20X3 was $522,000. There were no movements in the investments held during the year.

(c)   On 1 November 20X3, HI was informed that one of its customers, X, had ceased trading. The liquidators advised HI that it was very unlikely to receive payment of any of the $45,000 due from X at 30 September 20X3.

(d)   Another customer is suing for damages as a consequence of a faulty product. Legal advisers are currently advising that the probability of HI being found liable is 75%. The amount payable is estimated to be the full amount claimed of $100,000.

(e)   The income tax due for the year ended 30 September 20X3 is estimated at $1,180,000 and the deferred tax provision needs to be increased to $281,000.

(f)   During the year, HI disposed of old equipment for $11,000. The original cost of this equipment was $210,000 and accumulated depreciation at 30 September 20X2 was $205,000. HI's accounting policy is to charge no depreciation in the year of the disposal.

(g)   Depreciation is charged using the straight-line basis on non-current assets as follows.

Buildings	3%
Equipment and fixtures	20%

Depreciation is regarded as a cost of sales.

Required

Prepare the statement of profit or loss and other comprehensive income for HI for the year to 30 September 20X3 and a statement of financial position at that date, in a form suitable for presentation to the shareholders, in accordance with the requirements of IFRS.

Notes to the financial statements are **not** required.   **(25 marks)**

Question 4

The following are the financial statements relating to ST, a limited liability company, and its subsidiary company BE.

STATEMENT OF PROFIT OR LOSS AND OTHER COMPREHENSIVE INCOME

FOR THE YEAR ENDED 31 DECEMBER 20X5

	ST	BE
	$'000	$'000
Sales revenue	235,000	85,000
Cost of sales	(140,000)	(52,000)
Gross profit	95,000	33,000
Distribution costs	(12,000)	(5,000)
Administrative expenses	(45,000)	(8,000)
Dividend income from BE	5,000	–
Profit before tax	43,000	20,000
Tax	(13,250)	(5,000)
Profit for the year	29,750	15,000

STATEMENTS OF FINANCIAL POSITION AS AT 31 DECEMBER 20X5

	ST		BE	
	$'000	$'000	$'000	$'000
Assets				
Non-current assets				
Property, plant and equipment		100,000		40,000
Investments				
30,000,000 $1 ordinary shares in BE at cost		34,000		–
		134,000		40,000
Current assets				
Inventory, at cost	13,360		3,890	
Trade receivables and dividend receivable	14,640		6,280	
Bank	3,500		2,570	
Total assets		31,500		12,740
		165,500		52,740

Equity and liabilities
Equity

$1 Ordinary shares	100,000	30,000
General reserve	9,200	1,000
Retained earnings	27,300	9,280
	136,500	40,280

Current liabilities

Trade payables	9,000		2,460	
Dividend payable	20,000		10,000	
Total equity and liabilities		29,000		12,460
		165,500		52,740

Additional information

(a) ST purchased its $1 ordinary shares in BE on 1 January 20X1. At that date the balance on BE's general reserve was $0.5 million and the balance of retained earnings was $1.5 million.

(b) At 1 January 20X5 the total goodwill arising from the acquisition of BE was valued at $960,000. ST's impairment review of this goodwill at 31 December 20X5 valued it at $800,000.

(c) During the year ended 31 December 20X5 ST sold goods which originally cost $12 million to BE. ST invoiced BE at cost plus 40%. BE still has 30% of these goods in inventory at 31 December 20X5.

(d) BE owed ST $1.5 million at 31 December 20X5 for some of the goods ST supplied during the year.

Required

(a) Calculate the goodwill arising on the acquisition of BE.   **(2 marks)**

(b) Prepare the following financial statements for ST.

  (i) The consolidated statement of profit or loss and other comprehensive income for the year ended 31 December 20X5.

                                                                          (8 marks)

  (ii) The consolidated statement of financial position as at 31 December 20X5.   **(15 marks)**

Disclosure notes are not required.   **(Total = 25 marks)**

(Total for Section C = 50 marks)

Answers

**DO NOT TURN THIS PAGE UNTIL YOU HAVE
COMPLETED MOCK EXAM 1**

A plan of attack

As you turned the page to start this exam any one of a number of things could have been going through your mind. Some of them may have been quite sensible, some of them may not.

The main thing to do is take a deep breath and do not panic. It's best to sort out a plan of attack before the actual exam so that when the invigilator tells you that you can begin and the adrenaline kicks in you are using every minute of the three hours wisely.

Your approach

This paper has three sections. The first section contains 10 multiple choice questions which are compulsory. The second has six short compulsory questions. The third has two compulsory questions totalling 50 marks.

OTs first again

However you find the paper, chances are you should **start with the objective test questions**. You should be able to do at least a few and answering them will give you a boost. **Don't even look at the other questions before doing Section A**. Remember how long to allocate to the OTs? That's right, 36 minutes.

You then have a **choice**.

- Read through and answer Section B before moving on to Section C
- Read the questions in Section C, answer them and then go back to Section B

Time spent at the start of each Section B and the Section C questions confirming the requirements and producing a plan for the answers is time well spent.

Doing the exam

Actually doing the exam is a personal experience. There is not a single *right way.* As long as you submit complete answers to the MCQs in Section A, the six Section B questions and the questions in Section C, your approach obviously works.

One approach

Having done or guessed at the MCQs, work straight through Section B. The possible pitfall would be getting sucked too deeply into Section B and leaving insufficient time for Section C.

So lets look at the Section B questions in the paper:

- Question (a) is a straightforward calculation of income tax liability. It would be a good idea to begin by putting the information into T-accounts. Then the information just needs to be correctly presented. This can easily be done in 9 minutes.

- Question (b) is a discussion question on the relationship of accounting profit to taxable profit. Make a few notes before you start.

- Question (c) is more straightforward than it looks, but you must read it carefully so that you know exactly what to do. Then write your answer out methodically.

- Questions (d) and (e) are on statements of cash flows. Don't waste time digesting the whole of the financial statements. Look at the question to see what information you need to extract and get on with it. A methodical approach is really needed here.

- Question (f) requires you to know the definition of a liability and of a provision and then provide two examples of how the definitions improve reliability in the accounts. You might have found hard to think of the examples, but don't spend more than the allocated time here.

Having hacked your way through Section B, taking no more than 9 minutes per question, you should now be left with 90 minutes to do your Section C questions. These are worth 50 marks and you must aim to secure as many of them as possible. Read the questions **twice** if you need to.

For the Section C Questions you must proceed in a methodical way. Set out your formats and then work through the question requirements, doing neat, readable calculations and fill out the figures. Even if you do not finish, you will get marks for what you have done, so do the easy bits first.

Time allocation

Be disciplined. Allocate your time according to the marks available but never go over the time allocation. The last few marks in a question are the hardest to earn.

Be sure to follow the requirements. If four advantages are required, give four. No extra credit will be given for five. Two advantages will only get you half marks.

Answer all of the question. Having a go at every part of all the Section B questions you are required to do will put you in a better position to pass than, say, only doing five questions. However difficult that sixth question seems at first, there are marks to be earned.

If you have time left at the end of the exam ensure that you have attempted every part of every question. If you have, then scan through and ensure you complete any part of an answer you left earlier. Use the full three hours working towards a pass.

Marking the exam

When you mark your exam, be honest. Don't be too harsh though. Give yourself credit for the things you did well, but don't kid yourself with 'I would have done that in the real exam'. It may be worth your while making two lists; strengths and weaknesses.

Strengths will be areas of the syllabus you are confident with and also good exam technique. (Maybe you produced correct financial statement formats.)

Weaknesses will be holes in your knowledge and poor exam technique (maybe you ran out of time and couldn't answer all the requirements of the last question).

Making this list will help you focus your last days of revision on the areas which require attention whilst reminding you of the areas you excel in.

SECTION A

Question 1

1

	$
Taxable profit	100,000
Less: depreciation	10,000
	90,000
Add: tax allowable depreciation	25,000
Accounting profit	115,000

2   The correct answer is C.

	$	$
Accounting profit		300,000
Add: depreciation	35,000	
disallowed expenses (entertaining)	5,000	
		40,000
		340,000
Less: non-taxable income	10,000	
tax allowable depreciation	30,000	40,000
Taxable profit		300,000

3   A   A qualified opinion should be issued as the amount is material but not pervasive to the financial statements.

4   The correct answer is D.

	$
Output tax (230,000 × 15%)	34,500
Input tax ((113,000 – 10,000)/115 × 15)	13,435
Payable	21,065

5   The correct answer is B.

In the case where an entity is resident in more than one country, the OECD Model Tax Convention states that the entity will be deemed to be resident only in the country of its effective management.

6   D   The subsequent sale provides evidence of the net realisable value of the inventory as at the year end.

7   B $$\$(100{,}000 - 80{,}000) \times \frac{5}{5+4+3+2+1} = \$20{,}000 \times \frac{5}{15}$$

$$= \$6{,}667$$

8   B $20,938

	TWDV	Carrying amount
	$'000	$'000
01.04.20X0	200	200
Tax dep'n/Dep'n	(100)	(20)
31.03.20X1	100	180
Tax dep'n/Dep'n	(25)	(20)
31.03.20X2	75	160
Tax dep'n/Dep'n	(18.75)	(20)
31.3.20X3	56.25	140

Temporary difference 140,000 – 56,250 = 83,750

Deferred tax balance = 83,750 × 25% = $20,938

			20X2	20X3
9	C		$'000	$'000
		Costs to date	2,900	4,600
		Costs to complete	6,000	3,900
		Estimated total cost	8,900	8,500
		Projected profit	1,100	1,500
		Contract price	10,000	10,000
		Completed	30%	55%
		Cumulative profit	330	825
		Profit recognised	330	495

10   C   Number of shares issued:

$$\frac{2,000,000}{5} = 400,000 \text{ shares}$$

	$
Issue price	2
Nominal value	1
Premium	1

	$
∴ Total premium	400,000
Less issue costs	25,000
Net to share premium	375,000

SECTION B

Question 2

Marking scheme

			Marks
(a)	Tax expense	1	
	Tax payable	1	
	Deferred tax balance	1	
	Notes	1	
	Presentation	1	
			5

	$
Statement of profit or loss and other comprehensive income (extract)	
Tax expense (Note 1)	25,000
Statement of financial position (extract)	
Current liabilities	
Tax payable	50,000
Non-current liabilities	
Deferred tax (Note 2)	225,000

Notes to the financial statements

1	*Tax expense*	$
	Provision for the current period	50,000
	Decrease in deferred tax provision	(25,000)
		25,000

2	*Deferred tax*	$
	Balance brought forward	250,000
	Decrease in provision	(25,000)
	Balance carried forward	225,000

Marking scheme

		Marks
(b)	1 mark per well-presented point	5

In many sets of financial statements, there **may appear to be little relationship** between the figure reported as the profit before tax and the actual tax charge that appears in the statement of profit or loss and other comprehensive income. In a simple tax system, the tax charge would be the reported profit multiplied by the tax rate. However this will not normally be the case in real life, due to the complexities of the tax system and the estimates and subjective decisions that the directors must make in estimating the tax charge for the year.

The purpose of the reconciliation between the actual tax charge and the reported profit multiplied by the standard rate of tax is to highlight to the users of the financial statements these estimates and judgements. This reconciliation should **clarify the effect of adjustments** such as changes in tax rates, estimated tax charges differing from final agreed tax liabilities and other factors that have affected the amount that appears as the tax charge in the statement of profit or loss and other comprehensive income. Another factor which may affect the tax charge is deferred tax. The reconciliation will therefore draw attention to factors which may lead to an increased tax charge in the future.

Marking scheme

		Marks
(c)	Depreciation charges	2
	Revaluation loss	1
	Property, plant and equipment	2
		5

STATEMENT OF PROFIT OR LOSS AND OTHER COMPREHENSIVE INCOME (EXTRACTS)

	$'000
Depreciation charge	
North (($1.2m × 80%)/20 years)	48
Central (($4.8m × 140%)/40 years)	168
South ($2.25m/30 years)	75
	291
Loss on revaluation of North property (20% × $1.2m)*	240
Other comprehensive income	
Gain on revaluation of Central property ($4.8m × 40%)	1,920

STATEMENT OF FINANCIAL POSITION (EXTRACTS)

	Cost/ revaluation $'000	Depreciation $'000	Carrying value $'000
North	960	48	912
Central	6,720	168	6,552
South	2,250	75	2,175
	9,930	291	9,639

It is assumed that the properties are depreciated on a straight-line basis. At 1 January 20X0 the accumulated depreciation of the Central property is $1.2m, which represents 10 years' worth of depreciation, leaving 40 years remaining life. For the South and North properties, the respective lives in these calculations are 30 and 20 years.

* It is assumed that there is no previous revaluation surplus on the North property, so the loss in the current year is classed as an impairment, and is taken to profit or loss.

Marking scheme

		Marks
(d)	Net profit before taxation	½
	Depreciation	1
	Profit on disposal	1
	Finance cost	½
	Working capital adjustments	1½
	Cash generated from operations	½
		5

	$'000
Net profit before taxation	2,200
Depreciation (1,110 + 882)	1,992
Profit on disposal of plant (60 – 35)	(25)
Finance cost	600
Increase in trade receivables (W)	(150)
Increase in inventories (W)	(250)
Decrease in trade payables (W)	(70)
Cash generated from operations	4,297

Working

Inventories, trade receivables and trade payables

	Inventories	Trade receivables	Trade payables
	$'000	$'000	$'000
Balance b/d	1,500	900	800
Increase/(decrease) (balancing figure)	250	150	(70)
Balance c/d	1,750	1,050	730

Marking scheme

		Marks
(e)	*Cash flows from investing activities*	
	Purchase of property, plant and equipment	1
	Proceeds from sale of plant	1
		2
	Cash flows from financing activities	
	Proceeds from share issues	1½
	Dividends paid	½
	Borrowings repaid	1
		3
		5

Cash flows from investing activities

	$'000
Purchase of property, plant and equipment (W)	(1,977)
Proceeds from sale of plant	60
Net cash used in investing activities	(1,917)

Cash flows from financing activities

	$'000
Proceeds from issue of share capital (6,000 – 3,000 + 2,500 – 1,000)	4,500
Dividends paid	(500)
Borrowings repaid (7,000 – 2,400)	(4,600)
Net cash used in financing activities	(600)

Working
Property, plant and equipment

	$'000
Balance b/d	15,050
Disposals	(35)
Depreciation (1,110 + 882)	(1,992)
	13,023
Cash paid for additions (balancing figure)	1,977
Balance c/d	15,000

Marking scheme

		Marks
(f)	1 mark per well presented point	<u>5</u>

The *Conceptual Framework* defines a liability as a present obligation of an entity arising from past events, the settlement of which is expected to result in an outflow from the entity of resources embodying economic benefits. The obligation can be legal or constructive.

A provision is a liability of uncertain timing or amount.

Because it is regarded as a liability, a provision must meet the definition of a liability, as well as the recognition criteria in IAS 37, before it can be recognised in the financial statements.

The definition of a liability helps to improve the reliability of an entity's financial statements because it:

(a) prevents entities from recognising liabilities that are not true liabilities of the entity. For instance, the definition of a liability prevents entities from 'smoothing' profits by making provisions for future losses in years when profits are high in order to release those provisions in years when profits are lower. This is no longer possible because future losses are not a present obligation of the entity arising from past events and so cannot be provided for.

(b) helps to ensure that all liabilities of the entity are recognised, even if they are long term. For example, an entity which has an obligation to make good environmental damage because of past polluting activities is required to make a provision for the full amount as soon as the liability becomes apparent, rather than waiting until nearer the time.

SECTION C

Question 3

Marking scheme

	Marks
Statement of profit or loss and other comprehensive income	
Revenue	½
Cost of sales	1
Distribution costs	½
Administrative expenses	2
Overprovision	2
Profit on disposal	1
Investment income	½
Income tax expense	2
Other comprehensive income	2
	11½
Statement of financial position	
Property, plant and equipment	3
Available for sales investments	1½
Receivables	1
Revaluation surplus	1½
Retained earnings	1½
Deferred tax	1
Other provisions	1
Taxation	1
Restructuring accrual	1½
	13
Presentation	½
	25

HI
STATEMENT OF PROFIT OR LOSS AND OTHER COMPREHENSIVE INCOME

FOR THE YEAR ENDED 30 SEPTEMBER 20X3

	$'000
Revenue	9,415
Cost of sales (W2)	(4,410)
Gross profit	5,005
Distribution costs	(314)
Administrative expenses (W3)	(860)
Reorganisation costs overprovision (W4)	45
Profit on disposal of asset (W1)	6
Investment income	37
Profit before tax	3,919
Income tax expense (W5)	(1,205)
Profit for the year	2,714
Other comprehensive income:	
Gain on available-for-sale investments	30
Total comprehensive income for the year	2,744

HI
STATEMENT OF FINANCIAL POSITION AS AT 30 SEPTEMBER 20X3

	$'000	$'000
Assets		
Non current assets		
Property, plant and equipment (W1)		9,856
Available-for-sale investments (W6)		522
		10,378
Current assets		
Inventory	822	
Receivables (852 – 45)	807	
Cash at bank and in hand	1,409	
		3,038
		13,416
Equity and liabilities		
Equity		
Ordinary shares of $1 each	5,000	
Share premium	2,388	
Revaluation surplus (W6)	202	
Retained earnings (1,890 + 2,714 – 800)	3,804	
		11,394
Non current liabilities		
Deferred tax	281	
Other provisions (W3)	100	
		381
Current liabilities		
Trade payables	396	
Taxation	1,180	
Accruals: restructuring (W4)	65	
		1,641
		13,416

Workings

1   *Property, plant and equipment*

	Buildings $'000	Equipment and fixtures $'000	Total $'000
Cost			
Opening balance	11,200	2,625	13,825
Additions	–	–	–
Disposals	–	(210)	(210)
	11,200	2,415	13,615
Accumulated depreciation			
Opening balance	1,404	1,741	3,145
On disposals	–	(205)	(205)
Charge for year			
• $11,200 × 3%	336	–	–
• $2,415 × 20%	–	483	819
Closing balance	1,740	2,019	3,759
Carrying value	9,460	396	9,856

Profit on disposal:

	$'000	$'000
Sale proceeds		11
Carrying value		
Cost	210	
Accumulated depreciation	(205)	
		5
Profit		6

2   *Cost of sales*

	$'000
Per trial balance	3,591
Depreciation (W1)	819
	4,410

3   *Administrative expenses*

	$'000
Per trial balance	715
Bad debt written off (Note 1)	45
Provision for legal claim re faulty product (Note 2)	100
	860

Notes

1   Although the customer went into liquidation after the year end, this provides additional evidence of conditions existing at the year end. It is thus an adjusting event under IAS 10.

2   The obligation is probable, therefore a provision must be made.

4   *Reorganisation costs*

	$'000	$'000
Provision in 20X2 accounts		1,010
Reorganisation expenses	900	
Invoice received after y/e	65	
		965
Provision surplus		45

5   *Taxation*

	$'000	$'000
Income tax payable		1,180
Deferred tax		
Provision b/fwd	256	
Provision required	281	
∴ Increase required		25
Charge to statement of profit or loss and other comprehensive income		1,205

6   *Investments and revaluation surplus*

	Investments $'000	Revaluation surplus $'000
Per trial balance	492	172
Revaluation of investments to market value	30	30
	522	202

Question 4

Marking scheme

		Marks
(a)	Goodwill calculation	2

(b)   (i)   **Consolidated statement of profit or loss and other comprehensive income**

	Marks
Revenue	1½
Cost of sales	2
Distribution costs	1
Administrative expenses	1½
Tax	1
Profit for the year	1
	8

(ii)   **Consolidated statement of financial position**

	Marks
Goodwill	1
Property, plant and equipment	1
Inventory	1½
Trade receivables	1½
Bank	1
Share capital	1
Retained earnings	2½
General revenue	1½
Trade payables	1½
Dividend payable	1½
Presentation	1
	15
Total	25

(a)   **Calculation of goodwill**

	$	$
Consideration transferred		34,000
Net assets acquired		
Share capital	30,000	
Share premium	500	
Retained earnings	1,500	
		32,000
Goodwill		2,000

(b) (i) ST GROUP
         CONSOLIDATED STATEMENT OF PROFIT OR LOSS AND OTHER COMPREHENSIVE INCOME
         FOR THE YEAR ENDED 31 OCTOBER 20X5

	$'000
Revenue (235 + 85 – 16.8 (W1))	303,200
Cost of sales (140 + 52 – 16.8 + 1.44 (W1))	(176,640)
Gross profit	126,560
Distribution costs (12 + 5)	(17,000)
Administrative expenses (W2)	(53,160)
Profit before tax	56,400
Tax (13,250 + 5,000)	(18,250)
Profit for the year	38,150

(ii) ST GROUP
      CONSOLIDATED STATEMENT OF FINANCIAL POSITION AS AT 31 OCTOBER 20X5

	$'000	$'000
Assets		
Goodwill	800	
Property, plant and equipment (100 + 40)	140,000	
		140,800
Current assets		
Inventory (W4)	15,810	
Trade receivables (W5)	9,420	
Bank (3,500 + 2,570)	6,070	
		31,300
Total assets		172,100
Equity and liabilities		
Share capital	100,000	
Retained earnings (W8)	32,440	
General reserve (W7)	9,700	
		142,140
Current liabilities		
Trade payables (W6)	9,960	
Dividends	20,000	
		29,960
Total equity and liabilities		172,100

Workings

1 *Intragroup sale*

Sale price to be eliminated from consolidated revenue:

	$'000
Cost to ST	12,000
40% mark up	4,800
Cost to BE	16,800

Unrealised profit in inventory: $4,800,000 × 30% = $1,440,000

Gross profit = $95,000,000 + $33,000,000 – $1,440,000
            = $126,560,000

2 *Administrative expenses*

	$'000
ST	45,000
BE	8,000
Impairment of goodwill (W3)	160
	53,160

3   *Impairment of goodwill*

	$'000
Impairment at 1.11.20X4 (2,000 – 960)	1,040
Impairment during year (bal. fig.)	160
Impairment at 31.12.X5 (2,000 – 800)	1,200

4   *Inventory*

	$'000
ST	13,360
BE	3,890
Less unrealised profit (W1)	(1,440)
	15,810

5   *Trade receivables*

	$'000	$'000
ST	14,640	
Less dividend receivable	(10,000)	
		4,640
BE		6,280
Less intragroup		(1,500)
		9,420

6   *Trade payables*

	$'000
ST	
BE	9,000
Less intragroup	2,460
	(1,500)
	9,960

7   *General reserve*

	ST $'000	BE $'000
Per question	9,200	1,000
Less pre-acquisition general reserve		(500)
		500
Share of BE 500 × 100%	500	
	9,700	

8   *Retained earnings*

	ST $'000	BE $'000
Per question	27,300	9,280
Less PUP	(1,440)	
	25,860	
Less pre-acq'n retained earnings		(1,500)
		7,780
Share of BE: 100%	7,780	
Impairment of goodwill (2,000 – 800)	(1,200)	
	32,440	

CIMA

Financial Pillar

F1 – Financial Operations

Mock Exam 2

Question Paper
You are allowed three hours to answer this question paper.
You are allowed 20 minutes reading time *before the examination begins* during which you should read the question paper and, if you wish, highlight and/or make notes on the question paper.
You are strongly advised to carefully read ALL the question requirements before attempting the question concerned (that is all parts and/or sub-questions).
You should show all working as marks are available for the method you use.
ALL QUESTIONS ARE COMPULSORY
Section A comprises of 10 sub-questions.
Section B comprises of 6 sub-questions.
Section C comprises of 2 questions.
The country 'Tax Regime' for the paper is provided on the next page.

DO NOT OPEN THIS PAPER UNTIL YOU ARE READY TO START UNDER EXAMINATION CONDITIONS

COUNTRY X – TAX REGIME FOR USE THROUGHOUT THE EXAMINATION PAPER

Relevant Tax Rules for Years Ended 31 March 2007 to 2013

Corporate Profits

Unless otherwise specified, only the following rules for tax of corporate profits will be relevant, other taxes can be ignored:

- Accounting rules on recognition and measurement are followed for tax purposes.

- All expenses other than depreciation, amortisation, entertaining, taxes paid to other public bodies and donations to political parties are tax deductible.

- Tax depreciation is deductible as follows:

  o 50% of additions to property, plant and equipment in the accounting period in which they are recorded;

  o 25% per year of the written-down value (i.e. cost minus previous allowances) in subsequent accounting periods except that in which the asset is disposed of;

  o No tax depreciation is allowed on land.

- The corporate tax on profits is at a rate of 25%.

- No indexation is allowable on the sale of land.

- Tax losses can be carried forward to offset against future taxable profits from the same business.

Value Added Tax

Country X has a VAT system which allows entities to reclaim input tax paid.

In country X the VAT rates are:

Zero rated 0%

Standard rated 15%

Exempt goods 0%

SECTION A – 20 marks

Answer ALL ten sub-questions in this section

Question 1

1   An entity makes a taxable profit of $600,000 and pays corporate income tax at 25%. The entity pays a dividend to its shareholders. A shareholder, who pays personal tax at 40% receives a $6,000 dividend and then pays an additional $2,400 tax on the dividend.

The tax system could be said to be:

A   A classical system

B   An imputation system

C   A split rate system

D   A partial imputation system   **(2 marks)**

---

2   **Define** the term "tax avoidance"   **(2 marks)**

---

3   RS purchased an asset on 1 April 2010 for $375,000, incurring legal fees of $12,000. RS is resident in Country X. There was no indexation allowed on the asset.

RS sold the asset on 31 March 2013 for $450,000 incurring transaction charges of $15,000.

Calculate the capital gains tax due from RS on disposal of the asset.   **(2 marks)**

---

4   **State** the significance to an entity of having a permanent establishment in a country.   **(2 marks)**

---

5   Which ONE of the following would normally be subject to a withholding tax when paid to an entity in another country?

A   Consultancy fees

B   Payment for materials purchased

C   Dividends paid

D   Payments for plant and equipment imported from another country   **(2 marks)**

---

6   **Identify one** benefit of regulating published accounts for users of accounts **and** one benefit for preparers of accounts.   **(2 marks)**

---

7   The following are possible methods of measuring assets and liabilities other than historical cost:

(i)   Current cost
(ii)   Realisable value
(iii)   Present value
(iv)   Replacement cost

According to the IASB's *Conceptual Framework for Financial Reporting (2010)* (Framework) which of the measurement bases above can be used by an entity for measuring assets and liabilities shown in its statement of financial position?

A   (i) and (ii)

B   (i), (ii) and (iii)

C   (ii) and (iii)

D   (i), (ii) (iii) and (iv)   **(2 marks)**

8   Which **one** of the following bodies is responsible for the approval of interpretations of international financial reporting standards before they are issued?

    A   IASB

    B   IFRS Advisory Council

    C   IFRS Foundation

    D   IFRS Interpretations Committee   **(2 marks)**

9   The IASB's *Framework* identifies qualitative characteristics of financial statements.

Characteristics

(i)   Relevance
(ii)   Reliability
(iii)   Faithful representation
(iv)   Comparability

Which of the above characteristics are **not** fundamental qualitative characteristics according to the IASB's Framework?

    A   (i) and (ii)

    B   (i) and (iii)

    C   (iii) and (iv)

    D   (ii) and (iv)   **(2 marks)**

10   An external audit of XCD's financial statements has discovered that due to flooding of its administration offices a large proportion of XCD's financial records were destroyed. XCD's accountants have reconstructed the data to enable them to prepare the financial statements but there is insufficient evidence to enable the auditors to verify most of the sales and purchase transactions during the year.

State the appropriate type of audit report that the auditors should issue for XCD's financial statements.

                                 (2 marks)

                               (Total = 20 marks)

SECTION B – 30 marks

Answer ALL six sub-questions

Question 2

(a) Extracts from SF's statement of financial position at 31 March 2013, with comparatives, are shown below:

	2013 $000	2012 $000
Equity		
Ordinary shares	460	400
Share premium	82	70
Revaluation reserve	44	24
Retained earnings	273	246
Non-current liabilities		
Finance lease payables	98	60
Long term borrowings	129	105
Current liabilities		
Finance lease payables	10	6

Extracts from SF's statement of changes in equity for the year ended 31 March 2013:

	$000
Retained earnings:	
Retained earnings at 31 March 2012	246
Profit for the year	46
Dividends paid	(19)
Retained earnings at 31 March 2013	273

During the year ended 31 March 2013 SF's transactions included the following:

(i) Acquired property plant and equipment on a finance lease, debiting $55,000 to property, plant and equipment.

(ii) Repaid $25,000 of its long term borrowings during the year.

(iii) Issued some ordinary shares at a 20% premium.

(iv) Charged finance costs for the finance lease of $16,000 for the year.

Required

Prepare the "cash flows from financing activities" section of SF's statement of cash flows for the year ended 31 March 2013. **(Total = 5 marks)**

(b) XY has recently begun to lease an expensive machine. The lease agreement effectively means that XY takes on substantially the risk and rewards associated with owning the asset.

The managing director has instructed XY's finance director to treat the lease as an operating lease in order to show a better financial position.

Required

Explain any ethical issues that this may cause for the finance director. **(Total = 5 marks)**

(c) CD had 5,000,000 $1 ordinary shares in issue.

Subsequently, CD made a rights issue of 1 new ordinary share at $3.50 per share for every 5 ordinary shares currently held. At the same date CD's ordinary shares were trading at $4.75.

Required

(i) **Explain** the difference between a bonus issue and a rights issue of shares.

(ii) **Prepare** the journal entries required to record CD's rights issue in its financial records, assuming that all rights were taken up. **(Total = 5 marks)**

(d)   PU purchased machinery on 1 April 2011 for $350,000.

PU depreciates machinery over 10 years, using the straight line method assuming no residual value.

Required

(i)   **Explain** the meaning of "temporary difference" according to IAS 12 *Income Taxes.* Include an example to illustrate your answer.   **(2 marks)**

(ii)   **Calculate** the amount of deferred tax provision that PU should include in its statement of financial position as at 31 March 2013.   **(3 marks)**

(Total = 5 marks)

(e)   BZ received a salary of $34,000 for the year ended 31 March 2013. BZ also received a bonus of $1,700 and benefits in kind valued at $2,150.

BZ was entitled to a personal tax allowance of $5,750 for the year.

Personal taxation rates that apply to BZ are 20% for the first $20,000 of taxable earnings and 40% on the balance.

Required

(i)   **Explain** the meaning of "benefits in kind" for taxation purposes.   **(2 marks)**

(ii)   **Prepare** an income tax computation for BZ for the year ended 31 March 2013.   **(3 marks)**

(Total = 5 marks)

(f)   YN is an importer and imports goods in bulk. YN repackages the products and sells them to retailers. YN is registered for Value Added Tax (VAT) in Country X.

YN imports a consignment of goods costing $90,000 and pays excise duty of 10% and VAT at standard rate on the total (including duty).

YN pays $19,435 repackaging costs, including VAT at standard rate and then sells all the goods to retailers for $218,500 including VAT at 15%.

Required

(i)   **Calculate** YN's net profit on the goods consignment.

(ii)   **Calculate** the net VAT payable by YN on the goods consignment.   **(Total = 5 marks)**

(Total = 30 marks)

SECTION C – 50 marks

Answer BOTH of these questions

Question 3

BVQ's trial balance at 31 March 2013 is shown below:

	Notes	$000	$000
6% Loan notes (issued 2010, redeemable at par 2020)			600
Administrative expenses		357	
Leased delivery vehicles	(vi)	324	
Cash and cash equivalents		118	
Cost of sales		1,873	
Distribution costs		226	
Equity dividend paid 1 December 2012		70	
Income tax	(i), (iii)	27	
Inventory at 31 March 2013		198	
Land and buildings at cost	(vii)	2,553	
Loan interest paid		18	
Ordinary Shares $1 each, fully paid at 31 March 2013			1,400
Finance lease liability at 31 March 2012			268
Finance lease payment on 1 April 2012		74	
Plant and machinery at cost	(iv)	3,888	
Provision for deferred tax at 31 March 2012	(iii)		362
Provision for buildings depreciation at 31 March 2012	(v)		190
Provision for delivery vehicle depreciation at 31 March 2012	(v)		65
Provision for plant and machinery depreciation at 31 March 2012	(v)		2,489
Retained earnings at 31 March 2012			728
Sales revenue			4,364
Trade payables			176
Trade receivables		916	
		10,642	10,642

Additional information:

(i)   The income tax balance in the trial balance is a result of the under provision of tax for the year ended 31 March 2012.

(ii)   There were no sales of non-current assets during the year ended 31 March 2013.

(iii)   The tax due for the year ended 31 March 2013 is estimated at $180,000 and the deferred tax provision should be increased by $31,000

(iv)   Due to a general downturn in the economic environment property prices in Country X reduced during the year to 31 March 2013. BVQ also suffered a reduction in sales demand and decided to sell one of its specialist machines on 31 March 2013. The machine had cost $180,000 on 1 April 2011. The market value of the machine at 31 March 2013 was $73,000. BVQ's management was confident that they have a buyer ready to buy the machine at that price, but at 31 March 2013 the sale had not been agreed. It will cost BVQ $800 to get the machine ready to sell.

(v)   Depreciation is charged on buildings using the straight line method at 3% per annum. The cost of land included in land and buildings is $1,653,000. Plant and equipment is depreciated using the reducing balance method at a rate of 30% per year. All property, plant and equipment depreciation is treated as an administrative expense. Vehicles are depreciated using the straight line method.

(vi)   BVQ leased its fleet of delivery vehicles through a finance lease on 1 April 2011. The fair value of the vehicles at that date was $324,000. The lease is for 5 years and payments of $74,000 are made every April in advance. The interest rate implicit in the lease is 7.12%.

(vii)   BVQ carried out an impairment review of its land and buildings on 31 March 2013 and calculated that they had suffered impairment of $103,000.

Required

(a)   **Explain** why BVQ might have carried out an impairment review of its land and buildings on 31 March 2013.   **(3 marks)**

(b)   **Prepare** the statement of profit or loss and a statement of changes in equity for BVQ for the year to 31 March 2013 and a statement of financial position at that date, in accordance with the requirements of International Financial Reporting Standards.   **(22 marks)**

Notes to the financial statements are not required, but all workings must be clearly shown. Do not prepare a statement of accounting policies.

(Total = 25 marks)

Question 4

The draft statements of financial position at 31 March 2013 and statements of comprehensive income for the year ended 31 March 2013 for three entities, are given below:

Statements of financial position as at 31 March 2013:

	Notes	Road $000	Street $000	Drive $000
Non-current Assets				
Property, plant and equipment	(ii); (vi)	1,840	1,060	930
Investments	(i)	1,923		
Current Assets				
Inventory	(v)	310	236	287
Trade receivables		140	119	215
Cash and cash equivalents	(vii)	71	27	63
Total Assets		4,284	1,442	1,495
Equity and Liabilities				
Equity shares of $1 each		2,000	550	700
Share premium		500	150	200
Retained earnings		814	339	458
		3,314	1,039	1,358
Non-current liabilities				
Borrowings		700	250	0
Current liabilities				
Trade payables		270	128	137
Loan interest payable	(viii)	0	25	0
		270	153	137
Total Equity and Liabilities		4,284	1,442	1,495

Additional information:

(i)   Road's investments comprise the following:

- Road acquired 100% of Street's equity shares on 1 April 2010 paying $1,350,000. At this date Street's retained earnings were $122,000.

- On 1 April 2011 Road advanced Street a 10 year loan of $250,000.

- Road purchased its shareholding of 175,000 shares in Drive on 1 April 2012 for $323,000 when Drive's retained earnings were $350,000. Road exercises significant influence over all aspects of Drive's financial and operating policies.

(ii)   The fair value of Street's property, plant and equipment on 1 April 2010 exceeded its carrying value by $320,000. The excess of fair value over carrying value was attributed to buildings owned by Street. At the date of acquisition these buildings had a remaining useful life of 20 years. Road's accounting policy is to depreciate buildings using the straight line basis with no residual value.

(iii)   Road carried out an impairment review of the goodwill arising on the acquisition of Street and found that as at 31 March 2013 the goodwill had been impaired by $38,000.

(iv)   Road carried out an impairment review of its investment in Drive and found that as at 31 March 2013 its investment in Drive had been impaired by $20,000.

(v)   Road occasionally trades with Street. During February 2013 Street sold Road goods for $220,000. Street uses a mark-up of 25% on cost. At 31 March 2013 Road had sold 40% of the goods.

(vi)   Road sold a piece of machinery to Street on 1 April 2012 for $95,000. The machinery had previously been used in Road's business and had been included in Road's property, plant and equipment at a carrying value of $65,000. The machinery had a remaining useful life of 5 years at that date.

(vii)   Road had previously paid Street for half of the goods purchased and on 30 March 2013 Road transferred the balance of the amount due to Street for the goods purchased, $110,000. This was not recorded by Street until 3 April 2013.

(viii) At 31 March 2013 $25,000 loan interest due to Road in respect of its loan to Street was due and had not been paid. Street had accrued the loan interest due at the year end but Road had not accrued any interest income.

Required

(a) **Define** what is meant by control and **explain** how this is determined according to IFRS 10 *Consolidated Financial Statements.* **(5 marks)**

(b) **Prepare** the consolidated statement of financial position for Road as at 31 March 2013, in accordance with the requirements of International Financial Reporting Standards. **(20 marks)**

Notes to the financial statements are not required, but all workings must be clearly shown.

(Total = 25 marks)

Answers

DO NOT TURN THIS PAGE UNTIL YOU HAVE
COMPLETED MOCK EXAM 2

356

A plan of attack

This is the second mock exam, so you will now have some feel of what you have to get done in the exam.

Your approach

As before, this paper has three sections. All sections, and all questions, are compulsory.

Question by question

Section A has ten questions of two marks each. The questions include tax calculations, MCQs and narrative questions.

Lets look at the Section B questions in the paper:

- Question (a) is on the preparation of cash flows from financing activities (IAS 7).

- Question (b) relates to ethical issues facing a finance director.

- Question (c) is concerned with different types of shares and the journal entries to record a rights issue.

- Question (d) is on deferred tax (IAS 12).

- Question (e) deals with benefits in kind and income tax computation.

- Question (f) requires the calculation of profit and VAT payable.

The section C questions follow the pattern in recent exams of having one question on single entity financial statements and one on group financial statements.

Marking the exam

Marking the MCQs is not too difficult. You only have 2 marks to award. In the longer questions, give yourself credit where you used the correct method, even if your answer was wrong.

Most important, list out all the items you did not know or got wrong, and **make sure you revise them**.

Remember

Always **allocate your time** according to the marks for the question in total and then according to the parts of the question. And **always**, **always follow the requirements** exactly.

You've got spare time at the end of the exam ... ?

If you have allocated your time properly then you **shouldn't have time on your hands** at the end of the exam. But if you find yourself with five or ten minutes to spare, **go back to the questions** that you couldn't do or to **any parts of questions that you didn't finish** because you ran out of time.

Forget about it!

And don't worry if you found the paper difficult. More than likely other candidates will too. If this were the real thing you would need to **forget** the exam the minute you leave the exam hall and **think about the next one**. Or, if it's the last one, **celebrate**!

SECTION A

Question 1

1   A

2   Tax avoidance is tax planning to arrange affairs, within the scope of the law, to minimise the tax liability.

3

		$000
Sale:		
Selling price		450
Charges		15
		435
Less Purchase:		
Cost	375	
Fees	12	
		387
Profit		48
Tax (48 × 25%)		12

4   The OECD model tax convention states that business profits will only be taxable in a state if an entity has a permanent establishment in that country.

5   C

6   Any one benefit of regulating published accounts for users of accounts:

- Enable them to be relied upon by users
- Promote consistency to help interpretation
- Promotes comparability between entities

AND

Any one benefit for preparers of accounts.

- Helps to ensure principles are interpreted the same way every time
- Helps preparers format accounts in a consistent way
- Helps preparers provide relevant information
- Financial statements easier to prepare

7   D

8   A

9   D

10   A modified report, based on insufficient appropriate evidence, with a disclaimer of opinion.

SECTION B

Question 2

(a)

	Marks
Share issue	1.0
Long-term borrowings – increase/redemption	1.5
Lease payments	2.0
Dividends	0.5
Maximum for question	5.0

All figures in $000

Proceeds from issue of shares: (460+82) – (400+70) = 72

Proceeds from long term borrowing: 129 - (105-25) =49

Finance lease:

Balance b/fwd – non-current		60
Current		6
		66
New leases		55
		121
Interest charges for year		16
		137
Balance c/fwd – non-current	98	
Current	10	
		108
Repaid		29

SF Statement of cash flows (extract) for year ended 31 March 2013:

Cash flows from financing activities:	
Proceeds from share issue	72
Proceeds from increase in long term borrowings	49
Redemption of long term borrowings	(25)
Dividends paid	(19)
Payments on finance leases	(29)
Net cash inflow from financing activities	48

(b)

	Marks
Four main ethical issues	5
Maximum for question	5

As XY takes on substantially the risk and rewards associated with owning the machine, the lease should be treated as a finance lease.

The ethical issues that may arise as a result of the managing director's instruction include:

- Objectivity – the finance director would be allowing other people to influence his professional judgement if the lease was treated incorrectly in the financial statements.

- Professional behaviour – the finance director should follow relevant laws and regulations. That would include following the requirements of IFRSs including IAS 17 Leases, not to do so could cause a negative impact on his reputation.

- Integrity – he should not be associated with any information that contains materially false or misleading information. Incorrectly classifying the lease could be misleading to users of the financial statements.

- Professional competence and due care – the finance director needs to ensure that he keeps up to date and follows relevant professional and technical standards. He will therefore need to follow IAS 17 Leases and treat the lease appropriately.

(c)

	Marks
Explain the difference between a bonus issue and a rights issue of shares	2
Prepare the accounting entries to record CD's rights issue	3
Maximum for question	5

(i) Bonus issue of shares is an issue of shares to existing shareholders for free. A bonus issue is used to capitalise reserves, it does not raise new capital.

A rights issue is an issue of shares below full market price to existing shareholders. A rights issue is made to raise new capital from existing shareholders. They are issued at a discount to current market price to encourage the shareholders to subscribe for the rights issue.

(ii) Number of shares issued: 5,000,000/5 = 1,000,000

Transaction value: 1,000,000 shares at $3.50 = $3,500,000

Accounting entries required:

	Debit	Credit
Cash	$3,500,000	
Share capital		$1,000,000
Share premium		$2,500,000

(d)

	Marks
Define temporary differences and give an example	2
Calculate deferred tax	3
Maximum for question	5

(i)   Temporary differences are differences between the carrying amount of an asset or liability in the statement of financial position and the balance calculated according to the tax regulations, its tax base. This is caused by the timing difference in treatment between the accounting rules and the tax rules.

An asset is charged against the income statement by way of a depreciation policy which is adjusted at the end of its useful life by a gain or loss on its sale. This depreciation policy may not agree with the tax rules and although over the life of the asset the total allowance will be the same there may be differences in timing. The difference will be greater where a country has a high level of first year allowances that reduce the tax bill in the first year of an asset's life.

(ii)

	$ Accounting	$ Tax base
Cost 1 April 2011	350,000	350,000
Depreciation		(35,000)
Tax depreciation		(175,000)
Balance 31 March 2012	315,000	175,000
Depreciation		(35,000)
Tax depreciation		(43,750)
Balance 31 March 2013	280,000	131,250
Temporary difference		148,750
Deferred tax	148,750 × 25% =	37,187.5

(e)

	Marks
Define benefits in kind and give examples	2
Calculate tax due for the year ended 31 March 2013	3
Maximum for question	5

(i)   "Benefits in kind" are non-cash benefits given to an employee as part of the remuneration package often in lieu of further cash payments.

A benefit in kind can include any of the following:

- Company cars
- Private medical insurance
- Free loans or loans at very low rates of interest
- Living accommodation

(ii)   BZ income tax for the year ended 31 March 2013

	$
Salary	34,000
Bonus	1,700
Benefits in kind	2,150
	37,850
Personal tax allowance	5,750
	32,100

Tax due (20,000 × 20%) + (12,100 × 40%) = $8,840

(f)

Marking scheme

	Marks
Calculate VAT arising on sales and net VAT due to be paid	3
Calculate the profit on the consignment excluding VAT	2
Maximum for question	5

	$ Cost/sales	$ VAT	$ Total
Cost of goods	90,000		
Excise duty @ 10%	9,000		
	99,000	14,850	113,850
Repackaging cost	16,900	2,535	19,435
Total cost	115,900	17,385	133,285
Sales	190,000	28,500	218,500
	74,100	11,115	85,215

(i)   YN's net profit on the consignment is $74,100

(ii)   The net VAT due to be paid on the consignment is $11,115

SECTION C

Question 3

	Marks
Explain why BVQ carried out an impairment review	3.0
Prepare the statement of profit or loss – Revenue; Cost of sales; Admin & Distribution	4.0
Prepare the statement of profit or loss – Loss on assets held for sale; finance and tax	4.0
Prepare the statement of financial position – assets	5.0
Prepare the statement of financial position – equity and liabilities	5.0
Prepare the statement of changes in equity	1.5
Formats and presentation	2.5
Maximum for question	25

(a) IAS 36 *Impairment of Assets* requires BVQ to assess at each reporting date whether there is any indication that any assets may be impaired. If any indication exists, the recoverable amount must be estimated, that is, an impairment review must be carried out.

Due to the general economic downturn property prices have reduced during the year. This could suggest that BVQ's property has suffered an impairment.

BVQ has experienced a reduction in sales demand and is reducing its asset base by selling a specialised machine. This suggests that an impairment may have occurred to its plant and machinery.

Therefore BVQ needed to carry out an impairment review.

(b) BVQ - STATEMENT OF PROFIT OR LOSS FOR THE YEAR ENDED 31 MARCH 2013

		$000	$000
Revenue			4,364
Cost of sales			(1,873)
Gross profit			2,491
Administrative expenses	W3	(907)	
Distribution costs	W3	(291)	(1,198)
Profit from operations			1,293
Loss on non-current assets held for sale	W6		(16)
Finance cost	W4		(50)
Profit before tax			1,227
Income tax expense	W5		(238)
Profit for the year			989

BVQ STATEMENT OF CHANGES IN EQUITY FOR THE YEAR ENDED 31 MARCH 2013

	Equity Shares	Retained earnings	Total
	$000	$000	$000
Balance at 31 March 2012	1,400	728	2,128
Profit for the year		989	989
Dividend paid		(70)	(70)
Balance at 31 March 2013	1,400	1,647	3,047

BVQ STATEMENT OF FINANCIAL POSITION AS AT 31 MARCH 2013

	$000	$000
Non-current assets		
Property, plant and equipment (W1)		3,318
Current Assets		
Inventory	198	
Trade receivables	916	
Cash and cash equivalents	118	1,232
Non-current assets held for sale (W6)		72
Total Assets		4,622
Equity and liabilities		
Equity		
Share capital	1,400	
Retained earnings	1,647	
Total equity		3,047
Non-current Liabilities		
Loan notes	600	
Deferred tax (W5)	393	
Finance lease (W2)	134	
Total non-current liabilities		1,127
Current liabilities		
Trade payables	176	
Tax payable (W5)	180	
Interest payable	18	
Finance lease (W2)	74	
Total current liabilities		448
Total equity and liabilities		4,622

Workings - All figures in $000

(W1) *Tangible Non-current Assets*

Cost/Valuation	Land	Buildings	Plant & Mach.	Leased Vehicles	Total
	$000	$000	$000	$000	$000
Balance 31/3/12	1,653	900	3,888	324	6,765
Asset held for sale			(180)		(180)
			3,708		6,585
Depreciation:					
Balance 31/3/12		190	2,489	65	2,744
Charge for year		27	420	65	512
		217	2,909	130	3,256
Asset held for sale (W6)			(92)		(92)
			2,817		3,164
Carrying amount at 31/3/13	1,653	683	891	194	3,421
Impairment		(103)			(103)
		2,233	891	194	3,318

Depreciation

Buildings 900 × 3% = 27

Plant and machinery
Reducing balance = 3,888 – 2,489 = 1,399 × 30% = 420

Vehicle – 324 × 20% = 65

(W2) *Lease*

	Opening balance	Paid	Sub-total	Interest @ 7.12%	Closing balance
Year to 31/3/13	268	74	194	14	208
Year to 31/3/14	208	74	134		

Current liability = 74
Non-current liability = 134

(W3)

	Administration	Distribution
Per trial balance	357	226
Vehicle depreciation (W1)		65
Plant & machinery depreciation (W1)	420	
Land & buildings depreciation (W1)	27	
Land & buildings impairment	103	
	907	291

(W4) *Finance charge*

Year's loan interest	36
Finance lease (W2)	14
	50

(W5) *Tax*

Last year b/f	27
Current year	180
	207
Increase in deferred tax	31
	238

Deferred tax

Per trial balance	362
Increase in year	31
	393

(W6) *Non-current asset held for sale*

As per IFRS 5 Non-current assets held for sale and discontinued operations the proposed sale of the machine will be classified as held for sale.

Cost   180 two years ago

Depreciation $(180 \times 30\%) + (180 \times 70\% \times 30\%) = 54 + 37.8 = 91.8$

Carrying value $= 180 - 91.8 = 88.2$

Fair value less cost to sell $= 73 - 0.8 = 72.2$

Impairment $= 88.2 - 72.2 = 16$

Asset held for sale (SOFP) $= 72.2$ approx 72

Question 4

	Marks
Explain the meaning of control	5.0
Calculate goodwill arising on acquisition of Street	3.0
Calculate investment in associated entity	2.0
Prepare workings for consolidated property, plant and equipment	2.5
Calculate consolidated retained earnings balance at 31 March 2013	6.5
Prepare consolidated statement of financial position	6.0
Maximum for question	25

(a) According to IFRS 10 *Consolidated Financial Statements* control is the power to govern the financial and operating policies of an entity so as to obtain benefit from its activities.

There is a presumption that control exists where the investor entity owns over half of the voting power of the other entity. Where control over another entity exists that entity is regarded as a subsidiary.

IFRS 10 also sets out circumstances where control can be established with less than 50% of the equity votes, in each case where control exists the entity will be regarded as a subsidiary, even if less than 50% of the equity voting shares are held.

IFRS 10 provides the following instances where control can be achieved with less than 50% of equity shares:

- Power over more than 50% of voting rights by virtue of an agreement with other investors

- Power to govern the financial and operating policies of the entity under a statute or agreement

- Power to appoint or remove the majority of the members of the board of directors or equivalent governing body and control of the entity is by that board or body

- Power to cast the majority of votes at meetings of the board of directors or equivalent governing body and control of the entity is by that board or body

(b) *Workings (All workings in $000)*

(i) *Fair value of net assets of Street at acquisition*

Equity Shares	550
Share premium	150
Retained earnings	122
Fair value adjustment	320
	1,142

(ii) *Goodwill - Street*

Cost	1,350
Fair value of net assets acquired:	1,142
Goodwill	208
Impairment	38
Balance at 31 March 2013	170

(iii) *Investment in associate*

Cost	323
Add group share of post acquisition profits	
(458 – 350) = 108 × 25% =	27
	350
Impairment	(20)
Investment at 31 March 2013	330

(iv) *Intra-group trading*

Sale of goods from 100% owned subsidiary to parent
Mark up on cost 25% = 25/125 or 20% margin on selling price.
Selling price 220 ; unrealised profit = 44
Of which 40% is realised. Unrealised = 44 × 60% = 26.4 approx 26

	Dr.	Cr.
Consolidated retained earnings	26	
Consolidated current assets – inventory		26

Consolidated Trade Receivables

Road	140
Street	119
Less cheque in transit	(110)
	149

Consolidated Trade Payables

Road	270
Street	128
	398

(v) *Excess depreciation on fair value adjustment*

Fair value adjustment – 320
Economic life 20 years, straight line basis
Excess depreciation = 320/20 = 16 per year
Three years = 16 × 3 = 48

(vi) *Sale of machine*

Unrealised profit on sale of machine to Street – (95-65) = 30
Excess depreciation – one year – 30/5 = 6

(vii) *Consolidated Retained Earnings*

Road	814
Loan interest receivable	25
Street (339 - 122)	217
Drive (458 – 350) = 108 × 25% =	27
Goodwill impairment – Street	(38)
– Drive	(20)
Unrealised profit	(26)
Profit on sale of machine	(30)
One year's depreciation of excess	6
Excess depreciation on fair value adj.	(48)
Balance 31 March 2013	927

(viii) *Consolidated Property, plant and equipment*

Road	1,840
Street	1,060
Fair value adjustment	320
Profit on sale of machine	(30)
Add back machine excess depreciation	6
Excess depreciation	(48)
	3,148

ROAD - CONSOLIDATED STATEMENT OF FINANCIAL POSITION AS AT 31 MARCH 2013

	$000	$000
Non-current assets		
Property, plant and equipment (viii)	3,148	
Goodwill (ii)	170	
Investment in associate (iii)	330	
		3,648
Current assets		
Inventory (310+236-26)	520	
Trade receivables (iv)	149	
Cash and cash equivalents (71+27+110)	208	
		877
Total assets		4,525
Equity and liabilities		
Equity shares	2,000	
Share premium	500	
Retained earnings (vii)	927	
		3,427
Non-current liabilities		
Borrowings		700
Current liabilities		
Trade payables (iv)		398
		4,525

CIMA

Financial Pillar

F1 – Financial Operations

Mock Exam 3

Question Paper
You are allowed three hours to answer this question paper.
You are allowed 20 minutes reading time *before the examination begins* during which you should read the question paper and, if you wish, highlight and/or make notes on the question paper.
You are strongly advised to carefully read ALL the question requirements before attempting the question concerned (that is all parts and/or sub-questions).
You should show all working as marks are available for the method you use.
ALL QUESTIONS ARE COMPULSORY
Section A comprises of 10 sub-questions.
Section B comprises of 6 sub-questions.
Section C comprises of 2 questions.
The country 'Tax Regime' for the paper is provided on the next page.

DO NOT OPEN THIS PAPER UNTIL YOU ARE READY TO START UNDER EXAMINATION CONDITIONS

COUNTRY X - TAX REGIME FOR USE THROUGHOUT THE EXAMINATION PAPER

Relevant Tax Rules for Years Ended 31 March 2007 to 2014

Corporate Profits

Unless otherwise specified, only the following rules for taxation of corporate profits will be relevant, other taxes can be ignored:

- Accounting rules on recognition and measurement are followed for tax purposes.

- All expenses other than depreciation, amortisation, entertaining, taxes paid to other public bodies and donations to political parties are tax deductible.

- Tax depreciation is deductible as follows:

  o 50% of additions to property, plant and equipment in the accounting period in which they are recorded;

  o 25% per year of the written-down value (i.e. cost minus previous allowances) in subsequent accounting periods except that in which the asset is disposed of;

  o No tax depreciation is allowed on land.

- The corporate tax on profits is at a rate of 25%.

- No indexation is allowable on the sale of land.

- Tax losses can be carried forward to offset against future taxable profits from the same business.

Value Added Tax

Country X has a VAT system which allows entities to reclaim input tax paid.

In country X the VAT rates are:

Zero rated	0%
Standard rated	15%
Exempt goods	0%

SECTION A – 20 marks

Answer ALL ten sub-questions in this section

Question 1

1   Which **one** of the following is regarded as a direct tax?

   A   Value added tax

   B   Capital gains tax

   C   Excise duties

   D   Property tax   **(2 marks)**

2   In many countries employees' earnings have tax deducted by their employers before being paid to them. This is sometimes referred to as "Pay-as-you-earn".

   Identify two advantages of "Pay-as-you-earn" to employees.   **(2 marks)**

3   UI has the following details:

   (i)   Incorporated in Country A.

   (ii)   Senior management hold regular board meetings in Country B and exercise control from there, but there are no sales or purchases made in Country B.

   (iii) Carries out its main business activities in Country C.

   Assume all three countries have double taxation treaties with each other, based on the OECD model tax convention.

   In which country/countries will UI be deemed to be resident for tax purposes?

   A   Country A

   B   Country B

   C   Country C

   D   Countries B and C   **(2 marks)**

4   DF, a small entity resident in Country X, purchased its only item of plant on 1 October 2011 for $200,000.

   DF charges depreciation on a straight line basis over 5 years.

   DF's deferred tax balance as at 30 September 2013, in accordance with IAS 12 *Income Taxes* is:

   A $3,750

   B $11,250

   C $18,750

   D $45,000   **(2 marks)**

5   GH is registered for VAT in Country X and is partially exempt for VAT purposes.

GH's sales for the last VAT period, excluding VAT, were:

	$
Goods at standard rate	15,000
Goods exempt from VAT	10,000

During the period GH purchased materials and services costing a total of $12,075, including VAT at standard rate. These materials and services were used to produce standard rated goods and exempt goods.

Assume that GH had no other VAT related transactions in the period.

Calculate the net VAT due to/from GH for the VAT period.   **(2 marks)**

---

6   **Identify two** advantages of having an ethical code for accountants.   **(2 marks)**

---

7   **Identify** any **two** responsibilities of the IFRS Foundation.   **(2 marks)**

---

8   The IASB's *Conceptual Framework for Financial Reporting (2010) (Framework)* identifies faithful representation as a fundamental qualitative characteristic of financial information.

Which **one** of the following is **not** a characteristic of faithful representation?

A   Free from error

B   Verifiable

C   Neutral

D   Complete   **(2 marks)**

---

9   **Identify two** actions required under IAS 1 *(Revised) Presentation of Financial Statements* to ensure that "Financial statements shall present fairly the financial position, financial performance and cash flows of an entity."   **(2 marks)**

---

10   The IASB's *Framework* states that "materiality is an entity-specific aspect of relevance".

Describe the term "materiality" as used in the *Framework*.   **(2 marks)**

(Total = 20 marks)

SECTION B – 30 marks

Answer ALL six sub-questions

Question 2

(a)   An investment in another entity's equity is classified as an investment in a subsidiary, if the investor can exercise control over the investee.

AB acquired 4,000 of the 10,000 equity voting shares and 8,000 of the 10,000 non-voting preference shares of CD.

AB acquired 4,000 of the 10,000 equity voting shares of EF and had a signed agreement giving it the power to appoint or remove all of the directors of EF.

Required

Explain whether CD and/or EF should be classified as subsidiaries/a subsidiary of AB. You should refer to the provisions of IFRS 10 *Consolidated Financial Statements* in your answer.   **(Total = 5 marks)**

(b)   YZ purchased 100% of the equity shares in WX on 1 October 2012.

YZ and WX trade with each other. During the year ended 30 September 2013 YZ sold WX inventory at a sales price of $28,000. YZ applied a mark up on cost of $33^1/_3$%.

At 30 September 2013 WX still owed YZ $10,000 of the cost and had remaining in inventory $6,000 of the goods purchased from YZ.

Required

Prepare the journal entries to make the required adjustment in YZ's consolidated financial statements for the year ended 30 September 2013 for the above.   **(Total = 5 marks)**

(c)   UV purchased an asset for $50,000 on 1 October 2009, incurring import duties of $8,000. UV depreciated the asset at 10% per year on a straight line basis.

UV sold the asset for $80,000 on 30 September 2013, incurring costs of $2,000. The asset was subject to capital gains tax of 25% and the indexation factor from 1 October 2009 to 30 September 2013 was 14%.

Required

(i)   **Explain** the purpose of "indexation" when used in the calculation of capital gains tax.   **(2 marks)**
(ii) **Calculate** the capital gains tax arising on the disposal of UV's asset.   **(3 marks)**

(Total = 5 marks)

(d)   TY is resident in Country X.

TY's statement of profit or loss for year ended 30 September 2013 was as follows:

	$
Revenue	950,000
Cost of sales	(550,000)
Gross profit	400,000
Administrative expenses	(132,000)
Taxes paid to other public bodies	(1,900)
Entertaining expenses	(1,200)
Depreciation of plant and equipment	(47,500)
Distribution costs	(42,000)
	175,400
Finance cost	(3,500)
Profit before tax	171,900

TY has accumulated tax losses of $125,000 brought forward from 2011/12.

TY owns plant and equipment purchased on 1 October 2010 at a cost of $385,000 and plant purchased on 1 October 2012 at a cost of $90,000. TY charges depreciation at 10% per year on a straight line basis on all non-current assets.

Required

Calculate the tax payable by TY for the year ended 30 September 2013. **(Total = 5 marks)**

(e) You are a trainee accountant working for JHG, which owns a number of subsidiary entities.

A new Chief Executive has recently been appointed and has raised the following queries:

- JHG is a member of a tax group. What is a tax group?
- What are the benefits to JHG and its subsidiaries of being in a tax group?

Required

Prepare a short briefing note that answers the Chief Executive's questions. **(Total = 5 marks)**

(f)

Required

Explain the typical duties of an external auditor of an entity. **(Total = 5 marks)**

(Total = 30 marks)

SECTION C – 50 marks

Answer BOTH of these questions

Question 3

RDX'S TRIAL BALANCE AT 30 SEPTEMBER 2013 IS SHOWN BELOW:

	Notes	$000	$000
5% Loan notes (issued 2010, redeemable 2020)	(ix)		1,480
Administrative expenses		779	
Cash received on sale of equipment	(v)		23
Cash and cash equivalents		207	
Cost of sales		4,080	
Distribution costs		650	
Equity dividend paid 1 February 2013	(vii)	335	
Income tax	(ii)	24	
Inventory at 30 September 2013	(i)	1,055	
Land and buildings at cost at 1 October 2012		5,180	
Loan interest paid		37	
Equity shares $1 each, fully paid at 1 October 2012			5,650
RDX ordinary shares purchased	(viii)	135	
Plant and equipment at cost at 1 October 2012	(v)	4,520	
Provision for deferred tax at 1 October 2012	(iii)		282
Provision for buildings depreciation at 1 October 2012	(iv)		262
Provision for plant and equipment depreciation at 1 October 2012	(vi)		2,260
Retained earnings at 1 October 2012			1,990
Sales revenue			6,780
Share premium			565
Trade payables			300
Trade receivables	(x)	2,590	
		19,592	19,592

Notes.

(i)   RDX has always valued its inventories using a manual system. On 1 October 2012 RDX purchased and installed a computerised inventory system and changed its inventory valuation method to the industry standard method.

The impact on inventory valuation due to the change in policy was calculated as:

Inventory value increase at 30 September 2012 by $148,000.

Inventory value increase up to 30 September 2013 by $210,000.

(ii) The income tax balance in the trial balance is a result of the under provision for the year ended 30 September 2012.

(iii) The tax due for the year ended 30 September 2013 is estimated at $160,000 and the deferred tax provision should be decreased by $30,000.

(iv) Depreciation is charged on buildings using the straight line method at 3% per annum. The cost of land included in land and buildings is $3,000,000. Buildings depreciation is treated as an administrative expense.

(v)   During the year RDX disposed of old equipment for $23,000. The original cost of the equipment sold was $57,000 and its book value at 30 September 2012 was $6,000.

(vi) Plant and equipment is depreciated at 20% per annum using the reducing balance method. Depreciation of plant and equipment is considered to be part of cost of sales. RDX's policy is to charge a full year's depreciation in the year of acquisition and no depreciation in the year of disposal.

(vii) During the year RDX paid a dividend of $335,000 for the year ended 30 September 2012.

(viii) RDX purchased and cancelled 100,000 of its own equity shares on 30 September 2013 for $135,000. These shares had originally been issued at a 10% premium.

(ix)   Long term borrowings consist of loan notes issued on 1 April 2010 at 5% interest per annum.

(x)   On 22 October 2013 RDX discovered that ZZZ, one of its customers, had gone into liquidation. RDX has been informed that it will receive none of the outstanding balance of $230,000 at 30 September 2013.

Required

(a)   **Explain** how the change in inventory accounting policy should be recorded in RDX's financial statements for the year ended 30 September 2013, in accordance with IAS 8 Accounting Policies, Changes in Accounting Estimates and Errors.   **(3 marks)**

(b)   **Prepare** RDX's statement of profit or loss and statement of changes in equity for the year to 30 September 2013 AND the statement of financial position at that date, in accordance with the requirements of International Financial Reporting Standards.

Notes to the financial statements are not required, but all workings must be clearly shown. Do NOT prepare a statement of accounting policies.   **(22 marks)**

(Total = 25 marks)

Question 4

The financial statements of AWX for the year ended 31 March 2012 and 31 March 2013 are given below:

AWX STATEMENT OF FINANCIAL POSITION AS AT

	Notes	31 March 2013 $000	$000	31 March 2012 $000	$000
Non-current Assets					
Property, plant and equipment	(i) (ii)	4,191		4,500	
Intangible assets	(iv)	156		315	
			4,347		4,815
Current Assets					
Inventories		738		805	
Trade receivables		564		480	
Cash and cash equivalents		515		265	
			1,817		1,550
Total Assets			6,164		6,365
Equity and Liabilities					
Equity shares of $1 each		2,180		2,180	
Preference shares	(v)	700		–	
Share premium		968		968	
Revaluation reserve		469		353	
Retained earnings	(vii)	901		727	
			5,218		4,228
Non-current liabilities					
9% loan notes	(vi)	–		1,100	
Deferred tax		225		220	
			225		1,320
Current liabilities					
Trade payables		535		500	
Tax payable		84		218	
Provisions		90		–	
Interest payable		12		99	
			721		817
Total Equity and Liabilities			6,164		6,365

STATEMENT OF PROFIT OR LOSS FOR THE YEAR ENDED 31 MARCH 2013

	Notes	$000
Revenue		6,858
Cost of sales	(iii)	(3,552)
Gross profit		3,306
Administrative expenses	(viii)	(2,042)
Distribution costs		(816)
		448
Finance cost		(40)
		408
Income tax expense		(124)
Profit for the year		284

Notes.

(i)   Property, plant and equipment includes properties which were revalued upwards during the year.

(ii) Property, plant and equipment disposed of in the year had a net book value of $70,000; cash received on their disposal was $92,000.

(iii) Depreciation charged for the year was $675,000.

(iv) There were no additions or disposals of intangible assets during the year.

(v)   On 1 April 2012, AWX issued 700,000 5% cumulative $1 preference shares at par, redeemable at 10% premium on 1 April 2022. Issue costs of $50,000 have been paid by AWX and included in administrative expenses. The effective rate of interest is 6·74%. The cash received for the issue of the preference shares has been debited to cash and credited to equity.

(vi) On 1 May 2012, AWX purchased and cancelled all its 9% loan notes at par plus accrued interest (included in finance costs).

(vii) Equity dividends paid during the year were $75,000 and preference share dividends paid were $35,000.

(viii) AWX has been advised that it is probably going to lose a court case and at 31 March 2013 has provided $90,000 for the estimated cost of this case.

Required

(a)   (i)   **Explain** how AWX should treat its preference shares in its financial statements for the year ended 31 March 2013 according to IAS 32 Financial Instruments: Presentation AND,

      (ii)   **Calculate** AWX's revised profit before tax for the year ended 31 March 2013 in accordance with IAS 39 *Financial Instruments: Recognition and Measurement.*   **(6 marks)**

(b)   **Prepare** AWX's Statement of cash flows, using the indirect method, for the year ended 31 March 2013 in accordance with IAS 7 *Statement of Cash Flows.*   **(19 marks)**

Notes to the financial statements are not required, but all workings must be clearly shown.

(Total = 25 marks)

(Total = 50 marks)

Answers

DO NOT TURN THIS PAGE UNTIL YOU HAVE
COMPLETED MOCK EXAM 3

382

A plan of attack

This is the third mock exam, so you will now have some feel of what you have to get done in the exam.

Your approach

As before, this paper has three sections. All sections, and all questions, are compulsory.

Question by question

Section A has ten questions of two marks each. These include narrative and calculation questions on tax, and questions on regulations and ethics. Four of the questions are multiple choice in format

Lets look at the Section B questions in the paper:

- Question (a) is on the classification of subsidiaries (IFRS 10).

- Question (b) requires the journal entries to record consolidation.

- Question (c) is concerned with indexation and the calculation of capital gains tax.

- Question (d) requires the calculation of tax payable.

- Question (e) is on tax groups and the benefits of being in a tax group.

- Question (f) is on the duties of external auditors.

In section C the first question is relatively straightforward; the preparation of financial statements for a single entity, with the added complication of the repurchase of the entity's own shares. The second question in section C requires the preparation of a statement of cash flows, rather than group financial statements as has been the case in the last few exams. This question also asks the candidate to explain the treatment of preference shares in the financial statements.

Marking the exam

Marking the MCQs is not too difficult. You only have 2 marks to award. In the longer questions, give yourself credit where you used the correct method, even if your answer was wrong.

Most important, list out all the items you did not know or got wrong, and **make sure you revise them**.

Remember

Always **allocate your time** according to the marks for the question in total and then according to the parts of the question. And **always, always follow the requirements** exactly.

You've got spare time at the end of the exam ... ?

If you have allocated your time properly then you **shouldn't have time on your hands** at the end of the exam. But if you find yourself with five or ten minutes to spare, **go back to the questions** that you couldn't do or to **any parts of questions that you didn't finish** because you ran out of time.

Forget about it!

And don't worry if you found the paper difficult. More than likely other candidates will too. If this were the real thing you would need to **forget** the exam the minute you leave the exam hall and **think about the next one**. Or, if it's the last one, **celebrate**!

SECTION A

Question 1

1   B

2   The advantages to employees of being on PAYE (any two of the following):

- The employer is responsible for calculating the tax due
- The employer is responsible for paying the tax due to the tax authorities
- The costs of administering the system are borne by the employer
- Employees are not faced with large periodic tax bills
- Employees are not at risk of late payment or default

3   B

Where an entity is resident in more than one country, the OECD deems it to be resident only in the country of its effective management.

4   B

		Carrying amount $	Tax WDV $	Temporary difference $	Deferred tax (25%) $
01.10.11	Purchase	200,000	200,000		
30.09.12	Accounting depreciation ($200,000 ÷ 5)	(40,000)			
30.09.12	Tax depreciation ($200,000 × 50%)		(100,000)		
30.09.13	Accounting depreciation	(40,000)			
30.09.13	Tax depreciation ($200,000 – 100,000 × 25%)		(25,000)		
		120,000	75,000	45,000	11,250

5    $1,305

	$
VAT due on standard sales (15,000 × 15%)	2,250
VAT recoverable from purchases (12,075 × 15/115)	1,575
Partial exemption (1,575 × 15,000/25,000)	945

VAT due is $2,250 – $945 = $1,305

6   Any two benefits of having an ethical code for accountants from the following:

- Helps stakeholders to place reliance on the work carried out by accountants. Without this reliance financial markets cannot operate effectively.

- An ethical code helps maintain the reputation of the accounting profession as all accountants are obliged to adhere to an ethical code.

- Ethical codes are constantly evolving to adapt to changes in the business world and in society generally.

7   Any two responsibilities of the IFRS Foundation from the following:

- Develop a single set of IFRSs through the IASB
- Promote the use and rigorous application of those standards
- Take account of the financial reporting needs of emerging economies and SMEs
- Bring about convergence of national accounting standards and IFRSs

8   B

9   Any two actions required under IAS 1 from the following:

- Representing transactions in accordance with the recognition criteria set out in the *Conceptual Framework*.

- Compliance with IFRSs.

- Selection, application and disclosure of accounting policies in accordance with IAS 8.

- Presentation of information that is relevant and a faithful representation.

- Presentation of additional disclosures where this is necessary to give a full understanding of an event or transaction.

10   Information is material if its omission or misstatement could influence the economic decisions of users taken on the basis of the financial statements.

Information may be judged relevant simply because of its nature (eg the remuneration of management). In other cases both the nature of the information and its amount in the context of the financial statements will be taken into account.

There is no absolute measure of materiality; its determination is a very subjective exercise.

SECTION B

Question 2

(a) The important point in determining whether an investment is a subsidiary is **control**. In most cases, control will involve the holding company or parent owning a majority of the ordinary shares in the subsidiary (to which normal voting rights are attached). There are circumstances, however, when the parent may own only a minority of the voting power in the subsidiary, *but* the parent still has control.

IFRS 10 provides a definition of control and identifies three separate elements of control:

An investor controls an investee if and only if it has all of the following:

1   Power over the investee

2   Exposure to, or rights to, variable returns from its involvement with the investee; and

3   The ability to use its power over the investee to affect the amount of the investor's returns

If there are changes to one or more of these three elements of control, then an investor should reassess whether it controls an investee.

Power can be obtained directly from ownership of the majority of voting rights or can be derived from other rights, such as:

• Rights to appoint, reassign or remove key management personnel who can direct the relevant activities

• Rights to appoint or remove another entity that directs the relevant activities

• Rights to direct the investee to enter into, or veto changes to, transactions for the benefit of the investor

• Other rights, such as those specified in a management contract

In the case of CD, AB has 40% of voting rights and 80% of non-voting rights, therefore AB has no control over CD and CD is not a subsidiary of AB.

For EF, AB has a minority of voting rights (40%) but it has control in that it has the power to appoint and remove directors; EF is therefore a subsidiary of AB.

(b) The journal entries to make the required adjustments in YZ's consolidated financial statements are as follows:

	DR $	CR $
Group revenue	28,000	
Group cost of sales		28,000
Being the removal of intra-group trading		
YZ cost of sales	1,500	
Group inventories		1,500
Being the provision for unrealised profit		
Payables	10,000	
Receivables		10,000
Being the cancelling out of Intra-group balances		

Workings

Profit on intra-group trading = $28,000 x 33⅓/133⅓ = $7,000

Profit on goods held at year end = $6,000 x 33⅓/133⅓ = $1,500

(c)   (i)   Indexation is an allowance to provide relief for inflation which has occurred between the date of acquisition of an asset and the date of its disposal. In the UK this is known as the **indexation allowance** and it is based on the movement in the Retail Price Index (RPI) between those two dates. It is calculated as follows:

Indexation allowance = acquisition cost x indexation factor

(ii)   Capital gains tax arising from the disposal of UV's asset:

	$	$
Proceeds of sale (80,000 – 2,000)		78,000
Cost (50,000 + 8,000)	58,000	
Indexation allowance (58,000 × 14%)	8,120	
Total allowable cost		(66,120)
Capital gain		11,880
Tax payable (11,880 × 25%)		2,970

(d)   Calculation of tax payable by TY for the year ended 30 September 2013:

	$	$
Profit before tax		171,900
Add back non-allowable expenses:		
Taxes paid to other public bodies	1,900	
Entertaining expenses	1,200	
Depreciation of plant and equipment	47,500	
		50,600
Adjusted profit		222,500
Tax depreciation – plant and equipment (W1)	36,094	
Tax depreciation – additions in year (90,000 × 50%)	45,000	
		(81,094)
		141,406
Less: accumulated tax losses b/fwd		(125,000)
		16,406
Tax ($16,406 × 25%)		4,102

Working: tax depreciation

	$	$
Cost on 1 October 2010		385,000
Tax depreciation to 30 September 2011 ($385,000 × 50%)		(192,500)
		192,500
Tax depreciation to 30 September 2012 ($192,500 × 25%)		(48,125)
		144,375
Tax depreciation to 30 September 2013 ($144,375 × 25%)		36,094

(e)   BRIEFING NOTE

To: Chief Executive

From: Trainee Accountant

Date: 21 November 2013

Subject: Tax groups

A tax group is a group of companies that is treated as one entity for tax purposes.

In the UK, for example, losses of one group subsidiary may be set against the profits of another group subsidiary. When assets are transferred between group companies, capital gains tax is deferred until the

asset is sold outside the group. In effect, UK group relief rules treat the group as one entity for tax purposes.

This UK treatment is an example of **tax consolidation.** In general, if a group of enterprises are recognised as a **tax group**, it is possible for them to gain relief for trading losses by offsetting the losses of one group member against the profits of another group member. The rules for group relief will vary from country to country, as will the rules for recognition of a tax group (which may differ from the rules under which groups are recognised for financial reporting purposes).

Some countries also have their own regulations for recognising **tax groups for capital gains purposes**. It is not usually possible to offset capital losses and gains between the group members. However, there are usually provisions that allow the transfer of assets between group members without recognising a capital gain or loss. The calculation of the gain and the payment of the tax are usually **deferred** until the asset is sold outside the tax group. Good tax planning is needed to ensure that all asset sales to third parties take place through just one group member. These provisions can then be used to accumulate all the group's capital gains and losses in that member, thereby effectively obtaining offset.

Group relief may be used to save tax as the group company surrendering the loss may pay tax at a lower rate than the company receiving the loss. It also may enable tax relief to be gained earlier as instead of the company making the loss having to carry that loss forward, it can instead surrender it to a group company which can utilise it in the current year.

(f)   The external auditor of an entity has the following duties (any five duties from the following):

Truth and fairness of the financial statements	The auditor must give an opinion as to whether the statement of financial position shows a true and fair view of (presents fairly) the company's affairs at the end of the period and the statement of profit or loss and other comprehensive income (and a statement of cash flows) show a true and fair view of (present fairly) the results for the period.
Compliance with legislation	The auditor must give an opinion as to whether the financial statements have been prepared in accordance with the relevant legislation and applicable financial reporting framework.
Returns from branches	Report by exception if proper returns from branches not visited by the auditor have not been received.
Agreement of accounts to records	Report by exception if the financial statements are not in agreement with the accounting records.
Proper accounting records	Report by exception if adequate accounting records have not been kept.
Information and explanations	Report by exception if all of the information and explanations necessary for the audit have not been received.
Directors' disclosures	Report by exception if directors' disclosures (for example, emoluments) have not been properly made.
Consistency of other information	Report by exception if the other information presented with the financial statements is inconsistent with the financial statements.

SECTION C

Question 3

(a) The same accounting policies are usually adopted from period to period, to allow users to analyse trends over time in profit, cash flows and financial position. Changes in accounting policy will therefore be rare and should be made only if required by one of three things:

(i) A new statutory requirement

(ii) A new accounting standard

(iii) If the change will result in a **more appropriate presentation** of events or transactions in the financial statements of the entity

In the case of RDX the change in the inventory valuation method will result in a more appropriate presentation as it will comply with the industry standard.

IAS 8 requires **retrospective application** of a change in accounting policy, *unless* it is **impracticable** to determine the cumulative amount of the adjustment. Retrospective application means that all comparative information must be restated **as if the new policy had always been in force**, with amounts relating to earlier periods reflected in an adjustment to opening reserves of the earliest period presented. Comparative information should be restated unless it is impracticable to do so.

For RDX the opening inventory will need to be increased by $148,000 and the closing inventory increased by $210,000. The journal entries to account for these adjustments are as follows:

	$'000	$'000
DR Cost of sales	148	
CR Retained earnings		148

Being the increase in opening inventory resulting from the change in accounting policy

	$'000	$'000
DR Closing inventories	210	
CR Cost of sales		210

Being the increase in closing inventory resulting from the change in accounting policy

(b)

RDX STATEMENT OF PROFIT OR LOSS AND OTHER COMPREHENSIVE INCOME
FOR THE YEAR ENDED 30 SEPTEMBER 2013

	$'000
Revenue	6,780
Cost of sales (W1)	(4,452)
Gross Profit	2,328
Administrative expenses (W1)	(1,074)
Distribution costs (W1)	(650)
Finance cost (W4)	(74)
Profit before tax	530
Income tax expense (W3)	(154)
Profit for the year	376

RDX STATEMENT OF CHANGES IN EQUITY FOR THE YEAR ENDED 30 SEPTEMBER 2013

	Equity shares $'000	Share premium $'000	Retained earnings $'000	Capital redemption $'000	Total $'000
Balance at 1 October 2012	5,650	565	1,990	0	8,205
Prior year adjustment			148		148
Restated at 1 October 2013	5,650	565	2,138	0	8,353
Profit for the year			376		376
Repurchase of shares	(100)		(35)		(135)
Maintenance of capital			(100)	100	0
Dividend paid			(335)		(335)
Balance at 30 Sept 2013	5,550	565	2,044	100	8,259

RDX STATEMENT OF FINANCIAL POSITION AT 30 SEPTEMBER 2013

	$'000	$'000
Non-current assets		
Property, plant and equipment (W2)		6,656
Current assets		
Inventories (1055 + 210)	1,265	
Trade receivables (2,590 - 230)	2,360	
Cash and cash equivalents	207	3,832
Total assets		10,488
Equity and liabilities		
Equity		
Share capital		5,550
Share premium		565
Retained earnings		2,044
Capital redemption reserve		100
Total equity		8,259
Non-current liabilities		
5% Loan notes	1,480	
Deferred tax (W5)	252	
Total non-current liabilities		1,732
Current liabilities		
Trade payables	300	
Tax payable	160	
Interest payable (W4)	37	
Total current liabilities		497
Total equity and liabilities		10,488

Workings (All figures in $'000)

(W1)

	Cost of sales $'000	Administrative expenses $'000	Distribution Costs $'000
Trial balance:	4,080	779	650
Adjustment to opening inventory	148		
Adjustment to closing inventory	(210)		
Irrecoverable debt		230	
Gain on disposal of plant and equipment (23 – 6)	(17)		
Depreciation – buildings (W1)		65	
Depreciation – plant and equipment (W1)	451		
	4,452	1,074	650

(W2) **PPE**

Cost	Land $'000	Buildings $'000	P&E $'000	Total $'000
Balance b/fwd	3,000	2,180	4,520	9,700
Disposal (note (v))			(57)	(57)
Balance c/fwd	3,000	2,180	4,463	9,643

Accumulated depreciation	Land	Buildings	P&E	Total
Balance b/fwd	0	262	2,260	2,522
Disposal (note (v))			(51)	(51)
			2,211	
Depreciation – buildings (2,180 x 3%)		65		65
Depreciation – plant and equipment (4,463 – [2,260 – 51] x 20%)			451	451
Balance c/fwd	0	327	2,660	2,987
Carrying amount 30 Sept 2013	**3,000**	**1,853**	**1,803**	**6,656**

(W3) **Tax**

Under provision in respect of prior year	24
Current year	160
Decrease in deferred tax	(30)
	154

(W4) **Interest**

Paid in year	37
Due for year (1,480 × 5%)	74
Accrued	37

(W5) **Deferred Tax**

Balance b/f	282
Current year	(30)
	252

Question 4

(a) (i) According to IAS 32, the issue of preference shares creates an obligation on the part of the issuer to the holder, so preference shares are classified as a financial liability.

In this question AWX is obligated to pay the 5% dividend on the nominal value of shares each year and also to redeem the preference shares on 1 April 2022 and pay a premium of 10% of the nominal value at that time.

The treatment as described in note (v) is therefore incorrect as the net proceeds received on the issue of the preference shares should have been credited to non-current liabilities not to equity.

In addition, the issue costs should have been deducted from the proceeds received rather than be charged to administrative expenses. Therefore the preference shares would initially have been recognised as a non-current liability in the statement of financial position of $650,000 at 1 April 2012.

During the year AWX should recognise the finance charge of the preference shares using the effective interest rate of 6.74% and would show a finance charge of $44,000 ($650,000 x 6.74%). The actual dividend paid of $35,000 ($700,000 x 5%) would then reduce the liability at the year end. The year end liability would then be recognised at $659,000 ($650,000 + $44,000 - $35,000).

(ii) Calculation of revised profit before tax

	$'000	$'000
Profit before tax per SPL		408
Add: issue costs relating to preference shares, included in administrative expenses	50	
Less: finance charge on preference shares (650,000 x 6.74%)	(44)	
		6
Revised profit for the year		414

(b) AWX STATEMENT OF CASH FLOWS FOR THE YEAR ENDED 31 MARCH 2013

	$'000	$'000
Cash flows from operating activities		
Profit before taxation	414	
Finance cost (W5)	84	
Depreciation (note (iii))	675	
Amortisation (W2)	159	
Profit on disposal of PPE	(22)	
Decrease in inventory (W3)	67	
Increase in receivables (W3)	(84)	
Increase in payables (W3)	35	
Increase in provisions	90	
Cash generated from operations	1,418	
Interest paid (W4)	(162)	
Income taxes paid (W3)	(253)	
Net cash from operating activities		1,003

BPP LEARNING MEDIA

	$'000	$'000
Cash flows from investing activities		
Payments to acquire property, plant and equipment (W1)	(320)	
Proceeds of sale of property, plant and equipment	92	
Net cash used in investing activities		(228)
Cash flows from financing activities		
Equity dividend paid	(75)	
Repayment of long term borrowings	(1,100)	
Proceeds from issue of shares (700 – 50)	650	
Net cash used in financing activities		(525)
Net increase in cash and cash equivalents		250
Cash and cash equivalents at 31 March 2012		265
Cash and cash equivalents at 31 March 2013		515

Workings

1   *Property, plant and equipment*

	$'000
Balance b/d	4,500
Revaluation (469 – 353)	116
Disposal	(70)
Depreciation	(675)
	3,871
Additions (balancing figure)	320
Balance c/d	4,191

Alternative working:

Property, plant and equipment

	$'000		$'000
B/d	4,500	Disposal	70
∴ Additions	320	Depreciation	675
Revaluation in year	116	C/d	4,191
	4,936		4,936

2   *Intangible assets*

	$'000
Balance b/d	315
Amortisation (balancing figure)	159
Balance c/d	156

Alternative working:

Intangible assets

	$'000		$'000
B/d	315	∴ Amortisation	159
		C/d	156
	315		315

3   *Inventories, trade receivables and trade payables*

	Inventories	Trade receivables	Trade payables
	$'000	$'000	$'000
Balance b/d	805	480	500
Increase/(decrease) (balancing figure)	(67)	84	35
Balance c/d	738	564	535

4   *Income tax payable*

	$'000
Balance b/d - current	218
Balance b/d - deferred	220
Tax charge per SPL	124
	562
Income taxes paid (balancing figure)	(253)
Balance c/d – current (84) & deferred (225)	309

Alternative working:

Income tax payable

	$'000		$'000
∴ Tax paid	253	B/d: current tax	218
C/d: current tax	84	B/d: deferred tax	220
C/d: deferred tax	225	Charge per SPL	124
	562		562

5   *Interest paid*

	$'000
Balance b/d	99
Finance costs per **original** SPL	40
	139
Interest paid (balancing figure)	(127)
Balance c/d	12

Preference shares:

Finance charge for the year	44
"Dividends"/ interest paid	(35)

Summary:

Finance charge to be added back (40 + 44)	84
Interest paid (127 + 35)	(162)

MATHEMATICAL TABLES

PRESENT VALUE TABLE

Present value of $1 ie $(1+r)^{-n}$ where r = interest rate, n = number of periods until payment or receipt.

Periods (n)	1%	2%	3%	4%	5%	6%	7%	8%	9%	10%
1	0.990	0.980	0.971	0.962	0.952	0.943	0.935	0.926	0.917	0.909
2	0.980	0.961	0.943	0.925	0.907	0.890	0.873	0.857	0.842	0.826
3	0.971	0.942	0.915	0.889	0.864	0.840	0.816	0.794	0.772	0.751
4	0.961	0.924	0.888	0.855	0.823	0.792	0.763	0.735	0.708	0.683
5	0.951	0.906	0.863	0.822	0.784	0.747	0.713	0.681	0.650	0.621
6	0.942	0.888	0.837	0.790	0.746	0.705	0.666	0.630	0.596	0.564
7	0.933	0.871	0.813	0.760	0.711	0.665	0.623	0.583	0.547	0.513
8	0.923	0.853	0.789	0.731	0.677	0.627	0.582	0.540	0.502	0.467
9	0.914	0.837	0.766	0.703	0.645	0.592	0.544	0.500	0.460	0.424
10	0.905	0.820	0.744	0.676	0.614	0.558	0.508	0.463	0.422	0.386
11	0.896	0.804	0.722	0.650	0.585	0.527	0.475	0.429	0.388	0.350
12	0.887	0.788	0.701	0.625	0.557	0.497	0.444	0.397	0.356	0.319
13	0.879	0.773	0.681	0.601	0.530	0.469	0.415	0.368	0.326	0.290
14	0.870	0.758	0.661	0.577	0.505	0.442	0.388	0.340	0.299	0.263
15	0.861	0.743	0.642	0.555	0.481	0.417	0.362	0.315	0.275	0.239
16	0.853	0.728	0.623	0.534	0.458	0.394	0.339	0.292	0.252	0.218
17	0.844	0.714	0.605	0.513	0.436	0.371	0.317	0.270	0.231	0.198
18	0.836	0.700	0.587	0.494	0.416	0.350	0.296	0.250	0.212	0.180
19	0.828	0.686	0.570	0.475	0.396	0.331	0.277	0.232	0.194	0.164
20	0.820	0.673	0.554	0.456	0.377	0.312	0.258	0.215	0.178	0.149

Periods (n)	11%	12%	13%	14%	15%	16%	17%	18%	19%	20%
1	0.901	0.893	0.885	0.877	0.870	0.862	0.855	0.847	0.840	0.833
2	0.812	0.797	0.783	0.769	0.756	0.743	0.731	0.718	0.706	0.694
3	0.731	0.712	0.693	0.675	0.658	0.641	0.624	0.609	0.593	0.579
4	0.659	0.636	0.613	0.592	0.572	0.552	0.534	0.516	0.499	0.482
5	0.593	0.567	0.543	0.519	0.497	0.476	0.456	0.437	0.419	0.402
6	0.535	0.507	0.480	0.456	0.432	0.410	0.390	0.370	0.352	0.335
7	0.482	0.452	0.425	0.400	0.376	0.354	0.333	0.314	0.296	0.279
8	0.434	0.404	0.376	0.351	0.327	0.305	0.285	0.266	0.249	0.233
9	0.391	0.361	0.333	0.308	0.284	0.263	0.243	0.225	0.209	0.194
10	0.352	0.322	0.295	0.270	0.247	0.227	0.208	0.191	0.176	0.162
11	0.317	0.287	0.261	0.237	0.215	0.195	0.178	0.162	0.148	0.135
12	0.286	0.257	0.231	0.208	0.187	0.168	0.152	0.137	0.124	0.112
13	0.258	0.229	0.204	0.182	0.163	0.145	0.130	0.116	0.104	0.093
14	0.232	0.205	0.181	0.160	0.141	0.125	0.111	0.099	0.088	0.078
15	0.209	0.183	0.160	0.140	0.123	0.108	0.095	0.084	0.074	0.065
16	0.188	0.163	0.141	0.123	0.107	0.093	0.081	0.071	0.062	0.054
17	0.170	0.146	0.125	0.108	0.093	0.080	0.069	0.060	0.052	0.045
18	0.153	0.130	0.111	0.095	0.081	0.069	0.059	0.051	0.044	0.038
19	0.138	0.116	0.098	0.083	0.070	0.060	0.051	0.043	0.037	0.031
20	0.124	0.104	0.087	0.073	0.061	0.051	0.043	0.037	0.031	0.026

CUMULATIVE PRESENT VALUE TABLE

This table shows the present value of $1 per annum, receivable or payable at the end of each year for n years

$$\frac{1-(1+r)^{-n}}{r}.$$

Periods (n)	Interest rates (r) 1%	2%	3%	4%	5%	6%	7%	8%	9%	10%
1	0.990	0.980	0.971	0.962	0.952	0.943	0.935	0.926	0.917	0.909
2	1.970	1.942	1.913	1.886	1.859	1.833	1.808	1.783	1.759	1.736
3	2.941	2.884	2.829	2.775	2.723	2.673	2.624	2.577	2.531	2.487
4	3.902	3.808	3.717	3.630	3.546	3.465	3.387	3.312	3.240	3.170
5	4.853	4.713	4.580	4.452	4.329	4.212	4.100	3.993	3.890	3.791
6	5.795	5.601	5.417	5.242	5.076	4.917	4.767	4.623	4.486	4.355
7	6.728	6.472	6.230	6.002	5.786	5.582	5.389	5.206	5.033	4.868
8	7.652	7.325	7.020	6.733	6.463	6.210	5.971	5.747	5.535	5.335
9	8.566	8.162	7.786	7.435	7.108	6.802	6.515	6.247	5.995	5.759
10	9.471	8.983	8.530	8.111	7.722	7.360	7.024	6.710	6.418	6.145
11	10.368	9.787	9.253	8.760	8.306	7.887	7.499	7.139	6.805	6.495
12	11.255	10.575	9.954	9.385	8.863	8.384	7.943	7.536	7.161	6.814
13	12.134	11.348	10.635	9.986	9.394	8.853	8.358	7.904	7.487	7.103
14	13.004	12.106	11.296	10.563	9.899	9.295	8.745	8.244	7.786	7.367
15	13.865	12.849	11.938	11.118	10.380	9.712	9.108	8.559	8.061	7.606
16	14.718	13.578	12.561	11.652	10.838	10.106	9.447	8.851	8.313	7.824
17	15.562	14.292	13.166	12.166	11.274	10.477	9.763	9.122	8.544	8.022
18	16.398	14.992	13.754	12.659	11.690	10.828	10.059	9.372	8.756	8.201
19	17.226	15.679	14.324	13.134	12.085	11.158	10.336	9.604	8.950	8.365
20	18.046	16.351	14.878	13.590	12.462	11.470	10.594	9.818	9.129	8.514

Periods (n)	Interest rates (r) 11%	12%	13%	14%	15%	16%	17%	18%	19%	20%
1	0.901	0.893	0.885	0.877	0.870	0.862	0.855	0.847	0.840	0.833
2	1.713	1.690	1.668	1.647	1.626	1.605	1.585	1.566	1.547	1.528
3	2.444	2.402	2.361	2.322	2.283	2.246	2.210	2.174	2.140	2.106
4	3.102	3.037	2.974	2.914	2.855	2.798	2.743	2.690	2.639	2.589
5	3.696	3.605	3.517	3.433	3.352	3.274	3.199	3.127	3.058	2.991
6	4.231	4.111	3.998	3.889	3.784	3.685	3.589	3.498	3.410	3.326
7	4.712	4.564	4.423	4.288	4.160	4.039	3.922	3.812	3.706	3.605
8	5.146	4.968	4.799	4.639	4.487	4.344	4.207	4.078	3.954	3.837
9	5.537	5.328	5.132	4.946	4.772	4.607	4.451	4.303	4.163	4.031
10	5.889	5.650	5.426	5.216	5.019	4.833	4.659	4.494	4.339	4.192
11	6.207	5.938	5.687	5.453	5.234	5.029	4.836	4.656	4.486	4.327
12	6.492	6.194	5.918	5.660	5.421	5.197	4.988	4.793	4.611	4.439
13	6.750	6.424	6.122	5.842	5.583	5.342	5.118	4.910	4.715	4.533
14	6.982	6.628	6.302	6.002	5.724	5.468	5.229	5.008	4.802	4.611
15	7.191	6.811	6.462	6.142	5.847	5.575	5.324	5.092	4.876	4.675
16	7.379	6.974	6.604	6.265	5.954	5.668	5.405	5.162	4.938	4.730
17	7.549	7.120	6.729	6.373	6.047	5.749	5.475	5.222	4.990	4.775
18	7.702	7.250	6.840	6.467	6.128	5.818	5.534	5.273	5.033	4.812
19	7.839	7.366	6.938	6.550	6.198	5.877	5.584	5.316	5.070	4.843
20	7.963	7.469	7.025	6.623	6.259	5.929	5.628	5.353	5.101	4.870

Notes

Notes

Review Form – Paper F1 Financial Operations (01/14)

Name: _____   Address: _____

_____

_____

How have you used this Kit?
(Tick one box only)

☐ Home study (book only)

☐ On a course: college _____

☐ With 'correspondence' package

☐ Other _____

Why did you decide to purchase this Kit?
(Tick one box only)

☐ Have used the Study text

☐ Have used other BPP products in the past

☐ Recommendation by friend/colleague

☐ Recommendation by a lecturer at college

☐ Saw advertising

☐ Other _____

During the past six months do you recall seeing/receiving any of the following?
(Tick as many boxes as are relevant)

☐ Our advertisement in *Financial Management*

☐ Our advertisement in *PQ*

☐ Our brochure with a letter through the post

☐ Our website www.bpp.com

Which (if any) aspects of our advertising do you find useful?
(Tick as many boxes as are relevant)

☐ Prices and publication dates of new editions

☐ Information on product content

☐ Facility to order books off-the-page

☐ None of the above

Which BPP products have you used?

Text	☐	Success CD	☐	Interactive Passcards	☐
Kit	☑	i-Pass	☐	Home Study Package	☐
Passcard	☐				

Your ratings, comments and suggestions would be appreciated on the following areas.

	Very useful	Useful	Not useful
Passing F1	☐	☐	☐
Planning your question practice	☐	☐	☐
Questions	☐	☐	☐
Top Tips etc in answers	☐	☐	☐
Content and structure of answers	☐	☐	☐
'Plan of attack' in mock exams	☐	☐	☐
Mock exam answers	☐	☐	☐

Overall opinion of this Kit	Excellent ☐	Good ☐	Adequate ☐	Poor ☐

Do you intend to continue using BPP products?   Yes ☐   No ☐

The BPP author of this edition can be e-mailed at: helenajones@bpp.com

Please return this form to: Valli Rajagopal, CIMA Range Manager, BPP Learning Media, FREEPOST, London, W12 8BR

Review Form (continued)

TELL US WHAT YOU THINK

Please note any further comments and suggestions/errors below.